Fraynham

Revolution and Mass Democracy

Peter H. Amann

Revolution and Mass Democracy
The Paris Club Movement in 1848

Princeton University Press, *New Jersey*

Copyright © 1975 by Princeton University Press
Published by Princeton University Press
Princeton and London

All Rights Reserved

Library of Congress Cataloging in Publication Data will
be found on the last printed page of this book

Publication of this book has been aided by a grant from
The Andrew W. Mellon Publication Fund

This book has been composed in Linotype Monticello

Printed in the United States of America
by Princeton University Press, Princeton, New Jersey

Contents

	Illustrations	vii
	Abbreviations	ix
	Preface	xi
	Chronology of the Revolution of 1848	xx
1	The Urban Landscape	3
2	The World of the Clubs	33
3	The Eighteenth Brumaire of the People	78
4	The Mirage of Unity	111
5	The Popular Societies at Work	144
6	The Crisis of the Popular Movement	173
7	The Making of a *Journée*: May 15	205
8	Toward a Showdown	248
9	The June Days and After	294
10	Reflections and Retrospect	324
	Bibliography	338
	Index	351

Illustrations

Maps

1	The administrative divisions of Paris in 1848	9
2	The geography of wealth and poverty in Paris (1846)	15
3	Route of the demonstration of March 17, 1848	105
4	Route of the demonstration of April 16, 1848	174
5	Route of the demonstration of May 15, 1848	229

Plates

1	The traditionalist view of the Parisian social spectrum	12
2	Club membership cards	59
3	Two contemporary views of club sessions	66
4	Composite portrait of major club leaders and their revolutionary allies	69
5	Group portrait of the provisional government	74
6	The fracas over the dissolution of the elite companies	99
7	The 18th Brumaire of the people and the 18th Brumaire of the bourgeoisie	106
8	National elections, April 1848	153
9	Postelection crisis, April-May 1848	193
10	Antecedent of the June insurrection	284
11	The twilight of the club movement	317

Abbreviations

A.N. — Archives nationales

A.M.G. — Archives historiques du Ministère de la Guerre

A.S. — Archives du département de la Seine et de la Ville de Paris

A.P.P. — Archives de la Préfecture de Police

B.N. — Bibliothèque Nationale

B.H.V.P. — Bibliothèque historique de la Ville de Paris

B.A. — Bibliothèque de l'Arsenal

CdE — Commission d'Enquête (refers to the number stamped on given documents by the parliamentary commission investigating the June 1848 insurrection)

Amann, *Minutes* — P. Amann, "A French Revolutionary Club in 1848: The Société démocratique centrale," diss., Ph.D. University of Chicago, 1958. (Original MS A.N., C. 942)

DH Minutes — (manuscript) minutes of the Société des Droits de l'Homme, May 26-June 18, 1848.

CR — Comité révolutionnaire, Club des Clubs

DBMOF — *Dictionnaire biographique du mouvement ouvrier français*

Preface

One of the curious phenomena of intellectual history is the abruptness with which, for no obvious reasons, scholars will converge on certain problems and, much to their own surprise, find themselves becoming part of a movement. Adam Smith's "invisible hand," evicted from the realm of economics, may have found a cozier niche. This book is a case in point. I have long forgotten why, in the era of the Korean War, I should have become fascinated with nineteenth-century Parisian grass roots—or should one say paving stone?—revolutionary politics. Neither my teachers nor my fellow graduate students showed particular interest. I myself was unaware that, even as I began my own research, Soboul, Cobb, Rudé, and Tønneson were uncovering the behavior of revolutionary crowds, while Tilly was examining counterrevolution at the grass roots; or that E. P. Thompson was busily excavating his English working class, while Professor Hobsbawm (and I mention only a few prominent practitioners) was coming to terms with bandits and rural anarchists. Yet though this book was conceived in seeming isolation, quite inadvertently I now find myself modestly contributing to a vast and growing "history from below" movement.

More specifically, I hope to enlarge our understanding of nineteenth-century European history, first by renewing the history of the decisive months of the Second French Republic through a shift of perspective. Any serious student of the French Revolution of 1848 soon becomes aware that the key events of the crucial four months following the overthrow of the July Monarchy have been viewed through unfocused lenses. The events look fuzzy not only because, as P.-J. Proudhon was to note in his diary, revolutions are extraordinarily messy affairs, but also because the year 1848 in France has been viewed chiefly through the prism of the Provisional Government and its equally official successor, the Commission of the Executive Power. Yet in the face of a variety of popular pressures, these governments were bewildered, ill-informed, uncomprehending. Historians, reluctant merely to mirror bewilderment, have sought refuge in narrations of outward events or, if they tried to penetrate the facade of these events at all, in speculations. If the major episodes of the French Revolution of 1848 are to be rightly understood, the perspective of the revolutionaries themselves is indispensable; realistically, this means the perspective of the improvised mass organizations through which these tens and perhaps hundreds of thousands of revolutionaries expressed themselves. The history of the club movement, the most significant of these improvised mass organizations, therefore complements and illuminates the conventional political history of the Second French Republic.

The club movement may be viewed from a second angle, as an institution whose history helps us understand not only specific events but the overall dynamics of the revolution. If we reduce the political drama to its schematic essentials (and disregard its ideological and circumstantial context), the newly installed republican government's drive to regain the power monopoly traditionally enjoyed by the wielders of official authority becomes the central political issue in 1848. Between February and June 1848 that monopoly was challenged by institutions that owed their existence or their autonomy to the toppling of the monarchy; these paragovernments arrogated to themselves authority traditionally vested in the state. The National Guard, old and new, the craft unions headed by the Luxembourg delegates, Marc Caussidière's red-sashed police force, the unpredictable Garde Mobile, the National Workshops, and, last but not least, the club movement, all qualify as serious impediments, even rivals, to a government intent on restoring obedience. Understanding the career of the club movement—and that of other power blocs resisting traditional sovereignty—becomes essential if we want to grasp the intricate game of musical chairs which, by June 26, 1848, had eliminated all but one of the players —the government itself—and had ended by reestablishing that government's monopoly of power over its revolutionary competitors.

Finally, though this study concentrates on the revolutionary club movement at a particular point in time— 1848—and in a specific locale—Paris—I hope that my work may encourage others to consider revolutionary clubs as a historical phenomenon transcending these limitations. The club movement in a variety of forms was, I believe, a characteristic revolutionary phenomenon of a society in transition to modernity. Clubs belong to a certain stage of social development as much as to a given time and place. They are inconceivable in a society of rank, paternalism, and deference; they are obsolete in a world of assembly lines, recognized labor unions, and mass parties. In short, revolutionary clubs occupied a certain ecological niche which a changing social and political environment ultimately destroyed.

In concentrating on the club movement, I have kept general historical background to a minimum. As the clubs, more often than not, responded to events not of their own making, I have furnished a chronological table which dates important official acts, popular movements, and news from abroad in parallel columns. At the same time, this book is meant as a history of the club *move-ment*, not an exhaustive chronicle of all clubs that have left records of their activities. My focus has been on common elements rather than on particularities. Historians looking in this study for a coherent account of, say, the Society of the Rights of Man in 1848 will not find it, even though I accumulated the documentation for such mini-monographs.

An examination of the club or popular society movement (contemporaries used the two labels interchangeably) presents certain scholarly problems. The popular societies enjoyed the dubious distinction of being spied upon by numerous rival intelligence and security services, formal and improvised. Unfortunately, all this snooping has left precious little residue for the historian. Apparently the Ministry of the Interior discarded the dossiers of its club police in one of its periodic moves from one palace to another some time in the third quarter of the nineteenth century. The archives of the Prefecture of Police, save for some bundles protecting the Venus of Milo stored in the basement during the siege of Paris in 1870-71, were burned during the last week of the Commune— a case of the revolution devouring its predecessor's records, if not its own children. The files of what were possibly two distinct intelligence services operating out of the mayor's office in 1848 were also incinerated, together with the Paris City Hall, in 1871. As for gendarmerie dispatches, generally a useful source for any activities liable to disturb the authorities, many of them are missing. In any case, the jurisdiction of the gendarmerie only began at the city limits. Furthermore, as the revolution of 1848 triggered more than its share of apolitical disorders, the gendarmerie tended to disregard the "harmless" suburban popular societies. We are left with scattered police reports that found their way into the collection of the parliamentary commission charged with investigating the

June 1848 insurrection. We also have the confiscated papers of the Club of Clubs and a couple of less important organizations; and there are dozens of newspapers, many of them ephemeral, that reported club motions, petitions, and sessions; the record of the trial of club leaders implicated in the fiasco of May 15; and, finally, the 11,400 individual dossiers of the arrested June 1848 suspects—a historian's haystack full of needles.

My task has been to reconstruct a mosaic out of literally thousands of discrete bits, knowing that a high percentage of these historical tesserae have been irretrievably lost. In circumstances such as these, one runs the risk of detecting patterns where none exist, of projecting two or three isolated instances into a trend. I can only say in my defense that, aware of the problem, I have been deliberately conservative in assessing evidence. One reassuring experience may be worth noting: after working out one particularly troublesome problem—the genesis and implications of the so-called Banquet of the People in June 1848—on the basis of my usual fragmentary sources, I stumbled upon the complete archives of the banquet's organizers. My original appraisal, it turned out, had been reasonably accurate, though I had oversimplified and erred on details. Even so, I am sure that I have made mistakes that more satisfactory documentation could have eliminated.

The nature of my sources has also dictated considerable caution in the use of numbers and their statistical manipulation. While I am all in favor of quantitative measurement where figures or samples are reliable, I have been blessed with neither in this study. To cite one example: I was able to establish the professional background of half of the club presidents for whom I had names. Yet if I am certain of anything, it is that this 50 percent represents no random sample. Veteran republicans, journalists, men of letters, even students, all enjoyed a much higher visibility than humbler folk, but how much higher can be no more than a guess. Though I have sought to justify my guesses, I continue to wander in that impressionistic jungle that quantitative historians have so resolutely tried to leave behind.

After initial hesitation, I have emphasized analysis over narrative, explanation over evocation, historical distance over Rankean historicism. Second, and more prosaically, within the body of the book's text I have avoided French terms wherever possible. Though mention of the "Paris City Hall" instead of the Hôtel de Ville will jar all good francophiles, they might cast their minds back to their own reaction to untranslated Russian, classical Greek, or Chinese phrases. To avoid excessive consistency (and to avoid goading French specialists beyond endurance), I have compromised these good intentions in my footnotes: club names, for instance, are anglicized in the text but retained in French in the notes.

Like most scholars completing a book, I have a variety of debts to acknowledge. In the course of my research, I was awarded grants from Bowdoin College, Oakland University, the State University of New York, and the University of Michigan. A year in Paris in 1963-1964 as a John Simon Guggenheim Fellow and with the additional support of a Fulbright Senior Research Fellowship permitted me to explore French archives and libraries in much greater depth than I would have been able to do on my own resources.

Without the cooperation of archivists and libraries in many institutions in France and in the United States, I would have been stymied. I want to acknowledge help received at the French National Archives, and the archives of the Seine, the Paris Municipal Council, the Ministry of Foreign Affairs, the Police Prefecture of Paris, the Ministry of War, and the National Assembly; among Parisian libraries, I am indebted to the Bibliothèque nationale, the Bibliothèque historique de la Ville de Paris, the Bibliothèque de l'Arsenal, the Bibliothèque de l'Institute and the Bibliothèque de la Sorbonne. In the United States I imposed on the time and energy of interlibrary loan librarians at Bowdoin College, Oakland University, the State University of New York at Binghamton, and the University of Michigan-Dearborn. I also availed myself of the rich collections of the New York Public Library and of the university libraries of Harvard, Yale, Columbia, Cornell, Michigan, Michigan State, and Chicago.

A number of colleagues were helpful with their criticism. Professors Leo Loubère, John Bowditch, and George Fasel read an early draft of several chapters which their comments led me to rethink and recast altogether. Professor Melvin Cherno went over the entire typescript with great care, making numerous suggestions, with most of which I concurred. Professors Charles Tilly and Edward Shorter, as well as several anonymous readers, raised cogent questions to which I have since tried to address myself. Despite such varied assistance, I must obviously take the final responsibility for the contents of this book. The editors of the *Journal of Modern History* and of the *French Historical Studies* kindly permitted me to incorporate material that first appeared, in somewhat different form, in the pages of their respective journals.

Madame Liliane Ziegel was expert, efficient, and indefatigable in undertaking research assignments in Parisian archives and libraries. Marian Wilson, editorial assistant at Oakland University, not only typed the various drafts with skill, but also disentangled convoluted sentences and rectified cryptic footnotes along the way. Rita Edwards executed the complicated chronological table.

My wife Enne read or listened to variants of each chapter with what in retrospect appears as astounding good humor, tact, and intelligence. I trust that Paula, Sandra, and David, who grew up with the club movement as permanent house guest, will adjust to its departure.

Pontiac, Michigan
October 1973

Governmental Action Affecting The Clubs		Popular Demonstrations		Significant News From Abroad

February 1848

| 25 | Proclamation of the Republic. All political prisoners ordered released. Establishment of the National Workshops. Creation of the Garde nationale mobile. | 25-26 | Popular demonstrations in behalf of red flag. | |
| 28 | Establishment of the government's commission for the workers (the future Luxembourg Labor Commission). | 27-28 | Popular demonstrations for the "right to work" and the "organization of labor." | |

March 1848

1	Creation of a Commission of National Rewards (for veteran republicans).			
2	Stamp duty (on newspapers) suspended. Decree shortening the workday and prohibiting labor subcontracting (*marchandage*).			
4	Public funeral for the victims of the February Revolution.			
5	The date for the general elections is announced as April 9. Major provisions for these elections are made public.			5	Agitation in German states of Baden, Hesse, Württemberg.
6	Abrogation of the press restrictions of September 1835.			

7   Creation of government sponsored discount banks in Paris and other major cities. Election of noncommissioned officers and officers in the Paris National Guard set for March 18, 19, and 20, with general instructions for this election.

8   Rising Chartist agitation in London and England generally.

9   Detailed supplementary instructions concerning the general elections.

13 Deadline for registering for the Paris National Guard extended from March 13 to March 16.

14 Dissolution of the elite companies of the Paris National Guard. They are integrated into regular Guard units.

15 Paris National Guard elections are postponed from March 18 to March 25.

16 Emergency increase in the land tax by 45 percent (the 45 centimes).

16 National Guard demonstration versus dissolution of elite companies. (*Manifestation des bonnets à poil*).

17 Popular mass demonstration jointly sponsored by the clubs and the organized trades.

18 The elections in the Paris National Guard are postponed again, from March 25 to April 5.

18 Polish demands for independent Polish (Prussian) Posen.

19 Revolution in Berlin.

CHRONOLOGY OF THE REVOLUTION OF 1848

February 24–June 26, 1848

Governmental Action Affecting The Clubs	Popular Demonstrations	Signification News From Abroad
		20 Revolution in Vienna.
	23 ca.-April 10 Popular agitation for the remission of 6 months' rental due April 1.	24 Rising nationalist agitation in Ireland.
		25 Semi-insurrection of Poles in Cracow against Austria.
26 The general elections are postponed from April 9 to April 23. The opening date for the new National Assembly is set for May 4.		26 King of Bavaria's resignation.
27 Provisional list of registered voters to be published April 15. Final deadline for registration, April 20. Detailed instructions issued for the procedure to be followed in balloting for the various ranks to be elected within the Paris National Guard.		28 Mass demonstration bearing "monster" petition planned for April 10 by Chartists in London.
30 Commission to receive "patriotic gifts" created.		30 Piedmontese mobilization and impending war of National liberation versus Austria after Milanese revolution.

31 Announced reform of the sales tax on wine and liquor.

April 1848

5-7 Paris National Guard elections.

6 Government proclamation in behalf of fair treatment for foreign workers.

10 Mayor of Paris proclaims warning against intimidation of landlords and refusals to pay rentals due.

15 Abrogation of the salt tax announced for January 1, 1849.

16 Scheduled election of 14 National Guard staff officers by workers of the organized trades at the Champ-de-Mars.

1-7 Agitation versus foreign workers in Paris.

2 Club banquet on the Place du Châtelet.

16 Demonstration of the organized trades.

1 Hostilities between Denmark and Schleswig-Holstein.

3 Proclamation of Venetian Republic.

7 German "Pre-Parliament" meets in Frankfurt.

10 Revolt in Buda-Pest.

12 Chartist demonstration has fizzled.

15 Clashes between Poles and Prussians in Posen.

CHRONOLOGY OF THE REVOLUTION OF 1848
February 24–June 26, 1848

	Governmental Action Affecting The Clubs	Popular Demonstrations	Signification News From Abroad
17	Decree proclaiming April 20 (the scheduled National Festivities) a holiday.		
18	Decrees suppressing municipal entry taxes (*octroi*) on fresh meat and wine. Ordinance restricting the authority to call out the Paris National Guard to the Minister of the Interior and the mayor of Paris.		
19	Proclamation against armed clubs.		Agreement for disarmament of Polish irregulars in Posen reached but breaks down.
20	Day of National Festivities.		
22	Decree suppressing municipal entry taxes on pork and processed meat products.		
23-24	General elections in the department of the Seine and throughout France.		
25	Announcement of a festival (later labeled Fête de la Concorde) for May 4.		
28	Announcement of general election results in Paris.		
29		News of the *troubles* of Rouen and Limoges reach Paris.	
30			First indication that Piedmontese army stalemated versus Austrians. Posen partitioned; desperate resistance by Polish irregulars.

May 1848

1 Festivities scheduled for May 4 postponed to May 10.

2 Decree putting Commission of National Rewards under the jurisdiction of the mayor of Paris.

2 Revolution in Cracow; Polish defeats in Posen.

4 Opening day of the National Assembly.

4 First noted crowd (*rassemblement*) gathering in the evening on the northern boulevards. To occur almost nightly through following 6-7 weeks.

4 Cracow surrenders to Austrians.

8 Continuing defeats of Polish irregulars by Prussian troops in Posen.

9 Decree by the National Assembly granting executive authority to a 5-man Commission of the Executive Power.

10 Election of the Commission's members by the National Assembly.

14 Scheduled date (following postponement from May 4, then May 10) at Champ-de-Mars for a national Festival of Harmony (Fête de la Concorde) (postponed once again on May 13 to May 21).

15 National Assembly lifts the immunity of representatives (Barbès and others) implicated in the *journée* of May 15, authorizing their arrest.

15 Demonstration in behalf of Poland. Dissolution of National Assembly and abortive revolutionary government.

CHRONOLOGY OF THE REVOLUTION OF 1848

February 24–June 26, 1848

Governmental Action Affecting The Clubs	Popular Demonstrations	Significant News From Abroad
22 Decree dissolving the clubs of Blanqui and Raspail. Special supplementary elections to fill vacancies in the National Assembly occasioned by multiple elections, resignations, and nullified elections announced for June 4.		19 Polish commander prisoner; resistance virtually ended in Posen.
25 Decree ordering an inquiry into the problems of industrial and agricultural labor.		26 Revolution in Naples defeated.
June 1848	1-22 Continuing nightly *rassemblements* on boulevards. Mass arrests after June 7.	3 New revolution in Vienna.
4 Special supplementary elections for 11 seats to the National Assembly for the department of the Seine.	4-11 Height of agitation over Workers' Banquet.	6 Piedmontese victory at Peschiera.
7 Law against unlawful assembly passed by National Assembly.		

9 Announcement of election results in the department of the Seine.

14 Law against the acceptance of other salaried public employment by members of the National Assembly.

15 Louis Napoleon Bonaparte resigns as member of the National Assembly after having been elected in the special elections of June 4.

19 Minister of Public Works announces in the National Assembly that contingents of National Workshop workers are to leave Paris for the provinces.

20 Start of Austrian counteroffensive with capture of Vicenza.

22 Demonstration on Place du Panthéon and elsewhere against impending dissolution of the National Workshops.

23 Outbreak of June insurrection.

23 National Assembly proclaims emergency session (*se met en permanence*).

24 National Assembly declares Paris to be in state of siege and delegates all executive authority to General Cavaignac.

26 Recapture of Faubourg Saint-Antoine by government forces, effectively ending insurrection.

Revolution and Mass Democracy

1 | The Urban Landscape

On a sunny and cheerful February day, we climbed the tower of Notre-Dame. . . . "Paris, the storm-tossed sea" lay at our feet. The babble of a thousand voices, the clatter of a thousand carriages rose up to us like the sound of ocean surf to a lighthouse. On our right, majestic and somber, the massed houses of the Faubourgs Saint-Antoine and Saint-Marceau spread out before us, while on our left, the terraces and tree clumps of the Tuileries Gardens and the Champs-Elysées appeared bathed in colored light; the Seine, like a band of sparkling green emeralds, wound its way through the impressive urban landscape.[1]

i

This is how the French capital appeared to two young German revolutionaries early in 1849. By then, the revolution of 1848, having run its course, had become part of the mystique of a Paris where, as one of the young men put it, "every nook, every corner, every alley was alive with the memory of a great and potent past that had so often shaken old Europe to its foundations."[2] Yet revolution had not altered the city's physical appearance. In 1848 Paris was already an immense metropolis: thirty-two thousand houses sheltered a million people, far and

[1] Gustav Rasch, "Ein Immortellenkranz auf das Grab eines Märtyrers [Max Dortu]," *Der deutsche Eidgenosse* [German exile periodical published in London] (March 1865), p. 21. My translation.
[2] Ibid., p. 20.

away the greatest urban concentration in France and, indeed, on the European continent. The suburbs located between the second and third ring of boulevards (not annexed until 1859) added another quarter million to the capital's effective population.[3] Though population continued to increase throughout the nineteenth century, the Paris of 1848 was more crowded than it was to be in 1900, because the bulk of its inhabitants piled into the central districts. In 1848, even within the more confining city limits of the second boulevards, vast tracts along the eastern and western fringes on the Right Bank were hardly built up, while on the Left Bank most of the people occupied a mile-wide strip along the Seine. Beyond the city limits, but within the fortifications surrounding Paris, the intramural suburbs ranged from busy industrial centers like Belleville and La Chapelle-Saint Denis to rustic retreats like Passy. Between communities there still lay considerable agricultural land, particularly along the southern periphery.[4]

Twentieth-century tourists—or, for that matter, Pari-

[3] Statistique générale de la France, *Dénombrement des années 1841, 1846 et 1851* (Paris, 1855), p. 93.

[4] For the physical description of Paris I am largely indebted to David H. Pinkney, *Napoleon III and the Rebuilding of Paris* (Princeton, 1958), ch. 1. However, in Paris, Chambre de Commerce, *Statistique de l'industrie à Paris . . . pour les années 1847-1848* (Paris, 1851), pp. 43-47, there is an excellent survey of the economic geography of the capital that necessarily touches on physical features. For a discussion of the extremes of population density, I am indebted to Louis Chevalier, *Classes laborieuses et classes dangereuses à Paris pendant la première moitié du XIXᵉ siècle* (Paris, 1958), pp. 225-227; for a description of the southeastern suburbs, to Jean Bastié, *La croissance de la banlieue parisienne* (Paris, 1964), pp. 92-99, 143-146; and for an unscholarly but engaging description of the suburbs during the July Monarchy, to *La vie parisienne à travers les âges*, Louis Mazoyer, *La Banlieue parisienne des origines à 1945*, VI ([Paris], n.d.), 49-132.

sians—would be bewildered by the Paris of 1848. They would, of course, look in vain for the silhouette of the Eiffel Tower in the west and the white marble of Sacré-Coeur to the north; even the soaring spire on the roof of the cathedral of Notre-Dame had yet to be raised by Viollet-le-Duc. More important, they simply would not be able to find their way around the city. The great reconstruction of the capital undertaken by Napoleon III and his prefect, Baron Haussmann, creating the Paris of straight thoroughfares, long vistas, and respectably uniform facades, still lay in the future. Much of the Paris of 1848 was an overgrown medieval city, whose crooked, narrow streets admitted little sunlight, despite ancient ordinances regulating the height of buildings.[5] Actually, such regulations applied only to houses fronting a street, not to the warrens that had filled what had once been courtyards or even gardens. Most of central and eastern Paris was a vast slum, picturesque no doubt, but overcrowded, dilapidated, smelly, and unhealthy.[6]

Parisian life in the first half of the nineteenth century was much more localized, much less mobile than urban renewal and subways were to make it by the twentieth. Public transportation—horse-drawn cabs that were supplemented by several hundred horse-drawn buses adding to the city's congestion—was beyond the means of ordinary Parisians: the thirty centimes for bus fare amounted to almost ten percent of a worker's daily wage.[7] As the major thoroughfares slicing through the center of Paris

[5] For alterations of the capital during the constitutional monarchy, see Paul Léon, "Les transformations de Paris du Premier au Second Empire," *Revue des deux mondes*, No. 14 (1954), pp. 204-225.

[6] Pinkney, *Napoleon III*, pp. 7-13; Chevalier, *Classes laborieuses*, pp. 225-234.

[7] Henri d'Almeras, *La vie parisienne sous le règne de Louis-Philippe* (Paris, n.d.), pp. 3-5; Pinkney, pp. 17-18.

were not even on the drawing board in 1848, walking any distance entailed zigzagging through a maze of alleys, many of them lacking adequate sidewalks but provided with an open sewer running down the middle of the pavement.[8] Whether inadequate communications within the city were cause or effect or a little of both, most Parisians remained closely tied to their own neighborhood, generally residing, working, and shopping within an area of a few streets.[9] When politics became important in their lives in 1848, their political participation tended to be similarly circumscribed, save on very special occasions.

In one important respect, mid-nineteenth-century Paris broke with its own past. Before 1800, the French capital had taken hundreds of years of slow if uneven growth to reach the half-million mark; yet in the first half of the nineteenth century, the number of Parisians almost doubled. That such rapid growth aggravated all sorts of urban problems, from pauperism to municipal housekeeping, is clear enough. Whether, as one historian has recently suggested, one should describe the result as a major social crisis is another question.[10] Assuredly, the experience of Paris was not unique in its own time. Its rate of growth was paralleled or surpassed by other nineteenth-century European metropolises, while even in France such urban

[8] Pinkney, *Napoleon III*, p. 18; Chevalier, *Classes laborieuses*, pp. 238-239.

[9] Pinkney, *Napoleon III*, pp. 17-18. A very limited test of such localism is provided by Adeline Daumard, "Les relations sociales à l'époque de la monarchie constitutionnelle d'après les registres paroissiaux des mariages," *Population*, xii (1957), 457-461.

[10] This is, of course, the well-known thesis of Chevalier in his *Classes laborieuses*, the most charitable verdict on which is the Scottish "not proven." For a perceptive recent critique, see Richard M. Andrews, "Laboring Classes and Dangerous Classes," *New York Times Book Review*, November 4, 1973, pp. 7-8.

agglomerations as the Lille-Roubaix-Tourcoing textile complex grew at a far more spectacular pace with equally spectacular symptoms of social dislocation.[11] Yet it is also true that in Paris, despite the efforts of successive governments, municipal services had lagged, the quality of life for the lower classes had probably declined, and public health—witness the two devastating cholera epidemics of 1832 and 1849—had deteriorated.[12] Most noticeable for ordinary Parisians must have been the increasing housing shortage during the years of the July Monarchy. While population increased 34 percent between 1831 and 1846, new housing rose by only 22 percent.[13] This lag, as well as the apparent decline in the size of the average household, led landlords to carve up their buildings into smaller but more numerous apartments. The total number of rental units increased by almost 50 percent during the 1830's and 1840's.[14]

[11] See Pierre Pierrard, *Lille et les Lillois* (Paris, 1967), pp. 83-93, 96-104, 111-112. A. Laserre, *La situation des ouvriers de l'industrie textile dans la région lilloise* (Lausanne, 1952), passim; Dr. Villermé, *Tableau de l'état physique et moral des ouvriers* (Paris, 1840), i, 74-115.

[12] Chevalier, *Classes laborieuses*, pp. 228-234, 242-255, 313-359, 368-450; Pinkney, *Napoleon III*, pp. 18-24.

[13] Since the figures for the number of houses refer to 1829 and 1849 or 1850, respectively, the lag may have been somewhat greater (though population in Paris did not increase between the census of 1846 and that of 1851). See Adeline Daumard, *La bourgeoisie parisienne, 1815-1848* (Paris, 1963), p. 8, for the 1829 figure; *Statistique de l'industrie*, p. 19, for the later figure.

[14] See table, p. 10, in Daumard, *Bourgeoisie parisienne*. This trend was evidently reflected in the rapid rise in landlord revenues during the period 1833-1854, which amounted to 72 percent (compared to a 63 percent rise for 1812-1833 and 66 percent for 1854-1875). Adeline Daumard, *Maisons de Paris et propriétaires parisiens au XIXe siècle, 1809-1880* (Paris, 1965), pp. 116-124, esp. chart on p. 123.

Arrondissements and Quartiers of Paris, 1848

Arrondissement I
1 Roule; 2 Champs-Elysées; 3 Place Vendôme; 4 Tuileries
Arrondissement II
5 Palais-Royal; 6 Feydau; 7 Chaussée d'Antin; 8 Faubourg
Montmartre
Arrondissement III
9 Mail; 10 Saint-Eustache; 11 Montmartre; 12 Faubourg
Poissonière
Arrondissement IV
13 Marchés; 14 Banque; 15 Louvre; 16 Saint-Honoré
Arrondissement V
17 Faubourg Saint-Denis; 18 Bonne-Nouvelle;
19 Montorgueuil; 20 Porte Saint-Martin
Arrondissement VI
21 Porte Saint-Denis; 22 Lombards; 23 Saint-Martin-des-
Champs; 24 Temple
Arrondissement VII
25 Mont-de-Piété; 26 Saint-Avoye; 27 Marché Saint-Jean;
28 Arcis
Arrondissement VIII
29 Marais; 30 Popincourt; 31 Faubourg Saint-Antoine;
32 Quinze-Vingt
Arrondissement IX
33 Hôtel-de-Ville; 34 Arsenal; 35 Cité; 36 Île Saint-Louis
Arrondissement X
37 Invalides; 38 Faubourg Saint-Germain; 39 Saint-Thomas
d'Aquin; 40 Monnaie
Arrondissement XI
41 Luxembourg; 42 Ecole de Médecin; 43 Sorbonne;
44 Palais de Justice
Arrondissement XII
45 Saint-Jacques; 46 Saint-Marcel; 47 Observatoire;
48 Jardin des Plantes

1. The administrative divisions of Paris in 1848

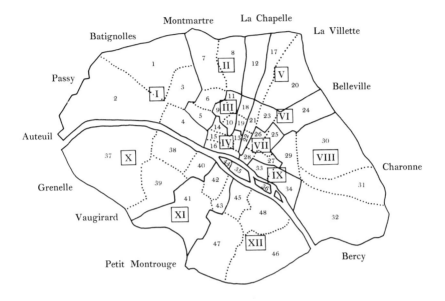

ii

As the administrative geography of Paris will from time
to time intrude on our story, the reader should try to vis-
ualize the ninety-degree arc of the Seine River entering
the city on the southeast and leaving it due west. This was
the boundary between the Right Bank, stretching out on
the north side of the river, and the much less important
Left Bank on its south side. With three-fifths of the city's
area, the Right Bank contained three-quarters of the population and five-sixths of Parisian industry. As the present twenty *arrondissements* were not drawn until the suburbs were incorporated in 1859, the modern district lines
coincide only very occasionally with the twelve districts
into which Paris was divided in 1848. *Arrondissements*
one through nine fanned out from west to southeast along
the Right Bank, though in defiance of the vaunted French
logic the eighth district—rather than the ninth—lay east-
ernmost. The Left Bank was shared, from west to southeast, by the tenth, eleventh, and twelfth *arrondissements*.

District boundaries made no serious attempt to equalize
area or population, or even to encompass a compact territory: both the third and fifth *arrondissements* had been
gerrymandered to resemble badly drawn figure eights. To
Parisians, their district was something administrative,
something artificial. Their focus of loyalty was their own
quarter (*quartier*), each of the districts being subdivided
into four such quarters. These neighborhoods, already
recognized during the Great Revolution, had genuine
character and their own traditions. Despite historic association with the capital, the communities beyond the
toll barrier but within the fortifications ringing Paris had
no direct administrative links to the city. These intramural outskirts, as well as the suburbs beyond the walls, together made up the thirteenth and fourteenth *arrondissements* of the department of Seine, in which Paris, with

over two-thirds of the population, played such a preponderant role.

Because the national capital had unique importance, the taste for political symmetry had been sacrificed to political realities. Ideally, French departments were put in the charge of a single official, the prefect, answering to the Minister of the Interior.[15] At a lower level, subprefects were accountable to the prefect and mayors to the subprefect. For Paris this scheme was abandoned, though the fiction of a Seine department as the fundamental administrative unit was retained. Since Paris was also the seat of the national government, the Minister of the Interior was constantly tempted to take a hand in governing the capital. Officially, however, direct administrative authority was divided between two appointees of the Minister of the Interior: a prefect of the Seine doubling as mayor of Paris, and, independent of the prefect of the Seine, a prefect of police. On a lower level, the twelve municipal districts were administered by *arrondissement* mayors and deputy mayors, who, like Victor Hugo in June 1848, were unpaid local notables. The subprefects administering the suburban thirteenth and fourteenth districts were regular career men.

iii

As background to our story, the flesh-and-blood realities of mid-nineteenth-century Paris count for more than the administrative and political framework that contained them. What was the human geography of Paris in 1848? Contemporaries habitually trotted out two somewhat inconsistent stereotypes. On the one hand, they perceived a Paris broken down into two cities: a bourgeois west end

---

[15] For a brilliant (and more complex) analysis of this problem, see Alan B. Spitzer, "Bureaucrat as Proconsul: The Restoration Prefect and the *police générale*," *Comp. Stud. Soc. and Hist.*, VII (1965), 371-392.

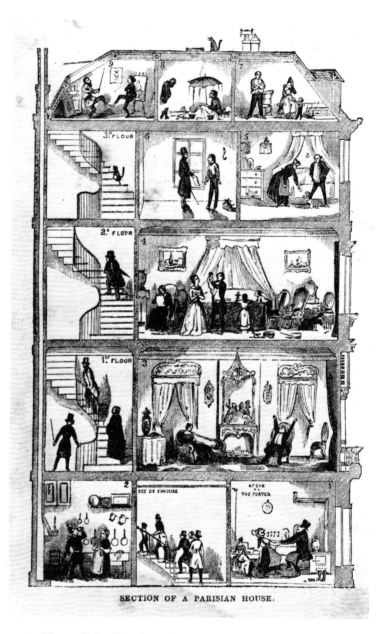

SECTION OF A PARISIAN HOUSE.

1.–The traditionalist view of the Parisian social spectrum

(the tenth district on the Left Bank, the first, second, and third on the Right Bank) opposing a proletarian east end (comprising the twelfth *arrondissement* on the Left Bank, the eighth, ninth, seventh, and sixth districts on the Right Bank). Running north–south between the two sides lay a strip of contested territory made up of the fifth, fourth, and eleventh *arrondissements*. On the other hand, contemporaries also evoked another, traditionalist vision of classes living in peaceful coexistence, quite literally, one on top of the other. "Once upon a time," reported the prefect of police in 1855, lamenting the exodus of workers from the central city and the passing of a golden age, "they [the workers] used to live in the upper stories of houses otherwise let to families of industrialists and other relatively well-off people. A sort of solidarity linked the inhabitants of the same house. They did favors for each other."[16] Less cheerfully, Balzac in his "Girl with the Golden Eyes" described the different levels of his typical Parisian apartment house in terms of Dante's circles of hell.[17] But he did not challenge the basic stereotype. Which of these perceptions corresponded to social realities in 1848?

Whatever life may have been like in the good old days, by 1848 the typical Parisian apartment house no longer displayed a cross section of Parisian society. Admittedly, the upper floors of a respectable building were subdivided into smaller apartments, occupied by humbler folk than the (French-style) first and second story, but the social range was unlikely to exceed the bounds of propriety. The entrepreneur from the first floor might well pass a

[16] Cited in Chevalier, *Classes laborieuses*, p. 233. A recent popular history of Paris elaborates on this theme in practically identical terms: *La vie parisienne à travers les âges*, Désiré Brelingard, *De 1600 à 1945*, III ([Paris], n.d.), 310-311.

[17] *The Works of Honoré de Balzac* (New York, n.d.), XIV, 279-287.

clerk from the fifth on the stairs; he was unlikely to encounter a worker.[18] Much more characteristic was a different type of integrated housing. Shabbier dwellings, in-
habited by the poor and the near-poor, could be found
interspersed among prosperous buildings. Appalling
slums could be found in the middle of the plush first district, and this was not unusual; within a few blocks of almost any fashionable address in Paris, streets could be
found whose residents rarely ate their fill. The converse
was no less true: islands of upper-middle-class comfort—
the Place des Vosges where Victor Hugo made his home
in the eighth *arrondissement*, the *quai* of the Île Saint-
Louis in the ninth—stood out in the midst of squalor.[19]
"Vertical stratification" may have been a myth, or at least
a vast exaggeration, but substantial middle-class families
could be found in every section of the capital.

There was more truth to the vision of a bourgeois west
confronting a working-class east. Though every district
had its middle class, this varied considerably in numerical
importance and in wealth. Perhaps the single most reliable divide between the poor—and the overwhelming majority of these were "working poor"—and those with pretensions to middle-class status was exemption from the
tax on rentals. Those occupying rooms or apartments
paying 200 francs rent per annum or less were excused
from a tax owed by all those with rentals above 200
francs. According to this criterion, the majority of tenants in every single *arrondissement* of Paris was officially

[18] Daumard, *Bourgeoisie parisienne*, p. 209. For the most
perceptive and well-informed discussion of the social distance
between the bourgeoisie and the "popular classes," see ibid.,
pp. 516-520. See also her broader "Relations sociales à Paris,"
pp. 445-466.

[19] Daumard, *Bourgeoisie parisienne*, pp. 207-208; and in
a broader context, p. 185.

2. The geography of wealth and poverty in Paris (1846)

A. Average tax on rental units per *arrondissement* (in francs)

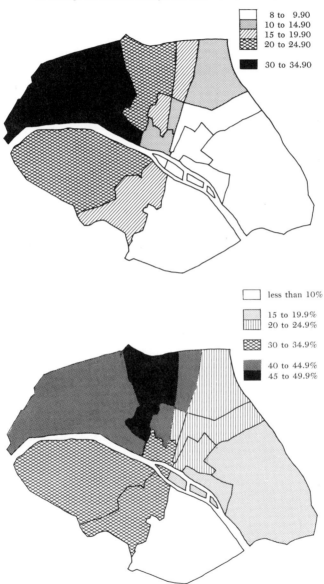

	8 to 9.90
	10 to 14.90
	15 to 19.90
	20 to 24.90
	30 to 34.90

	less than 10%
	15 to 19.9%
	20 to 24.9%
	30 to 34.9%
	40 to 44.9%
	45 to 49.9%

B. Percentage of taxed rental units (all units renting for less than 200 francs per year were exempt) in proportion to the total of rental units in each *arrondissement* classified among the poor.[20] Nonetheless, there were vast differences between western and eastern Paris in this respect. In the prosperous first, second, and third districts, between 40 and 50 percent of the tenants were among the taxed. In the west-central fourth, as well as in the two western *arrondissements* of the Left Bank, the tenth and eleventh, 30 to 35 percent were taxed. As one moved east, the proportion dropped to between 20 and 25 percent in the fifth, sixth, and seventh districts, to below 20 percent in the eighth and ninth, and to less than 10 percent in the twelfth *arrondissement*, which was notorious as the most poverty-stricken in Paris.[21] Obviously the Parisian middle class was more solidly rooted in its western home ground; moreover, the trend was toward greater residential segregation.[22]

Yet the mechanism by which the more concentrated bourgeoisie of western Paris established predominance in "its own" area is not so obvious. If we judge in terms of mass political participation in the weeks following the establishment of the Second Republic in February 1848, the record is unclear. Revolutionary clubs, frequented chiefly by the lower classes, sprang up in such bourgeois strongholds as the first and tenth *arrondissements*, just as they did in the proletarian Faubourg Saint-Antoine. Yet from the start, in the prosperous west end popular

[20] Daumard goes further, maintaining that at all times and in all *arrondissements* the poor constituted a majority of the population. However, the percentage of taxed rentals in the second district (48.3 percent) suggests an exception to this rule; since the average size of well-to-do households was larger than that of the poor, the former must have enjoyed a narrow absolute majority in the second district. See Daumard, *Bourgeoisie parisienne*, p. 182, for the map, p. 185 for the exact percentage, and p. 210 for her conclusion.

[21] Ibid., p. 182.

[22] Ibid., pp. 209-210, though the trend was barely perceptible at the end of the July Monarchy.

societies faced competition from clubs sponsored by local notables intent on keeping "their" workers from "foolish utopias." Social deference was evidently easier to exact where the well-to-do were ubiquitous than where they constituted a small and beleaguered minority. Even so, the contrast in mass political participation between eastern and western Paris remained blurred until the showdown of the June insurrection. Only then did the passivity of the workers in the westernmost districts of the capital bear out the effectiveness of bourgeois control.[23]

iv

Whatever the social geography of Paris, the prevalence of poverty among a large majority of the people is indisputable. On this point varied statistics converge: in 1846, 72 percent of all Parisian tenants were presumed unable to pay even the minimum tax of five francs on rentals; at least this was the rationale for exempting rents of under 200 francs per year. During the ten years prior to 1848, 73 percent of all funerals were paid for by the municipality, presumably because the survivors could not afford fifteen francs for a private service. During the same period, 79 percent of Parisian dead were buried in the French equivalent of potter's field, namely the pauper's ditch. Even if we allow for the smaller average size of

---

[23] Presumably—and the documentary evidence is very sketchy—the degree of ascendancy exercised by the middle class over the National Guard in the various districts is the key. In western Paris the middle classes not only monopolized the positions of leadership but also constituted a substantial portion of the rank and file. In eastern Paris they shared leadership positions with proletarian upstarts and were numerically insignificant among the rank and file. The result was that working class abstention in the west and bourgeois abstention in the east left the respective National Guard legions in opposing social hands in June. Louis Girard, *La garde nationale* (Paris, 1964), pp. 305-318, comes close to this conclusion.

working-class households and a higher working-class mortality, the fact remains that somewhere between two-thirds and three-quarters of all Parisians lived and died as paupers.[24]

In spite of the contemporary middle-class preoccupation with the "dangerous classes" and their supposed criminality, the great majority of the Parisian poor were no *Lumpenproletariat*.[25] For the most part, they were skilled, diligent artisans working at myriads of traditional trades. The industrial census undertaken, with official encouragement, by the Parisian Chamber of Commerce in 1849 listed 205,000 men, 113,000 women, and 25,000 youngsters under sixteen as employed in industry. To these should be added 33,000 masters working alone or with one assistant, who, for all practical purposes, were self-employed workers.[26] The chamber's census stopped at the city limits; a more realistic picture of working-class Paris would include as well at least 50,000 male and 25,000 female workers in the intramural suburbs, where a good deal of large-scale industry, particularly machine works, was located. The census also ignored workers in commercial (as against industrial) establishments, not to speak of a marginal population of casual laborers, scavengers, and peddlers.

Most Parisian workers were artisans employed by small

[24] Daumard, *Bourgeoisie parisienne*, pp. 6-12; on higher mortality rates among the lower classes, see Edmonde Vedrenne Villeneuve, "L'Inégalité sociale devant la mort dans la première moitié du XIXe siècle," *Population*, XVI (1961), 665-698, esp. 696-698.

[25] Cf. Chevalier, *Classes laborieuses*, pp. 454-468. As this chapter was completed before publication of Roger Price, *The French Second Republic* (Ithaca, N.Y., 1972), my description of the Parisian working class did not have the benefit of his synthesis. However, his depiction (pp. 6-10) and mine, largely based on the same source, match closely.

[26] *Statistique de l'industrie*, p. 48.

workshops, not factory hands. Even if we ignore the 33,000 independent workers already mentioned, the average "industrialist" employed no more than six or seven workers.[27] The emphasis was on the application of a great deal of highly skilled labor, rather than on elaborate machinery. As economists would put it, Parisian industry was labor rather than capital intensive, not so much because of French technological backwardness but because of economic conditions peculiar to the capital. In Paris space was at a premium, hence rentals, including industrial rentals, were expensive.[28] Waterpower was nonexistent, though the tanners of the twelfth district made use of the little river Bièvre for curing their hides.[29] Furthermore, the *octroi*, the toll levied on all goods entering the city (including raw materials and foodstuffs) raised both the cost of materials and, by driving up food prices, the level of wages. Paris therefore had to compete through skill, style, and inventiveness. An immense range of goods was produced in the capital: the chamber of commerce, after listing 325 distinct industries, apologized for lumping together related trades. The industries employing the largest number of workers were shoemaking and tailoring (with emphasis on ready-to-wear rather than on made-to-order), building, spinning and weaving, furniture, and the manufacture of the myriad of sundries and luxuries known under the collective name of "articles of Paris."[30] For the most part, industries had their traditional geographical location within the capital, with workers and employers living nearby. For example, the central fourth district was the garment center par excellence, while cabinetmakers dominated the Faubourg Saint-Antoine and the manufacturers of the "articles of

---

[27] Ibid., pp. 36-37.   [28] Ibid., p. 64.

[29] Ibid., p. 44; Pinkney, *Napoleon III*, p. 12; Chevalier, *Classes laborieuses*, pp. 249-250.

[30] *Statistique de l'industrie*, p. 48.

Paris" (from umbrellas to jewelry) were housed in the fifth, sixth, and seventh *arrondissements*.[31]

V

What composite picture of the male Parisian worker (and future club member) emerges from the statistics? In the first place, the term "Parisian" itself needs to be qualified. Apparently only four out of ten workers in 1848 were Parisians by birth; the rest were provincials, with a sprinkling of foreigners.[32] During the first half of the nineteenth century most of the migrants came, as Louis Chevalier has shown, from the departments surrounding the capital and, to a lesser extent, from eastern and northeastern France.[33] The city depended on immigrants not only for growth but for its very survival for children fifteen or under made up only 20 percent of the total population. A combination of early death and provincial retirement cut the percentage of Parisians over sixty years of age to 7 percent. Second, the age distribution was such that the twenty- to twenty-nine-year-olds constituted the

[31] Out of 31,138 journeymen cabinetmakers, 15,976 lived in these three *arrondissements*, and 2,276 masters out of 4,395. Ibid., p. 101. For a survey of the location of Parisian industry, district by district, see pp. 43-47.

[32] These not altogether precise statistics are derived from an analysis of the register of deported June 1848 insurgents, most (though not all) of whom were workers. Since inhabitants of the eighth *arrondissement* were greatly overrepresented for solely military reasons, while there were virtually no residents of the first, second, and tenth districts, the figures should be treated with considerable caution—though they do not appear to be out of line.

[33] Louis Chevalier, *La formation de la population parisienne au XIXᵉ siècle* (Paris, 1950), passim, but esp. pp. 14-15, 58-60. For a briefer, more general discussion of the Parisian population, see Charles H. Pouthas, *La population française pendant la première moitié du XIXᵉ siècle* (Paris, 1956), pp. 143-174.

largest group (23 percent), closely followed by the thirty-
to thirty-nine-year-olds (20 percent) and, more distant-
ly, by those in their forties (14 percent) and their fifties
(10 percent).[34] The age of the average Parisian forty-
eighter was somewhere in his thirties. Third, in terms of
economic rewards, by French standards of the time the
Parisian worker was well paid, though his money earn-
ings must be weighed against the higher cost of living of
the big city. The average daily wage for men was 3.80
francs, with not much differential from industry to industry, though the needle trades fared worst. Even so, 80
percent of all men earned between 3 and 5 francs.[35]
Fourth, three-fourths of all Parisian workers were properly established by contemporary standards; that is, they
owned their own furnishings, however modest.[36] Furnished rooming houses had, and deserved, a bad reputation in mid-nineteenth-century Paris, but a considerable
proportion of the roomers were seasonal migrants from
the Auvergne and the Limousin.[37] Finally, at a time when

[34] Chevalier, *Classes laborieuses*, p. 280. These statistics
date from 1851. The 1846 census did not include a breakdown
by ages. The extraordinarily small percentage of children would
rise a couple of points if the 15,000 nursing babies "exported"
annually to peasant nursemaids were included. See Armand
Husson, *Les consommations de Paris* (Paris, 1856), p. 39. In
any event, the proportion of Parisian children in 1821 was not
much more than one-half what it was for England (a rapidly
growing population with similar life-expectancies). See T. H.
Hollingsworth, *Historical Demography* (Ithaca, N.Y., 1969),
p. 347.

[35] *Statistique de l'industrie*, pp. 49-50. For scholarly controversy over the long-term trend of Parisian living standards
during the July Monarchy, see Jacques Rougerie, "Remarques
sur l'histoire des salaires à Paris au XIXᵉ siècle," *Annales*,
xxiii (1968), 71-108.

[36] *Statistique de l'industrie*, p. 69.

[37] For some hair-raising, first-hand descriptions of such
hovels see ibid., pp. 201-204; see also Chevalier, *Classes
laborieuses*, pp. 271-277.

nationwide more than two-fifths of all French recruits were illiterate, an astonishing 87 percent of male Parisian workers could read and write, and even 79 percent of the women could do likewise.[38] The chamber of commerce could conclude with some complacency: "During ordinary and normal times, the working population of Paris enjoys satisfactory living conditions in every respect. . . . The majority of workers are well-behaved, hard-working men, with a certain average education and not without morality. The wages they receive, though not always sufficient to safeguard them from the consequences of unexpected business slumps, at least permit them to live suitably."[39]

This last qualification provides the key to the puzzle of a well-paid labor force living in penury. Most Parisian workers could have lived "suitably"—no doubt in very modest circumstances—had their employment and their food costs remained stable. They were utterly without reserves in the face of an instability that was, unfortunately, "ordinary and normal." Most industries had their recognized off-seasons twice a year, forcing them to lay off some employees for a period of weeks or even months. More unpredictably, natural disasters introduced another variable. The failure of the grain crop in 1846, driving up the price of bread to twice its normal level over the course of an entire year, led to disastrous cuts in living standards. Bread was still the staple food of the lower classes, and expenditure for bread was the largest single item in a working-class family budget (though rent was a close runner-up in Paris). In this case, the effects of the grain shortage were made worse by the consequences of the potato blight of 1846, which drove up the price of the one food that could take the place of bread. Though the good harvest of 1847 brought bread prices down to nor-

[38] *Statistique de l'industrie*, pp. 68-69.
[39] Ibid., p. 61.

mal levels, most families must still have felt the earlier strain as they entered the year 1848.[40]

Unexpected business slumps, as the chamber of commerce's spokesman had recognized, posed the worst threat to lower-class living standards. The Second Republic did not invent depressions, the July Monarchy having experienced at least as many slow years as good ones. Yet the severity of the economic collapse that followed the February Revolution had no recent precedent. According to official figures gathered after the event, and almost certainly understating the problem, of 343,000 Parisian workers—men, women and children—186,000, or 54 percent, were completely out of work in the spring of 1848.[41] How many were put on short hours or a two-

[40] Neither 1847 nor 1848 saw a sharp rise in the death rate in Paris, though it is one or two per thousand above the average for 1841-1845. Chevalier, *Classes laborieuses*, pp. 405-406. What probably accounts for this relatively mild impact is that, despite a rise in bread prices from 25 centimes (average for 1841-1845) to 42 centimes per kilogram in 1847, public assistance lessened the shock. During the crisis of 1846-1847, 96,177 Parisians were put on relief, another 299,387 were granted bread coupons. Husson, *Consommations*, pp. 36-38.

There is no comprehensive scholarly account of the Parisian economic crisis of 1847. J. Markovitch, "La crise de 1847-1848 dans les industries parisiennes," *Revue d'histoire économique et sociale*, XLIII (1965), 256-260, is merely a rehash of the Chamber of Commerce survey of 1849 and does not deal with 1847 but only with 1848. André-Jean Tudesq, "La crise de 1847 vue par les milieux d'affaires parisiens," *Etudes*, "Société de l'histoire de la révolution de 1848," XIX (1956), 4-36, is not a comprehensive account either.

[41] *Statistique de l'industrie*, pp. 40-42. There are at least two reasons to suppose these figures to be gross underestimates. First, employment in 1848 was being compared with the "normal" base year of 1847. Economically, 1847 was a disaster year second only to 1848, with business bankruptcies in Paris 71 percent above the average for the years 1840-1846. (Daumard, *Bourgeoisie parisienne*, p. 428.) Presumably unemploy-

day work week is uncertain, because the organizers of the 1849 industrial census did not include the question on their list. In any event, the figures given do not include self-employed workers or small masters, who must have been equally hard hit, nor do they enumerate the unemployed of the Paris suburbs. This creeping catastrophe, which reached its worst in June 1848, makes intelligible lower-class agitation and its concern with work-relief. Mass unemployment goes far in explaining how a revolution begun in self-assertion and hope could collapse in despair and hunger four months later.

vi

It is easier to assess the economic role of the Parisian workers than to portray what the chamber of commerce census called their "habits and general living conditions." As the question was asked of employers, the editors of the industrial census of 1849 did not hesitate to sketch a "moral profile" of the Parisian working class. The tone was, as might be expected, utterly patronizing, and the judgments may reflect middle-class folk wisdom as much as the polltaker's data. Nevertheless, in the absence of

---

ment for 1847 was also above normal, thus making the comparison with 1848 relatively meaningless, if not actually misleading. Second, the undoubtedly even larger group of employers who, with or without bankruptcy, went out of business in 1848 was not polled by the Chamber of Commerce census takers. Reason (1) would raise the percentage of unemployed; (2) would raise the absolute numbers of both employed and unemployed without necessarily affecting the percentage. The only genuinely contemporary figures I have seen noted 52,000 of 337,500 male and female Parisian workers as fully employed by May 1848, 110,000 on a four-day week, and 175,000 without regular employment. There is no way of checking the accuracy of these statistics furnished without attribution by *Le Représentant du peuple*, May 20, 1848.

a French Mayhew indefatigably describing and classifying the Parisian laboring poor, the editors of the industrial census will have to do.

The editors appeared impressed by working-class intelligence, adaptability, and inventiveness, though on closer inspection they seem to have confined their admiration to certain types of workers, perceiving a sharp contrast between the improvidence of the unskilled and the self-respect of those who had completed their apprenticeship. In the larger factories (which, they noted, were little by little leaving the capital) rougher and less educated workmen created an atmosphere of turbulence quite unlike the quiet self-discipline governing most of the small shops. Evidently the chamber of commerce regarded the makers of the varied "articles of Paris"—actually only 12 percent of the labor force—as the ideal type of Parisian worker.[42]

To what extent Parisian workers were reconciled to their status we cannot tell. They do not seem to have married "above their station." In one parish of the first *arrondissement* that has been studied, unskilled workers and artisans married women three-quarters of whom were themselves workers and one-quarter servants; almost no other social groups were represented among the marriage partners.[43] Yet almost half of the petty bourgeoisie of small retailers was of "popular" origin. Slightly higher on the social scale, 69 percent of Parisian building contractors and 60 percent of other master artisans had begun their career without capital, strongly suggesting working-class origins.[44] Evidently there was some upward mobility. Yet the statistical chance of such success for an average worker was not great. Between 1815 and 1848,

[42] *Statistique de l'industrie*, pp. 62-65.
[43] Daumard, "Les relations sociales à Paris," pp. 448-450.
[44] Daumard, *Bourgeoisie parisienne*, pp. 259-262.

the Parisian bourgeoisie hovered around 15 percent of the city's rising population.[45] Save among the marginal petty bourgeoisie, there seems to have been little downward social mobility among members of the propertied minority. The number of openings for which ambitious workers might strive was therefore limited, and the chances for success did not appreciably improve during the constitutional monarchy.[46] Contemporaries, including the editors of the industrial census, noted a different sort of social mobility among workers, which might be described as lateral rather than upward: the skilled artisan who preferred humble self-employment to wage work. Apparently a cabinetmaker carrying the chair he had just finished to sell at a street corner or to a furniture dealer was a familiar figure.[47]

There was more to working-class life than labor and enforced idleness. Sunday was considered family day, churchgoing being the exception. "In the evening he takes a walk with his wife and children," unless a more ambitious outing has been planned: "For a population working within a great city, in neighborhoods where the streets are generally narrow and the buildings tall, . . . the need for an outing and for fresh air becomes overwhelming after a few days of assiduous labor. That is why one sees a tide of Parisians streaming out of the city every Sunday, and beautiful weather is a heavenly benediction to them."[48]

Unfortunately, in the editors' view, the lure of the open spaces was reinforced by that of cheap wine sold in the taverns beyond the toll barriers. Drink, the report as-

[45] Ibid., pp. 15-16.   [46] Ibid., pp. 285-286.

[47] *Statistique de l'industrie*, p. 72. Georges Duveau, *La vie ouvrière sous le Second Empire* (Paris, 1946), though I seem unable to find the page reference.

[48] *Statistique de l'industrie*, p. 70.

serted, was the bane of the worker. It was obviously also the bane of his employer, whose business suffered because even well-paid artisans would take Monday off as their "day with the boys."[49] The editors tempered their final verdict on the Parisian working class as "a population whose principal character traits are great mental liveliness, a remarkable facility for absorbing new ideas, a strong taste for pleasure, work habits favoring quick bursts of energy over perseverance, and little inclination to save money."[50]

vii

What about the political beliefs of this working class prior to the outbreak of the revolution of 1848? We know little about them, not only because the last years of the July Monarchy were fairly untroubled, but also because the files of the two agencies likely to keep track of lower-class opinions—the Prefecture of Police and the Paris municipality—have not survived. Working-class memoirs can be listed on the fingers of one hand.[51] The recollections of Martin Nadaud, a stonemason who made good, are quoted over and over, even though they were composed by an old man decades removed from the events he described.[52] The ballads of working-class *chansonniers*

[49] Ibid., p. 71. The contemporary French phrase is "le jour des camarades."

[50] Ibid.

[51] See their virtual absence, for example, from F. and J. Fourastié, eds., *Les écrivains témoins du peuple* (Paris, 1964). The lower-class nineteenth-century memoirists most often cited, aside from Nadaud, are Agricol Perdiguier, Sebastien Commissaire, and Anthime Corbon. By no stretch of the imagination can any one of these be considered a "representative" figure.

[52] *Mémoires de Léonard, ancien garçon maçon* (Bourganeuf, 1895; rpt. Paris, 1948).

merely attest to banal resentment of the worker's lot of hunger and insecurity.[53]

Undeniably, there were elements of militant opposition among the Parisian workers during the last years of the constitutional monarchy, but their numbers or importance can easily be exaggerated. Paris did have its splinter groups of true believers, with their "schools," their prophets, their struggling weeklies, their ten-centime pamphlets, their conspiracies engineered by *agents provocateurs*. The republican secret societies, in which neo-Jacobins quarreled with neo-Babouvists over ideology and tactics, were largely working class, with a membership between fifteen hundred and four thousand, figures that included an impressive contingent of police-spies.[54] The solemnly didactic weekly, *La Fraternité de 1845*, had its small band of materialist communist sympathizers.[55] The Fourierists, who were quite apolitical before

[53] Pierre Brochon, ed., *La chanson française: Le pamphlet du pauvre* (*1834-1851*) (Paris, 1957), passim.

[54] The police spy Delahodde, after elaborate and often tenuous calculations, reaches a maximum of 4,000 revolutionary republicans, though he puts the total of actual secret society members at no more than 1,000. Lucien Delahodde, *Histoire des sociétés secrètes et du parti républicain de 1830 à 1848* (Paris, 1850), pp. 402-403. Bernard Pornin, another secret society leader, put the total membership somewhat higher. Cf. Pornin, *La vérité sur la préfecture de police pendant l'administration de Caussidière: Refutation des calomnies Chenu* (Paris, 1850).

[55] See E. Labrousse, *Le mouvement ouvrier et les théories sociales en France de 1815 à 1848* (Paris [1952]), pp. 176-182, for a brief account of non-Icarian working-class "communism." Georges Sencier, *Le Babouvisme après Babeuf* (Paris, 1912), is tendentious and simple-minded. For a recent sympathetic account, see Samuel Bernstein, "Le néo-babouvisme d'après la presse (1837-1848)," in *Babeuf et le babouvisme* (Stockholm, 1960), pp. 247-276. There is an interesting comparison of *La Fraternité de 1845* with Cabet's Icarian *Le Populaire* in Christopher H. Johnson, "Communism and the Working Class before Marx: The Icarian Experience," *American*

1848, failed to get much proletarian support.[56] The Catholic-Socialists publishing *L'Atelier* were elite workers of such exemplary rectitude and moderation that their journal (maximum press run in 1847: 1,050 copies) ended up mostly in the hands of the middle class.[57] The largest working-class following in Paris looked to Etienne Cabet's Icarian communism, though its emphasis on nonviolence and, after 1847, its escapism (Cabet went on to found a commune in Illinois) may add up to less than "militant opposition." Cabet's paper, *Le Populaire* (selling 1,000 copies in the Paris area alone), was pitched to workers, the movement making an especially strong appeal to journeymen in depressed industries, such as shoemaking. There were several thousand Icarians in Paris.[58]

Yet if we add up the adherents of these diverse movements, the total comes surely to less than ten thousand. Cabet, the most successful, had one subscriber to every 350 workers![59] If we turn from the word to the deed, the impression of political lethargy is equally strong. The last major republican outbreak involving large numbers of workers in Paris had occurred in 1832; the last significant rebellion in 1834; the last abortive rising that of "the Sea-

---

Historical Review, LXXVI (1971), 642-689. See also Alexandre Zévaès, "La fermentation sociale sous la Restoration et sous la monarchie de juillet," *Revue internationale d'histoire politique et constitutionnelle*, No. 11 (1953), 206-234.

[56] Johnson, "Communism and the Working Class," p. 656. Labrousse, *Le mouvement ouvrier*, pp. 145-147.

[57] Armand Cuvillier, *Un journal d'ouvriers: l'Atelier (1840-1850)* (Paris, 1954), pp. 177-179.

[58] The highest attendance claimed by Cabet's Icarian club, the Société fraternelle centrale, during the spring of 1848 was 6,000, including 1,000 women. Not all of these were necessarily members or even active sympathizers. (*La Voix des clubs*, March 14, 1848.) Johnson minimizes Cabet's utopian escapism. See his "Etienne Cabet and the Problem of Class Antagonism," *International Review of Social History*, XI (1966), 403-443.

[59] Johnson, "Communism and the Working Class," p. 653.

sons" in 1839. After that, nothing—for the petty plots of the 1840's have the scent of police provocations.[60]

Such quiescence does not imply that the lower classes in Paris lived lives of total isolation, unmoved by collective interests, untouched by the currents of public opinion. Wineshops and rooming houses grouped men following the same trade or hailing from the same provincial village or district. Singing societies with a predominantly working-class membership, like the Choral Society of the Children of Lutèce, met regularly on Sundays at outdoor restaurants beyond the toll barriers. Adult education, of varying fare and sponsorship, tended to attract a proletarian elite. On a more prosaic level, some 7.5 percent of the Paris work force—nearly twenty-six thousand persons in 1846—belonged to "friendly societies" supporting their members in sickness, disability, and death. A dwindling number of journeymen carried on the tradition of the "wandering year"—the *tour de France*—by joining one of their guilds, the *compagnonnages*, with their elaborate ritual and their archaic and often bloody rivalries. Less picturesque and more hardheaded "resistance societies," like those that had won the great carpenters' strike of 1845, persisted in the shadows of illegality despite police repression. Popular undercurrents of republicanism came into the open on ceremonial occasions such as the funeral of some republican notable. Only five weeks before the February Revolution, for example, the burial procession of Caussidière senior, father of the republican conspirator and prefect-to-be, attracted vast crowds honoring the veteran of the First Republic.[61] Slo-

[60] It is no accident that our fullest account of the underground republican movement, Delahodde's *Histoire des sociétés secrètes*, should be by one of the most prominent "revolutionary" leaders—and a confessed police spy.

[61] R. Gossez, *Les ouvriers de Paris*, I: *L'organisation, 1848-1851*, "Bibliothèque de la révolution de 1848," XXIV (1967), 27-31, 41.

gans like "organization of labor," with connotations ranging from free collective bargaining to cooperative utopia, must have been widely repeated long before the first barricade ever went up. Yet there were limits to working-class sympathies: as late as March 1848, "communism"—a label sheltering phenomena as disparate as Cabet's Icaria and Blanqui's penchant for revolutionary dictatorship—was a dirty word.[62] The very imprecision of contemporary political terminology suggests that neither ideology nor politics had a central place in the lives of average Parisians prior to the February Revolution.

viii

It was a paradoxical revolution, over in three days, yet barely begun. Insofar as the July Monarchy was toppled on February 24, the revolution was over. Two days earlier, the slow-motion shadowboxing between the government and its opponents over the famous reform banquet of the twelfth *arrondissement* had unexpectedly turned vicious. The violence should have surprised no one: popular misery left over from last year's bread crisis, official arrogance, the diffusion of republican and socialist ideas, a small revolutionary underground, a disenchanted bourgeois militia added up to an explosive mix. Violence swelled as it proved effective in exacting belated concessions from a frightened regime. The inevitable "massacre" of unarmed demonstrators, the king's reluctance to resort to full-scale civil war did the rest. By February 24 the fighting had ended, as the king and his family made their way to England and a defeated and disorganized army garrison streamed out of Paris. The capital was left in the hands of the revolutionary crowds acclaiming, safeguard-

[62] For the hostility toward "communism" in the working-class Club des Quinze-Vingt in the Faubourg Saint-Antoine, see Forestier to Cabet, March 26, 1848, Cabet Papers, BHVP, série 25, carton II.

ing, and badgering a Provisional Government of their own making, but not necessarily after their own heart: respectable ex-deputies jostled feuding republican newspapermen. Albert, the machinist-named-minister, who owed his elevation to his leading role in the secret societies, was clearly no more than a conversation piece in this reluctantly revolutionary government—uncomfortable with revolutionaries, uncomfortable with power, and not least uncomfortable with a republic viewed as premature and proclaimed only under duress.

Yet on February 24, 1848, another revolution had just begun, jolting tens of thousands of working-class Parisians of "great mental liveliness, a remarkable facility for absorbing new ideas, a strong taste for pleasure" out of their narrow existence and into public life. For a few months, individual anxieties and desires came together in a collective drive for political and social transformation. Nothing like it had been seen since the great days of the 1790's. This burgeoning mass democracy desperately searched for ways to break through, for institutions through which its power could be made effective. This was the revolution that had just begun and this is what the Paris club movement of 1848 was about. When it was all over, its failure left an inarticulate sense of loss, like that of the journeyman glove-maker whose lassitude worried his solicitous employer. No, he wasn't ill and he wasn't unhappy where he was; but, he said, "It's stronger than me. I don't have my heart in the work any more. I keep arguing with myself, but it doesn't do any good. Ever since this revolution, I don't seem able to lift my arms."[63]

[63] *Statistique de l'industrie*, pp. 71-72.

2 | The World of the Clubs

The clubs are the living barricades of democracy.
. . . by way of the clubs, by way of this second National
Assembly always in session, always active, the new social
order must be erected.

From the Manifesto of the Republican Club of
Free Workers (March 1848)

i

On February 25, 1848, a mere twenty-four hours after
the revolution had ended, Auguste Blanqui, just released
from political prison, canvassed the possibility of overthrowing the newly installed Provisional Government.
Unable to find reliable allies for his own ultrarevolutionary followers, Blanqui, abandoning his insurrectionary
plans, founded instead the first Parisian club: the Central Republican Society.[1] This symbolic sublimation of
the revolutionary impulse is almost too pat. By March 1
there were at least 5 clubs; by March 10, 36; by March
15, 59. For mid-April 1848, when the club movement
reached its zenith, 203 popular societies have left traces
in greater Paris, 149 of them members of the same club
federation.[2]

---

[1] Suzanne Wassermann, *Les clubs de Barbès et de Blanqui
en 1848* (Paris, 1913), pp. 40-47.

[2] These figures are based on my own files and are almost
certainly incomplete by 10 or even 20 percent. They are much
smaller than the numbers contemporaries could cite because I

The numbers of people involved naturally paralleled the proliferation of organizations, though definitive figures are lacking. During the spring of 1848, newspapers occasionally published estimates of club attendance or club membership. The total for the eighteen popular societies publicized (less than one-tenth of all Parisian clubs!) came to well over twenty thousand.[3] This does not mean that there were two hundred thousand clubists in Paris—even though a club-sponsored demonstration on March 17 may well have attracted that many—for the press singled out the best attended popular societies. Besides, journalists did not usually distinguish between members and casual visitors. Still, my most conservative estimate puts the membership of the popular societies at fifty

---

exclude all clubs located beyond the fortifications of Paris and all special interest groups. The latter include not only such organizations as a Club des locataires-commerçants or the Société démocratique des hommes lettrés sans emploi but the numerous regional (e.g., Club républicain des ouvriers alsociens) or departmental popular societies (e.g., Club démocratique du Rhône) primarily concerned with organizing elections in their home region or department. However, a few such clubs did adhere to the Club des Clubs, Comité révolutionnaire and evinced general political interests.

[3] This figure is derived from the following sources: *La Commune de Paris*, March 9, 13, 1848; April 5, 14, 1848. *La Voix des clubs*, March 8, 13, 14, 15, 17, 20, 22, 1848. *L'Ami du peuple en 1848*, March 19, April 13, 1848. *La République*, March 2, 5, 1848. *Le Populaire*, March 2, 1848. *Le Courrier français*, March 5, 1848. *La Démocratie pacifique*, March 8, 1848. Archives nationales (hereafter A.N.), Commission d'Enquête (hereafter CdE) 8546, 8549. Bibliothèque nationale (hereafter B.N.), Lb[53] 565. Minutes, Société démocratique de La Villette, March 20, Buchez Papers, Bibliothèque historique de la Ville de Paris (hereafter B.H.V.P.). Undated poster, Club des travailleurs unis, B.H.V.P. Affiches, Seconde République.

thousand to seventy thousand.[4] A somewhat higher figure in the neighborhood of one hundred thousand seems more likely. To put this in homely terms: George Sand, the novelist, arriving at her Paris apartment one evening in mid-March 1848, found herself locked out. Not one of the three locksmiths whom she tried to summon could be reached; each one was attending a club.[5] Within a few weeks a mass movement had taken root.

ii

In trying to explain the origin of the club movement, we must, paradoxically, ignore some of the pioneering popular societies. Aside from Blanqui's Central Republican Society already mentioned, the first clubs to appear in Paris were atypical in the sense that they were carry-overs from the July Monarchy. The Central Democratic Society (not to be confused with Blanqui's own club) was

[4] I have used the following methods of computing these estimates: (1) I have assumed 200 clubs, a figure which is probably 10 to 20 percent too low. (2) Of the clubs for which I have attendance figures, I have dropped from consideration the six with the highest attendance on the ground that they are atypical. On the basis of scattered newspaper comment, I have assumed membership to total two-thirds of attendance. The average membership thus comes to 450. (3) For clubs for which I have membership or voting membership (none of which includes "name" clubs), I used the highest available membership figure. The average membership according to this approach is 600. (4) I assumed that clubs making the newspapers were likely to have a larger membership than average. I have therefore assumed the average membership derived in (2) and (3) for 100 clubs, one-half that average for the remaining 100. This provides a range from about 65,000 to 90,000. (5) I assumed that one-fourth of all clubists had membership in two clubs. This brings the range down to 50,000 to 70,000. These, in my judgment, are minimum figures.

[5] George Sand, *Correspondance*, VII (Paris, 1964), 356.

an offshoot of a prerevolutionary electoral committee; the Central Fraternal Society banded together the Icarian followers of the utopian communist, Etienne Cabet; the Republican Club of *L'Atelier* crystallized around a coterie of Christian-socialist workers who had collaborated on the newspaper by that name since 1840.[6] Because the very beginning of the club movement tells us nothing about why it snowballed, we can almost disregard these first stirrings. We may be equally cavalier in explaining the appearance of popular societies founded after mid-March 1848. Once the number of clubs had reached a certain critical mass, clubs proliferated by the momentum of imitation, until the scarcity of meeting places and the exhaustion of the public halted the movement. The question of origin should therefore be directed at the several dozen clubs that sprang up in the first two weeks of March 1848.

Perhaps even this question of origin should be narrowed. Why institutions for mass participation should have arisen in the circumstances of 1848 is virtually self-evident. The February Revolution was a social revolution in the sense of mobilizing tens of thousands of people who had previously been outside of the political process. Some form of revolutionary mass participation, be it workers' councils, brown-shirted storm-trooper units, or revolutionary militia, is a normal corollary of such a revolution. The questions we should raise, therefore, are: Why *not* soviets? Why *not* a workers' militia? Why *clubs*?

The questions may be answered both in terms of functional needs and of tradition. Though labor organization, long repressed by the French penal code, blossomed in

[6] For the Société démocratique centrale, see the introduction to my dissertation, "A French Revolutionary Club in 1848: The Société démocratique centrale," University of Chicago, 1958; I have alluded to the Icarians and the Atelier group in Ch. 1.

the tolerant atmosphere of the early days of the Second Republic, the unions' outlook was practical and craft-oriented.[7] Political unity was something that was imposed on them from above, and rather late in the day at that. Workers' councils, on the other hand, lacked the economic base that would make the Russian soviets so formidable in 1905 and 1917: large-scale industry. In the industrial warren of dwarf enterprise that was Paris, such councils would have been about as useful as family soviets. The Cuban response of the 1960's, a popular militia as organ of mass participation, was ruled out by the tradition of a Paris National Guard which was opened to the masses but was never really revolutionized by them. Clubs dovetailed with the needs, as well as the possibilities and traditions, of a particular revolutionary situation.

Where does this leave the conventional wisdom crediting the club movement of 1848 to the French revolutionary tradition? In one obvious respect, that tradition *was* potent: in the Paris of the 1790's, it took the sans-culottes two years to "invent" popular societies; in 1848 "the people" needed less than two weeks to rediscover them, no doubt aided by the promptings of revolutionary newspapers. Yet it is easy to exaggerate the human continuity between the Great Revolution and 1848. By the middle of the nineteenth century, only one Parisian in twenty-five was old enough—fifty-five years separated 1793 and 1848—to have lived through the storm of the 1790's as a young adult. Among club leaders, the proportion was the same: of forty-eight presidents for whom I was able to find a record of age, only two were men in their seventies. Their average age was thirty-nine, their median forty. Most were just old enough to recall the overthrow of the Bourbons eighteen years earlier.

[7] Gossez, *Les ouvriers*, passim.

Because our eyes leap to the Club of the Jacobins in 1848 (and there *were* three of them!), we are likely to overemphasize the persistence of symbols borrowed from the Great Revolution. The fact is that only 5 percent of club names deliberately raised the ghosts of the revolutionary past.[8] Among these, a historian is struck with the paucity of the tradition. By 1848, for example, the great Club of the Cordeliers had apparently vanished from folk memory insofar as no popular society during the Second Republic borrowed that name. Even among newly founded revolutionary newspapers (whose publishers were more likely to have been schooled in French history than the average club organizer), only 10 percent evoked revolutionary recollections by their title, and many of these were ephemeral sheets that folded after one or two issues.[9] The rhetoric of club posters and announcements also rarely appealed to the precedents of 1793, though

[8] Aside from the three Jacobin clubs mentioned, these comprised three named Club de la Montagne and one Club des Montagnards, one Club des amis du peuple celebrating Jean-Paul Marat's newspaper, and one Club de la Commune de Paris. A promised Club de la Convention nationale was stillborn.

[9] The historian of contemporary society able to use questionnaires and polling techniques has obvious advantages over the social historian dealing with an inscrutable past. See, e.g., the present-minded "Mémoire historique et usage de l'histoire chez les ouvriers français," by René Kaes (*Le mouvement social*, No. 61 [1967], pp. 13-32). As for contemporary newspapers, 18 of 171 postrevolutionary newspapers published in Paris between February 25 and June 22, 1848, bore nostalgic titles such as *Le Journal des sans-culottes*, *La Commune de Paris*, *L'Ami du peuple en 1848*, *La Carmagnole*. Of those, only three—*La Commune de Paris*, *L'Ami du peuple*, and *Le Père Duchêne*—were of any consequence. The list of newspapers is taken from Assemblée nationale, *Rapport fait au nom de la commission chargée de l'enquête sur l'insurrection qui a éclaté dans la journée du 23 juin et sur les évènements du 15 mai* (Paris, 1848), II, 277-280 (hereafter *Enquête*).

historical evocations fitted the overblown style popular in 1848.[10] The only exception—the frequent bows in the direction of Robespierre's proposed Declaration of the Rights of Man—is misleading: its popularity owed more to its use as a touchstone of true republicanism among the secret societies of the July Monarchy than it did to memories of 1793.

Though in a vague way the revolutionary tradition did inform the revolutionaries of 1848 that popular societies were a "good thing," the republican underground of the Orleanist period provided a much more tangible legacy. The importance of clubs had been emphasized by such neo-Babouvist organizations as the émigré French Democratic Society in London and the secret Egalitarian Workers in Paris, which agreed that popular societies should become the building stones for a postrevolutionary administration of France.[11] More directly, one of the most important clubs in 1848, the Society of the Rights of Man, took its leadership, name, organizational structure, and ethos from its defunct namesake of the 1830's. A number of other clubs incorporated structural features— mainly the subdivision of a popular society into "sections" or "cells"—taken directly from the secret societies of the July Monarchy.[12]

[10] For three such allusions—the only ones I found—see Club de la Montagne (du Carré Saint-Martin), in *Le Tribun du peuple, organe de la Montagne*, March 30, 1848; for Club républicain du Temple, announcement, B.N., Lb⁵³, 407; for Club des Jacobins (du Faubourg du Roule), *La Voix des clubs*, March 25, 1848.

[11] Georges Sencier, *Le Babouvisme après Babeuf*, pp. 274-275.

[12] For the "Instruction pratique concernant l'affiliation dans la Société des Droits de l'Homme," see *Enquête*, II, 84; for the complete organization of the *société*, see Haute-Cour de Bourges, session of March 21, *Le Moniteur universel*, March 23, 1849. For popular societies imitating this paramilitary organ-

iii

This impression of carry-over from the constitutional monarchy's republican underground is reinforced as soon as we examine the political background of the earliest club founders. Among some thirty-six clubs organized between February 25 and March 10, 1848, it has been possible to discover something of the political antecedents of seventeen club presidents or founders. Among these, militant veterans of the illegal republican underground movement constitute the single largest group, ten of the seventeen. This group comprised recent veterans of the secret societies, militants returned from exile, and, of course, Blanqui himself just released from his hospital-prison at Tours.[13] In terms of class, five of these founder-organizers were workers, five were of middle-class extraction or occupation.

The next group of four, only two-fifths as large as the illegal republicans, had been members of the legal republican opposition under the July Monarchy (calling itself "radicals," since the label "republican" had been outlawed). The distinction between "legal" and "illegal" republicans had originally arisen over questions of timing and tactics: many of the "legal" republicans, having begun their republican careers as flaming revolutionaries, had been tamed by the failure of political violence be-

---

ization, see among others: Club des travailleurs (du 1er arrondissement), B.N., Lb[53], 574; bylaws, Club de la fraternité, *Les murailles révolutionnaires*, ed. A. Delvau (Paris, 1852), pp. 238-240.

[13] It is ironical that one of the secret society men, Grandmesnil, cofounder of the Société populaire du XIe arrondissement, was still drawing a 100 francs per month pension from Louis-Philippe in January 1848 as a former political prisoner of the Restoration, having been condemned as a Carbonaro in 1822. (Archives de la Préfecture de Police, A[A], 366; hereafter cited as A.P.P.)

tween 1831 and 1834. In the case of returning long-time exiles, men with rather similar revolutionary backgrounds chose different sides: Joseph Guinard, back from England, opted for the "legals"; Napoléon Lebon, returned from Spain, chose the "illegals." The division was more one of temperament than of ideology; of the two like-minded neo-Jacobins in the Provisional Government, Ledru-Rollin would have had to be classified as a legal republican, Flocon as an illegal. At most, there was a tendency for clubs emerging from the republican underground tradition to be somewhat more socially conscious and more working-class-oriented. All four presidents of legal republican antecedents were, for example, solidly middle class.

Of the 178 club presidents whose names are on record, almost half can be identified by profession. Of these, 23 percent were workers, 22 percent intellectuals (writers, journalists, professors), 21 percent bourgeois (employers, proprietors, managers, *rentiers*—though this last category is ambiguous); 18 percent white-collar workers (ranging from clerk through bookkeeper to priest); 9 percent members of the "popular bourgeoisie" of wineshop owners, rooming house operators, modest greengrocers; and 5 percent university students. No doubt these statistics should be greeted with some skepticism: our sources, street directories and biographical dictionaries, tend to concentrate on the educated, the accomplished, and the propertied to the neglect of the humble. Even if we allow for this bias, we must conclude that the Parisian middle class (one-third of the capital's population) provided two-thirds of the club presidents, while the working class (two-thirds of the inhabitants) ended up with no more than one-third of the club presidencies.[14]

[14] Occupational identifications are derived from club announcements, printed accounts of club minutes, archives of the Club des clubs, campaign literature, the list of those arrested and booked after the June insurrection, the biographies

Two plausible, though unprovable, explanations may account for these disproportions. First, club leadership required an unusually high degree of verbal skill to manipulate the symbols of revolutionary ideology. In this respect, the education acquired by men of bourgeois background was an obvious advantage. Second, the 730 delegates of the organized crafts, meeting nightly at the Luxembourg, were unable to compete for positions of leadership in the popular societies. By and large, therefore, these natural leaders of the Parisian workers were lost to the club movement. Among some hundreds of club militants who have left some record of their activity, only three managed to combine trade union and club offices: Maury, president of the Republican Society of La Chapelle doubled as cofounder of the Railroad, Stagecoach, and Teamster Employees Association; the head of one guild of specialized cabinetmakers also chaired the Society of the Rights of Man of the twelfth *arrondissement*; Blanqui's friend Flotte combined his post as president of the cooks' union with the vice-presidency of the Central Republican Society.[15] Yet these were clearly exceptional cases.

---

in the new *DBMOF* and the Paris street and professional directory, the Didot-Bottin for 1847 and 1848 (which includes *only* middle-class residents), and the printed catalogue of the B.N. (excellent for intellectuals).

Using the new figures, I added 100 percent to the categories of workers, *bourgeoisie populaire*, and white collar workers, as being most likely to be overlooked by existing sources. I added 50 percent to the categories of bourgeoisie and professionals and 25 percent to intellectuals and university students as being least likely to have been ignored.

My social structure of Paris relies on the calculations of Daumard, *Bourgeoisie parisienne*, pp. 13-16, although I have attributed her 10 percent for military personnel (inapplicable after February) to "le peuple."

[15] Gossez, *Les ouvriers*, pp. 147, 213-222, 244.

iv

The weight of the middle-class club leadership, whatever the reasons for it, raises the question of the class base of the entire club movement and its relationship to the other great mass organization of 1848, organized labor. Did these two tap essentially separate layers of the Parisian population? Certainly we cannot accept club labels at face value. On closer examination, the fact that thirteen clubs featured "workers" (*ouvriers, travailleurs*) or "labor" (*travail*) as part of their name is inconclusive. For instance, the founding fathers of the Workers' Club of Fraternity included three or four lawyers, three government employees, several proprietors, as well as a dozen authentic artisans and journeymen.[16] Nor can one blame this confusion on deliberate deception: in 1848 the same semantic fog beclouded the term *travailleur* as enveloped the term "workingman" in Jacksonian America. *Travailleur* did not necessarily imply someone engaged in manual wage labor, though it did connote someone actively pursuing an occupation.

Neither can we postulate that all popular societies shared the same social basis. Self-consciously elite clubs —Blanqui's Central Republican Society, Barbès' Club of the Revolution, Guinard's Central Democratic Society —tended to middle-class membership for the good reason that the bulk of the revolutionary elite *was* bourgeois or petty bourgeois. At the other end of the scale, the membership of a given popular society might be characterized in terms of specific occupational groups, as, for example, the Republican Club of Workers was described as a gathering of four hundred "weavers and machin-

[16] Announcement, Club des ouvriers de la fraternité, B.N., Lb53, 672.

ists."[17] All this tells us is that there was some variety in the social composition of the clubs. On the whole, however, contemporaries were struck by the conspicuous presence, often by the predominance, of Parisian workers in the popular societies.

How, if at all, then, did club membership differ from that of organized labor, or the *corporations ouvrières* as the trade unions were known? Though we have no direct evidence, it seems probable that there was considerable overlapping between the two types of mass organization. Popular societies were generally local in character and met frequently, three to five times a week being typical. *Corporations ouvrières*, organized on a city-wide basis, met much less frequently. We happen to know, for example, that the tinsmiths-lampmakers held only twelve general meetings between the February Revolution and the June Days.[18] In other words, a tinsmith, and presumably other union members as well, could have attended his local popular society without any dereliction of duty to his trade. Such dual affiliation is made more probable in that the appeal and objectives of the *corporations* and of the clubs were complementary rather than inconsistent. Throughout the revolutionary phase of 1848, the unions were chiefly preoccupied with questions of full employment, collective bargaining, wage rates, hours, and working conditions, whereas the typical trade union objectives were never broached by the popular societies, which stressed political aims and political methods.[19] If there was a real split within the lower classes, most likely it was between the "mobilized" and the apathetic, rather than between those mobilized in the realm of economics and those activated by politics. The only known excep-

[17] Announcement, B.N., Lb[53], 565.
[18] Gossez, *Les ouvriers*, p. 156.
[19] Ibid., passim, but esp. pp. 48-110.

tion, as we noted, was the worker delegates to the Luxembourg Labor Commission, whom their duties excluded from club participation.

This is not to say that the rank and file of the popular societies merely coincided with that of the *corporations*. While the latter were restricted to skilled craftsmen, clubs, by contrast, were open to anyone who subscribed to the principles of the organization. This meant that popular societies reached both up and down: up into the middle classes, and not only in selecting leaders; down to the ranks of the unskilled and the unorganized. Though there are no reliable statistics for unskilled labor in the Paris of that period, it must have been a sizable minority group: 9 percent of those arrested and 10 percent of those deported in the wake of the June Days were listed as laborers. No doubt, with 35 percent of the Parisian population between them, the middle and lower middle class was numerically more important.[20] Yet most probably, both bourgeois and unskilled were underrepresented among club members. Given the radical complexion of at least two-thirds of all clubs, the average shopkeeper or manufacturer must have hesitated to take part. My guess is that no more than 20 percent of all club members were of bourgeois or petty bourgeois origin. We have no direct evidence on the participation of unskilled

[20] For statistics of unskilled workers arrested and/or sentenced as June insurgents, see Roger Price, *The French Second Republic: A Social History* (Ithaca, N.Y., 1972), pp. 165, 169. For the numerical estimate for the Parisian middle class, see, aside from Daumard's breakdown, the figures provided by the professional and street directory of Paris, the Didot-Bottin. This yearbook, which seems to have contained a reasonably complete listing of middle-class Parisian adult males, carried about 60,000 names in 1848. This figure also jibes with the prerevolutionary membership of 56,000 in the Paris National Guard.

laborers, but political sociologists may be correct in equating low status with a low level of political involvement.

However far the membership of the club and labor movement may have overlapped in practice, it is useful to regard the two as distinct in certain respects. At the most elementary level, this applies to an individual forced to decide whether to march behind the banner of his trade or that of his popular society, as in the popular demonstration of March 17. On this occasion, the clubs had clearly taken the organizing lead, yet both clubs and trade unions marched as self-contained entities. Similarly, in cooperating with the Revolutionary Committee, Club of Clubs, the unions were represented by their own block of fifty delegates, whom club delegates, incidentally, outnumbered seven to one.[21]

The official representation granted to labor delegates by Louis Blanc's Luxembourg Commission, in providing both an umbrella and leadership at the top, impelled the *corporations* toward a more active political role. By sponsoring their own slate of working-class candidates to the National Assembly, by organizing among themselves the demonstration of April 16, the Luxembourg workers for a short time captured the political initiative among the forces of the revolutionary Left. Their claim to the unswerving loyalty of tens of thousands of workers—which turned out to be somewhat exaggerated—momentarily intimidated, even overawed, the club movement. The failure of April 16 as a political move, as well as the defeat of the worker candidates at the polls, disappointed the organized trades as much as it disillusioned their allies. Within the revolutionary camp, the clubs regained their predominance in May, keeping it well into June. By that time, the former Luxembourg delegates began to set

[21] Gossez, *Les ouvriers*, p. 256.

up district affiliates throughout Paris.[22] The growth of these local organizations, which ignored craft lines and competed with the clubs, was cut short by the June 1848 insurrection.

V

Perhaps even more important than its links to the labor movement was the clubs' symbiotic relationship with the revolutionary press. Just as the revolution succeeded in bringing together masses of the formerly apolitical, so the Second Republic unleashed an avalanche of newspapers catering to the thirst of the newly mobilized for guidance, reassurance, and information.[23] Several hundred news-papers—the exact numbers vary with the definition—appeared in Paris between the February Revolution of

[22] Ibid., p. 297.

[23] The most complete and best informed study of the popular press in 1848 is R. Gossez, "Presse parisienne à destination des ouvriers (1848-1851)," pp. 135-166, in Jacques Godechot, ed., *La presse ouvrière 1819-1850*, "Bibliothèque de la Révolution de 1848," XXIII (1966). Individual newspapers may be checked against contemporary bibliographical guides, some of them annotated and all but one featuring supposedly typical, but often tendentious, excerpts. Listed roughly in the order of their usefulness and/or reliability are [H. Delombardy and H. Izambard], *Le Croque-Mort de la presse* (Paris, December 1848-January 1849); [Gaëtan Delmas], *Les journaux rouges: Histoire critique de tous les journaux ultra-républicains publiés à Paris depuis le 24 février jusqu'au 1er octobre 1848* (Paris, 1848); H.-A. Wallon, *La presse de 1848 ou Revue critique des journaux publiés à Paris depuis la Révolution de Février jusqu'à la fin de décembre* (Paris, 1849); H. Izambard, *La presse parisienne—statistique de tous les journaux . . . depuis le 22 février 1848 jusqu'à l'Empire* (Paris, 1853); Anon. [E. Pelletan], *Physionomy de la presse ou Catalogue complet des nouveaux journaux qui ont paru depuis le 24 février jusqu'au 20 août avec le nom des principaux rédacteurs* (Paris, 1848).

1848 and the June Days. As many sheets were either stillborn or died ingloriously after two or three neglected issues, the total of new journals does not tell the full story: the combined press run for all Parisian newspapers rose eightfold, from about fifty thousand before the revolution to four hundred thousand on the eve of the June uprising.[24] Allowing for the fact that some Parisian papers traditionally enjoyed a national as much as a local circulation, even the sale of perhaps three hundred thousand copies in a city of one million was astronomically high.

Popular societies had good reasons to seek the sympathetic collaboration of revolutionary newspapers. In the first place, clubs needed publicity in order to attract attention—and members. Initially, the founders of a club were likely to rely on placards, posters, and handbills to announce their opening, but in the long run continuing publicity in the newspapers—at least in one newspaper—was invaluable. Even more important than running announcements and statements of principles was the regular publication of club minutes that introduced potential recruits to the functioning organization. Second, in order for a club to have political impact, its decisions and resolutions had to get proper public exposure, and this meant publication in the daily press. This was even truer of club attempts to play an electoral role. What good was it to nominate and endorse candidates if such endorsements remained known only to the audience? Newspaper publicity was absolutely essential. Third, because clubs had few direct lateral ties to each other, a common newspaper could serve a significant coordinating function. Though on special occasions club delegates were sent to neighboring popular societies to garner support for some resolution or petition, most of the time club activists must have

[24] Gossez, *Les ouvriers*, p. 184.

relied on a common journal for their sense of what was happening in other popular societies. Though many neighborhood clubs originated in response to a spontaneous enthusiasm for political involvement, the club *movement* depended heavily on the collaboration of a revolutionary press.

In practice, such collaboration took a number of different forms. Least common was the co-option by a club of an established, prerevolutionary newspaper. The one, and perhaps only, example is the relationship of Xavier Durrieu's *Le Courrier français* to Blanqui's Central Republican Society of which Durrieu was vice-president. Until Taschereau's charges against Blanqui cooled his ardor, Durrieu faithfully published the minutes, announcements, and resolutions of Blanqui's club in the columns of his paper, which otherwise retained its normally staid format.[25] More common, but generally unsuccessful, were attempts by a single club to put out its own newspaper, presumably on the premise that the club's membership provided a stable nucleus of subscribers. The high rate of failure of such sheets is easy to explain: most of these club organs were amateur efforts that could not compete with professionally written and edited publications. Only an exceptional republican polemicist like François Raspail managed to combine the roles of president of the Society of the Friends of the People and editor of the newspaper *L'Ami du peuple en 1848*. The experience of J.-J. Danduran, who founded *La Propagande républicaine* as the "official" organ of the Society of the Rights of Man, seems to have been more typical: the paper folded after three issues. An informal "interlocking directorate" between professional journalists and club cadres often worked more smoothly. For example, Théophile Thoré, chief editor of a major revolutionary news-

[25] Wassermann, *Les clubs de Barbès et de Blanqui*, pp. x-xi.

paper, *La vraie République*, was also prominent as a member of Barbès' Club of the Revolution. *La vraie République*, though devoting little direct coverage to the club's sessions, generally mirrored its concerns and its outlook.

In yet another category were journalistic ventures that catered to widespread sentiments for closer cooperation among Parisian popular societies. The earliest of these promotions, *La Voix des clubs* (later changed to *La Sentinelle des clubs*), reproducing mainly club minutes and announcements, was floated by the undercover police: its editor, Victor Bouton, was a veteran police-spy of the July Monarchy. More serious, more effective, and relatively durable was *La Commune de Paris, Moniteur des clubs*, the recognized organ of the Club of Clubs and its affiliated member societies. It must have had a healthy circulation, since even in its declining phase—by then its founder was in prison in the wake of the May 15 affair— it still printed five thousand copies. In its heyday the paper seems to have been financially sound, backed by Joseph Sobrier's modest fortune as well as subsidized by those popular societies that wished to see their minutes in print. The offices of *La Commune de Paris*, or rather the government-owned palace in which they were housed, also served as a popular get-together for revolutionary militants.

During the weeks preceding the June insurrection, the polarization of politics reinforced the key role of the press. Editors of prominent revolutionary journals were invited to help club and labor delegates select the slate of revolutionary candidates for the special elections of June 4 and 5 and in ruling on the famous Banquet of the People shortly afterwards. When popular societies drew fire from the authorities in late May and early June, newspapers were hoisted as club banners. The Club of the Revolution, for instance, founded *Le Travail*, a paper enjoying press runs of up to ten thousand copies. The

Blanquist Club of the People under Alphonse Esquiros, himself a journalist and writer of note, put out *L'Accusateur public* in five thousand copies. The Club of Equality and Fraternity and the Democratic Club of the Arsenal cooperated in sustaining six issues of *Le Travailleur* between May 27 and June 24. Léon La Collonge, president of the Club of the Antonins and a future insurrectional mayor of the eighth *arrondissement* on June 24, launched *L'Organisation du travail.*[26] In yet another case, eviction by the municipal authorities from their usual school meeting place led the Peaceful Club of the Rights of Man to rally its members around an ominously titled newssheet, *Les Boulets rouges.*[27] Revolutionary clubs and revolutionary press alike were swallowed up in the June uprising and its suppression; neither ever fully recovered.

vi

Since we have so little direct evidence as to what led Parisian revolutionaries to found clubs in 1848, the proclaimed aims of those who did are worth considering. Some leading themes recur so consistently that they do tell us at least something about what people wanted to hear.

One major theme was the clubs' appeal to unity and fraternity, an appeal sometimes couched in the blandest clichés ("in unity lies strength"), at other times in what sounds like an 1848 version of agitprop: "We must join forces, coming together to funnel all divergences of opinion into one unified, dynamic viewpoint, dissipating through discussion any germs of dissension."[28] The siege

[26] Gossez, "Presse parisienne," pp. 139, 143-145, 150, 155-158.

[27] Izambard, *La presse parisienne*, p. 22; Delmas, *Les journaux rouges*, pp. 53-54; Wallon, *La presse de 1848*, p. 86.

[28] Announcement, March 1, 1848, Société populaire du XIe arrondissement, *Les murailles révolutionnaires* (1852 ed.),

mentality of such a statement, the premise that republicans were surrounded by enemies, was common. For this reason, unity for many clubs was a means, not an end: "Let us all prove by the constancy of our union," the Club of the Etoile concluded its initial statement, "that if some day the Republic were to be threatened, we would cease our parliamentary debates to take up arms again to defeat the Republic's enemies whomever they might be."[29] Fraternity was the other constant in such appeals, but its scope varied from club to club. In some cases, future members were invited to believe that the new Republic had already abolished all classes: "The words 'people,' 'bourgeois,' 'army,' 'workers,' must no longer be used to divide citizens into rival or hostile categories."[30] Other popular societies, rejecting such soft-headedness, defined fraternity as an incipient form of class solidarity: "Workers," the Republican Society of Passy proclaimed, "you are all citizens. This gives you both the right to participate and the duty to learn what your task is."[31] But either way, the burgeoning of clubs

---

p. 192. For other announcements stressing unity, see Club des prévoyants, *La Réforme*, March 8, 1848; Club de fraternité, B.N., Lb[53], 1555; Club de la Montagne (de Passy), B.N., Lb[53], 801.

[29] Club républicain de l'Etoile, B.N., Lb[53], 862. For similar sentiments, see Club des intérêts populaires, B.N., Lb[53], 812; Club des devoirs et des droits de l'homme, B.N., Lb[53], 738; Club démocratique du travail, B.N., Lb[53], 1548.

[30] Club des patriotes indépendants, n.d., *La Commune de Paris*, March 31, 1848. For similar sentiments, see Club des devoirs et des droits de l'homme (before March 25, 1848), B.N., Lb[53], 738; Club de l'Île Saint-Louis (before March 25, 1848), B.N., Lb[53], 738; Club des indépendants (de Charonne) (before March 29, 1848), B.N., Lb[53], 851.

[31] Société républicaine de Passy, March 10, 1848, B.N., Lb[53], 426. Other similar appeals: Club républicain de l'Etoile, n.d., B.N., Lb[53], 862; Club des travailleurs, March 21, 1848,

was viewed as an indication that the reign of fraternity was beginning.

A second, related theme praised the clubs as instruments of civic education for the newly enfranchised, places where an informed public opinion would be molded. As the Club of Socialist Republicans explained: "We [now] have the Republic, but we lack the habits suited to living as republicans. We must try with all our might to let fraternity take root in our lives. We must organize political education, create a political opinion."[32] For most clubs this meant more than just learning the procedural aspects of representative democracy. Civic education put social reform, particularly social reform benefiting the workingman, high on the agenda. Sometimes a club announcement spelled out in detail an entire program of social reform—or at least all the areas that the club would examine. At other times, cautious or less opinionated founders merely dropped slogans like "organization of labor," or the even blander "well-being of the people," promising that future sessions would clarify such concepts.

A third major theme centered on practical politics and the forthcoming political campaign. The clubs promised personal political involvement to prospective members. "Let us question the candidates," the Democratic Society of the First District urged. "Let us discuss their credentials so that our votes, after severe reflection, may be cast only for men who are sympathetic, resolute, and endowed with true republican sentiments."[33] Other clubs were

---

B.N., Lb[53], 574; Club de la Montagne (du Carré Saint-Martin), *Le Tribun du peuple*, March 30, 1848.

[32] Announcement (poster), Club des républicains socialistes du VIe arrondissement, n.d., B.H.V.P., Affiches (2e République).

[33] Société démocratique du Ier arrondissement, B.N., Lb[53], 371.

more specifically concerned with electing genuine old-line republicans: "The Club of the Mountain of Mont-martre will make every permissible effort to insure the election of as many as possible of the veterans of the struggles against the regime just overthrown."[34] In some popular societies the appeal was much more naïve, addressed to new voters obviously overwhelmed by the unfamiliar responsibilities of citizenship. To such prospective voters the Republican National Club of Belleville promised mutual aid: "We are all in need of enlightenment. How will we get it, unless we get together to exchange our ideas, our opinions? We are all voters and potential candidates for office. How will we become informed about the conduct of citizen such-and-such running for the National Assembly, if we don't know him? Let us therefore meet together, form societies, and we'll find a way out of our predicament."[35]

A final theme recurs in the form of club ambivalence toward the Provisional Government. In one sense, that government, proclaimed by the people-in-arms, embodied the legitimacy of the February Revolution. As symbol of the Republic it deserved support. In another sense, it was a government that had had to be coerced into proclaiming the Republic, a government that included men whose conversion to republicanism was suspect. In any case, whatever its intentions, the Provisional Government required the continued guidance of revolutionary opinion; hence the guidance of the popular societies. The Democratic Club of Quinze-Vingt tersely defined its mission: "surveillance and support of the new government."[36] The Club of the Socialist Republicans of the Twelfth District proclaimed its readiness to set aside at any time its regular agenda to give priority to "the crit-

[34] Club de la Montagne (de Montmartre), B.N., Lb[53], 748.
[35] Club républicain national, B.N., Lb[53], 425.
[36] *Le Courrier français*, March 4, 1848.

ical examination of all measures taken by the Provisional Government."[37] "Let us not forget," the Democratic Society of the Fifth District intoned portentously, "that governments are better served by remonstrance than by blind support. With regard to our own, let us act as the advance guard of public opinion, preserving it [the government] from the dizziness that power brings on."[38] Some popular societies wanted to concentrate on overseeing the choice of new officials, "to foil the intrigues of calculating egotists, of these job-seeking opportunists who suppose that the Republic was founded only to serve their own private interests."[39] All told, vigilant and conditional loyalty was the club stance toward the new government. The next weeks would put it to the test.

vii

Like most institutions, popular societies had their constitutional essence and their everyday existence. Except for the Society of the Rights of Man, which made a fetish of its organizational structure, there is no indication that essence influenced existence. Characteristically, club founders presented fully articulated bylaws to a membership that promptly ratified them. While these rules varied, they all made minimal provisions for electing officers, screening and inducting recruits, distinguishing between

[37] *Les murailles révolutionnaires* (1852 ed.), p. 272.

[38] March 5, 1848, B.N., Lb⁵³, 337.

[39] Club républicain du Temple, March 9, 1848, B.N., Lb⁵³, 407. For other expressions of more or less watchful loyalty, see Comité central du IIIe arrondissement, *La République*, March 5, 1848; Club des intérêts populaires, March 28, 1848, B.N., Lb⁵³, 812; Club des devoirs et des droits de l'homme, B.N., Lb⁵³, 738; Club démocratique du travail, B.N., Lb⁵³, 1548; Club des ouvriers de la fraternité (XIe arrondissement), B.N., Lb⁵³, 672; Club des Jacobins (du Faubourg du Roule), *La Voix des clubs*, March 25, 1848; Société des droits et des devoirs, B.N., Lb⁵³, 528.

members and visitors, and conducting meetings.[40] Most constitutions stipulated a frequent renewal of the leadership: in fact, it was not unusual for a club to be headed by three or four successive presidents in the period of four months following the February Revolution. Once bylaws had been approved and (usually) printed, they sank out of sight. I was unable to find a single instance where the subject recurred in club debates.

Regardless of formal structure, each popular society faced at least three practical but important decisions at the very start: where to meet, how to defray its expenses, and how often to meet. March in Paris was no time to hold meetings outdoors if there was any way of avoiding it. The most obvious solution was to rent a private hall: the Salle Montesquieu, for example, was preempted by Cabet's Icarians, several thousand of whom attended the sessions of the Central Fraternal Society. The Club of the Mountain of Montmartre installed itself in a disused dance-hall, the Petit Château-Rouge; some obscure clubs may well have begun their career in the back room of the local tavern. Geographically, most halls for hire were in the "better" districts of central Paris, few of them in the peripheral areas.

Under such circumstances, most club founders preferred to seek facilities in public buildings. Usually club officers applied to their district mayor for permission, or merely notified him that they were, for instance, preempting the local grade school's recess area during the evening

[40] Dozens of such constitutions were printed as posters or leaflets or in revolutionary newspapers. To cite but a sampling: Club du deux mars, *Les murailles révolutionnaires*, I, 313; Club de la fraternité (du Quartier Latin), ibid., pp. 238-240; Club démocratique du Ve arrondissement, B.N., Lb[53], 370; Club des Templiers, B.N., Lb[53], 406; Club des Montagnards de Belleville, B.N., Lb[53], 424; Club des travailleurs (du Ier arrondissement), B.N., Lb[53], 574; Société républicaine du Faubourg Saint-Denis, *La Voix des clubs*, March 20, 1848.

hours of certain days.[41] Sometimes they requested the
municipal authorities to put any locally available hall at
their disposal. Occasionally clubs seem just to have
moved in.[42] At other times the higher reaches of bureauc-
racy were alerted: it was the police prefect who opened
the exhibition hall of the Gobelins Manufacture to a popular society of the twelfth *arrondissement*. The Society
of the Rights of Man required the permission of the Minister of Public Works to install its general headquarters
in the Palais-National.[43]

During March and April 1848, space limitations may
have been the basic constraint on the proliferation of revolutionary clubs. As early as March 11, the mayor of the
seventh district, announcing publicly "that he could no
longer satisfy the legitimate demands for meeting places,"
called on all citizens to inform him of any local premises
that were suitable and available.[44] This practical limit de-
fies any attempt to make political sense out of the distribution of clubs throughout Paris. Some places, such as
public schools, were available everywhere, but certain
areas were better endowed than others. For this reason,
clubs seem to have been sparser in such revolutionary
strongholds as the ninth and twelfth *arrondissements* than
in the conservative first and second—which happened

[41] Such routine applications are mentioned as early as February 28 in Raspail's paper, *L'Ami du peuple en 1848*.

[42] For example, the former Church of the Assumption (Faubourg Saint-Honoré) was shared on alternate evenings by the
Club de la Butte des Moulins (duly authorized by the mayor)
and a Société du club de l'Ardeche (which had never shown
any authorization to custodian). Letter from Heil, *gardien*, to
mayor of Ier *arrondissement*, May 10, 1848, A.S., V 3 D⁶-23,
No. 14.

[43] For Caussidière's authorization of March 13, 1848, A.S.,
D4, AZ 32; for Marie's intervention, testimony Gayot de Montfleury, *Enquête*, I, 286.

[44] B.N., Lb⁵³, 457.

to include major public facilities like the Palais-National, as well as some of the largest private halls. In any event, clubs were anything but stationary: in less than four months, Blanqui's Central Republican Society met in five different halls; Barbès' Club of the Revolution in six.[45]

When the dust had settled, the overwhelming majority —four-fifths would be a conservative guess—of popular societies met in premises belonging to the municipality or the state. Most widespread was the use of grade schools—public and parochial—where the roofed-over recess area doubled as a club *local* at night. Homes for the aged and the disabled found new functions: two popular societies met at the Hospice des Quinze-Vingt and one at the National Institute for the Deaf-Mute. Willy-nilly, institutions of higher education admitted the masses to evening "classes": the Club of the Arsenal met at the Lycée Charlemagne; at the Ecole des Arts-et-Métiers, where future technicians studied during the day, the Society of the Rights of Man debated at night; the faculties of the University of Paris yielded their amphitheaters to almost a dozen different clubs, only two or three of which were dominated by university students. At the National Academy of Music, Blanqui's Central Republican Society enjoyed the finest concert hall in Paris, the Salle des Menus Plaisirs. As many as half a dozen clubs may have used the Palais-National, including one meeting during the day to give night workers a chance to attend. A small palace (demolished during the Second Empire) in the rue de Rivoli was turned over in its entirety to Sobrier, the founder of the club newspaper *La Commune de Paris*, who in turn granted office space to the Club of Clubs, Revolutionary Committee, which he had helped to organize in late March. Even churches, though officially out of bounds, were requisitioned. The disused Saint-Hya-

[45] Wassermann, *Les clubs de Barbès et de Blanqui*, pp. 26-30.

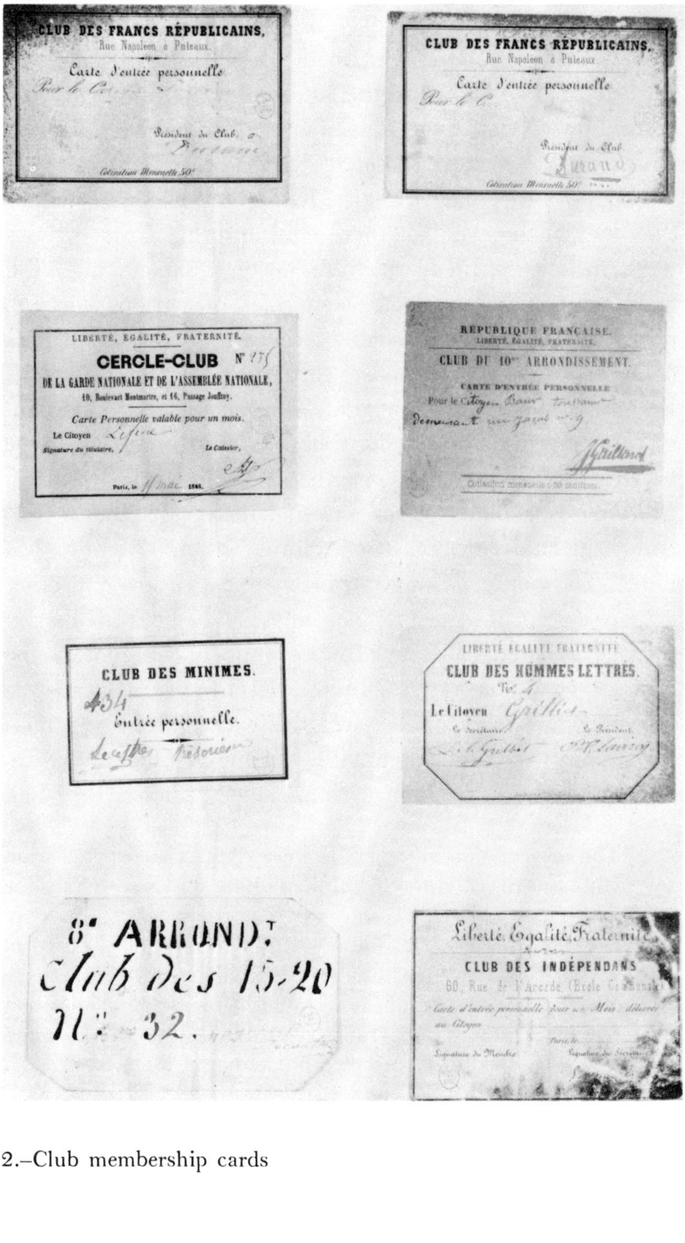

2.–Club membership cards

cinth chapel was in continuous club use and one late-blooming popular society met in the cellar beneath the towers of Saint-Sulpice.[46]

Whether or not they obtained a free meeting place had a good deal to do with the clubs' second practical concern: how to pay their bills. For all but the very largest clubs, even a modest rental fee could be prohibitive, particularly as popular societies had other expenses. Since they met in the evening, there were lighting costs; bylaws were usually printed, as were posters announcing club meetings. There were office supplies of various sorts to purchase. Some clubs, such as the Society of the Rights of Man, even paid a modest salary to their secretaries.[47] Relying on donations introduced considerable uncertainty, but charging high initiation fees and dues was likely to discourage potential members, particularly workers. Most clubs avoided either extreme. Etienne Cabet's Central Fraternal Society, for example, though it owed a nightly rental fee of 110 francs, managed by collecting a mere 5 centimes per session and per head from its numerous adherents.[48] The obscure Club of Chaillot in the first *arrondissement* got by on twenty-five centimes a month, while few popular societies exceeded ten centimes a night or one franc a month.[49] Though clubs were reluctant to put a strain on their members' purses, they had

[46] The information in the above paragraph is abstracted from my own extensive file on all Parisian clubs that have left some evidence.

[47] Dossier Charles-Jules Blue, A. 10188, Archives du Ministère de la Guerre; hereafter A.M.G.

[48] The Club des Templiers, stipulating a 5-franc initiation fee and monthly dues of 2 francs, was unlikely to attract many workers, even though it specifically exempted them from such assessments. (B.N., Lb[53], 406.)

[49] *Le Populaire*, March 4, 1848; session of the Société fraternelle centrale, March 11, *La Voix des clubs*, March 16, 1848.

no such scruples about demands on their time. A very few clubs began by scheduling only two evenings a week, but many met six or seven nights. Enough clubs, however, confined themselves to three or four weekly sessions to permit some club activists to participate in two popular societies, though most had their hands full in keeping up with one. Nightly meetings lasting from seven or eight o'clock to eleven, or even midnight, made for a grueling schedule for early rising workingmen. Ironically, growing unemployment, by easing this strain, may have helped sustain mass participation in the clubs.

When contemporaries talked about "the clubs," they were likely to point to a handful of what might be called "name" popular societies. These were, in the chronological order of their appearance, Auguste Blanqui's Central Republican Society, Etienne Cabet's Central Fraternal Society, the Society of the Rights of Man with a collegiate leadership among whom Léopold Villain and Napoléon Lebon were best known, Armand Barbès' Club of the Revolution, and François Raspail's Society of the Friends of the People. These organizations were singled out because they were known throughout the capital and drew their members and spectators from all over Paris. All of them were large gatherings, some of them regularly attracting audiences of four and five thousand. All of these popular societies—with the possible exception of the Society of the Rights of Man—were formed around one dominant and well-known republican personality. In all these respects, the "name" clubs were notably atypical of the general run of revolutionary clubs.

Partly because of its status as vanguard club, partly because of Blanqui's somewhat eerie charisma, the Central Republican Society was the great tourist attraction. A considerable number of old-line republicans of varying views, many of them intellectuals, had gathered around a working-class nucleus of secret society veterans faithful to Blanqui. This dichotomy was complicated further by the club's division into revolutionary members and moderate spectators, a distinction that made for a continuous dialogue that could momentarily degenerate into a shouting match between orchestra (members) and balcony (visitors). Though tourists visited the Central Republican Society to watch an emaciated, black-gloved Blanqui preside, icily passionate, the sessions were not simply Blanqui's show: they were filled with the rowdy give-and-take of debates from the floor and the podium in which Blanqui intervened, but which he made no attempt to dominate. Club organization was minimal; agendas were nonexistent or else were disregarded in practice; the stress was on debating the burning issues of the hour and on exercising control over a lukewarm Provisional Government.[50]

Very different was Etienne Cabet's Central Fraternal Society, which was also formed during the first week of the Second Republic. Where Blanqui was a revolutionary activist, just released from nine years' imprisonment for his part in the insurrection of 1839, Cabet was what contemporaries labeled a "chef d'école," the leader and prophet of a sect of true believers. Where before the revolution Cabet had disciplined his faithful Icarians by means of his newspaper, *Le Populaire*, the revolution of 1848, by sanctifying the right of free assembly, enabled Cabet to turn his following into a popular society, over which he then presided. Cabet's adherents were almost entirely lower class, yet quite unlike the militants who had almost followed Blanqui in rising up against the Provisional Government in the first days of the Republic. It is true that throughout March Cabet took initiatives that

[50] Wassermann, *Les clubs de Barbès et de Blanqui*, passim, but esp. pp. 1-5, 8-17, 31-39. For one tourist's view, see P. Guichonnet, ed., "William de la Rive: un témoin génèvois de la Révolution de 1848," *Etudes*, "Société de la Révolution de 1848," xv (1953), 161.

propelled him and his society into the forefront of the revolutionary movement; yet it is equally true that his club, though attended by as many as four thousand men and one thousand women, was no more than an orderly meeting of the faithful assembled to "get the word" from Cabet. Authoritarian by temperament, the Icarian leader created the Central Fraternal Society in his own image.[51]

The Society of the Rights of Man, by contrast, stood for a different sort of order. Organized by veteran republican revolutionaries who had been active in the original Society of the Rights of Man of the 1830's, the reborn society of 1848 set itself a paradoxical task: to revive the ethos of the most militant secret societies in the context of a popular meeting admitting all sympathizers. What resulted was a hybrid: a disciplined, militarily organized society prepared for combat and headed by professional revolutionaries but running club sessions that dealt mostly with local problems and current political questions of concern to a rank and file drawn mainly from the lower-class seventh district where the society had established itself. Of its professed aim—to serve as buffer between the enraged poor and the terrified rich—not much survived in day-by-day practice, though the professional staff of the organization, lodged in a separate headquarters in the Palais-National, may have continued to pursue longer-range goals.[52] Unlike other "name" clubs, the Society of the Rights of Man treasured an image of disci-

[51] Christopher Johnson, *Utopiar Communism in France: Cabet and the Icarians* (Ithaca, N.Y., 1974), ch. 6; Pierre Angrand, *Etienne Cabet et la République de 1848* (Paris, 1948), pp. 34-62. The club's activities, mostly in the form of Cabet's ex-cathedra oratory, are best documented in the columns of *Le Populaire*.

[52] The sessions of the Société des Droits de l'Homme—at least to the extent that these were public—can be followed virtually on a day-by-day basis for March and April 1848 in the columns of *La Voix des clubs*, *La Sentinelle des clubs*, and *La Commune de Paris*.

plined hierarchy; though the officers of the society were known, no one dreamed of referring to it as the Club Villain or the Club Lebon.

The Club of the Revolution, founded in mid-March, represented still another pattern. Popularly labeled the "Club Barbès" after its president, the Club of the Revolution gathered in all those ardent republicans—an elite among revolutionaries—who, for reasons personal or ideological, found Blanqui's leadership unacceptable. Armand Barbès himself offered sincerity, charm, and good will, but he was no more than a friend among friends. Certainly he was no prophet or master within his circle, nor even a dominating orator. Unlike the Central Republican Society with its nucleus of proletarian veterans, the Club of the Revolution attracted mostly democrats and revolutionaries of middle-class background, many of them journalists and lawyers. The two to three thousand militants attending the sessions expected not only to hear from the recognized leaders of the revolutionary Left, but to discuss seriously policy problems and policy alternatives.[53]

Of the major "name" clubs, François Raspail's Society of the Friends of the People, founded toward the end of March, was the last to be launched. In some ways it resembled Cabet's sectarian gathering in that people— women as well as men (though neither Cabet nor Raspail were full-fledged feminists)—came to listen to "Father Raspail" rather than to discuss, decide, or take action. Though Raspail did not ignore current events such as the national elections, his description of the once-a-week club session that attracted up to four thousand as "a course where I gave public lectures" was not far from the mark. Yet the relationship between Raspail and his

[53] Wassermann, *Les clubs de Barbès et de Blanqui*, passim, but esp. pp. 5-8, 18-24, 25-26, 28-30, 33-34, 37-39.

audience was not quite that of Cabet. Men and women flocked to Raspail because they knew, admired, and trusted him as the embattled doctor (minus a medical degree) of the poor, the crochety saint of the Faubourg Saint-Antoine.[54] In turn, Raspail addressed them in complete confidence that his role was to teach, their role to learn. The scope of his lectures was dazzlingly immodest. In a single scintillating and opinionated session, Raspail was capable of sweeping through the whole of world history to prove the cosmic inevitability of the Second French Republic.[55]

Evidently, the very fact of being singled out set the "name" clubs apart from the run-of-the-mill popular societies. Yet there probably was no typical club. Gustave Flaubert's portrait of a zanily tumultuous club session in his *Sentimental Education* was probably inspired by the real-life Club of Educated Men without Employment, and this was not pure imagination.[56] But neither was the club visited by the editor of the revolutionary paper, *Le Père Duchêne*: "The president and the members of the audience retained a stiff and pompous demeanor. They seemed colder to me than monks at Matins. When I saw all these Puritan faces, I thought I had entered not a club of patriots, but a synod of Scottish Presbyterians. Nonetheless, it was a club."[57] Though for the most part the club world was neither peopled by *Le Père Duchêne*'s Scottish Presbyterians nor by Flaubert's pathetic lunatics, sympathetic observers noted that it was "generally very agitated." Revolutionary journalists were ecstatic

[54] Dora B. Weiner, *Raspail, Scientist and Reformer* (New York, 1968), pp. 135-163.

[55] Suzanne Wassermann, "Le club de Raspail," *La révolution de 1848*, v (1908-1909), 589-605, 655-674, 748-762.

[56] To cite a paperback translation: (New York: New Directions, 1957), ch. 14, pp. 405-415.

[57] *Le Père Duchêne*, April 16, 1848.

3.—Two contemporary views of club sessions

whenever they discovered an orderly club.[58] What accounted for the habitual disorder?

On the most basic level, the club habit was a revolution in the daily lives of tens of thousands of common people, and revolutions are not noted for their calm. But revolutionary enthusiasm aside, the clubs confronted a number of tangible difficulties. Public speaking in an age before amplification posed practical problems. How many experienced speakers today would care to address an audience of five hundred, fifteen hundred, six thousand (the highest club attendance figure cited in 1848) without a microphone? Consider further that most potential club activists had never spoken before a crowd. Evidently, the more numerous the audience and the larger the hall, the more intractable the problem. It may be no coincidence that there was virtually no discussion in the two largest clubs of Paris, headed by Etienne Cabet and François Raspail, both of them experienced and inspirational orators.[59] Even in less formidable settings, a speaker had not only the problem of making himself heard (in 1848 the nine-hundred-man National Assembly was continually beset by cries of "We can't hear!"), but to hold the audience's attention, which was not easy. "The audience shows no charity toward the men of good will measuring themselves against the difficulties of the speaker's platform. As soon as the orator makes a slip, there are catcalls from all sides. The speaker becomes flustered and confused. There is laughter, there is hooting; and the un-

[58] Le Tam-Tam républicain, March 9, 1848. For comment on the Club de Chaillot, session of March 16, La Voix des clubs, March 19, 1848; for similar praises for Club de l'avenir, ibid., March 25, 1848.

[59] For Raspail's Club des amis du peuple, see Wassermann's analysis, "Le club de Raspail," pp. 589-605, 655-674, 748-762. Cabet's Société fraternelle centrale may be followed in his newspaper Le Populaire and in the numbered club speeches issued as pamphlets.

happy man naturally ends up by making a fool of himself."[60]

Inexperience showed in other ways. Chairmen, uncertain of their authority, tended to favor spontaneity over the etiquette of public debate. As one clubist complained in a letter to the editor: "In any meeting that deals with lively, pressing issues, everybody wants to speak at the same time. People are often more apt to start fighting than to listen to each other. . . . Thus, for example, a motion is developed: five, ten, fifteen members raise their hands at the same time. They should be inscribed, assigned a number permitting them to respond one at a time."[61]

Inexperience was compounded with democratic hypersensitivity. Club members were always ready to denounce anything that smacked of arbitrary authority. When it transpired, for example, that the executive board of the Club of the Butte des Moulins had nominated two delegates for campaign work in the provinces without the permission of the membership, "an extraordinary uproar disrupted the meeting. Fighting almost broke out. There was talk of expulsion."[62] And clubists had keen ears for the patronizing phrase. Even so prestigious a club leader as Auguste Blanqui had to be on guard: "In reading a list of candidates admitted to club membership, Blanqui said, 'Citizen Balard, an excellent citizen.' 'We are all good citizens! What does this mean? This is an insult!' And on it went for several minutes."[63]

Many times disturbances simply reflected genuine dif-

[60] *Le Tam-Tam républicain*, March 9, 1848.

[61] Letter to the editor, signed Vidal. *La Voix des clubs*, March 14, 1848. See the similar comments on the Club de l'émancipation de peuples, *La Commune de Paris*, March 16, 1848.

[62] *La Commune de Paris*, April 2, 1848.

[63] "William de la Rive: un témoin génèvois," p. 161.

4.–Composite portrait of major club leaders and their revolutionary allies.

Note: Originally this was one of several extant versions of a group portrait of the men accused of the invasion of May 15, 1848, of the National Assembly and tried before the High Court at Bourges in March 1849.

As was common among nineteenth-century graphic journalists, the artist, sketching during the trial, posed his subjects conventionally when in fact they never posed as a group. I took the liberty of faking this fake group portrait by excising those accused who were not involved in the club movement or had affinities with it and by inserting (with the authorization of Roger-Viollet, Documentation generale photographique) the portrait of Etienne Cabet, the only major club leader not implicated in the May 15 affair.

From left to right:

ALBERT, member of the Provisional Government, February-May 1848; vice-chairman of the Luxembourg Labor Commission.

LOUIS BLANC, member of the Provisional Government; chairman of the Luxembourg Labor Commission.

MARC CAUSSIDIÈRE, revolutionary police prefect of Paris.

FRANCOIS RASPAIL, president, Club of the Friends of the People.

JOSEPH SOBRIER, publisher of *La Commune de Paris, moniteur des clubs*; member, executive board, Club of Clubs, Revolutionary Committee.

ARMAND BARBÈS, president, Club of the Revolution.

LÉOPOLD VILLAIN, president, Society of the Rights of Man.

ETIENNE CABET, president, Central Fraternal Society (Icarians).

AUGUSTE BLANQUI, president, Central Republican Society.

ALOYSIUS HUBER, member, executive board, Club of Clubs; president, Centralizing Committee.

BENJAMIN FLOTTE, treasurer, Central Republican Society; officer, Cooks' Union.

ferences of political outlook, interest, or class among those attending. Friction between moderates and revolutionaries, bourgeois and proletarians was a commonplace, particularly where a popular society founded by local middle-class notables attracted workers with ideas of their own.[64] A basic disagreement over the aim of a given popular society could be equally disruptive. Foreigners, attracted by the name of the Club of the Emancipation of the Peoples, were understandably irritated at having to listen to schemes for a National Bank.[65] The distinction between visitors (allowed neither to discuss nor to vote) and full members required supernatural restraint on the part of impassioned visitors, superhuman tact on the part of the club chairman. For instance, when one of the Central Republican Society's speakers decried counterrevolution and royalism in the departments, he was greeted "by shouts, whistles, stamping of feet from people who, from timid interrupters, had gradually turned into shameless disturbers, forcing the orator to interrupt his speech. Justice was done . . . the disrupters were forcibly ejected, screeching insults and shouting 'assassin' as they gave ground."[66] A company of the Garde mobile, the newly created professionalized militia, preserved order on the following evening, but off and on agitation persisted in the Central Republican Society.[67]

Yet obviously this is not the whole story. Orderliness may not have been one of the revolution's cardinal virtues; but club minutes indicate that issues were discussed,

[64] See, e.g., Club de la Butte des Moulins, *Le Courrier français*, March 27, 1848; Club de la liberté, session of March 17, *La Voix des clubs*, March 22, 1848.

[65] Session of March 10, *La Voix des clubs*, March 14, 1848.

[66] Session of March 22, *La Voix des clubs*, March 24, 1848.

[67] *La Voix des clubs*. For later incidents, some related to the Taschereau charge against Blanqui, see *La Sentinelle des clubs*, April 5, 1848; *Le Messager*, April 11, 1848.

candidates examined and endorsed, decisions voted, officers elected and dismissed. Apparently, beneath the surface agitation, things did get done.

viii

The turbulence of the popular societies reflected their revolutionary origins and their continued dependence on revolutionary enthusiasm. Yet, though this was not immediately apparent, the clubs were equally dependent on the good will of the authorities or at least on their loss of nerve. The clubs were vulnerable on two counts. As most of them met on government or municipal property, their status as tolerated guests could be abruptly terminated by executive fiat. Furthermore, the popular societies were allowed to operate in a legal no-man's-land in which restrictive laws on the statute books remained unenforced against them: the Provisional Government, bowing to pressure, had repealed the hated Laws of September 1835 restricting civil liberties, including the right of assembly. But this repeal had left a string of earlier restrictions untouched. There were enough anticlub laws on the books, dating back all the way to 1790, to destroy the club movement at any time the government chose to enforce this temporarily dead-letter legislation.

The Provisional Government's ambivalent stance toward the club movement cannot be isolated from the government's definition of its own role after February 24, 1848. The dominant governmental majority sought to restore stability and confidence, while preparing the national elections that would create a national assembly to propose and dispose. The government defined its role as that of caretaker, intent on keeping the house neat until the new landlord could be consulted on major renovations. In political terms, the Provisional Government intended to do no more than was necessary to insure free elections.[68] Virtually every reform proclaimed in the first weeks of the Second Republic was therefore exacted from an unwilling executive, which, as its spokesman Alphonse de Lamartine was to reiterate, had only words for a shield.

The government, however, was not monolithic but, as a number of its members were to insist in retrospect, tripartite. The moderate republican majority comprised Dupont (de l'Eure) as figurehead premier, Arago in charge of the War Ministry, Crémieux for Justice, Lamartine for Foreign Affairs, Garnier-Pagès for Finance, Marie for Public Works, and Marrast as mayor of Paris. There were two distinct minorities: the worker Albert and Louis Blanc, both in charge of the Luxembourg Labor Commission, were labeled "communist-socialist" by their opponents; Flocon, Minister of Commerce, and Ledru-Rollin, Minister of the Interior, were the two neo-Jacobin members. In its dealings with the clubs, the government was even more fragmented. Lamartine, unconcerned with republican respectability, played his own secret games. Furthermore, the police prefect Caussidière, though not a member of the government, tended to take an independent course by tacking cautiously between socialists and neo-Jacobins.

The moderates dominating the Provisional Government tolerated the clubs because they could not afford to do otherwise. As the Minister of Public Works was to reminisce years later: "A hidden but active power paralyzed all the political plans of the government. This was the power of the club leaders, who sought to divert the

[68] See the words of the wife of the Minister of Justice, Crémieux, in writing to friends in early April: "Nous gagnons du temps, mes amies, et l'on peut maintenant arriver sans troubles jusqu'à l'Assemblée nationale. L'esprit des clubs est moins violent." (A. Crémieux, *En 1848—discours et lettres* [Paris, 1883], p. 223.)

revolution into a course of excess and violence where it
could not have halted. . . . What was most irritating were
the processions of workers, of women, with banners flying, without other aim than to display their poverty and
even more . . . their idleness. . . . Repression was impossible."[69] As soon as the revolutionary momentum began
to subside in April, the government reasserted its power.
When, by July 1848, outside pressures had disappeared
altogether, the members of the Provisional Government
that had been part of the moderate majority voted to a
man to restrict the right of free assembly. But in March
and April, besieged by revolutionary mobs, the government not only cooperated in finding meeting places for
the clubs but even in financing their campaign in the
provinces. In making these concessions, the government
was temporizing while it sought to restore its control over
revolutionary Paris. In the meantime, it also pursued a
secret policy of surveillance and of dividing the club
movement by discrediting some of its more militant leaders like Blanqui. Once the demonstration of April 16 had
demonstrated that Paris was again solidly in the hands
of the authorities, the government's hostility toward the
clubs became public.

Considerably to the left of his moderate colleagues,
Minister of the Interior Ledru-Rollin struck a neo-
Jacobin pose of responsiveness to popular aspirations.
But this did not mean that he favored social revolution.
Translated into a policy toward the clubs, this attitude
made for ambiguity, if not confusion. Unlike the moderate republicans who equated clubs with illegitimate agitation, Ledru-Rollin differentiated between "anarchist"
clubs, such as Blanqui's Central Republican Society, and
"good republican" clubs, such as Barbès' Club of the
Revolution. Ledru-Rollin seems to have been the prime

[69] Aimé Cherest, *La vie et les oeuvres de A. T. Marie* (Paris,
1873), p. 146.

5.–Group portrait of the provisional government

Top row:	FLOCON	DUPONT (de l'Eure)	ALBERT
Middle row:	LOUIS BLANC CRÉMIEUX	LEDRU-ROLLIN	GARNIER-PAGÈS
Bottom row:	MARIE FRANÇOIS ARAGO	LAMARTINE	ARMAND MARRAST

mover in the Provisional Government's effort to discredit Blanqui by exploiting (or manufacturing) what came to be known as the Taschereau document. When the Minister of the Interior feared a putsch from the Blanquists on April 16, he rallied to the moderates with only a minimum of hesitation. Yet he had also become the patron saint of the Parisian club federation, conferring nightly with sympathetic club leaders. Perhaps Ledru-Rollin even encouraged them to look to him as a potential Robespierre.[70] Yet the distinction between "good" and "bad" clubs was forgotten in the appointment of an old-line, antirepublican policeman, Carlier, to spy on all popular societies. Apparently Ledru-Rollin had no scruples about sharing Carlier's daily bulletins with his conservative colleagues.[71]

If Ledru-Rollin's course is uncertain, Lamartine's is murky. Though technically confined to foreign affairs, Lamartine apparently built up his own intelligence apparatus among the clubs, drawing on secret funds at his disposal.[72] He personally made several overtures to major club leaders such as Sobrier (whose "outpost" in the rue de Rivoli was ordered supplied with arms and ammunition by the Foreign Minister) and Blanqui.[73] Exactly what transpired between the poet-politician and his revolutionary guests is unclear, as are Lamartine's motives.

On the far left of the government, Louis Blanc sympathized with the club objectives without being intimately

[70] Alvin R. Calman, *Ledru-Rollin and the Second French Republic* (New York, 1922), pp. 137-149.

[71] Testimony Carlier, *Enquête*, I, 247; testimony Carteret, ibid., I, 248. Also L.-A. Garnier-Pagès, *Histoire de la révolution de 1848*, 2nd ed. (Paris, 1862-72), VII, 226-227.

[72] For example, Lamartine testified that he was forewarned "of what went on in the clubs" at 5 A.M. on April 16, 1848. Testimony Lamartine, *Enquête*, I, 305.

[73] *Mémoires de Caussidière*, II, 177-178.

involved with the clubs themselves.[74] Blanc was committed to the Parisian labor movement and to its political offshoot, the Central Committee of the Workers of the Seine. To the extent that organized labor was allied to the club movement, Blanc was an ally. He too, however, seems to have shared the general distrust of Blanqui.[75]

Caussidière, as police prefect, was also charged with surveillance of the clubs, though the intelligence that he gathered apparently rarely reached either the Minister of the Interior or the mayor of Paris. As a former secret society activist himself, but also as a former salesman for the neo-Jacobin daily, *La Réforme*, Caussidière had close links to the clubs, as did many of the secret society men whom he recruited into his police force. His closest tie was to Sobrier, with whom Caussidière had briefly shared the police prefecture during the first days of the Republic and who was to become a pillar of the club movement. The police prefect had his own reasons for opposing Blanqui: Caussidière not only deplored Blanqui's revolutionary tactics, but Blanquists also disrupted discipline at the police prefecture.[76]

As long as the popular societies wore the mantle of revolutionary legitimacy, as long as they could count on the demoralization of conservatives of every stripe, as long as they could take advantage of the fissures and rivalries within the government and the administrative apparatus, the clubs were safe. Once sympathizers in high places were purged or neutralized, once the authorities

[74] Louis Blanc's fellow "socialist-communist" (and the token worker in the Provisional Government), Albert, seems to have made no impact whatsoever, despite his background as eminent secret society leader and his chairmanship of the patronage-rich Commission des récompenses nationales that made awards to political victims of the July Monarchy.

[75] Leo Loubère, *Louis Blanc* (Evanston, Ill., 1961), pp. 93, 95.

[76] *Mémoires de Caussidière*, II, 47-56.

recovered their nerve, the vulnerability of the club movement became apparent. When the government withdrew
its toleration, secretly in May, publicly in June 1848, the
clubs discovered that they had no legal standing; evicted
from the meeting places they had long taken for granted
as their own, they faced a bleak future—in fact, in the
long run, no future at all.

3 | The Eighteenth Brumaire of the People

What a revolution! It's prodigious, marvellous, miraculous!
It's like magic, like a fairy tale!

Etienne Cabet, February 27, 1848

i

The clubs' penchant for high-flown rhetoric tends to
obscure their central preoccupation with day-to-day politics. Popular societies, haunted by the "sleight of hand"
that had supposedly robbed the republicans of the fruits
of victory in 1830, wanted above all to prevent history
from repeating itself in 1848. Clubs proclaimed that the
February Revolution had opened an era of social renovation, but the fervor with which they asserted their faith
substituted for a clear-cut program. In the absence of
such a program, immediate political pressures shaped
and defined club agendas. The "normal" pattern of activity that evolved in the weeks after February was for the
popular societies to slide from crisis to crisis.

From what little we know about the earliest phase of
club activity during the Second Republic, the clubs' initial
concern was with freedom of the press. To control the
press, the July Monarchy had relied on a stamp tax,
which, by raising subscription rates by one-third, had
helped put newspapers beyond reach of the "dangerous
classes." A graduated scale of security bonds (rising to
100,000 francs for Paris dailies) posted by prospective

publishers had guaranteed any eventual fines for violation of the press laws. Tight curbs on street vendors had made newspapers still less accessible to the lower classes.[1] With the overthrow of the monarchy and the cooperation of Etienne Arago, the new director of the postal service, enforcement of these restrictions ended, just as the laws prohibiting clubs were now ignored. In this heady atmosphere, new democratic papers like Lamennais' *Le Peuple constituant* or Raspail's evocative *L'Ami du peuple* sprang up almost immediately, to be followed by countless imitators and competitors. Established republican papers like *La Réforme* also reacted by lowering their subscription prices to reflect the disappearance of the stamp tax.

When the Provisional Government suddenly announced that neither security bonds nor stamp taxes had been rescinded, revolutionary republicans greeted the news with a mixture of disbelief and rage. That the government was chiefly influenced by a Minister of Finance anxious to restore business confidence through "fiscal responsibility" did nothing to lessen the shock of betrayal.[2] The clubs, however, intended to put first things first. Spearheaded by Blanqui's Central Republican Society, the earliest and—at least until mid-March—the most prestigious revolutionary club, the political societies were quick to demand that the government rescind its decision. They argued that the most pressing need was to propagate republicanism by means of a sympathetic and vital

---

[1] Irene Collins, "The Government and the Press during the Reign of Louis-Philippe," *English Historical Review*, LXIX (1954), 262-282.

[2] For Goudchaux's own attitude, see Peter Amann, ed., "A French Revolutionary Club: The Société démocratique centrale," Ph.D. diss., University of Chicago, 1958, p. 68. Hereafter cited as Amann, *Minutes*. Also see Garnier-Pagès, *Histoire de la révolution*, VI, 234-235.

press that could compete with the established monarchist newspapers. They bitterly resented the system of bonds and stamp duties as discrimination against the poor, deprived of a voice because they could not post bond, or deprived of intellectual nourishment because they could not afford the inflated newspaper subscriptions. Some sensed that the government's reactionary policy was not only ideologically unacceptable but unenforceable. Would the Second Republic imitate the July Monarchy by imprisoning a Lamennais and a Raspail for the same "crime" of upholding an unfettered press?[3]

In the face of general republican opposition—including that of groups like the workers of the newspaper *L'Atelier*, who were otherwise very moderate—the Provisional Government backed down, officially voiding security bonds and stamp tax on March 4, abrogating all the Laws of September (the most severe of the restrictive legislation on the books) on the day following. To what extent the clubs deserve credit for the government's capitulation is hard to say. Had the Provisional Government persisted in its press policy, apparently the clubs would have led a mass march to enforce their demands.[4] Even so, sentiment was so overwhelmingly against the official stand that without club agitation other republican pressures would have proved irresistible.

[3] *Le Populaire*, February 29, 1848; Société fraternelle centrale (still labeled Réunion icarienne), session of March 1, ibid., March 2, 1848; Société républicaine centrale, session of March 1, *La République*, March 2, 1848; Société républicaine de l'atelier, session of March 2 [?], ibid., March 3, 1848; poster, Comité démocratique de la Porte Montmartre, *Les murailles révolutionnaires*, II, 1-2; Amann, *Minutes*, pp. 50-60; Société des gens de lettres, March 1, *La République*, March 2, 1848.

[4] *La Voix des clubs*, March 8, 1848. Also Société républicaine de la Sorbonne, session of March 3, *La République*, March 5, 1848.

ii

The clubs' involvement in the question of the National Guard was more prolonged and far deeper. Club members spent hours criticizing registration procedures, fretting about uniforms and equipment, debating the qualifications of good National Guard officers, and actually considering officer candidates.[5] There was sound reason for club concern, for the Paris National Guard and its makeup played a more central role in the revolution of 1848 than historians have generally recognized. The incorporation into the Paris militia of all able-bodied males between the ages of twenty and fifty-five was one of the few truly revolutionary, if transitory, social changes initiated by the Second Republic. The old monarchical guard, made up of taxpayers who could afford to purchase their own uniforms and equipment, really amounted to the propertied classes in arms, guarding their stores, workshops, and houses against the lapping tide of the poor. To arm these same poor, entrusting the defense of property to those who had none, was an incalculable gamble that made a mockery of the National Guard's traditions.

The political leverage which an "open" civic militia offered to this propertyless majority was even more revolutionary. As long as a democratized National Guard remained the only effective armed force in the capital, it could hold the government hostage to its pledge of social transformation. This is why the issue of keeping the regular army out of Paris was to become so crucial and why it became closely linked with opening the urban militia to the masses: any infusion of troops unconditionally

[5] There is documentary evidence for the existence of 78 clubs up to March 17, 1848. For 26 of these I have found evidence of involvement in National Guard affairs.

loyal to the Provisional Government would dilute revolutionary influence.

What was equally important from the viewpoint of the ultrarevolutionaries was whether the democratized National Guard would have new spirit and leadership, or whether the old bourgeois cadres would merely assimilate—or was it digest?—the working-class recruits.[6] How much of the adult male population would be fully integrated into the guard? Were they to be properly armed and uniformed, on an equal footing with the veterans of the July Monarchy? Who or what was to finance the new guards' arms and equipment?[7] In the recast companies,

[6] For a representative, but incomplete, listing of popular societies in which some of the issues of democratizing the National Guard were discussed, see Société des Droits de l'Homme, session of March 7, La Commune de Paris, March 14, 1848; Club populaire de la Sorbonne, session of March 10, ibid., March 11, 1848; Société républicaine centrale, session of March 12, ibid., March 14, 1848; Club démocratique de l'avenir, petition, March 13, 1848, A.N., BB[30], 300, No. 2779; Société des Droits de l'Homme, session of March 15, La Commune de Paris, March 16, 1848; Club du progrès, session of March 18, ibid., March 21, 1848; Club républicain de Batignolles-Monceaux, session of March 21, La Voix des clubs, March 25, 1848; Club républicain des travailleurs, session of March 22, ibid., March 24, 1848.

For a discussion of the difficulties among responsible authorities, see General Guinard (deputy commander of the Paris National Guard) to (unnamed) district mayor. (Liesville Collection, B.H.V.P.) Daily staff orders, National Guard (Seine), A.N., F[9]*, Register 1251; circular letter, Ledru-Rollin to mayor of X[e] arrondissement, March 14, 1848, A.S., V[bis] 429, dossier 3.

[7] On the issue of arming the new guards, see Club de la fraternité universelle, petition to Provisional Government, March 12, 1848, A.N., BB[30], 300, No. 2949; Club de la Sorbonne, petition, March 9, La Commune de Paris, March 11, and ibid., March 16, 1848; Club du progrès, session of March 18, ibid., March 21, 1848, and session of March 20, ibid., March 23, 1848. For official reaction, see Mayor Marrast to

battalions, and legions, would middle-class old-timers or newly enrolled workers be elected to command? Would these new officers identify with the traditional concern of the National Guard—the defense of order—or with the construction of a "democratic and social republic"? Each of these questions broke down into technicalities, like registration and electoral procedures or the adequacy of the Paris arsenals to provide equipment, but the answers would determine who would control the revolution. As the club activists rightly sensed, effective power was the sum total of administrative trivia.

All this might have aroused considerable interest but no great passion had the government's timetable not provided urgency. As originally decreed, March 13 was the last day of registration for the National Guard; March 18 was the beginning of officer elections. Bureaucratic delays and obstructions were more than a nuisance: they might serve to thwart the effective democratization of the urban militia by permanently excluding tens of thousands of good republican workers. As far as the elections were concerned, these provided the first major test of whether the Republic would be a facade for the status quo or a real transfer of power from the haves to the have-nots. As every officer and noncom from the colonel commanding each district legion down to the humblest corporal

---

mayor of XIe *arrondissement*, March 19, 1848, A.S., V^{bis} 429, dossier 2; staff report, March 19, 1848, Paris National Guard, A.N., F^9*, 1251.

For the question of uniforms, see circular letter to new recruits by one Captain Leger, *La Voix des clubs*, March 17, 1848; Comité central républicain du IIIe arrondissement to Provisional Government, March 18, 1848, A.N., BB^{30}, 300, No. 2993; Réunion démocratique de la fraternité du Faubourg Saint-Antoine, poster, March 6, 1848, Liesville Collection, B.H.V.P.; also *Les Droits de l'Homme*, March 4, 1848; for the official provision, *Le Moniteur universel*, March 17, 1848.

was elected democratically, these elections involved elaborate and time-consuming mass meetings, starting with the entire legion and ending with each individual company. In addition, there were preparatory gatherings for each voting session.[8] If in the meantime the newcomers could be kept off balance, the veteran guards attending these electoral assemblies would have all the advantages of know-how, mutual acquaintance, and discipline; a shrewd, antirepublican minority might overpower an unorganized and unprepared democratic majority. The clubs were likely to dramatize the contest in stark class terms, bourgeois against worker.[9]

Because the organization of the clubs and that of the Paris National Guard dovetailed, there was good reason to believe that the popular societies could intervene effectively. Most clubs were rooted in the *quartier*, the administrative quarter section into which each of the city's twelve *arrondissements* was subdivided. Save for the handful of clubs attracting a citywide membership, clubs were likely to draw on a single neighborhood of a few blocks. The now democratized National Guard was equally local in its recruitment, with each *arrondissement* incorporated into a corresponding legion, each *quartier* with its battalion, and each battalion formed into eight or twelve companies recruited according to residence. Fellow club members were therefore also likely to be comrades in arms, enrolled in the same battalion and often in the same company. A somewhat more far-ranging popular society could readily arrange to have its members split up according to their respective guard unit when it was time to consider officer candidates for the

[8] *Bulletin des lois de la République française*, X^e série, 1er semestre de 1848 (Paris, 1848), i, 77-78.

[9] Société républicaine centrale, session of March 18, *La Voix des clubs*, March 20, 1848; Club du progrès, session of March 18, *La Commune de Paris*, March 21, 1848.

lower ranks.[10] For the highest echelons—colonel and lieutenant-colonel—for which an entire municipal district voted, club delegates from that *arrondissement* could meet to agree on common candidates.[11] In short, the parallel structure of clubs and militia units promised easy campaigning.

From the beginning, the clubs were torn between two conflicting conceptions of their role in these militia elections. For most popular societies the primary goal was the election of vigorously republican officers, with the secondary goal the election of enough workers as officers to provide class parity between the old and the new guard. The club role became ambiguous because most popular societies also provided a forum where any professed republican candidate (and who denied being a republican in 1848?) could state his case to potential constituents. With the exception of former legion commanders whom the government had replaced with trusted republicans, prerevolutionary militia officers had been allowed to keep their posts and were likely to seek reelection. Ironically, by granting access to many such veterans, the clubs may unwittingly have helped tighten the grip of the bourgeois incumbents on the newly enlarged National Guard.

Not that the ideological nature of the contests was always clearly defined. Revolutionary spokesmen were in the habit of depicting the National Guard elections as an epic struggle between angelic republicans and diabolical reactionaries. A reading of club minutes casts doubt

[10] Club républicain de l'avenir, session of March 20, *La Voix des clubs*, March 22, 1848; announcement, Club républicain de Montmartre, B.N., Lb[53], 943; Club de Chaillot, session of March 23, *La Voix des clubs*, March 26, 1848.

[11] See Club des hommes libres, session of March 27, *La Commune de Paris*, March 30, 1848, for such an arrangement for the second district.

on this simplistic interpretation.[12] A run-of-the-mill officer candidate with years of service in the prerevolutionary
guard stood for officer not from political zeal but because
election gave him status among his comrades and neighbors. The clubs were intent on politicizing elections that
were not naturally political. The clubs realized that militia officers without strong convictions were likely to follow orders, no matter what these were or who gave them.
By contrast, the conscience of a fervently republican National Guard officer could be relied upon to defy any
counterrevolutionary commands.[13]

The more militant clubs, therefore, sought to eliminate
not only antirepublicans but the apolitical as well. The
great demonstration of March 17 had done nothing to
bring the clubs nearer to a consensus on how this might
best be done. Asking old-line guards about their part in
the February fighting was a common opening. Less his-
torically minded clubs made officer candidates ratify the
club's statement of principles as the platform on which
they ran. The Club of the Incorruptibles went so far as
to draw up a special twelve-point "bill of rights" for the
occasion, to which all aspiring candidates had to subscribe. Prospective lieutenants in the Paris National
Guard swore not only to uphold "free and obligatory education provided by the state," but even to redress
France's demographic maldistribution.[14] To save time,
other clubs worked from the legion downward rather
than from the candidate upward. The Club Popincourt
persuaded the entire Eighth Legion to make adherence

[12] For example, Club de Chaillot, session of March 19, *La
Voix des clubs*, March 25, 1848.

[13] See, among others, Club de la Montagne (à Montmartre),
session of March 18, *La Voix des clubs*, March 23, 1848.

[14] Club de Chaillot, session of March 19, *La Voix des clubs*,
March 25, 1848; Club de la Montagne, session of March 18,
ibid., March 26, 1848; Club des incorruptibles, resolution of
March 27, 1848, A.N., C. 941, CdE 8872.

to Robespierre's Declaration of the Rights of Man a pre-requisite for nomination.[15]

However clumsy their methods, the clubs, moderate and revolutionary alike, never swerved very far from their down-to-earth preoccupation with safeguarding the Republic against its prospective enemies. Most club activists feared the election of a representative assembly hostile to the Republic. Again and again, would-be militia officers faced the question: What would you do if the National Assembly were to disavow the republican form of government or to abridge fundamental rights? A candidate who merely promised to resign his commission under such circumstances was considered a weak reed.[16] Clubists firmly believed that the National Guard needed devoted, energetic leaders, "willing to march against the Assembly . . . if it deviated from the great democratic and republican principles—unlimited freedom of the press and of assembly."[17] The decisive role that the Paris National Guard had played in February was a lesson well learned.

As the election date approached, the clubs became increasingly apprehensive.[18] In too many cases it was just

[15] La Commune de Paris, March 23, 1848; La Réforme, March 23, 1848.

[16] Club de la Montagne (à Montmartre) session of March 20 [?], La Voix des clubs, March 25, 1848; Comité électoral du XIe arrondissement, session of March 20, La Commune de Paris, March 25, 1848; Club des prévoyants, session of March 20, La Voix des clubs, March 22, 1848; Club de l'égalité, session of March 21, ibid., March 24, 1848; Club des hommes libres, session of March 25, La Commune de Paris, March 26, 1848; Club de Chaillot, session of March 19, La Voix des clubs, March 25, 1848; Club des prévoyants, session of March 20, ibid., March 22, 1848.

[17] Comité électoral du XIe arrondissement, session of March 20, La Commune de Paris, March 25, 1848.

[18] For resolutions to postpone the National Guard elections, see Société fraternelle centrale, session of March 10, La Voix

too late for the newly enrolled guards to become officer candidates or even to make intelligent choices between candidates in the running. This was considered not simply troublesome but sinister, for many clubs were convinced that they faced a vast conspiracy to insure the election of National Guard old-timers. At the same time, the clubs' concern was superimposed on a basic optimism: if only they had a chance to prepare "their" electorate adequately, they were convinced that the majority stood solidly behind the Republic, and a social Republic at that.

Within the Provisional Government, the clubs' concern was echoed by their ally, Louis Blanc, who strongly favored postponing the National Guard elections. During a meeting of the council on March 13, he was unable to persuade the majority of his colleagues, who refused to reschedule the vote. As a concession the government did extend the registration period by three days (through March 16). The Minister of the Interior was instructed to dissolve the elite companies of the National Guard (who wore distinctive uniforms, including, in some companies, towering bearskin buskins) and to integrate their members into the regular guard units. Though the clubs had paid little attention to the undemocratic proclivities of the elite companies, their dissolution forced the administration to put off the National Guard elections by one week.[19]

---

des clubs, March 13, 1848; Club populaire du Xe arrondissement, ibid., March 14, 1848; Société républicaine centrale, session of March 12, *La Commune de Paris*, March 14, 1848; Club des travailleurs, session of March 15, *La Voix des clubs*, March 14, 1848.

[19] Garnier-Pagès, *Histoire de la révolution*, VI, 390-392. I have found only one early protest against the elite companies: from the Société républicaine de l'Atelier, *La République*, March 4, 1848.

iii

The postponement of the nationwide elections was an issue that originally had nothing to do with the agitation to put off the voting for officers of the Paris National Guard. The idea of holding the latter elections a few weeks later was merely to prevent conservatives from taking advantage of the newcomers' confusion. The implications of postponing the national elections ran counter to official policy and the government's own view of its role in the revolution. Once the two demands had been fortuitously joined, the clubs came up with reasons for linking them. They pointed out that the original election schedule had allowed two weeks between the vote in the Paris militia and the balloting for the National Assembly; putting off the former election therefore also required delaying the latter. The argument may have had some practical merit, but it was clearly invented after both demands had been adopted for other reasons.

The pressure to delay the national elections apparently originated in Blanqui's Central Republican Society before the government's election schedule had been announced and before the issue of the National Guard's election date had heated up. As early as March 4, Blanqui's club voted unanimously to present three demands to the Provisional Government. First, encouraged by the government's surrender on the question of good-behavior bonds for newspapers, the club asked that all laws interfering with freedom of the press and of association be rescinded; second, the petition called for the ouster of all magistrates who had served the monarchy; third, the clubists demanded that elections to the National Assembly be postponed.

By March 7, when a club delegation headed by Blanqui presented these demands, two of them seemed passé. Only the day before, speaking for the Provisional Government, Lamartine had announced the nullification of the hated September Laws, the July Monarchy's most severe restrictions on civil liberties. Blanqui himself seems to have felt that the request to postpone the parliamentary elections was no longer appropriate: "We also had a petition to hand to the Provisional Government," he announced, "asking it to put off the date of the elections, which seem too near to us. But perhaps this comes too late." The reference was to a decree published on March 5 which announced the elections for April 9 and spelled out electoral procedures. Lamartine responded abruptly: "You are asking the government to reverse a decision taken for a reason of which you must be aware. I shall not debate the question with you."[20] The club delegates, if the official text may be believed, made no rejoinder.

Since this abortive petition inspired a succession of related petitions climaxed by the grand remonstrance of March 17, its arguments bear summarizing. The country, Blanqui's document maintained, was unready for elections because for fifty years only "the counterrevolution" had had an effective voice in France. The press, throttled by fiscal restrictions, had failed to penetrate the epidermis of society. Direct access to the masses was a monopoly of reactionary priests. Immediate elections were therefore bound to make a sham of the revolution. The solution proposed by the Central Republican Society was to postpone the general elections for three months, during which time citizens would be sent into the provinces to enlighten the rural population.[21]

The petition's revolutionary implications were not lost on Lamartine. It predicted (correctly, as it turned out) that the majority of the French people were by no means republicans and would not, if left to their own devices,

[20] Société républicaine centrale, session of March 4, *Le Courrier français*, March 5, 1848.

[21] *Le Moniteur universel*, March 8, 1848.

elect a genuinely republican National Assembly. The club called upon the government not merely to grant time (which was all that was implied in the National Guard postponement) but to utilize that time for a major effort to "make" the elections. In short, without actually saying so, the club asked for a transitional dictatorship, a demand that ran counter to the basic assumptions of the government.[22] As Lamartine was quick to point out to Blanqui and the club delegation: "I and my colleagues had considered that our first duty, after doing what we could to save liberty, was to restore as soon as possible to the nation itself the powers that we had seized for the common welfare and not to prolong the sort of dictatorship which we had assumed under the force of circumstances."[23] The battle between a liberal-democratic and a Jacobin conception of the revolution was joined.

iv

Though the central Republican Society may have expressed a widely shared impatience with the government's tiptoeing in the provinces, few clubs wanted a forceful governmental presence in Paris itself. Blanqui's initial petition and its seeming failure created no great stir

[22] Petition, Société républicaine centrale, March 6, 1848, A.N., BB[18], 301, No. 3587. The existence of two variants of the text of this petition points to considerable disagreement within the club over how long the elections should be postponed. The official text, which was never published, specifically called for three months' delay. The text published in Le Courrier français, March 12, 1848, whose editor was Blanqui's vice-president, does not spell out the length of the proposed postponement but does include the following sentence (missing from the official text): "Do not forget that as between a National Assembly elected tomorrow and a National Assembly elected six months from now, there is an abyss. . . ." (My italics.)

[23] Le Moniteur universel, March 8, 1848.

among other clubs, yet when rumors swept the capital that a regular army garrison was returning many clubs were immediately aroused. On March 8 the Society of the Rights of Man went on record as demanding the absolute expulsion of all regulars from the city.[24] By the following day the rumor had taken more definite shape: on the Left Bank the Democratic Society of the Sorbonne fumed over reports that thirty thousand soldiers had returned, while on the other side of the Seine River the Club of the Marais was enraged over twenty thousand.[25]

The clubs that protested the reentry of troops into Paris supported their protest with the same basic arguments. As they saw it, the regular army was not needed. In the first place, if the National Guard were properly democratized and tours of duty evenly distributed among a vastly enlarged militia, no one could complain of overwork. Second, if the government brought back only a small number of troops, they would only constitute a useless provocation. Third, if the government brought back a substantial military force, such a force might inhibit the elections and the subsequent deliberations of the National Assembly. Finally, the return of a major garrison to the capital would threaten the revolution. Clubists were quick to warn of monarchist army officers joining hands with antirepublican elements of the Paris National Guard. In any case, the whole issue was also symbolic, with "the soldier [as] the symbol of an anti-democratic authority."[26] This was as close as anyone dared to come

[24] *La Commune de Paris*, March 14, 1848.

[25] Club du Marais, *Le Moniteur universel*, March 12, 1848; Club de la Sorbonne, loc. cit., March 11, 1848, and *La Commune de Paris*, March 12, 1848.

[26] Club démocratique de la Sorbonne, *Le Moniteur universel*, March 11, 1848; also session of March 9, *La Commune de Paris*, March 11, 1848. Club du Marais, petition, March 11, *Le Moniteur universel*, March 12, 1848; Club socialiste de l'avenir, session of March 13, *La Voix des clubs*, March 16,

to the heart of the problem. In the final analysis, the ultrarevolutionaries, with good reason, did not trust the Provisional Government with the traditional instrument of repression in the capital.

v

The three club demands, then—postponement of the Paris National Guard elections, adjournment of the vote for a National Assembly, permanent removal of all regular troops from the Paris area—had been formulated independently of each other and for different reasons. They seem to have been combined into one "package" on March 10 at the Central Fraternal Society, which was, as I have indicated earlier, in many ways an atypical club that remained on the periphery of the club movement. At its regular session of March 10, Cabet reiterated two demands that were by now familiar: the speedy democratization of the National Guard and the withdrawal of the army from Paris. He was supplemented by Dr. Baudin, president of the Socialist Club of the Future, who also proposed the postponement of the National Guard elections and perhaps of the general elections as well. In any event, the club unanimously voted to protest the ar-

---

1848; letter of protest, March 13, 1848, A.N., BB[30], 300, No. 2779; Club populaire du X[e] arrondissement, *La Voix des clubs*, March 14, 1848; Club des hommes libres, session of March 14, *La Commune de Paris*, March 16, 1848; also editorial comment in *La Voix des clubs*, March 14 and 15, 1848. Not all political clubs disapproved of the return of the troops to Paris, but the troop issue is a reliable index of revolutionary fervor. Only moderate republican and crypto-republican clubs wanted to see the troops back. See, e.g., petition, Comité central républicain du IIIe arrondissement, March 13, 1848, A.N., BB[30], 299, No. 1656; petition, Club de la fraternité universelle, A.N., BB[30], 300, No. 2949. The former club comprised chiefly prerevolutionary opposition electors; the latter was Catholic in outlook.

rival of troops in Paris and to demand that the elections be put off. Even more significant was the club's resolution to enlist all other Parisian clubs in behalf of such a petition and to organize a mass demonstration capable of impressing (or coercing?) the Provisional Government. Blanqui's club had acted in isolation and had failed. Cabet's club hoped that a joint venture would have the proper impact.[27]

Though the evidence is fragmentary for the next several days, the Central Fraternal Society seems to have given the initial impetus to a united club demonstration, but after March 12 delegates from Blanqui's Central Republican Society played a more influential role in mobilizing clubs.[28] The immediate result of these efforts was a meeting of club delegates on March 14 under Blanquist sponsorship. The turnout to what came to be briefly known as the Central Committee of the United Clubs (a day or so later, the Commission of Thirty) was exactly half of

[27] *La Voix des clubs*, March 13, 1848; *Le Populaire*, March 19, 1848. The postponement of the parliamentary elections may have been added two or three days later. See *Le Populaire*, March 16, 1848. For the influence of Cabet's club, ibid., March 19, 1848, and Rapport des officiers de rondes de nuit du 15 au 16 mars 1848, Saisset, colonel, chef d'état-major, A.N., BB[30], 319, dossier 2. On the other hand, the Ministry of the Interior's secret club police was poorly informed. *Enquête*, II, 215.

[28] For evidence that this early preeminence was acknowledged, see Société républicaine centrale, session of March 4, *Le Courrier français*, March 5, 1848; Club des hommes libres, March 12, *La Commune de Paris*, March 14, 1848; Club de l'égalité, session of March 7, *La Voix des clubs*, March 20, 1848. Yet the petition against the troop return and for postponement of the election was generally to be attributed to Blanqui's club or "to the clubs," but not to Cabet's Société fraternelle centrale. See, e.g., Club des hommes libres, session of March 13, *La Commune de Paris*, March 15, 1848; Club des prévoyants, session of March 16, *La Voix des clubs*, March 22, 1848.

the thirty clubs which an optimistic newspaper announcement had anticipated. Yet if the delegates were discouraged by such lukewarm militancy, they must have been warmed by support from the Provisional Government's leftist minority. By reprinting the club petition in his *Bulletin de la République* circulated throughout France, Minister of the Interior Ledru-Rollin appeared to sanction the postponement of elections which came under his administrative jurisdiction. Another member of the Provisional Government, Louis Blanc, actually attended the March 14 meeting and tried to persuade his colleagues to postpone the parliamentary election (as he had already supported putting off the National Guard elections).[29]

Yet the delegates' approach was cautious. The few delegates to the March 14 meeting who proposed to exploit the demonstration to purge conservative members of the Provisional Government were overruled. Though the wording of the petition was agreed upon, Cabet's idea of an immediate mass demonstration was shelved. Instead, the Committee of the United Clubs decided to try

[29] Announcement, *La Voix des clubs*, March 14, 1848; Garnier-Pagès, *Histoire de la révolution*, VI, 394-395; *Le Populaire*, March 19, 1848. Garnier-Pagès mentions the immediate defection of the delegate of the crypto-Bonapartist Club Saint-Georges. As a summons to the Provisional Government of March 15, 1848, bears only 12 signatures, two additional delegates may have dropped out. Some clubs turned down the invitation in the first place because they rejected the proposals. See Société républicaine et patriotique de l'Atelier, letter to Provisional Government, March 15, 1848. A.N., BB[30], 301, No. 3457; petition to Provisional Government, Comité démocratique du Ve arrondissement, March 15, *La Démocratie pacifique*, March 22, 1848. Other clubs, like the Société républicaine du Faubourg Saint-Denis, did not hear of the movement until later. *La Voix des clubs*, March 22, 1848. For the title of the organization, see Club des hommes libres, session of March 15, *La Commune de Paris*, March 18, 1848.

a less dramatic gesture first by having club spokesmen present the demands to the government, with the mass demonstration held in reserve.[30] Consequently, the next day, March 15, the club delegates sent an open letter (placarded on Paris walls) to the Provisional Government requesting an immediate interview on a matter of vital importance. Apparently the government never answered this request.[31]

As this initial move had failed, the clubists chose to return to Cabet's original notion of a monster demonstration organized by the clubs. Perhaps the sympathetic Louis Blanc had warned that they would be snubbed, for, even while the club delegates were waiting for a response, news of the impending march was spreading throughout Parisian workshops. On the morning of March 16 fourteen club envoys met with fifteen representatives of the organized crafts, who claimed to speak for forty-five thousand Parisian workers.[32] The demands to be pre-

[30] I have found the text of a petition discussed at the Club des travailleurs (a satellite of the Société républicaine centrale of Blanqui) on March 15 that is probably the petition adopted on March 14 by the delegates and the one that the club now endorsed. The petition calls for removal of all troops beyond a thirty-mile radius of Paris, postponement of the National Guard elections until the completion of registration, arming of all citizens, the postponement of elections until all officials of the former regime have been purged and public opinion had time to be shaped by republican clubs, and the placing of newspapers under the supervision of competent *commissaires*. No dates are specified. *La Voix des clubs*, March 17, 1848; loc. cit., March 14, 1848; *Le Populaire*, March 19, 1848.

[31] *Les murailles révolutionnaires*, II, 297; see Société des Droits de l'Homme, session of March 15, *La Commune de Paris*, March 16, 1848, for an indication that the clubs were waiting for the outcome of this *démarche* before taking further steps; also *Le Populaire*, March 16, 1848.

[32] This seems to have been the figure bandied about by the organizers. Société républicaine du Faubourg Saint-Denis, session of March 18, *La Voix des clubs*, March 22, 1848. For the meeting of March 16, see *Le Populaire*, March 19, 1848.

sented seem to have been reworded once more. Where an earlier version had been vague as to how long the national elections were to be put off, the three months' delay, originally formulated in Blanqui's petition of a week earlier, was reinstated.[33]

By the morning of March 16 a mass demonstration to present the three demands had been agreed upon, though the date had yet to be set.[34] What were the prospects of the ultrarevolutionaries, clubists, and craftsmen? How large a demonstration could they expect to mount? The figure of one hundred thousand clubists advanced by one left-wing daily was absurdly high, particularly since there was considerable disagreement as to the wisdom of postponing the general elections. An estimate of twenty thousand club activists, mentioned by an informer to the secretary general of the Provisional Government, may have been closer to the mark, though this still exceeded the combined attendance figures of the twelve clubs whose delegates signed the March 15 request for an audience.[35] As to the numbers that organized labor could be expected to marshal, thirty thousand would be

[33] *Le Populaire*, March 19, 1848.

[34] The evidence that the popular demonstration was not scheduled until March 16 is circumstantial. It is almost inconceivable that the general police report for March 15 would have remained silent on a prospective mass march had it already been scheduled (*Enquête*, II, 215). The same applies to the numerous club reports (including several of those known to have been involved in the *démarche* of March 15), where the reports for the evening sessions of March 16 do talk of the morrow's demonstration. This is also confirmed by Caussidière, the police prefect (*Mémoires*, I). *Le Populaire*, March 16, 1848, still spoke of the demonstration in the conditional, the time to be posted if and when.

[35] Victor Bouton, *Attentat de la police républicaine contre la souveraineté du peuple* (Paris, 1848), p. 5. Bouton, an old police spy still under cover in March, predicted 20,000 to 40,000. By March 16 *La Voix des clubs* projected 40,000 under club banners at the demonstration (March 17, 1848).

a reasonable guess.[36] In short, as between clubs and labor unions, an impressive but not overwhelming demonstration of fifty thousand men seemed a likely prospect before the conservatives were to alter the picture.

vi

Since February 24, Parisian revolutionaries had encountered obstruction but no open opposition. The *journée* of March 16, later known as the Day of the Bearskin Buskins, was the first feeble attempt at counterrevolution since February. Just as the ultrarevolutionaries appealed to a variety of fears, so the conservatives played on a variety of resentments. On the lowest level, the demonstration reflected the distaste of the prerevolutionary middle-class-in-arms for many of the fruits of the revolution: the enrollment of "riffraff" in "their" National Guard, excessive guard duty because of the garrison's removal from Paris, the deepening business depression.[37] On a second level, the old National Guard reacted to the dissolution of the elite companies, distinguished by their fancy uniforms and headgear and their aristocratic reputation. Members of the dissolved companies resented their dispersion among strangers on the eve of the officer elections as much as the loss of their distinctive insignia.[38] Finally, the old-line guards regarded the dissolution of the elite companies as part of Ledru-Rollin's grand strategy of imposing a red dictatorship on France. Within this

[36] For the demonstration of March 17 from the perspective of the Parisian labor movement, see Gossez, *Les ouvriers*, pp. 244-245.

[37] See, e.g., the anonymous letter, dated March 8, 1848, from a veteran guard to the Provisional Government, A.N., BB[30], 319, dossier 2. The reactionary daily, *Le Garde national*, published from mid-March to mid-April 1848, also displayed similar attitudes, though somewhat less nakedly.

[38] Société des Droits de l'Homme, session of March 15, *La Commune de Paris*, March 16, 1848.

6.–The fracas over the dissolution of the elite companies

"Well, Euxodie, take my bearskin buskin. . . . Since from now on I am going to be deprived of the happiness of wearing it, I am giving it to you so that you can make a muff with it. At least I'll have the consolation of laying my eyes on it from time to time."

The demonstration of the old-line National Guard, March 16.

paranoid grand design, the Minister of Interior's circular
of March 12 (bombastically proclaiming that his commissioners to the departments had unlimited powers!),
the dissolution of the elite guard on March 14, and the
rising agitation for postponing the elections and removing
the regulars from Paris all seemed part of a pattern.[39]
Ledru-Rollin, who was not even a socialist, who lacked
stomach for a revolutionary dictatorship and was equivocal on the election issue, became the conservative National Guardsmen's symbol of anarchy.[40] As a police spy
reported, "He is called a dictator, and if he didn't immediately resign they would force him to; that his conduct was leading to civil war and causing all sorts of com-
motion throughout the country."[41]

The *journée* of March 16 was a failure that became a
joke (bearskin buskins were made for cartoonists and
this was the age of Daumier), yet the demonstration had
been more threatening than anyone has conceded. On
March 15 preliminary demonstrations on a smaller scale
had revealed open disagreement within the Provisional
Government over Ledru-Rollin's circular. The demonstration of March 16 itself involved not only the elite
companies but a substantial portion of the prerevolutionary National Guard.[42] The demonstrators appeared in

[39] For a good detailed account of the *journée* of March 16,
see Calman, *Ledru-Rollin*, pp. 120-124. For the association of
the garrison and election issues with that of the dissolution
decree, see Rapport des officiers de rondes, 15-16 mars, BB[30],
319, dossier 2.

[40] See Calman, pp. 75-76, for Ledru-Rollin's ideological
stance; for his attitude toward dictatorship, see pp. 114-119
(including the bulk of the text of the March 12 circular, pp.
129-134); for his view on the election, see pp. 124, 135, which
show him as undecided before March 17 but later opposed to
any delay except a brief two weeks for technical reasons.

[41] Police report, signed Carlier, March 16, 1848, *Enquête*,
II, 217-218.

[42] Thirty thousand according to Garnier-Pagès, *Histoire de
la révolution*, VI, 408. The lowest estimate was police prefect

uniform, armed with their service sabers—a gesture on the fine borderline of mutiny—and they were in a nasty mood. When the throng surrounded Ledru-Rollin in his carriage, a lynching was barely averted. The *journée* failed not only because the guardsmen hesitated to live up to their convictions but also because they were hemmed in on the Place du Châtelet by hostile lower-class crowds that streamed out of the central districts as news of the demonstration spread.

vii

The Day of the Bearskin Buskins at first appeared to be a fantastic stroke of luck for the ultrarevolutionaries, who had been planning their own demonstration. No doubt this would-be putsch by the reactionaries rallied to the Commission of Thirty many republicans who would otherwise have stayed home. So much was clear profit. Yet when the Commission of Thirty decided to take advantage of this heaven-sent opportunity by scheduling its own march for the next day, Friday, March 17, the clubists altered the significance of their demonstration. In the face of an antirepublican threat from the old-line National Guard, March 17 was no time for one group of republicans to coerce another. By staging a popular counterdemonstration, the Commission of Thirty willy-nilly let itself in for a republican love-feast. The Day of the Bearskin Buskins may have helped to triple or quadruple the number of republican marchers. By the same token, this mass influx of the uncritically enthusiastic deterred the leaders of the demonstration from a showdown with the Provisional Government.

We know that the flurry of March 16 mobilized republicans who had not responded to the earlier call for a rad-

---

Caussidière's figure of 4,000-5,000. For a much smaller "preliminary" demonstration by delegates of one battalion only, on March 14, see *Le Moniteur universel*, March 15, 1848.

ical demonstration. When the Republican Society of the Faubourg Saint-Denis, for example, heard that the Bearskins were demonstrating against Ledru-Rollin, the three hundred club members immediately proclaimed an unlimited emergency session. Dispatching delegates to other clubs to organize a republican countermarch, they ended up under the banners of the Commission of Thirty.[43] Other clubs dashed off messages of support to Ledru-Rollin and to the Provisional Government, expressing both their personal devotion and their support for the dissolution of the elite companies.[44]

It was in this atmosphere of excitement that the Commission of Thirty laid its plans for March 17. Labor and club delegates agreed that their respective followers—the clubs alone expected forty thousand—would use the broad avenue des Champs-Elysées all the way from the Etoile at the western city limits to the Place de la Concorde (recently renamed Place de la Révolution) for the morning's rendezvous and deployment. Some clubs, like the paramilitary Society of the Rights of Man, made their own special arrangements; the latter decided to gather in the inner court of the Louvre and join the march there.[45] Members of the Commission of Thirty decided to meet at nine o'clock, one hour before the march was

[43] Société républicaine du Faubourg Saint-Denis, session of March 18, *La Voix des clubs*, March 22, 1848.

[44] Club de l'avenir, session of March 16, *La Voix des clubs*, March 17, 1848; Comité central républicain du IIIe arrondissement, March 16, 1848, letter to Provisional Government, A.N., BB[30], 300, No. 2932; Club républicain du Faubourg Saint-Marceau, March 16, 1848, letter to Provisional Government, A.N., BB[30], 300, No. 2850; unsigned police report, March 18, 1848, *Enquête*, II, 223-224.

[45] For the clubs, *La Voix des clubs*, March 17, 1848; for the labor groups, see Gossez, *Les ouvriers*, pp. 244-245; for the Société des Droits de l'Homme, session of March 16, see *La Commune de Paris*, March 18, 1848.

scheduled to begin, at the fountain of the Palais-National (formerly Palais-Royal).[46] The events of March 16 called for an updating and rewording of the petition which the commission expected to approve at its morning meeting. Because so little time was left, the commission ruled out the printing of posters and decided to rely on word of mouth to announce the demonstration. Its envoys, fanning out all over Paris during the evening of March 16, intercepted workers as they were leaving their jobs. Delegates also made a point of notifying the clubs.[47]

An equally natural tendency to rally around the flag—in this case, the Provisional Government's—in a time of emergency was carefully nurtured by Marc Caussidière, police prefect and a political ally of Ledru-Rollin. Caussidière, an old revolutionary activist himself, was sympathetic to the club movement. In this instance he may have feared Blanqui's influence in the Commission of Thirty; in any case he opposed postponing the national elections as a tactical error. On the evening of March 16, Caussidière intervened directly by sending his uniformed officers (many of them former members of republican secret societies) throughout Paris "to announce that on March 17 the people were to proceed to the Hôtel de Ville to congratulate the Provisional Government on the decree it had promulgated and to promise support whenever its efforts tended to promote democratic institutions."[48] By making the Place de la Concorde the gathering place of the demonstrators, the police prefect was mobilizing his own crowd to insulate the Provisional Government from the mass of militant club and labor elements deployed further west and thereby consigned

[46] Garnier-Pagès, *Histoire de la révolution*, VI, 427-428. *Le Populaire*, March 19, 1848.

[47] Gossez, *Les ouvriers*, p. 245; Garnier-Pagès, *Histoire de la révolution*, VI, 429.

[48] Caussidière, *Mémoires*, I, 175.

to the rear of the procession. Caussidière also intervened indirectly by calling on some of his former secret society comrades headed by Joseph Sobrier. Sobrier had been co-police prefect during the first week of the Republic and had just begun publication of a club newspaper, *La Commune de Paris—Moniteur des clubs*. The Sobrier group printed and distributed a poster announcing the demonstration but omitting any mention of the petition that had originally prompted it. Like Caussidière, Sobrier made the Place de la Concorde the rendezvous of the demonstrators.[49]

The meeting of the Commission of Thirty on the morning of the demonstration of March 17 reflected both a broader base of support—delegates of at least a dozen new clubs joined the commission—and a softening of the original demands. The latter was not surprising: several of the newcomers had been completely unaware of any petition; other newcomers had disapproved its content. Though the dissenters bowed to the majority will, in all likelihood their reluctance had something to do with the altered tone of the petition's final draft, which bore the signatures of representatives from fifteen labor organizations and twenty-five clubs.[50]

Though the original demands stood, they had been

[49] Poster, March 17, 1848, B.N., Lb[53], 580. The other six were all signers of an earlier Manifesto of the Secret Societies (*Les murailles révolutionnaires*, I, 254-256) and of an appeal by an organization floated by Sobrier, the magniloquently titled "Commission instituée pour appeler tous les patriotes éprouvés à la défense de la République," *La République*, March 5, 1848.

[50] For a complete text, see *La Voix des clubs*, March 18, 1848; for the original of the petition presented, see A.N., BB[30], 299, No. 1798. For some indication of the nature of the meeting on the morning of March 17, see Société républicaine du Faubourg Saint-Denis, session of March 18, *La Voix des clubs*, March 22, 1848.

shorn of their revolutionary implications. The demand to postpone National Guard elections to April 5 was not tampered with, since it was the least controversial issue. It was the justification for postponing the general elections that had been drastically changed. Blanqui's harsh but plausible thesis that the provinces were politically hostile, that only a strong government determined to re-publicanize the country could succeed, had given way to

3. Route of the demonstration of March 17, 1848

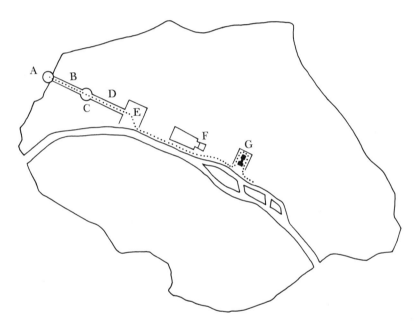

A. Place de l'Arc de Triomphe
B. Avenue de Neuilly
C. Etoile des Champs-Elysées
D. Avenue des Champs-Elysées
E. Place de la Révolution (formerly: de la Concorde)
F. Palais du Louvre

7.–The 18th Brumaire of the people and the 18th Brumaire of the bourgeoisie

The popular demonstration of March 17

The triumph of the National Guard before City Hall on April 16

twaddle about technical registration delays and the need for voters to be better acquainted with their candidates. The argument for withdrawing regular troops from Paris had been reduced to a constitutional formality: "The democratic principle that where the people and its representatives deliberate, only citizens should be present" was an argument invalidated by the recent decree granting soldiers the vote. The petition concluded: "Yesterday a threatening demonstration was seeking to undermine you. Today we respond to it by a peaceful demonstration to defend you and ourselves with you."[51] Between pressure and support, support loomed larger.

The *journée* of March 17, therefore, turned into a triumph of ambiguity that some club activists mistook for a triumph for their own cause. They were, above all, intoxicated by sheer numbers, for the demonstration turned out to be the largest unofficial outpouring of the masses of any *journée* of the revolution of 1848. Though estimates of crowds are usually unverifiable, there is no reason to question the figures of one hundred fifty thousand or two hundred thousand cited by contemporaries. Even hostile eyewitnesses were overawed by the discipline of the proletarian marchers who held the fate of the Provisional Government and of France in their hands that day.[52] Yet conservative observers may have been overimpressed by the novelty of the spectacle. They failed to note that even as the masses occupied the center of the stage, they were still cast as chorus rather than as actors. They came more to applaud than to demand.

The Commission of Thirty's position was doubly equivocal. In the first place, its leadership of the march-

[51] A.N., BB[30], 299, No. 1798.

[52] Lord Normanby, *A Year of Revolution from a Journal Kept in Paris in 1848* (London, 1857), I, 240-241. See also the tone of the anonymous (and usually hostile) daily police report probably prepared by Carlier, *Enquête*, II, 223-224.

ers was more apparent than real, for the majority of the demonstrators was probably unaware that one of the aims of the demonstration was to change government policy.[53] This political isolation must have been reinforced by the physical isolation of the leaders from their followers, who, thanks to the efforts of Caussidière and Sobrier, brought up the rear. In the second place, because March 17 was first and foremost a loyalty rally for the Republic, the Commission of Thirty had, as we have seen, sugarcoated its demands. The commission's flaccid arguments cried out for rebuttal.

The confrontation between the enlarged Commission of Thirty (comprising some forty delegates) and the Provisional Government revealed the weakness of the petitioners' position. In one respect this weakness was the result of a misunderstanding. The delegates received less support from Louis Blanc, their contact within the Provisional Government, than they had expected. The socialist minister, who had not been told of the last-minute addition of new club delegates, mistook the newcomers for dangerous anarchists.[54] Consequently, instead of supporting the commisioners' demand for an immediate answer to their petition, Blanc backed the government's right to deliberate in freedom.

Yet the petitioners could not rely on the crowd either, and the other official spokesmen, Ledru-Rollin and

[53] Testimony Carteret, *Enquête*, I, 249; *La Démocratie pacifique*, March 19, 1848; protestation of the workers of the Guillot Company, *Le Moniteur universel*, March 22, 1848; Garnier-Pagès, *Histoire de la révolution*, VI, 429.

[54] For the official account, see *Le Moniteur universel*, March 18, 1848. For Louis Blanc's role, see Loubère, *Louis Blanc*, pp. 98-99, and Gossez, *Les ouvriers*, p. 245. Blanc's own recollections are given in *1848: Historical Revelations* (London, 1858), pp. 306-307, and at somewhat greater length in *Pages d'histoire de la révolution de février 1848* (Paris, 1850), pp. 90-93.

Lamartine, were able to seize on the weakness of the arguments themselves. Ledru-Rollin, for one, convinced the delegates that the date for *national* elections could not be decided on the basis of the *local* registration difficulties with which they were familiar. Any decision, the Minister of the Interior conveyed, would have to be based on the reports from all over France that he had requested. Lamartine was equally successful in undermining the argument for removal of troops. Could a people that had won against eighty thousand regulars fear a few thousand soldiers guarding the tollgates of the capital? Besides, he continued, snapping another weak link in the petition's chain, how could continued discrimination against soldiers be justified under a Republic that had just granted them full civic rights? Earlier, Lamartine had been conciliatory on the National Guard election issue. Now, having scored a debater's point on the soldiers as citizens, Lamartine could get to the root of the matter, to what the clubs had meant rather than what they had said. "We will not, in the name of Paris alone," he affirmed, "set up a dictatorship of liberty, a liberty which, even though it was won right here, was won for all of France." And amidst applause, the Foreign Minister could end by warning the delegates against such mass demonstrations: "Unwittingly, the 18th Brumaire of the people might bring on the 18th Brumaire of despotism."[55] The rest of the day belonged to the cheering crowd that filed for hours past the Provisional Government.

Though the club and labor movement had not been able to master the Provisional Government on March 17, by the end of the day it was not clear who had won or lost. The prevailing republican exaltation in the wake of the *journée* precluded cool-headed appraisal. There were some plusses for the ultrarevolutionaries. On one point,

[55] *Le Moniteur universel*, March 18, 1848, p. 633.

that of putting off the National Guard elections to April 15, the government capitulated, though the election results were nonetheless to disappoint the Left. Within two weeks, the government consented to finance republican missionaries whom the clubs selected to be sent to the provinces, a proposal originally made in the Blanqui petition. Within about a week, the Minister of the Interior postponed the national elections by a fortnight, supposedly on purely administrative grounds. The debits were less obvious but longer lasting. March 17 notwithstanding, the Minister of War, more or less surreptitiously, recalled regular troops to Paris. By election time in April, these had grown to four regiments, by June to twenty-five thousand regulars. Above all, despite its secret underwriting of the club missionaries, the Provisional Government clung to Lamartine's refusal to set up "a dictatorship of liberty" to sway the elections. In this context of an official hands-off policy, even those club demands to which the government had acceded proved a disappointment to the revolutionaries.

From the start the clubs had preempted several roles. They had seen nothing incompatible in both supporting the Provisional Government against the forces of reaction and pressuring that government to live up to its revolutionary origins. Yet March 17 showed that in its aggressive role the club movement lacked conviction; even at the head of the Parisian masses the popular societies could only exact minor concessions. In retrospect, March 17 looks like a major turning point precisely because, when the point was reached, no turn was made.

4 | The Mirage of Unity

I have just left the Club of Clubs. It is laughable, it is dis-
tressing, it is frightful. A pseudoeducation has driven everyone
crazy.

P.-J. Proudhon, April 8, 1848

i

However inconclusive its outcome, the great street demonstration of March 17 had shown that the popular societies could cooperate in a common endeavor. What was
missing was organized and continuous cooperation, what
one newspaper early in March had labeled "living and
permanent links" binding the clubs.[1] March 17 had offered a unique occasion for common organization. The
government's announcement of general elections had
been even more fundamental in providing the needed
impetus to unity. While clubists, generally agreed on the
need for close cooperation if the revolutionary Republic
were to survive the trauma of manhood suffrage, there
was no agreement on how unity might be most effectively
achieved.

Between the beginning of March and mid-April 1848,
at least five separate campaign organizations tried to rally
the Parisian clubs. Three of these republican groupings,
the Central Democratic Society, the Central Committee
for General Elections, and the Central Committee of the

[1] *La République*, March 15, 1848.

Workers of the Department of the Seine, were organized outside of club circles but tried to enlist club support. Two other attempts, the Central Committee of Elections and the Revolutionary Committee, Club of Clubs, were generated within the movement itself.

ii

The Central Democratic Society was the first postrevolutionary organization with claims to republican leadership.[2] Technically the society was a carry-over from the July Monarchy, having been founded during the winter of 1847-48 by a group of socially minded upper-middle-class republicans who had become disenchanted with collaboration with liberal monarchists. The Central Democratic Society was thus a dissident offshoot of the Central Committee of the Electors of the Seine, in which the monarchist opposition and "legal" republicans had co-operated successfully to sweep the elections in Paris in 1846. Machiavelli once noted that nothing fails like yesteryear's success: the methods of the Central Committee that had worked in 1846 proved a burden to the Central Democratic Society working in a very different political climate. The minutes of the Central Democratic Society, unique in their completeness, reflect great ambitions but little adaptability to new conditions. As veteran republicans, the founders of the Central Democratic Society kept at arm's length the masses who had made the revolution. Self-confident and self-appointed, the *sociétaires* thought of themselves as democratic commanders conveying their orders to district societies. Such a vision of a passively obedient populace had no relation to reality. Though the Central Democratic Society included National Guard colonels and lieutenant colonels, district mayors and provincial commissioners, the society stagnated, exercising at best a shadowy moral authority over two

[2] Amann, *Minutes*, pp. 9-46.

score affiliated district committees and neighborhood clubs founded by society members. The society proved unable to broaden its base or to appeal to the dozens of nascent revolutionary clubs.

The Central Democratic Society's attempts to influence the national elections were pathetically amateurish. A few random members, volunteering to propagandize in their native departments, were granted full powers to speak for the society. In Paris the Central Democratic Society, increasingly troubled by its isolation, ended by cooperating with the proletarian Central Committee of the Workers of the Seine—though its own membership remained resolutely middle class. The bargain was unequal; in return for the Central Democratic Society's endorsement of twenty worker candidates selected by the organized crafts, the Workers' Committee promised to support General Joseph Guinard, the Central Democratic Society's president and second-in-command of the Paris National Guard. Perhaps the bargain was more equal than it seemed; nineteen of the twenty worker candidates went down to defeat anyway, while Guinard, even though the Central Committee of the Workers reneged on its support, narrowly won election. In any event, the Central Democratic Society never came close to exercising the influence to which it had aspired.

iii

The rival Central Committee for the General Elections to the National Assembly took a very different course.[3]

[3] For a more extensive discussion of this organization, though in a somewhat different context, see George Fasel, "The French Election of April 23, 1848," *French Historical Studies*, v (1968), 287-289; and "The French Moderate Republicans, 1837-48," Ph.D. diss., Stanford University, 1965, pp. 284-286, 293-299. My analysis relies on my own research in both contemporary newspapers and manuscript sources in B.H.V.P., Liesville Collection.

Where the Central Democratic Society inclined to secretiveness and behind-the-scenes maneuvering, the Central Committee thrived on publicity. Actually, the two organizations attracted men with similar middle-class republican backgrounds, many of them in the upper reaches of the administration installed by the Provisional Government. The similarity helps explain why some thirty members of the Central Democratic Society deserted it to participate in the activities of the Central Committee.[4] Yet there were differences: the Central Democratic Society was more genuinely committed to social change than the Central Committee.

The creation of the Central Committee for the General Elections during the second week of March offered a curious parallel to the formation of the Provisional Government several weeks earlier.[5] In both instances, moderate republicans, most of whom had ties with the newspaper Le National, constituted the original nucleus. The Central Committee's president, Dr. Recurt, doubled as deputy mayor of Paris. Other founding fathers included the municipal secretary and two recently appointed National Guard colonels. Then, just as the Provisional Government had broadened its original makeup by admitting new members identified with the leftist La Réforme, so did the Central Committee. In neither case did the latecomers set the tone. The committee's secretary, the archaeologist Philippe Lebas (who made the most of being the grandson of Robespierre's political ally) best expressed the organization's political mood by calling for a republic that would "provide for those who lacked

[4] Amann, Minutes, p. 23, for the relations of the Société démocratique centrale and the Comité central des élections générales.

[5] J. Gouache, editor of La Réforme, to Comité central, March 12, 1848, B.H.V.P., Liesville Collection. For the fusion, see Le National, March 13, 1848; La Réforme, March 14, 1848; Le Courrier français, March 17, 1848.

without taking from those who owned." He wanted, he said, "to lengthen the vests without shortening the coats," but gave no hint as to who would pay the cost of alteration.[6]

From the start, the committee's self-appointed leaders built public support by enlisting prominent republicans (even to the point of claiming for their cause republican notables who had never been consulted) and by making the Central Committee for the General Elections a clearinghouse for republican candidates.[7] By publicizing their existence in the hospitable columns of Le National, the committee began to gather data received from all over the country, accumulating information on a vast array of candidates to the National Assembly. Sifting eight to ten thousand names, the Central Committee for the General Elections ended by endorsing 850 duly certified republicans for the 900 seats at stake. The committee completed this task by April 15, one week before election day.[8]

The committee looked for club support for the same reason that it sought endorsement by prominent republican personalities—because such publicity was useful. Between March 17 and 21, Parisian clubs were invited to send delegates "to deliberate on how best to achieve republican election results everywhere."[9] At least a dozen

[6] Le Courrier français, March 26, 1848.

[7] For the attempt to "enlist" Barbès, and the ensuing controversy, see La Réforme, March 15, 1848. For the committee as a clearinghouse, see Le National, March 9, 1848; La République, March 11, 1848; L'Assemblée nationale, March 11, 1848; Le National, March 11, 16, 17, 1848; La Réforme, March 19, 1848; Le National, March 18-20, 1848; Le Peuple constituant, March 19, 1848.

[8] Le Courrier français, April 15, 1848.

[9] Comité central to Société des Droits de l'Homme, March 14, 1848, A.N., CdE 8362; for the general invitation, see Le Courrier français, March 21, 1848.

clubs complied, but their delegates felt that their views were ignored.[10] It soon became obvious both that the Central Committee for the General Elections had no intention of sharing power and that its political orientation was too conservative to please club activists.

The list of candidates endorsed by the Central Committee for the department of Seine, published on March 29, brought home this difference.[11] Where most clubs were unwilling to back the moderate members of the government (either because of distrust or because they would be elected in the provinces anyway), the Central Committee's slate featured the entire Provisional Government surrounded by a galaxy of republican officials and other respectable notables. Only five workers, most of them known antisocialists, were chosen. Not one of the prominent club leaders—Blanqui, Barbès, Lebon, Huber, Sobrier, Raspail—won the committee's stamp of approval; nor did a single leader of one of the socialist or communist "schools"—men like Cabet, Considérant, Proudhon, Pecqueur—make the grade. In short, the Central Committee for the General Elections to the National Assembly was willing to accept club support but was in no way willing to pay for it.

[10] There are letters relating to the following clubs in the (fragmentary) papers of the Comité central in the Liesville Collection of the B.H.V.P.: Club démocratique central de la garde nationale, Club de la société unitaire de propagande démocratique (Passy), Club de Puteaux, Club de Clichy, Société des Droits de l'Homme, Club de l'Abbaye, Club des Provençaux, Club républicain du Faubourg du Roule; also poster, Comité central des écoles, *Les murailles révolutionnaires*, I, 315-316. For the unhappiness of the clubists with the Comité's high-handedness, see the testimony of Delaire, *Enquête*, I, 172. Session of Club de la révolution (undated), *La Voix des clubs*, March 24, 1848.

[11] *Le Peuple constituant*, March 31, 1848.

iv

The social origin and aims of the Central Committee of the Workers of the Seine differed sharply.[12] Where both the Central Democratic Society and the Central Committee for the General Elections were dominated by substantial middle-class republicans accustomed to legal political opposition under the July Monarchy, the Workers' Committee was simply an organization of craft delegates embarking on their first venture into politics. The Central Democratic Society and the General Elections Committee dreamed of, and to some extent worked for, national influence. The Workers' Committee aimed at the more modest goal of sending a substantial number of their fellows to represent Paris in the National Assembly. This goal had initially been formulated on March 19 by a Club of United Workers in an open letter to the delegates of the Luxembourg Commission.[13] The club informed the Luxembourg delegates of its decision, taken at a meeting held "with the aim of electing at least twenty workers from the department of Seine to the national representation," that working-class sentiments could be most effectively expressed through the organized crafts. Specifically, the club urged the Luxembourg delegates to convoke the various crafts, which would then nominate provisional candidates, preferably from among the delegates themselves, in order to take advantage of their newly won political experience. These provisional candidates would then thin their own ranks to produce a slate of

[12] The fullest accounts of the Comité central des ouvriers de la Seine (whose archives have not survived) may be found in Loubère, *Louis Blanc*, pp. 110-117, and in Gossez, *Les ouvriers*, pp. 247-259.

[13] Petition from Club des travailleurs unis to Commission des travailleurs sitting at the Luxembourg, March 19, 1848, in the form of a poster. *Les murailles révolutionnaires*, II, 457-458.

final candidates whom the various crafts would promise to support.

Evidently this or a similar proposal convinced the Luxembourg labor delegates. On March 28 Louis Blanc, whose ascendancy over the delegates was unquestioned at this time, persuaded them in a passionate speech to abandon their plan of choosing candidates along craft lines, "which would lead to disastrous divisions."[14] Instead, he urged that the delegates' executive committee nominate the candidates to be discussed and the entire Assembly of Delegates make final selections. Blanc retained the Club of United Workers' figure of twenty proletarians (from a slate of thirty-four representatives allotted to the department of Seine). He suggested that the remaining fourteen seats be filled by well-known veteran republicans. In Blanc's view, fifty or a hundred determined representatives, backed by the people of Paris, could move the whole sluggish mass of provincial parliamentarians.

Almost immediately two committees were set up, drawn from Luxembourg delegates. A Central Committee of the Workers of the Department of the Seine was to deal with the political organization of the Paris working class. Within a day or two it had established liaison with the Central Democratic Society and had sent three delegates to the recently created Revolutionary Committee, Club of Clubs. It made no secret of its decision to nominate twenty workers as candidates from Seine to the National Assembly. In the meantime, on April 5 a second committee dealing specifically with elections set about its task of selecting worker candidates. This election committee relied on the seventy organized trades to nominate one member each. Apparently the task was

[14] For the full text of Blanc's speech, A.N., C. 929A, dossier 3, No. 84, "Recueil des discours prononces au Luxembourg par Louis Blanc," March 28, 1848.

completed by April 12, though the formal approval of
the nominees by the entire Assembly of Labor delegates
was delayed until April 17, just one week before election
day. At that time, in concert with the club federation, the
workers also agreed on which nonworkers to endorse. In
short, the Central Committee of the Workers of the Seine
offered cooperation to all groups, clubs included, willing
to accept its slate.

v

The Commission of Thirty, having led the mass demonstrations of March 17, did not survive its equivocal triumph. It was displaced by a new organization, the Revolutionary Committee, Club of Clubs, whose organizers
deliberately shouldered aside Blanqui and Cabet, who
had played so prominent a part in the commission. The
Club of Clubs grew out of an earlier Commission to Call
All Tested Patriots to the Defense of the Republic
headed by Joseph Sobrier in early March.[15] Not only was
Sobrier a key man in both organizations, but there was
overlapping leadership all along the line: an appeal for
a meeting on March 18 to launch the Revolutionary
Committee, Club of Clubs (and, as it turned out, a Club
of the Revolution as well), bore twelve signatures. Eight
of these twelve had also signed the manifesto of the
Tested Patriots two weeks earlier.

The timing of the move may have been determined by

[15] For the "Manifeste des sociétés secrètes," see *Les murailles
révolutionnaires*, I, 254-256. For the Commission instituée
pour appeler à la défense de la République tous les patriotes
éprouvés, *La République*, March 5, 1848. For acknowledg-
ment that the commission was the Club de la révolution's
predecessor, see the proclamation by the latter, *La Commune
de Paris*, March 29, 1848. For the call to the initial meeting
of what was to become both the Club de la révolution and the
Comité révolutionnaire, Club des clubs, see *La Commune de
Paris*, March 18, 1848.

the events of March 17, which had enhanced Blanqui's influence among Parisian clubs. The call for a meeting of delegates on March 18 may have been Sobrier's and his friends' challenge to Blanqui's leadership of the Commission of Thirty. The new element was the support of revolutionary luminaries like Armand Barbès and Martin-Bernard, prominent left-wing journalists like Thoré, Bianchi, and Cahaigne, as well as some of the cadres of the republican secret societies.[16]

The manifesto of this Revolutionary Committee for the Elections to the National Assembly identified its sponsors as convinced socialists. The document stressed that the impending elections would be crucial to achieving the goal of the Republic, the extinction of the proletariat. On a practical level, the meeting called for March 18 would set up electoral committees for the various districts of Paris.

This preliminary meeting of March 18 seems to have been neither a spectacular success nor an outright failure. Compared to the twenty-five clubs that had participated in the Commission of Thirty the day before, only eighteen responded to Sobrier's appeal. The clubs represented were not outstanding. Several were so conservative as to be only nominally republican; others, from some of the more rustic suburbs of the capital, were politically unsophisticated. This did not deter the sponsors from founding a dual organization: an elite, directing Club of the Revolution which, in turn, would sponsor a Parisian club federation, the previously advertised Revolutionary Committee, Club of Clubs.[17]

[16] For a text of the poster, see *La Commune de Paris*, March 18, 1848; for one of the clubs contacted by letter, see Club du progrès, session of March 18, *La Commune de Paris*, March 21, 1848.

[17] Longepied and Laugier, *Comité révolutionnaire*, pp. 31-32; Garnier-Pagès, *Histoire de la révolution*, VII, 77-78.

The founders of the Club of the Revolution and its nebulous offspring probably lacked any blueprint for the future of the revolutionary club movement. Armand Barbès, who was to be the president of the Club of the Revolution, was privately talking simply of "a truly democratic club to push public opinion in the right direction."[18] In public, Barbès' comrades said much the same, though less succinctly. In the words of the club's keynote speaker at its formal opening on March 21:

Create a revolutionary club in Paris: have it made up of men who have long given France shining pledges of their patriotism; republicans tested by struggle, by fire, by persecution, by martyrdom; thinkers and writers who have devoted long nights to the spelling out of the great reforming ideas. . . . To do so is to organize, from the first days of the revolution, an intellectual and moral force which may not be without influence on its march and destiny.[19]

The club had the dual purpose of fostering political action through the still uncreated Revolutionary Committee, Club of Clubs, and of providing a forum for communist ideas. In its attitude toward the Provisional Government, the Club of the Revolution professed ambivalence: enthusiasm for these ministers "truly embodying the spirit of the revolution"; reluctant support for the moderates "as Robespierre and the Jacobins defended the Constitution of 1791 on the eve of August 10."[20]

Two days later, on March 23, Blanqui's Central Republican Society, supported by eight less well-known clubs, counterattacked. Apparently by that time the

[18] Barbès to Alberny, March 19, 1848, in F.-F. Jeanjean, *Armand Barbès (1809-1870)*, II (Carcassonne, 1947), 85 87.

[19] Minutes, Club de la révolution, March 21, *La Commune de Paris*, March 24, 1848. See also Longepied and Laugier, *Comité révolutionnaire*, pp. 36-38.

[20] *La Commune de Paris*, March 24, 1848.

Commission of Thirty could not readily be reconvoked. Rather, Blanqui chose to challenge the yet unorganized Club of Clubs head on by posting his own much more militant call for club unity. Where the Club of Clubs had called for social reform, Blanqui demanded a thorough-going social revolution to emancipate the workers, to end "the reign of exploitation" and usher in a new order where labor would be free from the tyranny of capital. The organizational meeting for this new club federation was scheduled for the same Sunday as a widely publicized first session of the rival Revolutionary Committee, Club of Clubs.[21]

On March 26 club delegates faced the choice of at-tending three rival meetings, all of them supposedly dedi-cated to unity.[22] One of these, promoted by a Club of Equality, seems to have been ignored. The Blanqui-spon-sored meeting, scheduled for eleven o'clock in the morn-ing at the Palais des Arts et Métiers, caused enough stir to attract delegates from twenty-three clubs. The meeting itself merely went about the business of organizing a Cen-tral Committee for Elections, of which Blanqui became president, while two other club presidents were elected vice-chairmen. Delegates who, before committing them-selves, would have preferred to see what would come of the evening meeting of the Revolutionary Committee, Club of Clubs, were evidently outvoted.[23]

The organizational meeting of the Club of Clubs, held in the Hall of Battles of the Palais-National, outdid the Blanqui effort.[24] Amable Longepied, a founder of the

[21] Announcement, *La Voix des clubs*, March 26, 1848.

[22] Ibid.

[23] *Le Courrier français*, March 27, 1848.

[24] Minutes, Comité révolutionnaire, Club des clubs (here-after CR), March 26, 1848, A.N., C. 941, CdE 9021. These minutes are unusually sketchy and may be complemented with eyewitness reports in Longepied and Laugier, *Comité révolu-*

Club of the Revolution, welcomed two hundred delegates from some sixty clubs in a long-winded speech stressing the need for republican unity. The remainder of the session was devoted chiefly to practical matters. Delegates agreed that member clubs had to have an enrollment of at least one hundred before they could send delegates to the Club of Clubs. All delegates would have to provide themselves with proper credentials within three days. A committee elected from among the delegates would enforce standards of democratic orthodoxy in processing club applications for membership. Future meetings would be scheduled for the afternoon so that delegates could report on the day's deliberations to their own clubs in the evening. Temporary officers, headed by Longepied, were confirmed by acclamation. There seems to have been at least some talk about the organization's future role in reaching beyond Paris to France and the world. More to the point, delegates were to bring their clubs' preliminary lists of parliamentary candidates to the next meeting two days away, so that the Club of Clubs could begin immediately to draw up its own definitive list.

The rivalry between the two nascent club federations was short-lived. Within less than a week the Central Committee for Elections folded when Blanqui was temporarily eliminated from practical politics. On March 31 the journalist Taschereau's *Revue retrospective*, a collection of the July Monarchy's secret documents, singled out Blanqui as an erstwhile police informer.[25] Blanqui's reac-

---

tionnaire, pp. 42-46. Also *Le Courrier français*, March 27, 1848; and proclamation dated March 27 in *La Commune de Paris*, March 28, 1848.

[25] There is a considerable literature on the question of Blanqui's "guilt" or "innocence." Among the major contributors are Wassermann, *Les clubs de Barbès et de Blanqui*, pp. 105-136; Jeanjean, *Armand Barbès*, I, 170ff.; C. Geoffroy, *L'enfermé* (Paris, 1897), pp. 147ff. The most exhaustive scholarly de-

tion was to withdraw from club affairs for two weeks to devote himself to his personal defense. His rebuttal, not published until April 13, convinced his friends, failed to impress his enemies, and left nonpartisans uncertain. The net effect of Taschereau's charge was to undermine Blanqui's leadership, and without his guidance the Central Committee for Elections foundered. All but six of its member clubs moved over to the Revolutionary Committee, Club of Clubs, though probably some had joined both federations from the start. Former Blanqui adherents were made welcome in the Club of Clubs: at least two delegates from clubs originally under Blanqui's patronage were elected to the executive board of the Revolutionary Committee. The collapse of Blanqui's federation left the field free for the Club of Clubs, which by mid-April enrolled nearly one hundred and fifty Parisian clubs, at least two-thirds of those active at the time.

vi

The history of the Revolutionary Committee, Club of Clubs, is the history of political failure. As a campaign instrument geared to the elections in the Seine department, the Club of Clubs was wholly ineffectual. As a disseminator of revolutionary republican propaganda, the

---

fense of Blanqui is Maurice Dommanget's *Un drame politique en 1848* (Paris, 1948), passim; "Les 'faveurs' de Blanqui: Blanqui et le document Taschereau," *1848*, XLIII (1950), 137-166; and "Blanqui et le document Taschereau: attitude et règle de conduite de Blanqui en matière de défense personnelle," *Revue d'histoire économique et sociale* (1953), pp. 50-70. By a curious coincidence, shortly before April 14, Blanqui's club vice-president, Michelot (in his own right president of the Société populaire de la Sorbonne), was exposed and arrested as Juin d'Allas, a fraudulent bankrupt. *Le Moniteur universel*, April 14, 1848; *La Commune de Paris*, April 14, 1848; *Le Courrier français*, April 15, 1848; *La Réforme*, April 17, 1848; for his trial, see *Pilier des tribunaux, compte-rendu des assises* (August 1848).

role of the Club of Clubs is harder to assess. Recent local and regional studies of the French revolution of 1848 have generally minimized the impact of the Parisian organization and its provincial envoys.[26]

The two roles were related: the Club of Clubs' involvement in the provincial elections had a devastating effect on its effectiveness in Paris. The club federation's decision to extend its operations throughout France was made as early as March 28. The idea of republicanizing the countryside was nothing new. Blanqui and other organizers of the March 17 demonstration had urged postponement of the elections in order to allow time for republican propaganda among the rural masses. Since "it was the opinion of the Club of Clubs that the elections in Paris would take place under ideal conditions, but [as] there was fear that such would not be the case in the provinces," the club federation eagerly decided to put its energies where they[27] would truly count.

[26] The correspondence of the Club des clubs missionaries, the starting point for resolving this problem, has never been systematically exploited. It may be found, filed alphabetically by department, in A.N., C. 937, 938, and 939. It has been sampled most recently by Price, *The French Second Republic*, pp. 114-139. At least one recent regional study, John Merriman, "Radicalization and Repression: the Experience of the Limousin, 1848-1851," Ph.D. diss. University of Michigan, 1972, pp. 61-65, does assign to one particular Club des clubs delegate a key role in mobilizing the workers of Limoges and the department of Creuse in general.

[27] G. A. Leroyer, vice-president of the Club républicain du Faubourg de Roule to CR, undated, A.N., C. 940, CdE 8238, which summarizes the reports from the CR delegates received in his club. Such beliefs were not confined to club activists. See, e.g., *Le Courrier français*, April 13, 1848, for an almost identical appraisal. The decision to concentrate on the peasantry, already taken for granted at the Club of Clubs' meeting of March 31 (A.N., C. 941, CdE 9029) was apparently decided on March 28. Club du progrès, session of March 29, 1848; *La Commune de Paris*, March 31, 1848.

Not only was this a misreading of the ultrarepublican situation in Paris. Blanqui's proposal had assumed ample time—at least three months—and massive government intervention to carry republicanism to the peasants. The Club of Clubs had a mere four weeks and only lukewarm official backing. Four weeks to recruit, train, dispatch, and direct a corps of some five hundred propagandists! Even so, five hundred missionaries for ten million voters was not a very promising ratio. Yet in turning most of its energies to this national campaign, the Club of Clubs not only lost the political initiative locally, but undermined its independence from the government.

From the first, the proposal to send envoys to the departments was linked to official financial support for such a venture. As one club delegate put it: "We shouldn't be stymied by questions of money. The Provisional Government owes it to us. We'll ask for it and the government will come across."[28] A five-man committee was immediately sent to the Minister of the Interior to obtain funds, bearing what sounded more like an ultimatum than a petition. The Revolutionary Committee, Club of Clubs, had determined to dispatch "men chosen in the clubs and in the organized trades and sponsored by them; men of tested patriotism, full of drive, men of heart imbued with openly proclaimed principles, capable by virtue of their vocation, character and family connections . . . of introducing among the inhabitants, more stunned than enlightened, the sense of republicanism that ought to dictate the choice of representatives to the National Assembly."[29]

The petitioners made it clear that they would not be put off by "measly considerations of lack of money." The

[28] Minutes, CR, A.N., C. 941, CdE 9022 (March 28, 1848).

[29] The only surviving text of this letter, signed by 13 members of CR, headed by Sobrier, may be found in B.H.V.P., Liesville Collection.

Club of Clubs' sledgehammer approach impressed
Ledru-Rollin, who, two days later, successfully cham-
pioned the clubs' demand in the councils of the Provisional Government. A few hundred carefully chosen
"apostles," the Minister of the Interior argued, could do
little harm and might do some good. In any event, it was
wiser to keep an official eye on the operation by subsidiz-
ing it than to let the club envoys elude supervision.[30] By
accepting this argument, the moderate majority within
the Provisional Government put themselves in the awk-
ward position of oiling a political machine designed to
crush moderation.

The task now assumed by the Club of Clubs not only
took priority over all other concerns but required a very
different sort of organization from the loosely run mass
meeting of club delegates sitting at the Palais-National
almost every afternoon. A specially appointed commission of the federation's executives was given the responsibility of selecting and supervising the revolutionary
apostles. A battery of secretaries was hired.[31] The commission and its staff obtained office space in the palace
of the rue de Rivoli that housed Sobrier's headquarters
and newspaper. There the commissioners interviewed
prospective candidates every evening between seven and
ten.[32] As soon as they reached agreement on the nightly
list of provincial envoys, they reported to the Ministry
of the Interior, where the undersecretaries doled out
funds against signed receipts, while Ledru-Rollin himself
was kept abreast of the Club of Clubs' activities. Sometimes these conversations with the Minister of the In-

[30] Garnier-Pagès, *Histoire de la révolution*, VII, 235-236.

[31] A.N., C. 941, CdE 9009.

[32] Undated note introducing an Alsatian worker, Bige
Wenge, from Tard, mayor of Passy. A.N., C. 942, CdE 8144,
Testimony Delaire, *Enquête*, I, 172.

terior lasted until 1:30 and 2:00 A.M. The regular open sessions of the Club of Clubs, attended by delegates from member clubs during the afternoon, merely endorsed the envoys already chosen by the commission.[33]

The Club of Clubs also competed with the moderate Central Committee for General Elections in drawing up slates of candidates, department by department, for the whole country. To what extent the commission relied on reports from provincial republican campaign committees and to what extent it drew on the dispatches of its own traveling agents is not known.[34] What is clear is that this ambitious undertaking was never completed. About one week before the elections, the Club of Clubs, somewhat apologetically, released a list of approved candidates for a dozen departments—the only lists completed by that time. The names of hundreds of other endorsed candidates were filed but never published, though they may have been conveyed privately to the club federation's envoys in the departments.[35]

[33] Longepied and Laugier, *Comité révolutionnaire*, pp. 108-110. Testimony Delaire, *Enquête*, I, 172, 210. For example, minutes, CR, A.N., C. 941, CdE 9026. Undated (March 31, 1848?).

[34] Departmental clubs were summoned to affiliate with the CR, "in order to coordinate the active and common efforts of republicans on the question of principle which the social revolution of 1848 has raised." *La Commune de Paris*, April 11, 1848.

[35] The list contained some 750 names for the 900 seats in the National Assembly. A.N., C. 941, CdE 8952. A somewhat sketchy comparison, based on Robert *et al.*, *Dictionnaire des parlementaires français* (Paris, 1889-90), of the CR's list with that of the moderate Comité central des élections républicains confirms the suspicion that, with the exception of a few urban centers, there was no *national* split between moderate and socialist republicans in the spring of 1848—largely, I suspect, because there were not enough socialist republicans to go around.

vii

Its widened scope changed the Club of Clubs' character and altered its leaders' outlook. In order to administer the vast operation of departmental delegates that the funds from the Ministry of the Interior sustained, the Club of Clubs' commissioners became willy-nilly bureaucrats tied to office routines. The daily allowance of five francs which they collected—the wage of an average clerk—was symbolic of their new status and may have been a brake on revolutionary impulsiveness.[36] Yet the effect of the nightly conversations with Ledru-Rollin must have been more insidious: familiarity with the great is liable to feed the insider's illusion of power, corroding his independence more surely than bribes or subsidies.

Much depended on the character of the men who had been thrust into the Club of Clubs' leadership. The permanent executive board, formally elected on April 2, consisted of Aloysius Huber, president; Louis Deplanque, vice-president; Laugier, treasurer; Amable Longepied, chairman of the commission; with Adrien Delaire, Napoléon Lebon, Joseph Sobrier, Louis Cahaigne, and Hippolyte Gadon[37] members of the board, some of whom

[36] Testimony Delaire, *Enquête*, i, 210.

[37] For an evaluation of Huber's background and career, see P. Amann, "The Huber Enigma—Revolutionary or Police Spy?" *Int. Rev. of Social History*, xii (1967), part 2, 190-203. The *notice* in DBMOF, ii, 354, is poorly informed. For Deplanque, see autobiographical letter, unaddressed, March 7, 1848, B.H.V.P., Liesville Collection, complemented by my own club files. For his skulduggery, see *Le Populaire*, April 22, 1848. Laugier, a lawyer and writer, commanded a battalion of the Twelfth Legion under Barbès and also sat on the Commission des récompenses nationales, which itself indicates that he had been active in the illegal republican movement of the monarchy. Laugier also coauthored the only history of the Club des clubs. Police prefect Caussidière, rightly or wrongly, considered him financially unscrupulous. (Wassermann, *Les clubs*

also staffed the commission. Huber, Lebon, and perhaps Sobrier, though not names to conjure with, were revolutionary leaders familiar to any old-line Parisian republican. Longepied and Delaire, and possibly Cahaigne, Gadon, and Laugier, were men at least widely acquainted in revolutionary circles. Deplanque was breaking the political surface for the first and last time.

The antecedents of these men confirm the ascendancy which the Club of the Revolution, headed by Barbès, exercised on the Club of Clubs. Of the nine-man board, four members—Longepied, Laugier, Sobrier, and Cahaigne—were also active in the Club of the Revolution. Laugier, moreover, was a National Guard battalion commander in the Twelfth Legion of which Barbès was colonel. Two other members, Huber and Lebon, sat with Barbès on the executive committee of the reactivated

---

de Barbès et de Blanqui, p. 21.) For Longepied, his "profession de foi," see April 6, 1848, C. 942, CdE 9070. His family and financial troubles can be traced in C. 942, dossier 11. For Delaire, DBMOF, II, 41-42 and 44 (there are two *notices* about him), his interrogation in *Enquête*, I, 170-171, and his "A tous mes frères de l'industrie," in *La Commune de Paris*, April 3, 1848. Lebon has an autobiographical "profession de foi," Société des Droits de l'Homme, April 3, ibid., April 6, 1848. For his early career, see the index of G. Perreux, *Aux temps des sociétés secrètes, 1830-1834* (Paris, 1931) and of G. Weill, *Histoire du parti républicain, 1814-1870* (Paris, 1928). DBMOF, II, 456, is inadequate for Lebon, but excellent for Sobrier (III, 410-412). See also the autobiographical introduction for both Sobrier and his coeditor, Cahaigne, in their *La Commune de Paris*, March 20, 1848. Cahaigne's police dossier is in A.N., C. 934, CdE 2774. Gadon, a former secret society activist associated with the Commission des récompenses nationales in 1848, can be traced throughout the spring of 1848 in CR, as well as in his earlier connection with the Club des hommes libres whence he was ousted as president for striking a fellow member. (Wassermann, *Les clubs de Barbès et de Blanqui*, p. 23.)

Society of the Rights of Man. As the Club of the Revolution was strongly socialist in word but very cautious in deed, the Club of Clubs may have absorbed much of its mother society's political orientation.

Yet paradoxically the majority of the Club of Clubs' leaders had been genuine revolutionaries, men of action. Huber, having joined the Society of the Rights of Man in his teens, had been involved in two successive plots to kill the king. Until the February Revolution freed him, he spent ten years behind bars, wracked by chronic tuberculosis. Lebon claimed to have been active as a militant republican for twenty-three years, his record dating back to the Carbonari of the Restoration. Longepied had been involved in the bloody republican uprising of 1832 and claimed to have been among the handful of Guard officers to defect to the revolutionaries at the onset of the February Revolution. Sobrier and Cahaigne had been republican conspirators under the July Monarchy. Sobrier had made his mark in the bitter fighting around the Château d'Eau on February 24, before seizing the police prefecture with his friend Caussidière. Gadon, a vetteran of the secret societies, proudly wore the medal of a July combatant, while Deplanque claimed to have suffered for his political writings under the July Monarchy. In short, of the nine-man executive board of the Club of Clubs, all but two claimed some sort of "resistance" record.

Equally striking is the predominance of men of modest middle-class standing among these leaders. Take Lebon, who had dropped out of medical school in the early years of the July Monarchy, or Deplanque, a professor of accounting at the Arts-et-Métiers. Longepied, a science teacher by training, had gone bankrupt running a boarding school. Sobrier was a provincial drawn by the University of Paris. A former law student enjoying a family inheritance, he had led the life of a republican man-about-town. Cahaigne could look back on a varied career as noncommissioned officer, traveling salesman, occasional republican journalist, and manufacturer of chemicals in 1848. Nothing is known of Laugier's law practice. Gadon is a cipher, though almost certainly a middle-class cipher. Huber can only be classified as a professional revolutionary despite his early years as an apprentice currier. Delaire stood alone as the token proletarian, having come to the attention of republicans as what was patronizingly called "an intelligent worker."

Aside from Delaire, enough Club of Clubs officers clung to the fringe of middle-class society to evoke the cliché of the *déclassé* as revolutionary. Probably this is a misleading impression. In their own eyes, Huber—republican martyr and popular orator—and Cahaigne—manufacturer and republican editor—must have seemed successful self-made men. Sobrier may strike us as a law school dropout, but contemporaries saw nothing shameful in a man living on his patrimony. Lebon and Longepied had gone down in the world: Longepied was a recent bankrupt at his wits' end; Lebon must have been unable to come to terms with a career, for in 1848 at the age of forty he still styled himself "medical student." But even in these two cases the label of *déclassé* is misleading. Lebon had abandoned his medical studies to immerse himself in the Society of the Rights of Man in the early 1830's; Longepied had probably been blacklisted by the state-sponsored secondary schools, where men of his training found their best opportunities. In short, they lost status by being revolutionaries; they did not become revolutionaries because they were *déclassés* in the first place.

Discussions of club affiliation, of revolutionary and social background, unfortunately skirt the central problem, that of the Club of Clubs' political failure, which had to do with the way its authority was husbanded. It could rely only on moral authority. In a politically semiliterate society gripped by revolution, moral authority needed to be personified. Yet no charismatic leader emerged in the Club of Clubs, whose collective leadership evinced a blend of insouciance, mediocrity, and self-seeking that ignored the dynamics of 1848. One might start with Huber, presiding at the Club of Clubs' sessions, who announced one April day that he was off to Indre-et-Loire to run for a parliamentary seat.[38] Another board member, Cahaigne, departed for Poitiers to do likewise. Delaire juggled his time between the Club of Clubs, the rival Central Committee for General Elections, and the promotion of his candidacy to the National Assembly from Paris. When the Club of Clubs failed to endorse him, Delaire left. Sobrier, who excused his own absence from the club federation's meetings on the grounds of ill health, nonetheless managed to keep his newspaper afloat and to announce *his* candidacy. Lebon divided his time between the Club of Clubs, the Society of the Rights of Man, and his personal campaign for parliament. Deplanque seems to have used his post to blackmail other club leaders into supporting his bid for the Assembly. By mid-April seven of the nine board members were on the campaign trail. Who could say where republican fervor left off and irresponsibility began?

This is not to imply that the executives of the club federation were dishonest by their own lights. On the contrary, they took justifiable pride in having well over a hundred thousand francs pass through their hands without any of its sticking to their fingers.[39] As deserving re-

---

[38] Huber to CR, April 7, 1848, A.N., C. 940, CdE 8388; minutes of CR, April 7, 1848, *La Commune de Paris*, April 9, 1848.

[39] Longepied and Laugier, *Comité révolutionnaire*, pp. 48ff.

publicans, they no doubt felt that they were finally modestly rewarded. Slightly intoxicated by their sudden access to the antechambers of power, they remained small men, industriously organizing the departure of the provincial missionaries and taking care of the paper work. But this was office management, not leadership. To prepare the Club of Clubs to meet its multiple responsibilities in Paris was beyond them.

viii

Above all, what the club federation had to offer was practical guidance in the elections to the Constituent Assembly scheduled for April 23 and 24. As the president of the Club of Reform explained to his members, "this committee [the Revolutionary Committee, Club of Clubs] has been created to eliminate all candidates from the election who do not sincerely embrace the democratic Republic with all its consequences."[40] For this effort to have any chance of success, the Club of Clubs would have had to do three things: nominate promptly a plausible slate of candidates for the Seine department; coordinate the political education of the club rank and file; see to the organization of the working-class electorate to be sure that sympathizers were registered and that they really voted. These facets of political campaigning were linked. Unless the Club of Clubs could nominate candidates without delay, there would not be enough time to make them known. Unless the club federation kept its adherents in line, their votes might be scattered among hundreds of candidates (an estimated two thousand were actively running in Paris!) or else converge on the handful of familiar names. Even if candidates were endorsed in time and adequately publicized, unregistered or apa-

[40] Minutes, Club de la réforme, March 29, 1848, A.N., C. 941, CdE 8651.

thetic voters could still mean defeat. The record of the Club of Clubs turned out to be abysmal on all counts.[41]

When it came to organizing the voters, the Club of Clubs' practical accomplishments were nil. During one of the early sessions, the delegates turned down a suggestion to set up district election committees in Paris on the curious grounds that such "regimentation" infringed on the voters' freedom. Later they did enter into correspondence with the Provisional Government to propose that the general elections in the capital be held in one place, the parade ground of the Champ-de-Mars (where the Eiffel Tower now stands). The Club of Clubs may have hoped to shame the workers into participating by making the national elections into a monster patriotic demonstration. Countering official objections, the club federation's officers drew up an elaborate scheme by which voters, divided into units of ten thousand, would assemble at the Champs-Elysées and parade past the ballot boxes on the Champ-de-Mars before dispersing along the *quais* of the Left Bank. In spite of official objections, the club federation continued to play with the idea. On the eve of the

[41] The account that follows is circumscribed but I hope not distorted by the available documentation. MS "raw" minutes, some close to verbatim and a few in more than one variant, have survived for all or most of the Club of Clubs' sessions through April 3. The problem for this first period is that the minutes are not dated. Through April 7, the official published minutes are available, though one or two sessions may be missing. From April 8 through election day there are no minutes of either description, only announcements, proclamations, and tantalizing hints by a couple of participants, scattered correspondence, most of it incoming. There is a ledger listing member clubs and their date of membership; there is also a tally sheet for the deliberations on the candidates to endorse, but no record of the later negotiations with the Luxembourg workers. The gaps in the record are less serious for reconstructing what happened than in gauging why it happened.

elections, the Club of Clubs invited Parisian workers to gather at the Champ-de-Mars prior to voting. Apparently only a few hundred showed up.[42]

A second aspect of the campaign, the political indoctrination of the electorate, was contingent on the third, the early announcement of the Club of Clubs' official slate of candidates for the Seine department. This search for authorized candidates makes a depressing story of procrastination and incompetence. At its very first full-fledged meeting on March 26, the Club of Clubs had resolved that delegates were to bring to the next session "a preparatory but not a final list of their [club's] candidates." Yet for the next five days the question of general qualifications of candidates preempted the discussion until several speakers proposed moving on to specific nominees. By this time, the president of the member Republican Society of the Faubourg Saint-Denis expected "our central committee" to submit its list of recommended candidates to the early ratification of participating clubs. Indeed, by April 1 "the nomination and establishment of the list of candidates for the National Assembly" was the only item of business on the Club of Clubs' agenda, prompting another club president to predict successful completion by the end of that week. But the end of the week passed. April 10 became a new target date, a deadline for accepting provisional lists handed in by member clubs. On April 13 the Club of Clubs solemnly announced that its final list of candidates would be drawn up during the next three days. This proved optimistic. After further delays, the Club of Clubs' official list of

[42] Minutes, CR (March 31, 1848), A.N., C. 941, CdE 9025. Boulard, secretary to Flocon (Minister of Commerce) to Sobrier and/or Longepied, April 16, 1848, A.N., C. 940, CdE 8359. Also undated draft letter, CR to Provisional Government, B.H.V.P., Liesville Collection.

candidates was finally completed and released on April 22—only twenty-four hours before the polls opened.[43]

The way the Club of Clubs was organized and managed goes far to explain why it had so much trouble getting things done. The organization had an indeterminate membership of up to several hundred, with no permanent committees and no effective officers except a chairman. Delegates' terms of office were revocable from one day to the next, and the turnover correspondingly rapid. The presiding officer had no notion of parliamentary procedure but did have an emotional commitment to the right of unlimited debate. Under such circumstances, it was an uphill task to nominate within two weeks a slate of thirty-four candidates for a crucial election in which hundreds were running. The problems faced by the Club of Clubs also included fluctuating attendance, meetings that rarely started on time, agendas that were often disregarded. When one outspoken delegate dared to complain about the absence of rules, "the anarchy in our deliberations," he was shouted down as a troublemaker. Chairman Huber might claim to do his best to keep everybody happy, but his best did not prevent what vice-president Deplanque admitted were "endless and often

[43] Garnier-Pagès, *Histoire de la révolution*, VIII, 272-273, 279; minutes, CR, March 26 and 31, 1848, A.N., C. 941, CdE 9021, 9025-9027; minutes, Société républicaine du Faubourg Saint-Denis, undated, *La Sentinelle des clubs*, April 2, 1848; minutes, CR, April 1, 1848, A.N., C. 941, CdE 9031; minutes, Société des Droits de l'Homme, session of April 2, *La Commune de Paris*, April 7, 1848; minutes, CR, April 7, ibid., April 9, 1848; announcement, CR, no date, ibid., April 13, 1848, listing April 13-15 as the days devoted to drawing up the final list of candidates. A printed circular, dated April 13, gives April 14-16, A.N., C. 941, CdE 8963; for the list, see *La Commune de Paris*, April 22, 1848, and *Le Populaire*, April 23, 1848.

aimless speeches."[44] An unstable mass meeting made up of people unaccustomed to working together, lacking committees assigned specific responsibilities, and without officers able to impose discipline, was an unlikely body to reach decisions.

An unwieldy structure and a loose leadership also helps account for the numerous distractions that diverted the Club of Clubs from its primary objectives. The daily formality of ratifying the commission's choice of departmental missionaries could degenerate into acrimonious exchanges between the commissioners and the club delegates whose offer to serve had been refused. Minor chores such as verifying a delegate's accreditation could become the subject of passionate and fruitless debate. Was Citizen Grégoire entitled to represent the Club of the Foresighted after being ousted from its presidency? Was he simply removed from office or had he and his adherents been actually booted out—or was it his opponents who had been expelled? Or were there really two clubs now where one had existed before: the original Club of the Foresighted competing with a Club of the Tenacious Foresighted?[45] The discussion may have been absurd, but it was time-consuming.

What about the Club of Clubs' duty to respond to emergencies and assume moral leadership? What was the proper role of the organization, for example, in the face of the wave of xenophobia that swept Paris, directed against the competition of foreign workers? Under pres-

[44] Minutes, CR, April 6, *La Commune de Paris*, April 9, 1848.

[45] Minutes, CR, April 6, ibid., and March 31, A.N., C. 941, CdE 9025-9027; Delbrueck and Danse de Boullonges to CR, April 2, 1848, A.N., C. 940, CdE 8370. For the resolution, see open letter by Ernest Grégoire "Aux membres du Club des prévoyants qui se sont séparés du fondateur," *La Commune de Paris*, April 16, 1848, and the new president Treulé's answer, ibid., April 17, 1848.

sure from member clubs, the Club of Clubs debated its
stand, resolving that "the people of Paris . . . remain true
to its principles by allowing our brothers from other na-
tions to enjoy the benefits of our civilization rather than
to drive them out of our workshops by violence and intimidation."[46] Nor could one simply ignore the pleading
of republican delegates from some provincial town, who
had traveled all the way to Paris to lay their case against
their antirepublican municipality before the Club of
Clubs. They had to be heard, questioned, and given public support.[47] Even closer to home, the Paris National
Guard elections rescheduled for April 5 and 6 were a
kind of emergency. Could the Club of Clubs afford to ignore the qualifications of the officers entrusted with the
future of the Republic? The board of the Club of Clubs
was ordered into executive session to recommend candidates for all ranks above that of lieutenant; the general
assembly of delegates devoted precious hours to reporting election-day abuses.[48] It is hard to see how such last-
moment intervention could be effective; but, justifiable
or not, these side excursions prevented consideration of
the Parisian candidates to the national elections.

The steps by which the Club of Clubs proceeded to
choose candidates to the National Assembly were themselves invitations to delay. It was logical but not very
sensible that the delegates began by discussing funda-
mentals. Should the people's representatives sit in a constituent assembly as free agents or as spokesmen bound

[46] Resolution, CR, April 4, 1848, A.N., C. 841, CdE 9032;
Club de l'unité républicaine du VIᵉ arrondissement and the
Club de la Butte des Moulins raised the issue in the CR, A.N.,
C. 941, CdE 8454, 8667.

[47] Minutes, CR, April 7, *La Commune de Paris*, April 9,
1848; resolution, CR, A.N., C. 941, CdE 9039. The plaintiffs
were from Vendôme.

[48] Minutes, CR, April 1, 1848, A.N., C. 941, CdE 9031;
April 6, *La Commune de Paris*, April 9, 1848.

by the voters' stated preferences? The consensus that "any citizen who is granted power must by that very fact be held in legitimate suspicion" implied a binding mandate; but should this consist of a detailed set of policies or merely basic principles? In opting for the latter, how could the majority decide what principles were fundamental and what were derivative? Was the "recall of unworthy officials" on a par with "the right and duty of revolution" or "support for the organization of labor"?[49] When the club delegates bypassed these questions by accepting Robespierre's Declaration of the Rights of Man as the basis for the binding mandate to be imposed on the nation's representatives, they embroiled themselves in an article-by-article analysis of that historic document which dragged on until April 6. Ironically, the final version of the proposed mandate—"to support, apply and develop the Declaration of the Rights of Man in all its democratic consequences"—was so jejune that it could have been reached without discussion.[50]

This drawn-out debate on basic principles may have been a way of killing time, for the Club of Clubs was forced to wait for its member clubs to furnish provisional lists of candidates from which the final selections might be made. Unfortunately, most neighborhood clubs were preoccupied with the pending National Guard elections. Busy interrogating prospective captains and majors, they did not turn their attention to the general elections until the officers of the civic militia had been elected on April 6. In desperation, the Club of Clubs announced April 10

[49] The phrase is that of delegate Lefèvre of the Club des hommes libres. Minutes, CR, March 28, 1848, A.N., C. 941, CdE 9022; for the text of the binding mandate proposed by the delegate of the Société républicaine du Panthéon, no date, A.N., C. 941, CdE 9017.

[50] Minutes, CR, April 3, 1848, A.N., C. 941, CdE 8498; April 6, *La Commune de Paris*, April 7, 1848.

as the last date for accepting nominations of candidates to the Assembly from member clubs. By that time two weeks had been wasted.

By catering to its member clubs, the Club of Clubs may have compromised its initiative; by deferring unconditionally to organized labor, it surrendered its independence. Details of this obscure story are hard to untangle. As early as March 31, the debate over general qualifications for candidates to the National Assembly narrowed down to the question of worker candidates. For two days delegates who maintained that social origin was irrelevant in the new society argued against those who wanted Paris represented by genuine manual workers. When the latter won on April 1, Adrien Delaire, the only worker on the Club of Clubs' executive committee, was ordered to get in touch with the trade unions, whose worker candidates the club federation promised in advance to endorse by acclamation. Just as earlier the Club of Clubs had had to await the decisions of its member clubs, now it had to await the action of the Central Committee of the Workers of the Seine, which did not complete its nominations until April 17. Originally the Club of Clubs expected to prevail in choosing the fourteen nonworker candidates by agreeing to the Central Committee's twenty workers, but the labor action committee had become conscious of its bargaining power: it insisted that only six names were subject to negotiation with the club federation.[51]

This tangle accounts for the final travesty of political management in which the Club of Clubs became involved. Having begun its career by erring on the side of democracy, the Club of Clubs ended by imposing rigid control over its members—a pledge to support the official slate before it was actually drawn up—in order to satisfy the demands of its labor allies. In the final haggling, the

[51] Minutes, CR, March 31, 1848, and April 1, 1848, A.N., C. 941, CdE 9025, 9027, 9031. *Le Populaire*, April 23, 1848.

preferences of member clubs meant nothing. In any case, their preliminary lists had been drawn up before the twenty—later changed to twenty-eight—nominees had been selected by labor. A single example suffices: though thirteen clubs had chosen Lamennais and Kersausie had received only one vote, the Club of Clubs threw out Lamennais (an outspoken critic of Louis Blanc and the Luxembourg Commission) and endorsed Kersausie (a socialist and a friend of Barbès). Then, in the final negotiations with the Central Committee of the Workers, Kersausie was evidently also eliminated. The newspaper releases and the hundreds of thousands of printed handbills betrayed the haste and confusion of the final decisions: many of the names were mangled beyond recognition.[52]

To popularize the slate of candidates finally adopted would have taken considerable time and energy. The twenty workers sponsored by organized labor were mostly obscure men, though they did include revolutionary veterans like Huber and Martin-Bernard and Babouvist ideologues like Adam and Malarmé. Only the four left-leaning members of the Provisional Government were endorsed, including Ledru-Rollin, who was no socialist and seemed likely to win in the provinces anyway. The remainder of the list was a grab bag—a couple of radical officials like Caussidière and Etienne Arago, a handful of club leaders, most of them from the Club of Clubs or the "mother" Club of the Revolution. To spring such a list on the electorate on the eve of the vote was extraordinarily naïve.

[52] Register of the CR indicating what clubs endorsed what candidates, no date, no CdE number, but filed following A.N., C. 941, CdE 9560. Since the distorted spellings of candidates appeared in the sympathetic *La Commune de Paris*, this was carelessness, not sabotage. According to printers' bills in the CR archives, the CR ordered at least 230,000 ballot lists printed on April 21 and 22, 1848. A.N., C. 942, CdE 9167, 9171.

Yet in the week before the elections true believers were becoming scarce. Fewer delegates attended the Club of Clubs' daily meetings: no more than a quarter of a paper membership of over four hundred took part in the last, supposedly crucial, deliberations.[53] The Club of Clubs' ineffectuality left a vacuum that lesser clubs vainly tried to fill. Half a dozen of them, led by the Free Men and the Salvation of the People, sponsored a meeting of delegates to get on with the nomination of the Assembly candidates. A Club of Fraternal Union took a similar step, expressing the rising panic in club circles. "Election day approaches," it announced, "and we anxiously await the few remaining hours."[54] The phrase might serve as epitaph for the Club of Clubs, which had been founded to allay just such anxieties.

[53] *Le Populaire*, April 23, 1848. By election time, the CR had acquired 149 member clubs, each entitled to 3 candidates, plus 50 from organized labor and additional ones for the army and Garde mobile.

[54] Lithographed circular addressed to Club de Bercy, signed by Gen. Griardon, by President Colfavru of the Club des hommes libres, and by the Abbé Raymond for the Club du salut du peuple, plus a fourth illegible signer, April 18, 1848, B.H.V.P., Liesville Collection. This initiative seems to have been an electoral trick by candidate Raymond. *Le Père Duchêne*, April 23, 1848. Resolution, Club de l'union fraternelle to Société des Droits de l'Homme du IIIe arrondissement, April 18, 1848. A.N., C. 941, CdE 8619.

5 | The Popular Societies at Work

The people have reconquered all their rights. Called but yesterday to the public life of the citizen, their political education
is yet to be undertaken. . . . This is the mission of the popular
societies. Their goal and their purpose are to elaborate and to
illuminate questions of progress and of social organization;
to propagate generous ideas of emancipation and order among
workshops and cottages, even to the darkest, most isolated
hovels where the proletarian suffers.

> *President Fontaine,*
> *Club of Democratic Progress*

i

Neither the massive demonstration of March 17 nor the
organization of a Parisian club federation in the days
following changed the direction of the club movement.
The demonstration of March 17 had raised three major
issues: opposition to the return of an army garrison, postponement of the National Guard elections, and a three
months' delay in holding national elections. Only one of
these demands was fully met by the government: the National Guard officer elections were postponed by two
weeks, though the political effect of the delay may have
been imperceptible. As to the regular troops' return to
Paris, the petitioners of March 17 had received reassuring phrases, leaving the Provisional Government free to
pursue its own course. The controversy over the date of

the national elections was ended when the government decreed a two weeks' postponement to April 23.

This retreat from militancy appears most clearly in the changing attitudes toward the return of an army garrison to Paris, bitterly opposed by the popular societies before the March demonstration. The issue at stake remained unaltered: as long as the Provisional Government lacked armed force, it had to bend to popular pressures. The return of an army garrison, a goal that François Arago, the Minister of War, pursued with purposeful duplicity, would insulate the government from such pressures.[1] In retrospect, the clubs' misgivings appear well grounded: army regiments reintroduced into the capital in March and April crushed the revolutionary insurgents in June.

Nonetheless, after March 17 club resistance melted rapidly. Initially, most clubs had been strongly suspicious of the army, and particularly of its commanders, those "favorites of despotism and corruption."[2] Therefore, the first reports that regulars had filtered back into the suburbs to man the capital's tollgates were greeted with indignation.[3] Opposition to such a move could always evoke the precedent of the Great Revolution, which had deliberately barred regular troops from Paris to insure the Republic's freedom.[4] But indignation was not the end of it. Was it really fair, the National Republican Club countered, to discriminate against the very army which,

[1] Testimony François Arago, *Enquête*, I, 225. Commanding general of Vincennes to commander of first military region, March 2, 1848, A.M.G., F¹, carton 2.

[2] Société des Droits de l'Homme, session of March 20, *La Commune de Paris*, March 21, 1848.

[3] Club républicain des travailleurs, session of March 22, *La Voix des clubs*, March 24, 1848.

[4] For example, E. Chevalier (a member of the Club de la révolution) to *Le Populaire*, April 22, 1848, Cabet Papers, B.H.V.P., Liesville Collection.

by capitulating to the revolutionary people in February, had insured the revolution's success?[5] Was it politically expedient to isolate the troops from those who would instill in them the proper republican sentiments?[6] The moderate Circle of Liberty, making a virtue of necessity, petitioned the government to bring back a few regiments with the specific aim of having them fraternize with the people and the National Guard of Paris.[7]

Republican equity and political expediency were buttressed by fatigue and fear. The capital's army garrison had not only served the monarchy but had helped keep law and order in an underpoliced metropolis haunted by crime and violence.[8] The troops' retreat had shifted the burden of routine policing from the regulars to the militiamen of the National Guard. As most of the nighttime patrols relied on bourgeois veterans rather than on the working-class newcomers, the former objected strenuously to what they considered overwork. Their objections were echoed in petitions sent to the government by several clubs with middle-class membership.[9] Yet these

[5] Club républicain national, petition to Provisional Government, March 30, 1848, *Le Moniteur universel*, March 31, 1848.

[6] Session of Club Saint-Maur, n.d., *Le Monde républicain*, April 5, 1848.

[7] Cercle de la liberté, petition to Provisional Government, March 26, 1848, A.N., BB[30], 306, No. 6356.

[8] Chevalier, *Classes laborieuses*, passim.

[9] Club des Halles, petition to Provisional Government, March 24, *Le Moniteur universel*, March 25, 1848; Club de l'union fraternelle, petition to Provisional Government, April 18, 1848, A.N., BB[30], 310, No. 8774; Club républicain national, petition to Provisional Government, March 30, *Le Moniteur universel*, March 31, 1848; Cercle de la liberté, petition to Provisional Government, March 26, 1848, A.N., BB[30], 306, No. 6356; Société démocratique de La Villette, petition to Provisional Government, March 31, 1848, A.N., BB[30], 303, No. 4464.

"overworked" veterans avoided the obvious solution of tapping larger numbers of newly enrolled militiamen for service. Evidently the return of an army garrison had other implications than relief from unwanted duties. The return of the regular troops may well have symbolized a return to the "normal" prerevolutionary social equilibrium by stressing once again the protection of property from the "dangerous classes."

Within a surprisingly short time, these converging pressures changed the clubs' response to the return of a garrison. By the end of March, *La Commune de Paris*, the semiofficial organ of the club movement, took for granted that the Provisional Government would recall some regulars, expressing concern only that these returning soldiers be exposed to the healthy republicanism of the Parisian people.[10] The Provisional Government was able to go ahead with its plans without interference, as the inability of the Society of the Rights of Man to arouse club opinion indicated.[11] A military festival on April 20, officially billed as the great fraternization of the regular army with the democratized Paris National Guard, was made the occasion for bringing back permanently five army regiments, the nucleus of a garrison.[12] There was no outcry from the clubs.

ii

The National Guard elections of April 5-7 proved a serious setback to club hopes, though the full extent of the revolutionary defeat cannot be documented. At the level of legion commanders, where the contest had been be-

[10] *La Commune de Paris*, March 31, 1848.

[11] Club du IIIe arrondissement, Société des Droits de l'Homme, April 14, 1848, A.N., C. 941, CdE 8579.

[12] For two of many detailed accounts of these celebrations, see *Le Représentant du peuple*, April 21, 1848, and *Le Monde républicain*, April 22, 1848.

tween old-line republicans and converts of convenience,
republicans had prevailed; but where the chief contenders
were moderate republicans opposing revolutionaries the
moderates came out ahead. Barbès was the only victor
with whom club activists wholly identified, though a number of quasi-official candidates who won—Colonel Yautier in the Ninth, Colonel Forestier in the Sixth, Lieutenant-Colonel Schoelcher in the Second, D'Alton-Shée
in the Second suburban Legion—were much more sympathetic to the revolutionary position than was realized
in club circles. On the battalion and company levels, the
election of incumbent prerevolutionary officers over-
shadowed the success of some working-class candidates
in the eastern districts of Paris and in proletarian suburbs
like Belleville and Montmartre. The victory of middle-
class candidates was sufficiently one-sided to embarrass
the Provisional Government, which would have been far
more upset by a sweep of revolutionary proletarians. As
a token gesture, the government decreed the election of
fourteen National Guard staff officers to be chosen from
among themselves by the capital's organized trades on
April 16. This supplementary balloting, transparently a
consolation prize, advertised the workers' incapacity to
win a free election.

Why did the revolutionaries, led by the clubs and pa-
tronized by the labor movement, fail in electing their
own? In the vote for colonel and lieutenant-colonel of the
various legions, revolutionaries were at a severe disad-
vantage in what usually amounted to a triangular contest.
On the right was a barely disguised monarchist candidate, usually the officer who had held command under
the monarchy; in the center was the moderate republican,
often leaning toward Ledru-Rollin rather than toward
Marrast and company, who, having been appointed by
the Provisional Government, enjoyed the advantages of
incumbency; on the left, the revolutionary republican,

though in some districts no revolutionary candidate was in the running. Typically, the decisive second ballot was between conservative and moderate, in the public mind between monarchy and republic. Where, as in the sixth district, the run-off was between the "official" republican and the revolutionary candidate, the clubs proved unable to dramatize barely detectable ideological differences.[13]

Elections of battalion and company officers raised the problem of the scarcity of revolutionary working-class candidates rather than their defeat at the polls. The reluctance of newly enrolled workers to try for officer, despite club encouragement, is no mystery. Though in contrast to bourgeois officer candidates many Parisian workers had extensive military experience, they lacked familiarity both with the militia unit to which they had been assigned and with the service routine of the Paris National Guard in general. In addition, they faced the prospect of the expense of officer uniforms, not to speak of the old guard's systematic hostility.[14]

During the elections themselves and the nominating meetings that preceded them, the abstention of a large percentage of newly registered guards was noted. In one company of the First Legion, for instance, only 200 of 660 enrolled militiamen were present to vote for non-

[13] Lagrange, the perennial insurgent par excellence, was no more socialist than Ledru-Rollin. He is ideologically indistinguishable from his successful competitor, Colonel Forestier. For Lagrange, see *DBMOF*, ii, 415-416; for Henri-Joseph Forestier, see E. Vapereau, ed., *Dictionnaire universel des contemporains*, 1st ed. (Paris, 1858), p. 679.

[14] An editor of *Le Courrier français* (March 21, 1848), who claimed to have attended several preparatory meetings for the elections of the National Guard, accused the veteran guards of deliberately monopolizing the proceedings. For evidence of the cost of officer's insignia as deterrent, see General Guinard to unnamed district mayor, March 31, 1848, B.H.V.P., Liesville Collection; *La Réforme*, April 1, 1848.

commissioned officers.[15] In the words of Léopold Villain, president of the Society of the Rights of Man, a counterrevolutionary minority had taken advantage of proletarian abstention.[16] As an explanation, this is not very helpful. First of all, there were abuses in the election process: polling places, closed during the morning hours when workers wanted to vote on their way to their jobs, were closed again by the time they came home; delays were caused by inadequate preparation, as when electoral assemblies ran out of ballots.[17] Second, and more significant, was the incredible cumbersomeness of the entire selection process, which was likely to discourage all but the most zealous. A truly conscientious National Guardsman might have to attend at least four preliminary meetings (at which nominations would be made and nominees introduced) followed by as many as eight voting sessions, for at each stage a candidate's failure to win an absolute

[15] *La Commune de Paris*, April 11, 1848. For comments on working-class abstention, see *La Réforme*, April 3 and 6, 1848; the circular letter from the mayor of Paris to district mayors, April 6, 1848, A.S., V[bis], 429, dossier 2, No. 394; *La Commune de Paris*, April 8, 1848; Société des Droits de l'Homme, session of April 8, *La Commune de Paris*, April 8, 1848; *Le Représentant du peuple*, April 10, 1848. For similar reports for the suburbs, see report of Club des clubs' delegates, April 7, 1848, A.N., C. 939, CdE 6956.

[16] Société des Droits de l'Homme, session of April 8, *La Commune de Paris*, April 11, 1848.

[17] For these and other reports of abuses, see Société des Droits de l'Homme, session of April 8, *La Commune de Paris*, April 11, 1848, and editorial comments of the same issue. Circular letter, mayor of Paris to district mayors, April 6, 1848, A.S., V[bis], 429, dossier 2; Mornet, member of Comité démocratique du Xe arrondissement, to mayor of X[e], April 8, 1848, A.S., V[bis], 429, dossier 2. On the other hand, the tobacco workers of the Gros-Caillou *quartier* left work en masse when antirepublican candidates were on the point of winning and tilted the balance. See *La Réforme*, April 9, 1848.

majority made a run-off vote mandatory.[18] Furthermore, the elections took at least four days and in some cases even longer. The invidious distinction between middle-class guards, whose businesses could spare them for a few days, and working-class guards, privately employed or on work-relief, who needed every day's wages, was obvious. Even the workers in the National Workshops, though compensated for the final two days of the militia elections, could attend nominating meetings only at their own expense.[19]

The impact of the National Guard elections on the clubs may have been more perceptible than all that the popular societies had done to dominate the militia elections. As a practical matter, these elections preempted many of the club meeting places: no less than four hundred polling places were temporarily requisitioned throughout Paris, forcing many clubs to suspend their sessions for as long as a week.[20] Even where clubs managed to carry on, their members must have been preoccu-

[18] For some sense of the complexities, see, e.g., the instructions issued by the *mairie* of the first district, n.d., B.H.V.P., Liesville Collection.

[19] For a report from April 4 that the National Workshop members were afraid to leave work to participate, see *La Réforme*, April 5, 1848. For the proclamation granting time off with pay to April 10, see *La Réforme*, April 6, 1848. For a report of the tactlessness with which this was announced by those in charge, see police report by Carlier, April 5, 1848, *Enquête*, II, 175. For the fact that few National Workshop members voted, see *La Commune de Paris*, April 7, 1848.

[20] *La vraie République*, April 6, 1848; *La Commune de Paris*, April 7, 1848. For a typical announcement of a temporary club closing, see Club patriotique des Blancs-Manteaux, B.N., Lb⁵³, 745; the Club des hommes libres was unable to resume its sessions until April 13; see *La Commune de Paris*, April 15, 1848; for a club that vigorously fought eviction, Société des Droits de l'Homme, see *La Commune de Paris*, April 7, 1848.

pied with National Guard business. Where, as in some
of the suburbs, clubs had flourished by appealing to bewildered new militiamen, the officer elections had a devastating effect. Club attendance was down by as much as
80 percent.[21] In any case, the voting served to slow the
momentum of the revolutionary club movement.

iii

Some clubs had needed no prompting to begin screening candidates for the National Assembly. For many
others, the Club of Clubs' instructions to submit a slate
of candidates served as a catalyst. Because most clubs
were deeply involved in the choice of militia officers, the
deadline for submitting parliamentary candidates had to
be extended several times, with April 10 as the final date.
The quickest way to respond to this pressure was to arrange for nominations from the floor, with the membership voting for or against each proposed name. The
thirty-four candidates having the highest number of affirmative votes would make up the club's approved list.
In this way, for example, the Club of Universal Fraternity considered sixty-one candidates, the Republican
Society of the Faubourg Saint-Denis one hundred twenty-
six.[22] But there were drawbacks. Was democracy simply
a matter of counting hands, of recording decibels of approval and opposition? Or did a genuine democracy also
imply rational and time-consuming discussion?[23] To rely

[21] Nogué to Comité révolutionnaire, April 12, 1848, A.N.,
C. 939, CdE 6962. For example, the Club des Amandiers
dwindled in attendance from 300 before the elections to 40 on
April 11.

[22] Club de la fraternité universelle, session of March 19, *La
Commune de Paris*, March 22, 1848; Société républicaine du
Faubourg Saint-Denis, n.d., *La Sentinelle des clubs*, April 2,
1848.

[23] A compromise proposed (but apparently not acted upon)
at the Club de la fraternité universelle was to vote on well-

8.–National elections, April 1848

Left: A cynical view of the national elections of April 1848: "Many are called, but few are chosen."
The little money-bags labeled "25" refer to the amount of the daily allowance to be granted the newly elected representatives.

Below: Armand Marrast, mayor of Paris, announcing the names of the representatives elected in the Seine department (evening of April 28, 1848).

on such crude popularity contests was tantamount to naming only candidates who were already widely known: members of the Provisional Government, municipal officials, revolutionary heroes, Parisian notables. What did this do to the hope that universal suffrage would uncover new political talents?

This issue was faced by indirection in the debates on worker representation in the National Assembly. The Club of Workers' proposal to the Luxembourg Labor Commission put forth in mid-March that at least twenty of the thirty-four Parisian representatives be working class, and its subsequent adoption by the Central Committee of the Workers of the Seine, has been noted earlier. Similar sentiments could be encountered in club circles. Adrien Delaire, cabinetmaker and poet, delegated by the Republican Club of Passy, echoed the same proletarian consciousness before the Society of the Rights of Man: "To represent the people, to understand them, one must belong to the people; one must have undergone hunger and cold; one must have suffered."[24] The statement triggered a debate as to whether French society remained bourgeois-dominated despite formal equality, a debate so acrimonious that the club president called a halt. Understandably, proletarian candidates were likely to emphasize the need to redress the neglect of the past. Charles Guillemette, a twenty-six-year-old machinist, defended his candidacy in incendiary images: "Fear no longer to seek out the humble and modest genius in his narrow garret, making him the arbiter of your destinies. Bother no longer with those . . . who, while seeming to plead the people's cause, have used it as a steppingstone

known candidates without discussion but to invite lesser-known candidates to appear before the club. *La Commune de Paris*, March 22, 1848.

[24] Session of March 21, *La Commune de Paris*, March 23, 1848.

to fortune. Let me repeat, you ought to give your support to the man of action who hides the sparkling fire of purest patriotism under his worker's smock."[25]

Revolutionary intellectuals tended to agree, provided that people like themselves were made honorary proletarians. At the Republican Club of Free Workers, the socialist writer Robert (du Var) gave workers credit for special aptitude as constitution makers: "He [the worker] is more up to this task than are the rich, fettered as they are by their status. It is scarcely possible for the rich to launch a completely new revolution made by and for the proletarian. The rich will not be able to accept such a revolution in its entirety because they will not have grasped it. In this case, wealth is like a ring embedded in the rock, to which they remain chained no matter how hard they strain."[26] Yet Robert's exemplars of likely proletarian representatives read like a roster of contemporary socialist intellectuals. At the Club of the Mountain (of the Carré Saint-Martin), the novelist and newspaperman Alphonse Esquiros proposed that "scholars and writers as much as workers" should be considered suitable for the National Assembly, and his motion carried.[27] Esquiros' proposal, often stretched to include government officials, became the club norm. Most clubs made a point of recommending some manual workers for seats in the forthcoming parliament; not one club endorsed a purely proletarian slate.

Club hesitations over disqualifying their bitterest political enemies show the popular societies at their anti-Machiavellian best. The Club of the Emancipation of the

[25] Club républicain des travailleurs, session of March 22, *La Voix des clubs*, March 24, 1848.

[26] Session of March 22, *Le Peuple souverain*, March 26, 1848.

[27] Session of March 27, *Le Tribun du peuple*, March 30, 1848.

Peoples, very moderate by club standards, had raised the issue by voting a resolution to bar the 225 ex-deputies who had supported the Guizot government.[28] In its rounds of Parisian clubs, this resolution ran into unexpected opposition. In spite of arguments for broadening and sharpening political punishment, club consensus opposed political vengeance. At the Central Republican Society, for example, the resolution was headed for defeat before it was rescued by President Blanqui's persuasiveness.[29] Most club members felt that the ex-deputies were sufficiently discredited. Extending the loss of civic rights to former officials, clubists argued, was punishing the lackeys for the misdeeds of their masters. Elsewhere the resolution was rejected by what amounted to a democratic self-denying ordinance. Napoléon Lebon, veteran revolutionary leader of the Society of the Rights of Man, insisted that true democracy could brook no limitations, not even limitations imposed on its enemies. In a republic, public execration took the place of outlawry.[30]

Such democratic scruples could be carried to excessive lengths. If it was unfair to deprive a man of his civic rights on the basis of his political past, was it equitable to oppose him politically if he appeared repentant? The Democratic Club of Blancs-Manteaux seemed willing to swallow the candidacy of General Piat, an old-line liberal, once he had pledged allegiance to Robespierre's famous Declaration and had publicly announced his faith in "the organization of labor."[31] Even more naïve was the Club of the Friends of the People's "almost unanimous" endorsement of Henri de Larochejaquelein, scion of one

[28] *La Commune de Paris*, March 21 and 23, 1848.

[29] Société centrale républicaine, session of March 20, *La Voix des clubs*, March 22, 1848.

[30] Société des Droits de l'Homme, session of March 22, *La Commune de Paris*, March 23, 1848.

[31] Session of April 7, A.N., C. 941, CdE 8481.

of France's great legitimist families. Members of Raspail's club were evidently willing to take at face value his credo "as democratic as any democrat's with ten years of republican service to his credit."[32] The Prince de la Moscowa, son of the ill-fated Marshal Ney and a hereditary Bonapartist, was treated with equal indulgence.[33] Not all clubists were as credulous. Some took obvious pleasure in unmasking false republicans, like the Dominican Father Lacordaire and Marchal (de Calvi) by publicizing their antirepublican writings dating from the days of the monarchy.[34]

Receiving no guidance from the Club of Clubs on how to select candidates to the National Assembly, individual clubs improvised their own methods as they had for the National Guard elections. Means of weeding out the unfit varied widely. Robespierre's Declaration of the Rights of Man, popularized by the republican secret societies and taken up by the Club of Clubs, turned out to be a very coarse sieve, for most candidates proved ready to endorse that historic document's ambiguous rhetoric. The elaborate statements of principles which some clubs had already tried on officer candidates provided a finer mesh. The ultimate in screening was a formidable list of embarrassing questions with which to net secretly antirepublican candidates. The difficulty of this candidate-by-candidate approach was that it was almost entirely negative:

[32] Club des amis du peuple, session of April 1, *L'Ami du peuple en 1848*, April 2, 1848; *La Sentinelle des clubs*, April 5, 1848.

[33] See, among others, Club républicain de Batignolles, session of March 23, *La Commune de Paris*, March 25, 1848; but the endorsement was apparently rescinded on March 26. *La Commune de Paris*, March 28, 1848.

[34] Open letter signed by members of six clubs, *La vraie République*, April 13, 1848, and April 15, 1848. *La vraie République*, April 13, 1848. Société des Droits de l'Homme, April 15, 1848, *Enquête*, ii, 112-113.

it was easy enough to discard those who failed the tests but hard to select candidates from among those who passed. Dr. Alphonse Baudin, president of the Club of the Future, may have been the first to propose some general principles. He suggested that the slate of candidates carried in the Seine department reflect every nuance of republicanism, socialism, and communism.[35] Generally, this ideal of ideological diversity within the democratic camp was widely adopted in club circles, though the specific balance between candidates of varying persuasions differed from club to club.

Theoretically, once a neighborhood club had turned in its list of favored candidates to the Club of Clubs, it had fulfilled its appointed role; neighborhood clubs affiliated with the club federation had pledged to abide by the official list to be announced. In practice, making candidates jump through the hoop had become so much a part of the daily routine of club meetings that it continued until election time. This prolonged exposure to campaign oratory and to the question-and-answer period that followed may have furthered the political education of club members. At the Society of the Rights of Man,

[35] Club du deux mars, n.d., *La Commune de Paris*, April 10, 1848, for the disqualification of Victor Considérant, editor of the Fourierist *Démocratie pacifique*, because he would not subscribe. Club de la fraternité universelle, session of March 22, *La Commune de Paris*, March 25, 1848; Club Soufflot, session of March 21, *La Voix des clubs*, March 24, 1848. Poster, Club des francs républicains (Montmartre), March 28, 1848, B.N., Lb53, 814; poster, Club de la sentinelle constituante, April 8, 1848, B.N., Lb53, 1023.

For the Baudin statement, see Société des Droits de l'Homme, session of March 21, *La Commune de Paris*, March 23, 1848. For a list of candidates reflecting varying leftist "schools," see Club démocratique des Blancs-Manteaux, session of April 3, 1848, A.N., C. 941, CdE 8482.

for example, the audience learned to be impatient of rhetoric, demanding that candidates propose specific programs to cope with the pressing needs of Parisian workers. As far as ideological indoctrination was concerned, popular societies did expose a good many workers to articulate socialists and to their ideas.[36] Not that the examination of candidates was automatically enlightening. In unanimously endorsing a local notable, the river-shipper Lavaux, the Democratic Society of La Villette merely lent a republican patina to traditional habits of deference.[37] The unwillingness of most clubs to go behind a candidate's statements to his past performance indicated political naïveté, as did the clubs' disregard of any given candidate's chances of success. Popular societies were also extraordinarily lax in their electoral bookkeeping. Seemingly they often failed to keep track of how many candidates had already been endorsed, recommending far more than the 34 for which there were slots. Finally, the preoccupation with nominating candidates may have been the opium of the club movement, divert-

[36] The examples of the examination and endorsement of candidates by neighborhood clubs in the period after April 10 are numerous. For three (of many) instances taken at random involving clubs belonging to the Club des clubs: Société des Droits de l'Homme (Club du IIIe arrondissement), session of April 14, La Commune de Paris, April 16, 1848; Club du deux mars, session of April 14, 1848, A.N., C. 941, CdE 8600; Club démocratique des Blancs-Manteaux, session of April 17, 1848, A.N., C. 941, CdE 8477. Session of March 28, La Commune de Paris, March 30, 1848; session of March 29, ibid., March 31, 1848; session of March 30, ibid., April 1, 1848. Club fraternel des Quinze-Vingt, session of March 22, La Voix des clubs, March 25, 1848; Club républicain de Batignolles Monceaux, session of March 31, La Commune de Paris, April 2, 1848, where, for example, the socialist peer D'Alton-Shée campaigned.

[37] Session of March 20, 1848, B.H.V.P., série 25.

ing popular societies from grubby but needed door-to-door electoral canvassing.[38]

Judged by success or failure at the polls, the whole effort turned out to be unprofitable for clubs and candidates alike. Not a single candidate relying for his campaign on club appearances seems to have been elected, while most of the 34 winners succeeded without ever appearing on a club platform.[39] Why? Most of the winners were moderate republicans, ideologically out of tune with the club movement and therefore unlikely to patronize it. The majority of successful candidates were also men whose names were generally known, who needed no personal introduction. Moreover, a candidate who focused his efforts on appearances in neighborhood clubs was demonstrably headed for political suicide. If we assume an average club attendance of 500 and hardworking candidate Y campaigning 30 days with two club appearances per evening, candidate Y would have polled only 30,000 votes if every one of his listeners—and only his club listeners—had voted for him. By contrast, the least popular of the 34 winners garnered nearly 105,000 votes. Since this was somewhat predictable, serious candidates put their efforts elsewhere. Club appearances were not a political kiss of death, but clubs tended to attract those hoping against hope—the obscure, the penniless, the crackpots.

[38] It was the exceptional club that set up a commission to investigate the political background of candidates soliciting endorsement. See Club de l'égalité et de la fraternité, session of April 13, La Commune de Paris, April 15, 1848. Occasional proposals to have club delegates mount a registration drive in Parisian workshops and labor organizations, like that of the Club de la Montagne (Montmartre), were never acted upon. A.N., C. 941, CdE 8551, March 29, 1848.

[39] Cabrel de Nurelé to Despeux, Sunday, n.d., A.S., V 3 D⁶, 23, No. 14, for indication that the Protestant minister Coquerel, elected in the Seine department, did meet with club delegates—the only such evidence that I uncovered.

The majority of candidates originally favored by neighborhood clubs reflect these facts of life. A sample of 20 neighborhood popular societies of varying political hues submitted 198 names to the Club of Clubs for the 34 seats at stake in the election. The ultimate fate of these recommended candidates is instructive: on election day, 117 of the 198 received less than 5,000 votes of 300,000 cast, 152 less than 50,000. Of the scattered 30 candidates who turned up among the victors of the April elections, most were connected with the Provisional Government and not one had campaigned in a club. Evidently it was the political losers who sought—and obtained—club endorsement.

iv

The clubs' preoccupation with the elections left them little time and less inclination to explore social and political ideas. Exceptional in this respect were clubs that had grown out of utopian groupings dating back to the July Monarchy, such as Etienne Cabet's Central Fraternal Society, which inherited his large Icarian following in Paris, or clubs founded by ideologues for the specific purpose of doctrinal propaganda, of which the Fourierist Commission for the Propagation of Social Science may serve as exemplar.[40] The analysis of Robespierre's Declaration of the Rights of Man, forced upon the clubs by the affiliation requirements of the Club of Clubs, was inherently artificial and inevitably somewhat antiquarian. Club audiences, despite or because of their continual exposure to the programs of candidates seeking endorsement, showed a low tolerance for fine-spun

[40] Minutes of the first session of its provisional executive commission, April 5, 1848, A.M.G., dossiers des insurgés de juin, A 3669bis; for another example, Jules Lechevalier's Club central de l'organisation du travail, *La Commune de Paris*, April 6, 1848.

ideologies.[41] Abstract ideas could not compete with the fascination of the revolutionary drama unfolding day by day.

Club ideologies tended to crystallize around immediate, concrete problems, though the preconceptions on which they were based had been there all along. The government's decree of March 16, imposing a surtax of 45 percent, was a case in point. Revolutionary republicans agreed unanimously that the measure, however sound fiscally, would alienate the peasants from the Republic.[42] In the clubs, the decree stimulated discussion of alternatives that ranged from state bankruptcy, paper money inflation, and a capital levy on the rich to the confiscation of the famous billion indemnity granted the émigrés of the French Revolution and the taxation of mortgage holders.[43] Yet because the debate was after the fact—the Central Republican Society's vote to have the tax rescinded was purely academic—and because club members were not directly and immediately affected by the decree, club grumbling never solidified. Club audiences were fatally attracted to symbolic acts. Rather than discuss fiscal policy, clubists much preferred to take up a collection for the government, overriding objections that "quantitatively, this will be small potatoes. You will have

[41] For example, Société des Droits de l'Homme, session of April 13, La Commune de Paris, April 20, 1848.

[42] See, e.g., Société républicaine centrale, March 23, La Voix des clubs, March 26, 1848; Club de la Sorbonne, March 25, Le Courrier français, March 27, 1848.

[43] Club des hommes libres, session of March 21, La Commune de Paris, March 22, 1848; Club de la révolution, early April, La vraie République, March 13, 1848; Société des Droits de l'Homme, sessions of April 2 and 8, La Commune de Paris, April 7 and 11, 1848; Club de la Sorbonne, session of March 25, Le Courrier français, March 27, 1848; Société républicaine de Passy, n.d., La Voix des clubs, March 26, 1848; Société centrale républicaine, session of March 23, La Voix des clubs, March 26, 1848.

emptied the pockets of the poor, of those who are in greatest need, because the poor are patriotic and patriots always sacrifice themselves for their country."[44]

Club audiences were personally more affected by the catastrophic tightening of business credit than by the government's fiscal plight. By the third week of March, many employers were unable to pay their workers, either because banks refused to discount commercial paper or because employers were unable to change their banknotes into the smaller denominations needed to meet their payrolls.[45] Although there was a good deal of talk in various clubs about issuing banknotes in denominations of 25 francs or less, improving the operation of the newly created discount banks, reviving confidence by weeding out the minority of unsound firms, dealing with capitalists hoarding their wealth or foreigners welshing on their debts, these matters were too technical to be resolved in open debate. Only an occasional resolution emerged from the *ad hoc* committees in which such problems tended to be interred.[46]

[44] The objection is that of Lamieussens, a somewhat suspect veteran of the secret societies, Société républicaine du Faubourg Saint-Denis, session of March 20, *La Commune de Paris*, March 21, 1848. See also Société des Droits de l'Homme, session of March 20, *La Commune de Paris*, March 21, 1848; Club du progrès, session of March 29, ibid., March 31, 1848; Club Saint-Georges, petition to Provisional Government, March 10, 1848, A.N., BB[30], 306, No. 6205; Club de l'Homme-Armé, n.d., *La vraie République*, April 11, 1848; Club de la fraternité des ouvriers, n.d., *La Commune de Paris*, April 12, 1848.

[45] *La Voix des clubs*, March 22, 1848.

[46] For pertinent debates on such questions, see Club des hommes libres, session of March 17, *La Commune de Paris*, March 18, 1848; Société républicaine du Faubourg Saint-Denis, session of March 20, *La Voix des clubs*, March 24, 1848; Société des Droits de l'Homme, session of April 2, *La Commune de Paris*, April 7, 1848; Club du IIIe arrondisse-

Similarly, most club discussions of "socialism" or "organization of labor," unless they were brought to a meeting by a visiting candidate, grew out of the prevailing economic depression. Considering that Paris suffered from unprecedented mass unemployment—for which the National Workshops were never more than an inadequate palliative—the surprise is not that the problem should occasionally have surfaced at club meetings but rather that it did not dominate the proceedings. The often repeated assertion that the revolution of 1848 was social rather than political was more autosuggestion than fact, unless one assumes a tacit division of revolutionary labor that allotted socioeconomic reforms to Louis Blanc and organized labor and left "pure" politics as the peculiar domain of the popular societies.

Whatever the reason, the record of the clubs in formulating economic reforms is relatively barren. One detailed proposal originated with the Republican Club of Workers, which, though led by a mathematics professor and an attorney's clerk, was largely working class. By a unanimous vote, the club petitioned the Provisional Government to step in and run any enterprise that had closed down. Management might be retained by the owner (who would in any case receive rent for his building and equipment) or be granted to the associated workers.[47] Even

---

ment (Société des Droits de l'Homme), session of April 14, ibid., April 16, 1848; Club de la révolution, session of April 13, *La vraie République*, April 15, 1848. For petitions to the Provisional Government on such topics, see Club des prévoyants, *Le Moniteur universel*, March 29, 1848; Club des républicains socialistes, B.N., Lb[53], 9145; Club de la révolution, *La Réforme*, April 10, 1848.

[47] For discussion and text of the petition, see Club républicain des travailleurs, sessions of March 19 and 22, *La Voix des clubs*, March 22 and 24, 1848. For its delivery to the Provisional Government's secretary, who suggested addressing it

more ambitious was a petition of the Club of Republican Socialists influenced by Saint-Simonian ideas. Dealing with the everyday plight of manufacturers enmeshed in punitive bankruptcy laws, the club outlined a new procedure by which shaky firms could suspend operations short of bankruptcy, in order to clear the decks for economic recovery. As the only agency able to generate credit, the state would then take over ailing firms, leaving their operation in the hands of the former owner, advised by a workers' council. This policy would be paralleled and supplemented by the immediate resumption of railway construction under state sponsorship, the organization of agricultural armies, and the foundation of a national bank that would issue paper money with private landed wealth as backing. Such measures would assure "workers a steady livelihood, a normal and secure existence." This petition apparently also influenced Barbès' Club of the Revolution to demand increased paper money and the nationalization of the Bank of France and of all insurance companies, railroads, mines, and canals.[48] Not all such reform proposals were so sweeping. A Club of the Union of Workers' earnest discussion of a producers' cooperative for a few dozen epaulette weavers or the Society of the Rights of Man's naïve trust in Louis Blanc as the fountainhead of all needed reform may have been more typical.[49]

Other evidence points to club reluctance to cross the

---

to the Luxembourg Commission, *Le Moniteur universel*, March 24, 1848.

[48] "Adresse au gouvernement provisoire pour réorganiser l'industrie nationale," Club des républicains socialistes, April 13, 1848, B.N., Lb[53], 9145. Club de la révolution, session of April 13, *La vraie République*, April 15, 1848.

[49] Club de l'union des travailleurs, n.d., *Le Courrier français*, April 12, 1848; Société des Droits de l'Homme, session of April 12, *La Commune de Paris*, April 15, 1848.

fine line separating revolutionary politics from social issues that lay beyond conventional politics. Had the clubs
been searching for a rousing popular cause in late March
1848, they could not have helped but stumble on the controversy over payment of apartment rentals.

The problem was massive and immediate because
landlord–tenant relations in Paris were governed by an
intricate traditional etiquette. Rents for unfurnished
apartments, which comprised the bulk of the capital's
housing, were payable in advance, six months' rental at
a time, on April 1 and October 1. When the term fell due,
a Parisian working-class family had to raise a lump sum
of seventy-five to two hundred francs, an average workingman's wages for twenty to fifty-three days. Conditions
since the February Revolution aside, working-class sav-
ings must already have been depleted by the prolonged
high bread prices and economic slowdown of 1846-47.
Then came the revolution: "The workers who left their
workshops on February 23 and 24 to man the barricades
have not been able to get back to their trades. . . . In any
event, the factories have for the most part remained
closed. This is why the workers currently find it absolutely impossible to pay their rent."[50] Spontaneous agitation spread throughout the capital, particularly in the
eastern working-class districts, as tenants banded together to cajole or threaten their landlords into canceling the
April term. Black flags were hoisted over the doors of
proprietors who had refused to give in. The police prefect, his revolutionary antecedents notwithstanding, intervened on the side of property rights.[51]

Only the faintest echoes of this conflict can be detected
in the clubs, which also stayed away from a demonstra-

[50] Petition to Provisional Government, March 31, 1848,
Club républicain des travailleurs, A.N., BB[30], 304, No. 5459.
[51] Caussidière, *Mémoires*, I, 254-257.

tion in behalf of the rent moratorium.[52] The proletarian Republican Club of Workers seems to have stood alone in petitioning the government to cancel rent payments and in protesting against police intervention on the landlords' side. The Club of Free Men discussed at considerable length whether the six months' rent due April 1 should not be turned over to the Provisional Government, a move not at all designed to relieve the tenants.[53] A couple of weeks later, the associates of the Rights of Man can be found muttering against the mayor of their district for ordering the removal of flags and posters honoring "cooperative" landlords. And this is all in a period in which the least misstep in registering workers for the National Guard was hashed over in a dozen popular societies!

This reticence also contrasts with club reaction to threatened mob violence that displayed more traditional political overtones than the tenant–landlord conflict. Toward the end of March and in early April, one, and perhaps two, newspapers, habitually critical of the new Republic came under pressure from hostile street crowds. The threat to Emile de Girardin's *La Presse*, which en-

[52] *La vraie République*, April 4, 1848. The demonstration, which goes unmentioned in most accounts of the French revolution of 1848, took place on the Champ-de-Mars and may have attracted 100,000 people. I have not found any copy of the posters advertising it and have no idea of the identity of its organizers or sponsors. There seem to have been no ties between it and a banquet of clubs announced also for April 2, but at the Place du Châtelet near the Hôtel-de-Ville, Club des incorruptibles to Club des clubs, n.d., A.N., C. 941 CdE 8586.

[53] March 31, 1848, A.N., BB[30], 304, No. 5459. Club des hommes libres, sessions of March 19 and 21, *La Commune de Paris*, March 21 and 22, 1848. This scheme had originated in the Société républicaine du Faubourg Saint-Denis, session of March 16, *La Commune de Paris*, March 17, 1848. Session of April 12, ibid., April 15, 1848.

joyed the largest daily circulation in Paris, was real; the danger to *Le Constitutionnel*, formerly an organ of the Dynastic Left, turned out to be imaginary. The rent controversy had pitted poor against rich; the *La Presse* incidents raised the issue of the rights of free speech in its most unpopular form, namely that of an antirepublican editor's freedom to attack the Republic in print without fear of reprisal. Yet this was precisely the area where club principles were clear. The Club of the People's Salvation, strongly protesting any attack on the freedom of the press, sent delegates to other clubs in support of the resolution. Eight of the nine clubs contacted complied, usually by unanimous votes. Some days later the Society of the Rights of Man was drawn in when President Villain announced that he had received warning that *Le Constitutionnel*'s presses were about to be smashed. Citing Article 5 of the Declaration of the Rights of Man "which consecrates in absolute terms the right to publish one's opinions and even though the Society protests against the doctrines of this paper," Villain called for twenty-five volunteers to protect the newspaper. One hundred and fifty members responded to what turned out to be a false alarm.[54]

Similarly, the persecution of foreign workers that broke out in Paris during March was readily identified as an offense against fraternity. This agitation against foreigners was far more widespread than any random threats

[54] For the story of the *La Presse* incidents told to magnify the police prefect's role in calming the crowd, see Caussidière, *Mémoires*, I, 242-244. For a contemporary mention of intimidation of *La Presse*'s hawkers, see *La vraie République*, April 1, 1848. For rumors of threats against *Le Constitutionnel*, see police report by Carlier, April 5, 1848, *Enquête*, II, 175. Club du salut du peuple, 13th session, *La Commune de Paris*, April 7, 1848; Société des Droits de l'Homme, session of April 4, ibid., April 7, 1848.

to the press. As the manager of a metal-working shop complained to the Provisional Government: "Brutal force, violence, constrain us to dismiss workers who have been with us for a long time, for the sole reason that they happen to be foreigners." Rising unemployment had released a latent xenophobia that singled out the lowest-paid foreign workers, mostly Savoyards and Belgians, as chief victims.[55] As in the case of the beleaguered newspapers, the clubs' response was one of principle rather than political expediency; regardless of hard times, the Republic owed fraternity and protection even to those who who were not her citizens. A number of clubs passed resolutions, placarded neighborhood walls, protested to the government, alerted the Club of Clubs to take an official stand. By mid-April, newspapers no longer reported antiforeign mobs. This may merely mean that violence had become commonplace; probably it does indicate that this ugly episode had run its course. Whether or by how much the clubs' actions had shortened its duration or lessened its intensity is anyone's guess.

[55] Letter from Moulin to Provisional Government, March 25, 1848, A.N., BB[30], 302, No. 4165. See also the delegation of port workers protesting to the government against the employment of Savoyards (Savoy being still Piedmontese). *Le Moniteur universel*, March 27, 1848. To the inhabitants of Montmartre, even Parisians were foreigners to be kept away from employment on "their" public works. Ibid., March 28, 1848. For description of antiforeign street gangs, see *La Réforme*, April 2, 1948.

The Provisional Government and Ledru-Rollin as its Minister of the Interior may have encouraged the "invasion" of Belgium by a column of Belgian ex-residents of Paris partly to avoid trouble in the capital. Caussidière, *Mémoires*, I, 200-201. Savoyards were induced to organize a mass exodus—*colonnes de départ*—with no such political coloration. See *La Réforme*, April 7, 1848.

v

Intervention on behalf of the foreign workers revealed the clubs' willingness to oppose both the prejudices and the interests of their own constituents in the name of fraternity. Giving encouragement to foreign revolutionaries eager to leave France posed no such unpopular dilemmas. Club attitudes testify to the power of the myth of France as standard-bearer of universal revolution. In the spring of 1848, every week brought news from abroad that seemed to confirm that myth. No wonder that clubs were ready to extend considerable sympathy and some aid to foreign revolutionaries, particularly to departing exiles carrying the torch to their homelands.

This is a long way from claiming that international solidarity was a burning or even a major issue for most clubs before May 1848. A popular society like the Club of Progress might be tempted into issuing a magniloquent manifesto addressed "To our Brothers in Germany, Italy and Poland," to circulate among other clubs for their approval.[56] Yet aside from competing stylistically with France's major lyric poet and a master at international manifestos, such expression of verbal solidarity came cheap. Elsewhere the Club of the Emancipation of Peoples lived up to its name by founding a French Central Committee for the Liberation and Defense of Poland, while the Club of the Garde nationale mobile extolled immediate military intervention in that dismembered country. An obscure poet went from club to club singing a hymn to Poland and was fervently applauded.[57] Be-

[56] Session of March 24, *La Commune de Paris*, March 26, 1848.

[57] For the announcement about the Club de l'émancipation des peuples, see *Le Monde républicain*. I have no information on the effectiveness of the new organization. For intervention in Poland, see Club de la garde nationale mobile, session of April 5, *Enquête*, II, 82-83.

The proud author-composer seems to have gone from club

cause its vice-president was of Italian origin, the Club of Popular Interests took a special interest in the fate of the Lombards, newly freed from Austrian domination but threatened with annexation by reactionary Piedmont. Sympathy for the English Chartists led the university students of the Club of Equality and Fraternity to prepare a rally in their behalf, only to call it off as the Chartist balloon began to sag.[58] More generally, good—meaning "revolutionary"—news from other capitals of Europe was likely to be read aloud and "thunderously" cheered.[59]

How many of these gestures were truly spontaneous is impossible to determine because Parisian clubs were continually solicited for aid and comfort by "foreign brothers" whose claims were hard to deny. Most insistent and popular among these exiled revolutionaries were the Poles, who lost no time in enlisting club backing for their efforts to bring revolution and independence to their divided and oppressed homeland. The Poles publicly called upon "club presidents and secretaries to become the treasurers of the Polish cause" in order to finance the return of the armed exiles to create the conditions in which

---

to club to sing his masterpiece. See Club de l'égalité et de la fraternité, session of March 23, *La Voix des clubs*, March 25, 1848; and Club de la Montagne (du Carré Saint-Martin), session of March 23, *Le Tribun du peuple*, March 26, 1848.

[58] Poster of motion passed on April 1, 1848, B.N., Lb[53], 895. For its vice-president, Barnabo, see *DBMOF*, I, 154.

For the announcement that a rally was being planned "in several Parisian clubs," see *La vraie République*, April 10, 1848; for its abandonment, see Club de l'égalité et de la fraternité, session of April 13, *La Commune de Paris*, April 15, 1848.

[59] See Société républicaine centrale, session of March 23, *La Voix des clubs*, March 26, 1848; Club de la Montagne (du Carré Saint-Martin), session of March 24, *Le Tribun du peuple*, March 26, 1848. The "thunderous applause" greeted news of the Prussian revolution. Société républicaine centrale, session of March 20, *La Voix des clubs*, March 22, 1848.

France would be able to "uphold Poland with your arms." A steady stream of emissaries from the Polish Central Committee passed through the clubs to plead, appeal, and beg. The first departure of Polish volunteers was made the occasion of a demonstration to which clubs were invited. Polish spokesmen may have been in back of a successful petition to the Minister of the Interior from the Democratic Society of Batignolles-Monceaux requesting that the families of the departing Poles receive relief.[60] The organizers of the German democratic legion under the poet Herwegh and of the Italian revolutionaries under Mazzini's inspiration were only slightly less ubiquitous and equally strapped for funds. A passionate appeal by Pole, German, or Italian, followed by the tinkle of copper into the collection plate, became routine at club meetings.[61] Club members were unfailingly sympathetic, polite, and patient. Yet, when all is said and done, European solidarity occupied a small niche in a dimly lit background. French revolutionary politics was never crowded from the stage.

[60] Poster, March 31, 1848. Appeal from Comité central [polonais] for patriotic gifts, B.N., Lb⁵³, 887. The appeal also appeared in revolutionary newspapers like *La vraie République* and *La Commune de Paris*. For example, the Club de la Montagne (du Carré Saint-Martin). See *Le Tribun du peuple*, March 26 and 30, 1848. Club républicain de Batignolles-Monceaux, sessions of March 26 and 31, *La Commune de Paris*, March 28 and April 2, 1848.

[61] Club de l'égalité et de la fraternité, session of March 28, *La Commune de Paris*, March 30, 1848; Club des Quinze-Vingt, letter to *La Réforme*, April 1, 1848; Société centrale républicaine, session of March 23, *La Voix des clubs*, March 26, 1848; Club du progrès, n.d., *La Commune de Paris*, April 2, 1848.

6 | The Crisis of the Popular Movement

Today we are the defeated, and I will speak to you as one defeated, that is, with hatred in my heart and with vengeance in my hand.

Auguste Blanqui,
Evening of April 16, 1848

From that day of April 16 on, everything became easy for the government.

Alphonse de Lamartine

i

Most of the "critical" days of the Second Republic's revolutionary phase seem much less crucial in retrospect. March 17, as we saw, ended as a standoff decked out in revolutionary rhetoric. The demonstration in behalf of Poland on May 15 was too botched an enterprise to be taken seriously. The June Days burned like a straw fire that a provincial tide would have drowned had the local fire brigade failed to douse it in time. Even if we include the national election of April 23 on our list of crises, its results merely confirmed widely held expectations that universal manhood suffrage would never endorse social revolution in a society of peasant proprietors and would-be peasant proprietors.

By contrast, the *journée* of April 16, which drastically altered the balance of forces between Parisian revolutionaries and the authorities, was genuinely decisive. By successfully calling on the Parisian National Guard—old and new—to overwhelm a massive workers' demonstration that Sunday, the Provisional Government destroyed the possibility that 1848 would reenact 1793. After April 16, militants' hopes of imposing their views on a beleaguered government and, in time, on a besieged National Assembly were dead. Had the demonstration succeeded and the mobilization of the Guard failed, revolutionary Paris might have looked forward to overawing the conservative provinces and their elected representatives as their sans-culotte ancestors had done.[1] The Provisional Government's ascendancy after April 16

4. Route of the demonstration of April 16, 1848

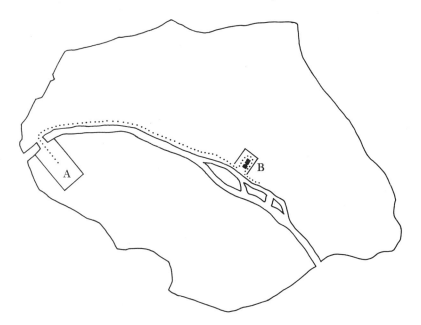

A. Champ-de-Mars, point of departure of the demonstrators

B. Paris City Hall (Hôtel-de-Ville), destination of the demonstrators

[1] See, e.g., Louis Blanc's speech to the Luxembourg workers on March 28, summarized in Loubère, *Louis Blanc*, p. 111.

doomed what was usually labeled "a democratic and social Republic" that only direct Parisian pressure could
have sustained.

ii

The outward events of April 16 make a straightforward
enough story that may be quickly summarized. To com-
pensate for the workers' poor showing in the National
Guard elections, General Guinard, the militia's chief of
staff (and, incidentally, president of the left-leaning Central Democratic Society), allotted fourteen staff officers
of their choice specifically to organized labor. These elections were arranged through the organized crafts, the
corporations ouvrières, that already enjoyed public recognition in the Luxembourg Labor Commission headed
by Louis Blanc. Scheduled for the afternoon of Sunday,
April 16, at the Champ-de-Mars, the staff officer elections
drew some tens of thousands of workers, who arrived
with banners flying. Some of them had attended a campaign rally earlier in the day called by the brigadiers of
the National Workshops on the west side of Paris. The
fact that the workers brought prepared banners (calling
for "organization of labor" and the end of "exploitation
of man by man") and had drawn up a petition to the
Provisional Government in advance proves that the demonstration of April 16 was not an impromptu affair. Having completed the balloting and passed the hat for
a "patriotic donation," the workers formed their ranks,
setting out along the Right Bank toward City Hall. The
authorities, meanwhile, had alerted the National Guard.
In response, the Guard surrounded the Hôtel-de-Ville,
hemmed in the marching workers, cut and isolated their
columns, hooting the demonstrators to the cries of "down
with communists!" The demonstrators' delegation was
barely permitted to squeeze through serried ranks of
bayonets to offer the workers' patriotic collection and to

present their petition in behalf of a more socially oriented policy. Snubbed by the Provisional Government, the delegates were sternly admonished by a mere deputy mayor who received them. Subjected to harassment and threats along the line of march, the workers were humiliated upon reaching their destination.[2]

There is a consensus on some aspects of the demonstration of April 16. Give or take a few concealed pistols, the marchers went unarmed to City Hall.[3] Had the *journée* been planned as an insurrectionary seizure of power, the prospective insurgents, as in June 1848, would have availed themselves of their National Guard rifles; April 16, therefore, was clearly not an attempt at an armed coup. Second, participants at various levels of the demonstration were to claim afterwards that their intentions had been entirely peaceful, that their sole aim was to convey the people's aspirations to the Provisional Government. We may be tempted to dismiss such declarations when drafted by the official leaders of the march, but why should an ordinary upholsterers' delegate go to the trouble of writing a personal letter to the government to the same effect?[4] And why should another participant,

[2] Garnier-Pagès, *Histoire de la révolution*, VII, 369-409; Caussidière, *Mémoires*, II, 18-36; Louis Blanc, *Révélations historiques* (Brussels, 1859), 15-35. For typical contemporary newspaper accounts, see *Le Moniteur universel*, April 17, 1848; *Le Représentant du peuple*, April 18, 1848; *Le Courrier français*, April 17, 1848. Careful reconstruction of the events of April 16 may be found in Loubère, *Louis Blanc*, pp. 104-109; Gossez, *Les ouvriers*, pp. 260-263. For the reception of the workers' delegation by Edmond Adam, see Garnier-Pagès, *Histoire de la révolution*, VII, 402-403.

[3] For a participant's assertion that orders were to go unarmed, see testimony Prot, Haute-Cour de Bourges, March 19, 1849, *Le Moniteur universel*, March 22, 1849.

[4] The protestation of "innocence" by the Luxembourg workers' delegates appeared in the left-wing press and is reproduced in Blanc, *Révélations*, pp. 28-30. The upholsterer's letter is in A.N., BB[30], 308, No. 7100.

the printer Mairet, recall privately that "we went to this meeting strictly 'on the up and up' [*en bonnes têtes*]? If there was anything fishy about this parade, my comrades and I knew nothing about it."[5] If the demonstration was meant to be revolutionary, apparently the rank and file had been left completely in the dark. Third, there is general agreement that the organized trades represented at the Luxembourg Labor Commission constituted the core of the demonstration, though it is uncertain whether they were joined by other organized groups along the line of march.

Nonetheless there was probably more to the *journée* than met the eye. It was common knowledge that Louis Blanc exercised a dominant influence over organized labor. The chances are that the minimum aim of the demonstrators of April 16 was to assure Louis Blanc, their patron, a more secure position within the government, a position that any future National Assembly would be forced to respect. The minimum aim of the demonstration—Louis Blanc's later denials notwithstanding—may therefore have been to extort the creation of a "Ministry of Progress" headed by Blanc to replace the impotent Luxembourg Commission.[6] Quite plausibly, the demonstrators may also have aimed at a more ambitious maximal objective. Their petition was couched in extraordinarily peremptory terms: "le peuple veut"—the people demand—has the ring of an ultimatum. Finance Minister Garnier-Pagès subsequently explained that the wording of the manifesto was deliberately insulting so as to induce moderates like himself to resign rather than to bow to its terms.[7] Quite possibly such a purge *was* intended. Yet all

---

[5] Cited in Chauvet, *Les ouvriers du livre*, pp. 191-192.

[6] Blanc, *Révélations*, pp. 17, 22. Loubère, *Louis Blanc*, p. 105. For one eyewitness statement to this effect, see testimony Prot, Haute-Cour de Bourges, March 19, 1849, *Le Moniteur universel*, March 22, 1849, p. 964.

[7] Garnier-Pagès, *Histoire de la révolution*, VII, 338.

we can say with assurance is that for Louis Blanc and his supporters, a Ministry of Progress under any circumstances would have been a step in the right direction. The government's successful mobilization of the National Guard against the marchers made minimum and maximum aims equally unattainable.

Perhaps the actual plans for the *journée* of April 16 are of less consequence than the rumors which determined the government to act as it did. We know that several days in advance, Louis Blanc had informed his colleagues that a peaceful demonstration by workers would take place on April 16, a demonstration over which he disclaimed any influence.[8] In the face of this announcement, the government was sharply divided between those who took the news (soon reinforced by wild rumors of impending insurrection) as a serious threat and those who made light of it.[9] According to a letter written to friends by his wife, the Minister of Justice, Crémieux, was convinced that Blanqui was about to attempt a coup.[10] Garnier-Pagès, who had access to gendarmerie reports, was also alarmed.[11] The most decisive of the

[8] Elias Regnault, *Histoire du gouvernement provisoire* (Paris, 1850), pp. 289-293; testimony Carteret, *Enquête*, I, 252; Alphonse de Lamartine, *History of the French Revolution of 1848* (London, 1852), pp. 456-457; Garnier-Pagés, *Histoire de la révolution*, VII, 344-353, 370-371.

[9] Testimony Crémieux, *Enquête*, I, 265-266.

[10] Crémieux, *En 1848*, pp. 237-238.

[11] Garnier-Pagès, *Histoire de la révolution*, VII, 360. Of the daily reports from the First Legion of the gendarmerie (whose jurisdiction extended to the whole of the department of the Seine except the capital itself) those for April 8, 11, and 12 have survived. None bear out Garnier-Pagès' misgivings. The only reference to impending trouble is the report of a rumor (as of April 15) that a secret club was being formed in the suburbs with the aim of overthrowing the government, a report issued from the headquarters of the Garde mobile. A.M.G., F¹ 5.

alarmists appears to have been the deputy mayor of Paris, Buchez. Buchez claimed to have been jolted by vague but persistent reports of subversive recruitment in the suburbs, reports that may have been the distorted echo of a campaign speech delivered by Blanqui before the workers of the Northern Railway shops. Unable to persuade his superior, Mayor Marrast, of the impending danger, Buchez did succeed in extracting permission to take any precautionary measures he saw fit: it was he who notified the National Guard commanders to stand by for an emergency.[12] Marrast, who went off to review a suburban National Guard legion on the morning of Sunday, April 16, was not alone in being unconvinced. Foreign Minister Lamartine, who prided himself on his personal contacts with leading ultrarevolutionaries, had a long and friendly interview with Blanqui on the morning of April 15. The Foreign Minister assured his moderate colleagues that they had nothing to fear from that quarter.[13] Certainly there is no evidence that anyone was

[12] For Blanqui's speech before the railway workers, testimony Gosset and Lavoie, Haute-Cour de Bourges, March 22, 1849, *Le Moniteur universel*, March 24, 1849, p. 1009. Buchez memorandum on April 16, Buchez Papers, B.H.V.P. This unsigned, detailed memorandum is a draft of a letter written to Garnier-Pagès (in the early 1850's?) in response to the latter's request for information in the preparation of his multivolume *Histoire de la révolution de 1848*. As far as I know, Buchez' recollections, which challenge some of the conventional wisdom on the *journée* of April 16 (that is, the crucial role of Ledru-Rollin in ordering the National Guard to arms), have escaped the attention of twentieth-century historians. I have verified the handwriting as Buchez', and there is good reason to believe that the account is substantially correct—though one man's perspective.

[13] Testimony Lamartine, Blanqui, Courtais, Haute-Cour de Bourges, session of March 15, 1849, *Le Moniteur universel*, March 18, 1849, p. 905; Caussidière, *Mémoires*, II, 12-14. For Lamartine's reassurances to his colleagues, testimony Marie, *Enquête*, I, 319.

trying to precipitate a crisis or that anyone was acting on precise and accurate intelligence: the picture is one of men groping amidst conflicting rumors that some took seriously, others not.

Was there any substance in the rumors of a Blanquist plot? In the spring of 1849, before the High Court of Bourges, Blanqui was to admit having been at the Champ-de-Mars on April 16, although only, he maintained, to distribute his flyer rebutting the charges against his revolutionary honor levied by the notorious Taschereau document.[14] Other testimony at the same trial suggests that some of Blanqui's followers may have appeared at the Champ-de-Mars with hidden weapons. Yet Blanqui was in no position to lead any coup, for his position had been shaky ever since the end of March when he had been accused of having informed on his fellow revolutionaries in 1839. His refusal to cooperate with a revolutionary "jury of honor" (stacked by his opponents, he claimed) did not enhance his position. He had been isolated by the charges, his attempt to consolidate a larger following in a club federation of his own having fizzled. Blanqui's public justification, belatedly issued on April 13, was viewed as a counterattack rather than as irrefutable proof of his innocence. In these circumstances, Blanqui was a general commanding a company instead of an army. What brought Blanqui to the Champ-de-Mars on April 16 was, no doubt, rumors that the demonstrators were about to purge the Provisional Government. Such a move would open up unexpected opportunities

[14] Testimony Blanqui, Haute-Cour de Bourges, session of March 13, 1849, *Le Moniteur universel*, March 15, 1849, p. 859; session of March 19, 1849, ibid., March 21, 1849, p. 848. Testimony Prot, session of March 14, 1849, ibid., March 17, 1849, p. 890. For the (contested) testimony claiming that some Blanquists had hidden pistols, see Klein, Haute-Cour de Bourges, session of March 22, 1849, *Le Moniteur universel*, March 24, 1849, p. 1009.

of which Blanqui meant to take advantage. The most plausible explanation of Blanqui's behavior on April 16 is that he was playing jackal to the Luxembourg workers' lion.

Neither was the *journée* of April 16 prepared in other club circles. At a meeting of the Society of the Rights of Man on April 11, a member suggested another mass demonstration to galvanize the Provisional Government. President Villain argued that it was imprudent to call the people into the streets again where "a few evil-intentioned men could stir them up to provoke terrible events." Besides, the earlier demonstration of March 17 had been unable to shake the Provisional Government out of its lethargy. The motion for a mass demonstration was withdrawn.[15] Nor does the demonstration of April 16, sponsored by the Luxembourg workers, seem to have been discussed in the popular societies prior to April 15. The elite Central Democratic Society took up the subject that evening, having learned of the demonstration from the Luxembourg workers with whom it had been negotiating an electoral alliance. Evidently the society had heard rumors of a purge of moderates; for, while it endorsed pressure on the Provisional Government to impel it in a progressive direction, the club voted down any demonstration directed against specific persons. Characteristically, rather than join the working-class demonstrators on Sunday afternoon, the society decided to present its own petition to the Provisional Government in the morning.[16]

Only on April 15 were clubs being asked to join the April 16 demonstration, presumably by delegates from

[15] *La Commune de Paris*, April 15, 1848. Garnier-Pagès, *Histoire de la révolution*, VII, 332, deliberately distorts the evidence by implying that the proposal was approved.

[16] Amann, *Minutes*, pp. 352-366; Garnier-Pagès, *Histoire de la révolution*, VII, 355-357.

the organized trades. A police report on the evening session of April 15 at the Club of the Revolution reveals its members' perplexity in the face of inadequate information. As the aims of the demonstration were explained, they included showing the government where the people stood, demanding the dismissal of incompetent departmental commissioners, and purging the Provisional Government of its "weak and incapable" members. The Club of the Revolution, obviously uneasy, postponed action, while an *ad hoc* committee looked into the situation. News that the mayor of the second district was on the verge of arresting Blanqui also encountered a wait-and-see reaction from the club.[17] Through the evening of April 15, the scanty evidence suggests, the club seems to have been singularly ill-informed about a demonstration that they had evidently been asked to join at the last moment.

For the crucial night of April 15-16, our evidence, however tenuous and circumstantial, allows us to sketch the rough outlines of that crisis. During the night, Lamartine was to claim, he had had word of an impending "communist" coup. Presumably his source was Sobrier, whom the Foreign Minister had cultivated, and, in spy-thriller fashion, had "turned around."[18] In club circles the rumors were more specific: Blanqui and his adherents were identified as the would-be putschists. No one knows the origin of the rumor, but what counted was that the clubists clustered in the Club of the Revolution, the Club of Clubs, and the Society of the Rights of Man shared the

[17] Session of April 15, *Enquête*, II, 104. Proudhon, a member who attended, confirms the prevalence of uncertainty (*Confessions*, pp. 27-28). So does George Sand (*Œuvres autobiographiques*, II, 1188-1189).

[18] Testimony Lamartine, Haute-Cour de Bourges, March 15, 1849, *Le Moniteur universel*, March 18, 1849, p. 905; also his testimony, *Enquête*, I, 305.

conviction that the report was true.[19] If Blanqui really threatened to overthrow the Provisional Government with the aid of the Luxembourg demonstrators on the morrow, emergency measures were called for. For weeks these club leaders had enjoyed nightly confidential chats with Interior Minister Ledru-Rollin in which they had weighed the establishment of a "purer" revolutionary government. Suddenly faced with a workers' demonstration that they could not halt, the overthrow of the Provisional Government an immediate prospect, and the dictatorship of Blanqui as the likely outcome, the anti-Blanquist club leaders turned to Ledru-Rollin as the only possible savior. During the night, anti-Blanquist leaders, probably with Caussidière's blessing, approached the Minister of the Interior: would Ledru-Rollin head a Committee of Public Safety to head off Blanqui's dictatorship? By this time they had probably drawn up a list of other prospective members in such an ultrarevolutionary government.[20]

The anti-Blanquist clubists were in a bind because they

[19] The rumor seems to have been general. See Club de la fraternité, session of April 15, where the *manifestation Blanqui* is condemned. *Enquête*, ii, 105. Barbès' comments in session of April 16 of Club de la révolution are pointed, though he does not name specific names. *Enquête*, ii, 104-105. Carlier, the government's inept undercover police chief, claimed that Barbès, Blanqui, and Ledru-Rollin were coconspirators (though Blanqui and Barbès were deadly foes and Ledru-Rollin refused even to meet with Blanqui). *Enquête*, i, 244, testimony Delpech, Haute-Cour de Bourges, March 13, 1849, *Le Moniteur universel*, March 15, 1849, p. 860. For the conviction in the Club des clubs, testimony Grégoire, Haute-Cour de Bourges, March 22, 1849, *Le Moniteur universel*, March 24, 1849, p. 828; testimony Carteret, *Enquête*, i, 250.

[20] Alfred Delvau, *Histoire de la révolution de février* (Paris, 1850), pp. 289-293; testimony Marrast, *Enquête*, i, 322; Garnier-Pagès, *Histoire de la révolution*, vii, 369-370; Lamartine, *French Revolution of 1848*, pp. 454-457.

had no alternative should Ledru-Rollin refuse their proposal. When he did, Barbès, Sobrier, and company continued to follow the minister's lead when, instead of seizing power, he decided to neutralize the demonstrators by
an overwhelming display of force. Militarily, Ledru-
Rollin's about-face (though perhaps it was no more than
a quarter turn) was not really decisive, for deputy mayor
Buchez had already summoned the National Guard into
the streets. Ledru-Rollin's action did have the effect of
carrying the anti-Blanquist leaders and their troops with
him in his show of solidarity with the government's moderates. When the alarm roused the militia, Armand
Barbès appeared at the head of the Twelfth Legion; Sobrier turned his headquarters in the rue de Rivoli into a
stronghold of law and order; the Society of the Rights of
Man mobilized its forces—all measures undertaken to
defeat plans that Blanqui had probably never made.[21]

iv

For several days following April 16, Paris was in
the throes of hysteria. There was a wave of hatred against
"communists," chiefly victimizing the inoffensive Cabet
and his Icarians, whom a fearful landlord temporarily

[21] For Barbès, whose legion responded first to the alert, see
testimony Ledru-Rollin, Haute-Cour de Bourges, March 19,
1849, Le Moniteur universel, March 21, 1849, p. 947. For
Sobrier, see testimony Grégoire (president of Club des prévoyants and member of the commission, Club des clubs), Haute-
Cour de Bourges, March 11, 1849, Le Moniteur universel,
March 13, 1849, p. 828, and La Commune de Paris, April 17,
1848; testimony Léonard Gallois, Haute-Cour de Bourges,
March 23, 1849, Le Moniteur universel, March 25, 1849, p.
1031. For Société des Droits de l'Homme, testimony Villain,
and note to Sobrier, April 16, 1848, Haute-Cour de Bourges,
March 22, 1849, Le Moniteur universel, March 24, 1849;
also P. Collet to Villain, April 16, 1848, A.N., C. 942, CdE
8364. For Club des clubs, Foulquier to Longepied, April 16,
1848, A.N., C. 940, CdE 8383.

barred from the Salle Valentino.[22] For several days daily alarms disrupted city life. On April 18 at 2:00 A.M. the commander of the National Guard alerted his colonels that the Tuileries and the Hôtel-de-Ville were to be attacked at dawn. Other rumors singled out the police prefecture as an objective of the impending attacks. According to others, the communists were sacking the Faubourg Saint-Antoine. National Guards dashed through the streets shouting that their guard posts had been stormed and burned during the night. Once again the capital became an armed camp tensely waiting for a blow that never fell. In fact, none of the rumors that circulated was ever verified.[23]

The pointless panic of April 18 had a sobering effect on the revolutionaries who had rallied behind Ledru-Rollin and the Provisional Government on April 16. That evening the events of the day still seemed glorious; Sobrier crowed that within two hours thirty thousand citizens had made his newspaper offices a focal point of resistance against the "agitators."[24] Yet Sobrier must have been perturbed when, in the midst of "victory," his own secretary was being mauled by National Guards for hawking *La Commune de Paris* in the streets.[25] By April 19 even Sobrier was willing to admit that "those who shouted 'down with the communists' will shout 'down with the republicans' tomorrow."[26] Other left-wing papers

[22] *La Démocratie pacifique*, April 18, 1848; *Le Populaire*, April 20, 1848.

[23] For Courtais' letter to Provisional Government, see Garnier-Pagès, *Histoire de la révolution*, VIII, 30; *La Réforme*, April 19, 1848; Société des Droits de l'Homme, session of April 19, *La Commune de Paris*, April 29, 1848; Caussidière to Provisional Government, April 19, 1848, *Enquête*, I, 171. Sand, *Correspondance*, VII (April 18-19), 421-424.

[24] *La Commune de Paris*, April 17, 1848.

[25] *Le Courrier français*, April 20, 1848.

[26] *La Commune de Paris*, April 19, 1848.

were more outspoken, tallying up contradictory rumors about Sunday's demonstration that canceled each other out. *La Réforme* summed up the growing revolutionary consensus: "We were right to be mistrustful. Yesterday's [April 16] *journée* was nothing but a day of dupes. Unawares, the National Guard lent itself to an infamous machination, serving as accomplice to reactionaries crying victory." By April 20, in an open letter to his Twelfth Legion, not even Barbès seemed quite sure whether "this cowardly phantom of anarchy" had ever been flesh and blood.[27]

Though the major effect of the *journée* of April 16 was to strengthen the armed might of the Provisional Government (confirmed, by sheer coincidence, by a great military review on April 20 that camouflaged the reintroduction of regiments of regulars as a Parisian garrison), April 16 may also have been a turning point in the club movement.[28] For the first time since the February Revolution, shouts of "down with the clubs" were heard in the capital.[29] For the first time, the government issued a warrant to arrest a major club leader; though Blanqui eluded detention and though the warrant was quashed on May 3, a precedent had been set.[30] For the first time, the government legislated against popular societies by

[27] Garnier-Pagès, *Histoire de la révolution*, VIII, 50.

[28] For a detailed, relatively detached eyewitness account of the military review of April 20, see *Le Monde républicain*, April 22, 1848. For the official account, *Le Moniteur universel*, April 21, 1848. Before the end of the month the military command was already planning for the intervention of the Paris garrison "in defense of order." A.N., F⁹, 1248, Dispatch from the Commander of the First Military Region, April 29, 1848.

[29] Testimony Villain (president of Société des Droits de l'Homme), Haute-Cour de Bourges, March 21, 1849, *Le Moniteur universel*. March 23, 1849, p. 991.

[30] Testimony Carteret (undersecretary of Ministry of the Interior), *Enquête*, I, 248. Caussidière, *Mémoires*, II, 50-52; Garnier-Pagès, *Histoire de la révolution*, VIII, 36-45.

prohibiting armed clubs.[31] The decree, based on false rumors, may never have been enforced, yet it helped to make suppression thinkable.

To what extent the hysteria following April 16 affected the outcome of the general elections in Paris is a moot question. In any case, it did not affect them decisively. The festivities of April 20 seem to have had a calming effect, as the daily alarms to which the National Guard had been subjected ceased. The electoral failure of the revolutionaries almost surely owed more to political incompetence than to a wave of unreason. Yet the great fear of "anarchists" and "communists" may have nudged some of the confused and the undecided to vote for authoritative figures who stood for stability and order in a mad and unsettled world.

v

While the first results of the elections began to trickle in from the provinces within a day or two of the polls' closing on April 24, the size of the Seine department's electorate slowed the counting. Not until the evening of April 28 were the local winners proclaimed from the steps of the Paris City Hall: the moderate republicans had won overwhelmingly. Of the slate of thirty-four candidates put forward by the Club of Clubs and the Central Committee of the Workers of the Seine, a mere handful—six to be exact—had won election. Whether the clubs could justifiably take credit for even a single one of these winners is questionable. Four of them—Albert, Louis Blanc, Flocon, and Ledru-Rollin—had probably been elected as members of the government and not because of club and labor endorsement. In number of votes, they lagged far

[31] Garnier-Pagès, *Histoire de la révolution*, VIII, 46-47. The decree was decided upon by the Provisional Government during the evening session of April 19. For text, *Le Moniteur universel*, April 20, 1848.

behind the more conservative members of the Provisional Government. Caussidière, the police prefect, had managed to endear himself to many conservative elements grateful for his "keeping order with disorder," to quote his clever public relations slogan. Agricol Perdiguier, though nominated by the Luxembourg workers, had showed considerable strength elsewhere. Perdiguier, admired as the apostle of the journeymen's guilds, enshrined by George Sand as protagonist of one of her novels, was notoriously antisocialist and therefore eminently acceptable as a token worker to many moderates and conservatives.[32]

The blow was not altogether unexpected, for newspapers close to the clubs had voiced misgivings even before the bad news became known. On April 27 two newspapers published by club sympathizers, Thoré's *La vraie République* and Raspail's *L'Ami du peuple en 1848*, published official though incomplete figures for the number of registrants and voters in eleven of the twelve administrative districts of Paris. In contrast to the very high turnout in the provinces, only two-thirds of registered voters in the capital had cast their ballots. Thoré surmised that the figures reflected widespread working-class abstention, though in fact the percentage of abstainers in the capital's most prosperous district, the first, slightly exceeded that of the twelfth, generally rated as the most impoverished. *La vraie République*'s assertion that workers had stayed away in droves because of administrative chicanery or pressure from their employers was a theme that would be fully orchestrated once the revolutionaries' defeat became definitely known.

What had happened to the one hundred fifty thousand or two hundred thousand marchers of a month before who now failed to support the "social and democratic Republic" with their ballots? Well-known club leaders

[32] *Le Représentant du peuple*, April 30, 1848.

like Cabet, Blanqui, Huber, Raspail, and Barbès had garnered between twenty thousand and sixty-four thousand
votes as against the one hundred five thousand awarded
the least popular of the thirty-four official winners. In the
first place, aside from the higher rate of absenteeism, the
election results in Paris are comparable to what took
place in the provinces. There the "great notables" who
had run France under the constitutional monarchy
stepped aside in a moment of panic induced by the February Revolution. By and large, the masses turned to a
second string of prominent men for their representatives.[33] Paris, which had never owed allegiance to "great
notables" in the past, turned to ersatz notables in 1848—
members of the Provisional Government and their more
visible associates—as reassurance in a troubled time.
Second, to the extent that the revolutionary tradition governed the outlook of the Paris lower classes, political
campaigning and voting had never been part of that tradition. Parisians were likely to associate revolution with
demonstrations, riots, insurrections, the intimidation of
elected legislatures, with militancy within popular societies or sections—but not with the prosaic discipline of
organized voting. The more recent experience of the July
Monarchy could only have reinforced the tradition. Nor
can the Parisian experience be considered aberrant in the
context of preindustrial Europe, where common people
habitually vented their grievances in the street, leaving
political machinations to their betters. Third, in eliminating most of the members of the Provisional Government
from their list of candidates, the clubs had probably
alienated a majority of ordinary workers. This, after all,

[33] André-Jean Tudesq, *Les grands notables en France (1840-
1849)* (Paris, 1964), pp. 1054-1072, for comments on the
April 1848 elections; pp. 246-349, for comments on the traditional lack of genuine Parisian notables because of the sheer
size and complexity of the capital.

was *their* Provisional Government, anointed by the people in arms on February 24. Finespun distinctions between desirable and undesirable republicans, between adherents of *La Réforme* and supporters of *Le National*, must have been lost on thousands who had manned barricades in February and would man them again in June.

This is, finally, to say that the clubs and organized labor had dismally failed in educating their constituents, a failure borne out by the sorry record of the Club of Clubs and the Central Committee of the Workers of the Seine. The dimension of this failure that can be most clearly demonstrated is organizational: the overwhelming defeat of the revolutionaries in Paris was not as unavoidable as the election returns seemed to show. In April 1848, to judge by all candidates receiving more than five thousand votes, the revolutionaries were a minority within the Seine department, but a much more sizable minority than the list of winners indicates. As *La vraie République* was first to point out, the revolutionaries had scattered their votes among a legion of losing candidates, while the moderate republicans had concentrated their votes on a much smaller number of successful nominees. The number of votes for all successful and unsuccessful candidates receiving more than five thousand votes each added up to 7,920,000. Of these, 2,320,000 were cast for former monarchist deputies, for republicans whose place in the political spectrum is uncertain, or for local notables whose political affiliation is altogether obscure. Seventeen clearly labeled moderate republicans were elected by 3,550,000 votes, which failed to elect another ten moderates. Yet less than half a million votes were thrown away on these ten losers. By contrast, though the vote for club favorites ranging from Blanqui to Ledru-Rollin numbered 2,050,000, those votes elected only six (or at most seven) candidates. Where the moderate republicans had wasted only half a million votes on ten unsuccessful runners, the revolutionaries expended 1,200,000 on thirty-three losers. If the electoral statistics for candidates receiving less than five thousand votes had been preserved, the total of the revolutionary vote would, I suspect, run even higher, further illustrating this same scatter effect.

vi

The clubs had little opportunity to mull over the lessons of the April elections before they were distracted by ominous news from Normandy, which, having reached the government by April 28, became generally known in Paris on the following day.[34] Disappointed over the defeat of the Jacobin-Socialist slate, workers in Rouen and nearby Elbeuf expressed their chagrin in what became a minor riot. A charge by the middle-class National Guard mortally wounded a worker, and barricades went up in the working-class sections. With cannon and rifles on one side, paving stones and iron bars on the other, the insurrection was suppressed within twenty-four hours, but only after considerable—and one-sided—bloodshed. To add to revolutionary bitterness, the prosecutor investigating the disturbance after it was over was the notorious Frank-Carré, who had demanded the death penalty for Barbès and Blanqui in 1839.[35] Moreover, in Limoges,

[34] For the first detailed telegraphic dispatch summarizing events in Normandy for the government, see Dispatch No. 843, A.N., F⁹⁰, carton 774. For initial response of the government, *Procès verbaux du gouvernement provisoire et de la commission du pouvoir exécutif* (24 février-22 juin) (Paris, 1950), p. 206.

[35] Garnier-Pagès, *Histoire de la révolution*, VIII, 291-320; the official speech by Sénard justifying the repression is in *Le Moniteur universel*, May 9, 1848, pp. 987-988. For a modern account, though also written from a conservative viewpoint, see André Dubuc, "Les émeutes de Rouen et d'Elbeuf (27,

where the workers' nominees had also been swamped by conservatives, workers seized power by disarming the bourgeois militia. Not a drop of blood was shed, in vivid contrast to Rouen. After tempers had cooled, workers meekly turned over control of Limoges to the constituted authorities.[36]

The Rouen "massacre" created a storm in the clubs. On the evening of April 30, *La Réforme*'s report on Rouen was read aloud before the Society of the Rights of Man. The reading evoked demands for an immediate punitive expedition against Rouen, "for if today reactionaries rise up in arms in Rouen, tomorrow it will be the turn of Paris." Others called for the removal and indictment of the Provisional Government's moderate majority. President Villain urged caution, reminding his listeners that the government would have to account for its actions to the forthcoming National Assembly. If the latter were to accept explanations unsatisfactory to the people, that same people might send the gentlemen representatives packing. "In that case, if there were to be a fight, the Society of the Rights of Man would know how to impose respect for the rights of the people."[37] The next day, May 1, the society's manifesto created a sensation when it appeared posted on Paris walls. It warned the retrograde supporters of the old order against persisting in their resistance, promising that "the day of the struggle you will find our organized sections in the vanguard

28, et 29 avril 1848)," *Etudes d'histoire moderne et contemporaine*, ii (1948), 243-275.

[36] See V. Chazelas, "Un épisode de la lutte de classe à Limoges," *La révolution de 1848*, vii, 161-180, 240-256, 326-349, 389-412; viii, 41-66. Some of the basic sources may be found in A.N., BB[30], 333. An excellent recent account discussing the Limoges incidents in a regional context is Merriman, "Radicalization," pp. 101-127.

[37] *Enquête*, ii, 105.

9.–Postelection crisis, April-May 1848

Left: The aftermath of the Rouen massacre through revolutionary eyes: Prosecutor Franck-Carre, impersonating Judge Jeffries of "Bloody Assizes" notoriety, is captioned as saying, "Look at the cunning Norman. He plays dead just to escape justice!!!"

Below: The invasion of the hall of the National Assembly on May 15, 1848.

and then your brothers will no longer be speaking of FORGIVENESS but of JUSTICE." Ironically, the posters had no connection with the Rouen troubles. Originally printed and publicized in early March, the society decided to post them again to answer rumors in the wake of the *journée* of April 16 that the Society of the Rights of Man was "anarchist" or "communist."[38] Barbès Club of the Revolution was equally incensed, naming and dispatching a commission headed by its president with the double aim of demanding an explanation from the government and proceeding to an on-the-spot fact-finding mission in Normandy. The club also voted a resolution demanding that the government arm in self-defense all workers in manufacturing towns.[39] Blanqui's Central Republican Society thundered against what it called "a Saint Bartholomew's massacre of workers" in a manifesto so violent that billposters were being harassed by National Guard patrols. Blanqui's explosive rhetoric was accompanied by four demands: dissolution of the Rouen National Guard; arrest of the officials in charge of the repression; arrest and trial of the regular and guard officers who had directed the massacre; and, finally, the immediate withdrawal of the Paris garrison to avoid an even big-

[38] The text of the manifesto of the Société des Droits de l'Homme may be found in most left-wing contemporary newspapers; for instance, *Le Peuple constituant*, May 2, 1848, repr. in *Les affiches rouges* (Paris, 1851), pp. 159-160, and in Wassermann, *Les clubs de Barbès*, pp. 149-150. A. Delvau, in *Les murailles révolutionnaires* (1852 ed.), I, 261, correctly places the original poster (undated) in very early March 1848. This point would not be worth emphasizing were it not for the fact that Wassermann, misconstruing the original date of the document as being at the end of April, relies on the manifesto as proof of Barbès' break with moderation. It proves nothing of the sort.

For the motives of the Société des Droits de l'Homme, see session of April 19, *La Commune de Paris*, April 29, 1848.

[39] *La Réforme*, May 3, 1848.

ger massacre of workers in the capital.[40] The Club of Equality and Fraternity in the Latin Quarter reluctantly shelved its motion to have Barbès' Twelfth Legion march on Rouen in favor of a protest against the role of Frank-Carré.[41]

The controversy was kept alive when the reactionary Central Democratic Club of the National Guard—one of a handful of "counterclubs"—publicized its commendation to the Rouen guard for "the example you have just furnished."[42] The Club of United Republicans, blaming the Democratic Club of the National Guard as the voice of a minority, extended its sympathy to "our brethren of Rouen."[43] Similarly, the Club of Montagnards of Belleville protested against this "appeal to civil war" and the commendation of those who had spilled French blood.[44] The Club of the Antonins, eight hundred strong, waited for the National Assembly to convene before launching a blistering attack on those it held responsible for the slaughter.[45] Less militant clubs nonetheless petitioned against the entry into Paris of the Twenty-Eighth Regiment that had taken part in the Rouen fighting.[46] As late as May 9 a branch of the Society of the Rights of Man was still protesting to the

[40] *Le Représentant du peuple*, May 3, 1848; *Les affiches rouges*, pp. 153-157.

[41] *La Commune de Paris*, May 5, 1848.

[42] Read and included in the minutes of the Club des républicains unis de Montmartre, *La Commune de Paris*, May 6, 1848.

[43] Loc. cit.

[44] *La Commune de Paris*, May 10, 1848.

[45] *Enquête*, ii, 126-127. The manifesto was turned over to the Ministry of Justice for possible indictments. See A.N., BB[30], 363(3), dossier M, No. 5272A. For a more moderately worded petition, Club de l'unité démocratique, session of May 6, *La Commune de Paris*, May 11, 1848.

[46] Club démocratique de Saint-Maur, session of May 3, *La Commune de Paris*, May 6, 1848; Club Servandoni, session of May 8, *La Commune de Paris*, May 10, 1848.

Minister of Justice against the Rouen incidents.[47] None of this agitation had any visible effect, but the clubs were right in sensing that the Rouen "massacre" had changed the set on the revolutionary stage: in the contest over the nature of the revolution of 1848, April 16 had made anti-revolutionary repression thinkable; the Rouen bloodletting made it respectable.

vii

The excitement over Rouen veiled the threatened disintegration of the club movement during the second half of April. Club statistics, though not completely reliable, point to a striking decline in the number of clubs still operating in May and June 1848. During March and April, about two hundred clubs in greater Paris can be documented; for May and June, less than sixty clubs have left traces of their existence. Even if we surmise that newspaper coverage of club meetings was declining because of lagging interest, such an abrupt decline cannot be shrugged off. To cite but one specific example: according to the mayor of the first district, of eight clubs that had met in municipal buildings in March and April, only half were continuing their sessions by early May 1848.[48]

Much of this decline may be attributed to a postelection letdown, to the widespread idea that clubs were campaign instruments to be discarded with the torn-up election posters. The rash of placards put up during the last week of April and early May by long-established clubs

[47] *Enquête*, II, 113-114. An abortive grand finale was reached when Barbès, as an elected representative from Aude, tried to demand an accounting for Rouen from the outgoing Provisional Government. He was ruled out of order. *Le Moniteur universel*, May 9, 1848, pp. 987-988.

[48] A.S., V 3 D⁶-23, No. 14.

announcing that their meetings were resuming or continuing speaks of popular societies deserted by their members. Occasionally, as in the Club of Socialist Republicans, the officers promised to reorient their society from campaign efforts to the study of social issues, which were spelled out in one formidable program.[49] In other instances, previously autonomous clubs consolidated, as when the Socialist Republicans of the sixth *arrondissement* merged with the Club of Republican Unity, or the Club of Fraternal Friends with the Club of Triumph. A new Club of the Antonins absorbed no less than four popular societies of the Faubourg Saint-Antoine.[50]

The coordinating body for the club movement, the Revolutionary Committee, Club of Clubs, also had difficulty in weathering the elections. The elections had undermined the Revolutionary Committee's prestige; for even though criticism in the left-wing press was muted it took no great insight to conclude that the club federation had mismanaged the campaign. In any case, the end of the elections meant the end of the Revolutionary Committee's announced role, moving some members of the executive board to hand in their resignation.[51] Furthermore, the Club of Clubs had come to depend on the secret funds of the Ministry of the Interior, yet no one nur-

[49] *La Commune de Paris*, April 25, 1848; also Club démocratique fraternel de Quinze-Vingt, ibid., May 2, 1848; Club du progrès, ibid., April 27, 1848; Club de la révolution, May 3, 1848.

[50] Letter to Commission executive, June 20, 1848, Pagnerre Papers, A.N., 67 AP, dossier 4. The Antonins comprised the Club dèmocratique de la rue Charonne, Club démocratique de la rue Traversière, Club démocratique de la rue Popincourt, and Club démocratique de la rue Saint-Bernard.

[51] Deleau to Longepied, April 29, 1848, A.N., C. 940, CdE 8371. Withdrawal of the Club Popincourt, *La Réforme*, April 30, 1848.

tured illusions that this official munificence would outlast a Provisional Government about to surrender its powers to a National Assembly.

The stricken organization was further rent by internal dissension. Shortly after the elections, Napoléon Lebon, stalwart of the Society of the Rights of Man, and Sobrier, publisher of the *Commune de Paris*, resigned in protest against the actions of the executive committee.[52] The two apparently objected to a visit made by Longepied, Laugier, and others to Lamartine, assuring him that the Club of Clubs had no insurrectionary plans against the Provisional Government. Possibly the moderates on the Club of Clubs, headed by Longepied, may have been looking for a new patron and benefactor, though there is no evidence that they found one in Lamartine. In a second, postelection interview, Longepied even tried to enlist the Foreign Minister as an ally in the event of an insurrection against an antirepublican Constituent Assembly.[53] The upshot of this conflict within the Club of Clubs was a complete revamping of the organization. At a meeting called by Huber on April 28 to which not only club delegates but commanders of Garde mobile units were invited, the Club of Clubs and its Revolutionary Committee were declared abolished and superseded by a new Centralizing Committee.[54]

Except for Huber, who stayed on as president of the new organization, there was an almost complete turnover of personnel. The three best-known members of the old

[52] *La Commune de Paris*, April 28, 1848.

[53] Longepied and Laugier, *Comité révolutionnaire*, pp. 103-108.

[54] For an invitation to a Garde mobile commander (which, characteristically, did not reach him in time to attend), Cournot to Foulquier, April 29, 1848, A.N., C. 940, CdE 7288; *La République*, May 1, 1848. This list of members includes two other holdovers, whose names do not recur on the manifesto published in *La Commune de Paris*, May 7, 1848.

Club of Clubs—Barbès, Lebon, and Sobrier—were replaced by men who had been active as club delegates but
who had not been officers. One of the new vice-presi-
dents, Jean-Jacques Danduran, was a typical *républicain
de la veille*, an old-timer who had done his share of street
fighting, prison, and exile. After long years in Belgium
and England, he had established himself as a prosperous
contractor specializing in a patented method for drying
out masonry. Since February 1848 he had seen his own
newspaper born and die, while presiding over the Club
of Republican Propaganda in the unreceptively bourgeois
second district.[55] Emile Lambert, named secretary, was
a journalist and secondary school teacher who had published, among other tracts, a work on "Practical Ways
of Organizing Labor." Lambert had chaired the Club of
the Institut Oratoire, from where he had launched an unsuccessful campaign for a seat to the National Assembly.[56] These were hardly names to conjure with. The new
Centralizing Committee's launching made no waves and
neither did its jejune manifesto, delayed until May 7.

viii

Just as the abrupt end of the electoral busy work posed
a problem to the survival of the clubs, so the election of
a representative assembly threatened to suborn the mystique of the club movement. Revolutionary ideologues
had raised the club movement to the status of beneficiary-
in-chief of a homemade theory of revolutionary sovereignty, summed up in a few simple propositions. First,
to their undying credit, the revolutionary masses in Paris
had not only overthrown the July Monarchy but determined that the February Revolution would be social as
well as political. Second, through their actions the revolu-

[55] Danduran to the Executive Committee, Club des clubs,
n.d., A.N., C. 940, CdE 8366. Also *DBMOF*, ii, 11.
[56] Lambert's *profession de foi*, A.N., C. 941, CdE 8881.

tionary people of Paris had truly embodied the general will. Finally, the clubs in turn constituted the apex, the revolution *en permanence*, the popular will organized, institutionalized, sharpened.[57] Free national elections undercut this myth of the clubs as the fountainhead of popular sovereignty. Once freely cast votes were counted, would club militants or duly chosen representatives of the whole French people guide France's revolutionary destiny?

The simplest approach to this new problem of club legitimacy was to deny that it existed, to deny that the elections had altered anything. "The people, by delegating the exercise of their sovereignty," read the Club of l'Homme Armé's poster, "have in no way abdicated their original creative sovereignty, their right of examination, their powerful initiative. We shall have to oversee what is done, to evaluate plans, to seek . . . the solution of the fearful problems posed."[58] The Democratic Club of Blancs Manteaux was even blunter: "The members of the Assembly are our delegates, yet the sovereign people does not relinquish its powers and must watch over the discussions of the deputies. The clubs must necessarily be the voice of the people and the expression of its will."[59]

More circumspectly, a newspaper close to the club movement, Proudhon's *Le Représentant du peuple*, suggested a division of labor between clubs and National

[57] This analysis is my extrapolation made on the basis of many casual allusions of this sort, not a summary of a doctrinal statement. There is a superficial resemblance between the Marx–Engels conception of the communists as the proletarian vanguard and the relationship between clubs and *peuple*. Yet unlike the communists, who were said to owe their leadership to their grasp of the world historical process, the popular societies were merely an organized expression of the legitimate revolutionary tradition of the people of Paris.

[58] B.N., Lb[53], 1859.   [59] B.N., Lb[58], 1837.

Assembly now that the first phase of the revolution was over. By shedding light on social questions, the daily club discussions would prepare the National Assembly's legislative debates as "the indispensable corollary." This flattering vision of a dual power, with the clubs representing "the poorest and most numerous parts of the population," apparently proved seductive.[60] On the day before the National Assembly was inaugurated, a club delegation sought an audience with Ledru-Rollin to demand that a special section of the balcony be reserved for club delegates. After several days of bargaining, in the course of which an offer to provide for three delegates from clubs enjoying official "clearance" had been indignantly rejected, the clubs' petition was granted. By May 12, forty club delegates met daily at Sobrier's palace, rue de Rivoli, before trekking over to the brand new but ramshackle wooden hall housing the deliberations of the nine hundred representatives of the people.[61] This concession did not still more ambitious demands. Sixteen clubs formed a commission that drew up an elaborate petition to the National Assembly, which was placarded for good measure on Paris walls. The commissioners, obscure men delegated by little-known clubs, wanted no less than the official recognition of a parallel chamber of club delegates—"the authentic organ of the people"—to take their seats in the unused former Chamber of Deputies.[62]

[60] *Le Représentant du peuple*, April 28, 1848.

[61] Garnier-Pagès, *Histoire de la révolution*, VIII, 390-391; announcement, Club de l'Arsenal, May 3, *La Commune de Paris*, May 6, 1848; announcement, Club républicain de la fraternité, *Le Courrier français*, May 7, 1848; Amann, *Minutes*, p. 480.

[62] B.N., Lb⁵⁴, 25. Students of the theory of revolution may be struck by the extent—which a fuller quotation would make even more striking—to which these views foreshadow the much more sophisticated analysis of "dual power" by Leon Trotsky, *The Russian Revolution*, ed. F. W. Dupee (New York, 1959),

If the request was ever answered, the reply has not come down to us.

The convocation of the National Assembly on May 4 did nothing to allay the clubs' frustrations. The popular societies had long considered what they would do should the new legislature refuse to confirm the Republic. They had not considered what Sobrier had predicted even as the election returns were coming in: that its enemies would proclaim the Republic as a delaying tactic, while awaiting a more opportune moment to fill the vacant throne.[63] The clubs, meanwhile, were in disarray, peppering the National Assembly with miscellaneous suggestions and petitions, while waiting for the conservative majority to remove its mask. The Club of Democratic Unity, over which the socialist peer D'Alton-Shée presided, offered a plan for dealing with representatives elected in more than one constituency.[64] Several clubs disinterred that old chestnut of the July Monarchy, *cumul*, by which officials parlayed their position into elective office in the legislature. The popular societies came out against such multiple officeholding.[65] Clubs proposed vast school building

---

pp. 199-208. Though there is no lineal connection, the fragmentation of authority was as obvious in France in 1848 as in Russia in 1917. Both situations invited explanation. See also P. Amann, "Revolution: A Redefinition," *Political Science Quarterly*, LXXVII (1962), 36-53.

[63] *La Commune de Paris*, April 30, 1848.

[64] Ibid., May 7, 1848.

[65] Club démocratique de l'Arsenal, session of May 11, *La Commune de Paris*, May 13, 1848, petition to National Assembly, May 12, 1848, *Le Moniteur universel*, May 13, 1848, p. 1023; Club du salut du peuple, petition of May 10, *La Commune de Paris*, May 14, 1848; Club de l'égalité (*Le Représentant du peuple*, May 10, 1848) wanted to make any public, private, or honorary post incompatible with the status of representative. The Club démocratique fraternel du Faubourg Saint-Antoine (*La Commune de Paris*, May 8, 1848) attacked double salaries rather than multiple officeholding.

programs to sop up unemployment, the legalization of labor unions accompanied by arbitration boards, the construction of meat markets to service each of the forty-eight quarters of Paris.[66] The United Republicans of Montmartre looked to the salvation of France in the expropriation of Louis-Philippe's extensive properties, while the Democratic Club of Quinze-Vingt proposed the immediate nationalization of the railways.[67]

There is an unreality about all this moving and petitioning, which a *cause célèbre*, embraced by the popular societies during the National Assembly's first week, underlines. The hubbub was caused by the election in Paris of one J.-B. Schmit, a respectable functionary in the Ministry of Cults, who during his campaign had described himself as a worker on the strength of having helped his father—a tailor—as a child. What confused electorate and election officials alike was that a shoemaker named Schmit, too, at one time a Luxembourg labor delegate, was also in the running. There had been piles of ballots for plain "Schmit," piles for "Schmit, writer" (the official in the Ministry of Cults had published some pamphlets!), and a third heap for "Schmit, worker." Clubists were enraged that all three had been awarded to the bureaucrat whose republicanism was suspect, instead of to the honest shoemaker. In fact, the National Assembly immediately annulled this election. Schmit the shoemaker, however, turned out to be a man of dubious credentials, having been relieved of his post as craft delegate in early April and refused admittance to the Central Democratic

[66] Club Servandoni, session of May 8, *La Commune de Paris*, May 10, 1848; Comité républicain du IIIe arrondissement, May 8, 1848, A.N., BB³⁰, 309, No. 7381; Club du Xe arrondissement, B.N., Lb⁵⁴, 45.

[67] Club des républicains réunis de Montmartre, *La Commune de Paris*, May 6, 1848; Club démocratique de Quinze-Vingt, A.N., BB³⁰, 310, No. 8332.

Society on the grounds of questionable republicanism.[68] The clubs, in short, had blunted a battering ram to break open an unlocked door that was hardly worth entering. They stood in obvious need of a new mission that would justify their continued existence.

[68] For the Schmit affair from the clubs' vantage point: Club républicain du progrès, *Le Courrier français*, May 3, 1848; Société démocratique centrale, *La vraie République*, May 3, 1848, and Amann, *Minutes*, pp. 428, 430, 432, 450, 492; Club socialiste de l'avenir, *La vraie République*, May 5, 1848; Club démocratique fraternel du Faubourg Saint-Antoine, *La Commune de Paris*, May 7, 1848; statement by the shoemakers' delegates, *La vraie République*, May 8, 1848. For the National Assembly deliberations, *Le Moniteur universel*, May 7, 1848, pp. 966-967. To complicate things further, six variant spellings were current: Schmit, Schmitt, Smith, Smit, Schmidt, and Schmith.

For now to crush by force an Assembly organized by cunning
would be a greater confession of error without undoing the evil.
                    François Raspail, April 29, 1848

i

At a time when the clubs were floundering, an international emergency came to their rescue. The plight of the
Poles, bombarded by Austrian forces in Cracow and har-
ried by Prussian regulars in Posen, suddenly blossomed
as the perfect political cause, that of solidarity with the
Polish independence movement. Pro-Polish sentiment
had long enjoyed a place of honor in the French revolutionary tradition. By 1848 it was indissolubly linked to
a popular and pervasive revolutionary imperialism appealing to a wide spectrum of forward-looking French-
men. After the divisive agitation over the Rouen "massacre" and the anticlimactic idiocy of the Schmit affair,
the issue of coming to the aid of the beleaguered Poles
promised the popular societies readmittance into the
mainstream of revolutionary politics. This was the promise that the club demonstration of May 15, 1848, was to
shatter rather than to fulfill.

While the events leading up to May 15 appeared tan-
gled and confused to participants, in retrospect the historian can usefully distinguish several phases. During the
first week, from May 2 to 10, the idea of a pro-Polish
mass demonstration originated and was popularized with-

out leading to specific plans. Several aspects of this "talking-up" phase stand out. First of all, the idea of a march on the National Assembly to press for aid to the insurgent Poles did not originate with the clubs. Second, individual clubs responded enthusiastically to the proposal regardless of their political orientation. Finally, far from taking the initiative in organizing the club demonstration, a preoccupied Centralizing Committee temporized until it was virtually forced to assume leadership because of pressure from neighborhood clubs.

The impetus for the Polish demonstration came from the Poles themselves, more specifically from the Committee of Polish Emigration in Paris, which was in turn prompted by news of the bombardment of Cracow by Austrian forces. On May 2 and on succeeding evenings, emissaries from the Polish émigré committee appeared at many Parisian clubs to read an "appeal to the French people" that demanded arms for the Polish revolutionaries. They also proposed a monster petition supported by a mass demonstration on the day of the Constituent Assembly's inauguration (May 4) to reflect the French nation's will to help.[1] While some club speakers seconded this Polish proposal, too little time remained to organize such a demonstration for inauguration day.[2] But the idea took root.

Any club, moderate or ultrarevolutionary, could iden-

---

[1] For the full text of the appeal (prompted by events in Cracow rather than the later collapse in Posen), see *Le Peuple constituant*, May 5, 1848. Two convenient summaries of and reflections on the problem of Polish nationalism in 1848 are M. Handelsman, "1848 et la question polonaise," *La révolution de 1848*, xxix, No. 179, 24-38; and B. Goriély, "La Pologne en 1848," in *Le printemps des peuples*, ed. F. Fejto (Paris, 1948), ii, 269-317.

[2] Société des Droits de l'Homme, session of May 2 (unsigned police report), *Enquête*, ii, 106-107.

tify with the Polish cause. The Democratic Club of the Montorgueil Quarter that leaned toward Ledru-Rollin published its announcement that "today the abolition in fact and in law of the reactionary treaties of 1815 having been proclaimed in the name of the Republic, Poland needs something more than good wishes and sympathy."[3] The Club of Democratic Unity, slightly more leftist in outlook, called for "an energetic demonstration of the sort that would sow terror in tyrants' souls" and even made a serious, if abortive, attempt to launch a pro-Polish demonstration under its own leadership.[4] The Club of the Friends of the People, whose president Raspail enjoyed a somewhat undeserved reputation as a fire-eater, petitioned parliament to make the Polish cause its own, peacefully if possible, by force of arms if need be.[5] The Society of the Rights of Man, which had a paramilitary structure and a tradition of militance, proposed that the civic festival announced for Sunday, May 14, be turned into an impressive show of support for Poland, Only if such a peaceful step failed to move the National Assembly was the society prepared to consider more energetic measures.[6] The newspaper La Réforme's claim

[3] Club démocratique du quartier Montorgueil, session of May 6, La Réforme, May 8, 1848.

[4] Session of May 8, La Commune de Paris, May 11, 1848; also a placard, B.N., Lb54, 1954; and session of May 11, La Commune de Paris, May 14, 1848.

[5] L'Ami du peuple en 1848, May 7, 1848. For the full text of the club resolution, see B.N., Lb54, 41. This club, one of the largest in Paris, claimed a membership of 500 women and 4,000 men. See Wassermann, "Le club de Raspail en 1848," pp. 589-605, 655-674, 748-762.

[6] Société des Droits de l'Homme, rue Albouy branch (unsigned police report), session of May 9, Enquête, II, 113-114. As late as May 12, Carlier, chief of the Interior Ministry's club police, was talking of a demonstration set for Sunday, May

that "all the republican clubs have voted by acclamation to invite the National Assembly to have France intervene immediately in the affairs of Poland" may have been only slightly inflated.[7]

During this initial phase of the pro-Polish agitation, the Centralizing Committee played a passive role. Like other clubs, the committee had been contacted by a Polish emissary about May 2 or 3 at a time when the committee was still in the process of organization. Its executive, headed by Huber, was preoccupied with the draft of a manifesto with which the Centralizing Committee hoped to gain more widespread club support. The committee's only response to the Poles was to dispatch a delegation to remonstrate with Foreign Minister Lamartine, but its delegates were never admitted. Even though individual club petitions in behalf of Poland began to pour in on the Centralizing Committee, President Huber actively opposed the mass demonstration that many of them called for. Vice-president Danduran was equally negative, perhaps because rumors were circulating that Marrast, the mayor of Paris, was planning to interfere. Yet the Centralizing Committee was in no position to hold back. Its manifesto, published on May 7, had evoked a disappointing response. As club opinion obviously favored a demonstration, such a demonstration would be held with or without the Centralizing Committee. On May 10 Huber and his executive capitulated in the face of urgent demands from Raspail's Club of the

14, though he also noted the lack of agreement among the clubs. *Enquête*, ii, 222.

[7] *La Réforme*, May 8, 1848. In the minds of the clubists, intervention in behalf of Poland was often linked to intervention elsewhere, particularly in Italy. The Club des intérêts du peuple et de la Garde nationale mobile favored simultaneous intervention against Austria, Prussia, Piedmont, Great Britain, and Turkey. *La Commune de Paris*, May 10, 1848.

Friends of the People. Reluctantly the Centralizing Committee agreed to lead a demonstration in behalf of Poland, though as yet no date was set.[8]

Between May 2 and 9 the character of the announced demonstration was never at issue. Most clubists believed that a show of mass support for Poland would encourage both the government and the National Assembly to do the right thing. Isolated individuals like Huber opposed the demonstration not because it was risky but because it was superfluous or inexpedient. The Assembly, Huber believed, would act on Poland in any case, and a private interview with Lamartine might accomplish more than one hundred thousand club demonstrators on the Place de la Révolution.

ii

By destroying such illusions, May 10 ushered in a second and stormier phase in the preparations. On the same day, Parliament was to demonstrate not only its lack of sympathy for social reform but also its coolness toward the Polish cause. The decisions of the Assembly had immediate reverberations among clubists, some of whom threatened to turn the impending demonstration into a revolu-

[8] The most detailed source for the role of the Comité Centralisateur is the testimony of its president, A. Huber, at his trial before the Haute-Cour de Versailles (*Le Moniteur universel*, October 11, 1849, p. 3044), which is far more instructive than his letter to the Commission d'Enquête of August 1, 1848. *Enquête*, I, 107-111. With slight modifications of detail and emphasis, his account is corroborated by Danduran, vice-president of the committee (letter to the editor, *Le Représentant du peuple*, May 30, 1848; testimony Danduran, Haute-Cour de Bourges [*Le Moniteur universel*, March 12, 1849, p. 843]; and testimony Danduran, Haute-Cour de Versailles [*Le Moniteur universel*, October 12, 1849, p. 3049]; and by Delbrouck, a member of the Comité Centralisateur's executive board (testimony Delbrouck, Haute-Cour de Versailles [*Le Moniteur universel*, October 13, 1849, p. 3064]).

tion. Though in the ensuing power struggle among the organizers the cautious leaders of the Centralizing Committee recaptured control of the Polish demonstration, its character had been irreversibly altered in the contest.

The parliamentary drama took place in two acts. During the morning session of May 10, prompted by Prussian armed intervention in Polish Posen, Representative Wolowski followed a reading of the latest plea from the embattled Poles with his own proposal for French action. A staid laissez-faire economist who had long been a naturalized French citizen, Wolowski was anything but a rabble-rouser. Indeed his recommendation—gentle pressure on Berlin and Frankfurt—was hardly breathtaking. Though his speech was politely applauded, parliament's more telling response was to put off debate on the Polish question (and other foreign policy matters) to Monday, May 15. A delay of five days at a time when Prussian regulars were rooting out the last remnants of Polish self-rule in Posen spoke for itself.[9]

The afternoon's second act, if less unexpected, was even more dramatic. Louis Blanc, who as former member of the Provisional Government had headed the Labor Commission at the Luxembourg, invited the National Assembly to create a Ministry of Progress, a somewhat symbolic demand widely regarded by the labor and club movements as a test of parliament's good faith. Blanc's proposal was literally hooted down in favor of an investigation "to find out if the poor were really poor," as one left-wing newspaper put it.[10] Timidity abroad and immobility at home seemed the order of the day.

[9] Cf. petition of Club des socialistes réunis, May 10, *La Commune de Paris*, May 13, 1848; for the speech and response, *Le Moniteur universel*, May 11, 1848, pp. 1005-1006.

[10] *Le Moniteur universel*, May 11, 1848, pp. 1007-1008, for Blanc's speech and the reaction to it. For detailed commentary, see Loubère, *Louis Blanc*, pp. 118-120.

The intensity of club reaction to Louis Blanc's debacle can hardly be exaggerated. Much in the manner of labor groups such as the ex-Luxembourg delegates and the Typographers' Council, the club response was immediate, aggrieved, and curiously personal, as though the integrity of Louis Blanc rather than the future organization of French society were the main issue. For example, the Club of Equality and Fraternity claimed to be "imbued with admiration for the devotion and civic spirit which you have evinced by accepting so difficult an assignment as the one confided to you by the revolutionary people on February 24. . . . Our club, which holds its sessions in one of the most populous and impoverished *faubourgs* of Paris, is made up of men destined to labor and to sacrifice. . . . As for ourselves, men of the *blouse* [the workingman's smock] and the hammer, we have wanted to tell our brother, the worker of intellect, that he has served his fatherland well."[11] The Democratic Central Committee of the Eleventh District (affiliated with the bourgeois Central Democratic Society) also assured Blanc that "he would not be abandoned by the people, no matter what the diatribes of his foes."[12] Other proclamations combined support for Blanc with a denunciation of the "renegade" worker Peupin, who had attacked Blanc's pro-

[11] The Conseil typographique in its announcement (B.N., Lb⁵⁴, 1943) had refused its participation in the festivities scheduled for May 14 (later postponed to May 21) on these among other grounds: "That our representatives received the proposals concerning the organization of labor in an almost mocking manner." The Luxembourg delegates (B.N., Lb⁵⁴, 1942) objected to "the reneging on the promises of February 25." Club de l'égalité et de la fraternité, session of May 11, *La vraie République*, May 13, 1848.

[12] Proclamation of Comité central démocratique du XIe arrondissement, May 11, 1848. Original is in Thoré-Bürger Papers, Bibliothèque de l'Arsenal, No. 7916 (ix); reprinted in *La vraie République*, May 13, 1848.

posals from the floor of the National Assembly. Though the cliché "traitor to his class" had yet to be coined, the sentiment behind it was fully mature.[13] As late as May 14, a Club of United Workers ended its session with cries of "Long live the organization of labor! Long live Louis Blanc!"[14] The Assembly's rebuff to Louis Blanc continued to reverberate.

In direct response to parliamentary inaction and insult, a group of revolutionaries around Joseph Sobrier, publisher of the club newspaper *La Commune de Paris*, made an attempt to take over the Polish demonstration and turn it into insurrectional channels. Sobrier's palace not only housed his newspaper and the offices of the Club of Clubs (in which he had played a major role until its dissolution) but was a general rendezvous for assorted clubists and revolutionaries. From a purely military viewpoint, Sobrier's headquarters had the only ammunition depot to which clubists had access.[15]

To what extent Sobrier himself was the brains behind the abortive "conspiracy" that began to unfold is unclear. The conclusion that there was some sort of plot in which at least his entourage was involved seems inescapable.

[13] Club de l'égalité et de la fraternité, session of May 11, *La vraie République*, May 13, 1848; Club des Droits de l'Homme et du Citoyen du XIIe arrondissement, *La vraie République*, May 15, 1848.

[14] Club des travailleurs unis, session of May 14 (police report), A.N., C. 933, CdE 1452; for Robert, see Wassermann, *Les clubs de Barbès et de Blanqui*, p. 12.

[15] For the ambiguous relationship of Sobrier's headquarters with the government and the police prefecture, see testimony of F. Arago, *Enquête*, I, 227, and that of Caussidière, ibid., 143-145. There were 400 rifles and 30,000 cartridges deposited at Sobrier's, though Caussidière claims to have removed both just before May 15—an unlikely story (A.N., C. 934, CdE 3010). In any event, on May 15, 78 men in police uniforms were arrested at the Sobrier palace.

The editorial policy of his newspaper provides the historian with the initial cue. From April 29 through May 10, *La Commune de Paris* was continually pleading for calm, for giving the Constituent Assembly its chance to deal with the pressing problems besetting French workers. On May 11 there was an abrupt change of tone: after reviewing both the Wolowski incident and the defeat of Blanc's Ministry of Progress, the editorial writer declared: "It is done. With sorrow but with conviction we must say that the time of vain hopes has passed. The day of dupes is at hand. Who knows? Will the hour of justice perhaps soon strike?" And the article concluded with the ringing slogan of the Lyon insurgents of 1834: "To live by working or to go down fighting!" While succeeding issues of the newspaper never called for immediate violence, they included directions for the home manufacture of gunpowder and clearly anticipated a rising in the very near future.[16]

Yet there is more direct evidence. A Dr. Royer, invited to the meetings of one of Sobrier's pet projects, his Agricultural Committee (which also met at the palace on the rue de Rivoli), became convinced that a coup was being hatched under cover of the Polish demonstration. Royer tried in vain to warn the government of this threat.[17] Nor is there any doubt that sometime between May 12 and 14, Seigneuret, one of Sobrier's journalistic associates, drafted a series of revolutionary decrees that presupposed

[16] *La Commune de Paris*, May 13, 1848.

[17] Testimony Royer, *Enquête*, I, 193-194. Between the time of his testimony before the Commission d'Enquête in July 1848 and his appearance at the trial of the alleged instigators of May 15 in March 1849, Royer had been won over to left-wing republicanism and tried to soft-pedal his original charges. But Interior Minister Recurt's testimony bears out Royer's original statement. *Les accusés du 15 mai devant la Haute-Cour de Bourges* (Paris, 1869), pp. 233-234.

a Committee of Public Safety founded in the wake of a popular demonstration.[18]

The group's first move seems to have been to announce the Polish demonstration for Saturday, May 13, in posters and newspapers on the eleventh.[19] More significant was an invitation to a preparatory meeting to be held on May 12 at Dourlans, a garden restaurant just beyond the toll barrier near the Etoile. The announcement restricted the meeting to club officers and delegates and —a new note—to men who had commanded barricades during the February Days. Of the nine signatures, Sobrier's was the only well-known name.[20]

[18] It is conceivable that Seigneuret (whose draft decrees can be dated because they take the National Assembly's new rules on petitions passed on May 12 into consideration) drew up his decrees, as he was to claim, without the knowledge of Sobrier. By May 14 the latter seems to have abandoned the project of an armed demonstration. For the decrees (one is missing), see *Enquête*, ii, 268-271; for Seigneuret's justification, see Haute-Cour de Bourges (*Le Moniteur universel*, March 25, 1849, p. 1031).

[19] The only evidence linking this announcement with Sobrier is little better than hearsay. The club policeman Carlier assumed that Sobrier was its sponsor. Police report, May 12, *Enquête*, ii, 222. Indeed, it may be significant that the announcement did appear one day earlier in Sobrier's newspaper than elsewhere. For the text, see *La Commune de Paris*, May 12, 1848; *La Réforme*, May 13, 1848.

[20] The text of the placard is in *Affiches rouges* (Paris, 1851), pp. 172-173. At his trial, Sobrier claimed he had not drawn up or signed the summons to the Dourlans meeting, yet a draft of it (though not in Sobrier's handwriting) was found in the offices of *La Commune de Paris* on the evening of May 15. Haute-Cour de Bourges, *Le Moniteur universel*, March 12, 1849, p. 823. Save for Sobrier, I can tentatively identify only one of the remaining eight, who seems to have been a member of the Société républicaine de Chaillot. Huber claims to have recognized the names of all but one of the signatories. Haute-Cour de Versailles, *Le Moniteur universel*, October 11, 1849, p. 3044.

Huber's own detailed account of the Dourlans meeting of May 12 is largely corroborated by other eyewitnesses.[21] Until he happened to see a poster on a city wall on the afternoon of the twelfth, Huber claims to have been unaware of the announced meeting. Puzzled, he hurried out to Dourlans in company with a colleague from the Centralizing Committee to find five hundred or six hundred men in animated discussion in the garden restaurant. Huber, something of a celebrity in revolutionary circles, was recognized and invited to chair the meeting, which was debating the Polish demonstration. He was shocked to find that a majority of the speakers agreed on an armed showdown, although they continued arguing about details. Huber, on the contrary, abandoned the chair to insist that the demonstration be unarmed and peaceful and that it halt on the Place de la Révolution across the Seine from the National Assembly's palace. He also advocated postponing the demonstration from May 13 to May 15 so that all clubs could be informed of the decisions taken and public opinion be reassured. Huber's speech ended in a shouting match between his supporters and opponents until he finally stalked out in a rage after announcing that he was through presiding over a bunch of raving lunatics. Huber's exit seems to have had a sobering effect, for a motion of postponement to the fifteenth actually passed, though Huber had no way of knowing this.[22] Upon his return to the Centralizing Committee, its executive immediately drew up a procla-

[21] For Huber's own account, see Haute-Cour de Versailles (*Le Moniteur universel*, October 11, 1849, p. 3044). For other testimony on the Dourlans meeting given at the same trial, see testimonies Dagneaux, Moulin, Stévenot, Maurice, Delbrouck (ibid., pp. 3060, 3061, 3064). Huber probably exaggerated his own isolation, but it is clear that there was strong sentiment for decisive action.

[22] Testimony Dagneaux, Haute-Cour de Bourges, *Le Moniteur universel*, March 12, 1849, pp. 822-823.

mation announcing the date of the Polish demonstration as Monday morning, May 15, and calling on all democrats to ignore any other summons.[23]

Huber's intervention may have forestalled open insurrection, but it was only half successful in preventing a demonstration in behalf of Poland on May 13. Apparently neither the postponement voted by the Dourlans meeting nor the Centralizing Committee's announcement had deterred a few thousand demonstrators. They gathered around a nucleus of several hundred club delegates beefed up by delegations from the organized trades, the Ecole Polytechnique, and the National Guard, who came uniformed but unarmed.[24]

Despite its modest dimensions and inoffensive character, the demonstration taught some instructive lessons. In the first place, May 13 showed how difficult it was to maintain discipline even among a few thousand demonstrators in the face of an aggressive National Guard. Originally, the marchers had planned to halt at the Madeleine, half a mile short of the National Assembly. Yet when the first and second legions—the most conservative in Paris—were called out against them, the demonstrators resumed their march on the Assembly amidst violent altercations, stopping only at the bridge facing the Palais Bourbon. In the second place, good timing played a vital role in keeping the demonstration within bounds. The bridge might have been forced if the crowd had been larger and if a delegation had not been promptly received by a deputy known for his Polish sympathies.[25] In the

[23] Testimony Dagneaux (ibid.) mentions this decision.

[24] Estimates of the May 13 demonstration crowd run from a low of 3,000-4,000 men (report by Carlier, A.N., C. 932A, CdE 1458) to a high of 5,000-6,000 (*La vraie République*, May 14, 1848).

[25] Contemporary newspaper accounts of the march disagree on whether the bulk of the demonstrators halted at the Madeleine or whether they proceeded to the bridge facing the Na-

third place, by demonstrating once again its indifference to the fate of Poland as well as its hostility to popular pressure, the Assembly virtually insured that May 15 would be more than a harmless gesture. When Representative Vavin attempted to read the demonstrators' petition on the floor of the Chamber, he was shouted down as out of order.[26] As the head of the government's undercover police noted with satisfaction, May 13 had been a complete failure.[27]

During the last phase of the preparations from May 13 on, Huber and his committee were in uneasy control of an enterprise that now evoked increasing misgivings. Having been unable to stem the momentum of the demonstration, the Centralizing Committee set out to counteract its more obvious dangers.

On the afternoon of May 13, Huber consummated his victory over the militants at the Centralizing Committee's meeting with delegates from numerous revolutionary clubs. The shrinking minority that still proposed an armed demonstration "to avoid being flattened by the bourgeois" (a statement that set off another cane-smashing rage on Huber's part) was defeated by a lopsided margin.[28] At this same gathering the practical details of

tional Assembly building. Cf. *La vraie République*, May 14, 1848; *La Réforme*, May 14, 1848; *Le Représentant du peuple*, May 14, 1848. In opting for the last version, I consider decisive the testimony of the police inspector who received the demonstrators on the bridge. Testimony Doussat, Haute-Cour de Bourges, *Le Moniteur universel*, March 12, 1849, p. 824.

[26] *Le Moniteur universel*, May 14, 1848, p. 1034.

[27] Police report for May 13, A.N., C. 932A, CdE 1458.

[28] Testimony Danduran, Haute-Cour de Bourges, *Le Moniteur universel*, March 13, 1849, p. 823; ibid., October 12, 1849, p. 3057; letter to the editor, *Le Représentant du peuple*, May 30, 1848; testimony Huber, Haute-Cour de Versailles, *Le Moniteur universel*, October 11, 1849, p. 3044; testimony Thomas, ibid., p. 3064.

the march seem to have been hammered out: the column, as Huber had first suggested at Dourlans the day before, would halt at the obelisk in the center of the Place de la Révolution and make this its nearest approach to the National Assembly. Only Huber and five delegates would then cross the Pont de la Révolution to present their petition to the Assembly.[29] The moderates had seemingly won their battle for control of the demonstration.

If so, it was an ambiguous victory. What the Centralizing Committee had really done was to persuade club delegates to take part in an unarmed demonstration that would remain peaceful provided—and this was a crucial proviso—the demonstrators were not attacked. If they were attacked, they would rush to take up arms and the battle would be joined. The key question therefore was what would determine the *casus belli civilis*. After what had happened in Rouen two weeks earlier, tens of thousands of demonstrators would scarcely wait till they were fired upon before deciding that they were indeed the victims of aggression. For most of the participants, as Huber and his friends knew, "aggression" would be equated with the *rappel*, the drumming of the National Guard to arms. Yet this itself was unclear: would a localized *rappel* in one or two *arrondissements* (such as had taken place on May 13) set off the critical reaction? Or would the demonstrators await the sinister roll of drums announcing *la générale*, the emergency alarm that called the entire National Guard of Paris to arms?

The organizers of the demonstration were not blind to the possibility of a clash, even though they apparently never worked out a coherent battle plan. On the eve of the demonstration, members of the Alsatian Club (of which Huber was honorary president) were reminded

[29] Testimony Huber, Haute-Cour de Versailles, *Le Moniteur universel*, October 11, 1849; Danduran, letter to the editor, *Le Représentant du peuple*, May 30, 1848.

that both rifles and ammunition were available at Sobrier's in case of need.[30] There is some testimony that the
Society of the Rights of Man was engaged in casting bullets on the days before the demonstration.[31] In any event,
members were instructed to join the demonstration as individuals. They were told that if some unexpected incident triggered a struggle, they were to go home, arm
themselves, and await orders.[32] There is also evidence
that the Centralizing Committee itself was in touch with
Girard, the commander of the Garde républicaine's artillery at the Hôtel-de-Ville. In response to Girard, who had
offered to march on the Assembly with his cannon in case
of a showdown, the vice-president of the Centralizing
Committee wrote: "The Centralizing Committee is aware
of your patriotism and knows that you will be ready for
any eventuality. If Monday we should respond to the attacks of the reactionaries, all patriots will do their
duty."[33]

Yet given the arrangements made for the demonstration, "patriots" would be hard pressed "to do their duty"
very effectively. Sobrier's palace, though within easy distance of the Place de la Révolution, contained only a few
hundred rifles and limited stocks of ammunition. In any
serious emergency, most of the demonstrators would
have to scurry back through a hostile, mobilized Paris to
their own neighborhoods (chiefly in the eastern half of
the capital) to pick up their rifles at their own homes;

[30] *Enquête*, II, 228.   [31] Ibid., pp. 85-93.
[32] Police report signed Carteret, A.N., C. 932A, CdE 1446.
[33] Though Girard's original letter was not offered in evidence, Danduran's reply was. It may be worth noting that
the latter claimed that Girard had addressed his offer to
Sobrier and that he, Danduran, had only answered in Sobrier's
absence. This episode may therefore have been connected to
the earlier Dourlans "conspiracy." Testimony Danduran, Haute-
Cour de Bourges, *Le Moniteur universel*, March 12, 1849,
p. 823; *Les accusés*, p. 67.

and unless they raided the district armories, they would still lack cartridges. No wonder that just before the demonstration the club leaders, Armand Barbès and Auguste Blanqui, usually bitterly antagonistic to each other, concurred in deploring the march, while even Sobrier was reported to be profoundly depressed.[34] The same mood gripped Huber's friends, who pressed him to appeal directly to the mayor of Paris on Sunday morning, May 14. "For God's sake, Citizen Marrast," Huber wrote, "for the sake of the Republic's salvation, do not misconstrue the aims of the citizens who will assemble on the Place de la Bastille tomorrow."

Above all do not beat the call to arms. Everything would be lost. There would be a terrible, perhaps a bloody, collision and, whatever the final outcome, the cause of the Republic would be compromised. . . . If . . . by means of a show of force by the National Guard, the government were to challenge our right of petition, then, despite my efforts, I would be powerless to control the indignation. An inevitable struggle would ensue and a horrible butchery like in Rouen.

Let us avoid this, citizen, I beg of you. . . . Instead of ordering the drums to beat the *rappel*, reassure, enlighten the National Guard and permit us to exercise freely and in peace a right which you have often seen the English people enjoy.[35]

[34] For Barbès, testimony E. Arago, Haute-Cour de Bourges (*Le Moniteur universel*, October 14, 1849, p. 846); testimony Detours (ibid., October 18, 1849, p. 907); police report on the Club de la révolution, May 14, A.N., C. 933, CdE 1450). For Blanqui, testimony Blanqui, Haute-Cour de Bourges (*Le Moniteur universel*, March 15, 1849, p. 849); testimony Trinité and Bertrand (ibid., March 16, 1849, p. 872); testimony Fomberteaux, Legré, Quentin, Frichot, Pireault, Lehsner, Lachambeaudie (ibid., March 24, 1849, p. 1009). For Sobrier's disposition, the testimony of L. Gallois (ibid., March 25, 1849, p. 1031); testimony Boyer (*Les accusés*, p. 179, which is more complete than that in *Le Moniteur*).

[35] Since Huber's letter is central to my interpretation both of the demonstrators' own attitudes and plans and the government's countermeasures, it is unfortunate that we have its text

Huber's keen awareness of the demonstration's explosive potential accounts for his reiterated misgivings about the whole affair. On the very eve of the demonstration he told the Centralizing Committee of his conviction that the National Guard—that is, the old-line bourgeois Guard that had never been reconciled to the Republic— was only waiting for its chance to pounce on the revolu-

---

(in fact, only a draft) from Huber himself, who was hardly a disinterested party. Haute-Cour de Versailles, *Le Moniteur universel*, October 11, 1849, p. 3044. Yet Marrast in his testimony before the Haute-Cour de Bourges not only acknowledged receiving a letter from Huber on May 14 but paraphrased its contents as "he let me know about the march and requested me not to beat the *rappel*. 'If that's how it goes,' he said, 'I give you my word of honor that the demonstration will be peaceful. If we encounter bayonets, the torrent will carry all before it.' " *Le Moniteur universel*, March 22, 1849, p. 963. Marrast's deputy, A.-E. Adam, also testified to the existence of Huber's letter, though he was vague in his recollections, first (wrongly) attributing it to Barbès, who disclaimed it. *Le Moniteur universel*, March 14, 1849, p. 847. Huber claimed to have sent a copy of his letter to Marrast to A. Recurt, who, as Minister of the Interior, was the (nominal) superior of the mayor of Paris. In his testimony before the Haute-Cour de Bourges, Recurt speaks of police reports on the evening of the fourteenth assuring him that the demonstration would be peaceful, and he does not mention Huber's letter; but then Recurt was not questioned on this point. Recurt explained the government's reluctance to beat the *rappel* as response to complaints that daily alerts were bad for business. *Le Moniteur universel*, March 22, 1849, pp. 968-969. L.-A. Garnier-Pagès accepted the authenticity of the text of the letter Huber had read at his trial. Garnier-Pagès, *Histoire de la révolution*, IX, 111-113.

The letter to Marrast and Recurt jibes with another letter that Huber had written to Barbès, president of the Club de la révolution and one of the luminaries of the Left, at about the same time. It indicates Huber's hesitations about holding the demonstration and reflects his attempts to keep it peaceful. Summation by the presiding judge, Haute-Cour de Versailles, *Le Moniteur universel*, October 13, 1849, p. 3082.

tionary republicans. "If we were sure to bring together
two hundred thousand men, well, then I wouldn't hesitate," Huber confessed publicly.[36] At the close of the
meeting on the evening of May 14, Huber made a last
peace gesture that had been suggested from the floor. The
president of the Centralizing Committee drew up a proclamation denying false rumors about "the anarchical and
malevolent intentions of the petitioners," which he submitted to the editor of *La Réforme* for insertion in the
morning edition.[37]

iii

A well-informed and moderately perceptive observer of
the club movement could have predicted disaster for the
demonstration of May 15: its organizers had not left the
slightest margin for error. *If* the marchers came unarmed
as planned, *if* they remained disciplined, *if* they halted
short of the National Assembly, *if* the National Guard
behaved with utmost tact, *if* there was no drumming to
arms, *if* the authorities effectively blocked the bridge
from the Place de la Révolution to the Palais Bourbon,
then all would go well. What actually occurred on May
15 was a combination that neither the demonstration's

[36] Anonymous police report on the Comité centralisateur,
session of May 14. A.N., C. 933, CdE 1453.

[37] *La Réforme*, May 15, 1848; testimony Huber, Haute-
Cour de Versailles, *Le Moniteur universel*, October 11, 1849,
p. 3045. In his testimony Huber claims that until May 13 he
was still hoping that the announced national festival (scheduled for May 14) would turn into a spontaneous demonstration
for Poland and make the demonstration of May 15 superfluous.
The postponement of the festivities left hundreds of provincial
delegates stranded. They were in fact actively wooed by organizers of the Polish demonstration. Police report, May 14,
A.N., C. 932A, CdE 1443. See also L. Lévy-Schneider, "Les
préliminaires du 15 mai 1848," *La révolution de 1848*, vii,
219-232.

organizers nor the authorities had foreseen. An unarmed crowd, after dissolving the Constituent Assembly, set up a short-lived revolutionary government without recourse to arms.

The first official reaction to rumors of an impending demonstration in behalf of Poland came from Philippe Buchez, former assistant mayor of Paris, former Christian-Socialist sage, and the recently installed chairman of the Constituent Assembly. Buchez, apparently acting on erroneous police reports of a pro-Polish demonstration planned for May 9, wrote to Caussidière, the police prefect, demanding that the demonstration be prevented.[38] At the same time, Buchez used his authority to mobilize part of the National Guard's Eleventh Legion to defend the National Assembly against the threatened demonstration. This order caused something of a panic: the officers of the alerted legion were so convinced that the Constituent Assembly was in mortal danger that they refused their colonel's order to disband after waiting all day for nonexistent demonstrators.[39] Buchez' false alarm, by discrediting official security measures and by demoralizing National Guards called up unnecessarily, may have helped set the scene for the debacle of May 15.

Caussidière, in the meantime, answered Buchez on May 9, explaining that he did not want to issue an official proclamation discouraging a demonstration, on the grounds that this would merely provide free publicity for the organizers. By "bringing to bear on people's minds an influence which is no less effective for being indirect,"

[38] Buchez' demand is reconstructed from Caussidière's responding letter, which survived and was printed in *Enquête*, I, 165. The incident was never brought up at either trial of the accused of May 15 and was not elucidated by the Commission d'Enquête.

[39] Open letter from the Comité central du XIe arrondissement, *Le Courrier français*, May 11, 1848.

he promised to forestall any march on the Assembly.[40] Exactly what Caussidière meant by this cryptic assurance is not clear, save that official proclamations had failed to quiet the earlier agitation over the Rouen "massacre." Whether a private appeal to club leaders, with most of whom the police prefect was on good terms, would be more effective was an open question. Yet Caussidière, the only socialist still clinging to power since the National Assembly had convened, was in a highly vulnerable position if police measures failed to stop the proposed Polish demonstration. Though direct evidence is lacking, it is possible that the police prefect spread the rumor that the Polish demonstration was a trap set by Marrast, the mayor of Paris. Marrast's role in opposing any concessions to socialist and neo-Jacobin elements was suspected or known, making a charge of provocation plausible.[41] In any event, whatever their origins, rumors that the mayor's fine hand was stirring the Polish agitation may account for the reluctance of most major club leaders to welcome the proposed demonstration.

Marrast's actual policy toward clubs and club leaders seems to have been more cautious. At the center of the municipal patronage machine, Marrast controlled not only relief, city jobs, and considerable discretionary funds but had recently brought a reorganized Commission of

[40] *Enquête*, I, 165.

[41] For echoes of such rumors, see testimony Huber, Haute-Cour de Versailles, *Le Moniteur universel*, October 12, 1849, p. 3044; testimony Raspail, Haute-Cour de Bourges, *Les accusés*, p. 49. Despite the fact that Caussidière's letter to Buchez was printed, the police prefect is silent on his exchange with Buchez on and about May 9 in his memoirs. For a specific mention of the feared coup, see Club des hommes libres, session of May 14 (unsigned police report), A.N., C. 933, CdE 1451. For a reconstruction of Marrast's role in the closing days of the Provisional Government, see Fasel, "The French Moderate Republicans, 1837-1848," pp. 318-321.

National Rewards under his wing. The commission, set up under the worker Albert to dole out compensation to old-line republicans victimized by the July Monarchy, was reconstituted into two sections in early May, headed by Joseph Guinard, a neo-Jacobin, and Chilmann, a socialist friend of Barbès—under the supervision of the mayor's office.[42] From this power base the mayor of Paris pursued a cagey two-pronged policy of wooing and taming receptive club leaders, while preparing to undercut popular societies by withdrawing privileges upon which they depended.

Direct evidence links several of the former leaders of the Club of Clubs to Marrast, apparently shortly after the Club of Clubs was dissolved. "My dear Longepied," Laugier wrote to his colleague, "Deplanque, Gadon and I have spoken to Marrast. Go see him. It must not happen that a fatal error should deprive you of a position to which your old-line patriotism entitles you, for we have been very satisfied with the answer that he has given to those of your comrades who continue to be your friends."[43] We have no evidence that Longepied followed the advice. We do know that he continued to associate with these same "comrades" and that, just before May 15, they sought to launch a new—and avowedly moderate—superclub together, the Society of the Friends of the Republic.[44] So much for the carrot.

The mayor also prepared to prod popular societies meeting in public buildings. Clubs, though tolerated, had

[42] *Le Moniteur universel*, May 3, 1848, p. 931. Under Albert's chairmanship the Commission had fallen hopelessly behind in its work of processing applications. The reorganization was completed between May 5 and 7. *Enquête*, II, 63; testimony Moulin, Chilmann, Haute-Cour de Versailles, *Le Moniteur universel*, October 12, 1849, pp. 3060-3061.

[43] Laugier to Longepied, no date (late April, early May 1848), A.N., C. 942, CdE 9078.

[44] Longepied and Laugier, *Comité révolutionnaire*, p. 131.

no legal right to such premises. Marrast began his campaign by requesting his district mayors to check the authorizations of all clubs using public facilities.[45] Presumably armed with the responses, Marrast's ally and nominal superior, Minister of the Interior Recurt, gained the Executive Commission's consent on May 14 to oust all clubs from municipal and state-owned buildings.[46] Though the decision was made in secret, it immediately leaked to the left-wing press.[47] Had the *journée* of May 15 never occurred, Marrast might well have succeeded in neutralizing the revolutionary club movement without a head-on clash.

What then becomes of the charge that the authorities deliberately invited the invasion of the National Assembly in order to trap and destroy the demonstrators? Marrast and Recurt, who jointly have been credited with such a coup, lacked sufficient control over official preparations to engineer so delicate an operation: in the emergency created by the impending Polish demonstration, mayor and Minister of the Interior were superseded by the Executive Commission acting in a body.[48] Whether a

[45] The evidence I found related only to the first district (I was unable to locate the corresponding files for other *arrondissements*), and I cannot prove that the inquiry was initiated by Marrast, though it is extremely likely. A.S., V3D⁶-23, No. 14. That this was not yet general government policy is demonstrated through the actions of Marie, Minister of Public Works under the Provisional Government, then member of the Commission du Pouvoir exécutif, who, despite his personal distaste for popular societies, was still making public buildings available to them. See testimony Gayot de Montfleury, *Enquête*, I, 257; and "Les papiers de Marie," *La révolution de 1848*, I (1904-1905), 155-156.

[46] Garnier-Pagès, *Histoire de la révolution*, IX, 125.

[47] *La Commune de Paris*, March 14, 1848, under "faits divers."

[48] For the case for Marrast and Recurt as the puppeteers staging the *journée* of May 15, cf. Henri Guillemin, *La tragédie de quarante-huit* (Geneva, 1948), pp. 231-257, which

government as divided and hesitant as that five-man directory would have been capable of devising and carrying out such a Machiavellian stratagem is dubious. That the political risks would have been enormous is not. Created by the National Assembly, the Executive Commission and its appointees were at its mercy. To stake out that Assembly as goat for the revolutionary tiger—by permitting an invasion of the parliamentary chamber in order to snare the invaders—would have been a suicidal gesture for the executive. Whether it was in fact the result of a ruse, of negligence, or of error, May 15 was almost as disastrous for the government as it was for the clubs. The effect on the clubs, whose leaders went to prison, was visible and immediate. The effect on the Executive Commission was screened by delay. Yet as soon as another political emergency arose—the June Days—the National Assembly hastened to exchange a discredited executive for General Cavaignac's dictatorship.

Practical politics therefore circumscribed the government's response to the Polish demonstration. In essence the Executive Commission could try to prevent the march, to crush it militarily, or to permit the demonstration to proceed amidst adequate security precautions. As to the first of these options, in May 1848 no one could ignore that a regime had recently been overthrown after prohibiting the gathering of an opposition. The Executive Commission flirted only very briefly with the idea of outlawing the Polish demonstration, by issuing sweeping but unenforceable orders to arrest major club leaders on the morning of May 15.[49] The second option—to let the

---

is brilliant but tendentious, and Fasel, "The French Moderate Republicans, 1837-1848," pp. 327-346, which is plausible but overlooks some crucial details.

[49] The minutes of the Commission exécutive, session of May 15 at 8:00 A.M., reveal that after receiving reports on the state of preparedness and the latest news it "ordered the Min-

march proceed in order to smother it with the Paris National Guard—would have amounted to a declaration of civil war, as Huber's letter to Marrast had made clear. From what evidence we have, among responsible officials only Carlier, the head of the undercover police, favored "a clash begun as a result of a vigorous act by the authorities." But Carlier, a holdover from the July Monarchy, was distrusted by his superiors as politically unreliable and morally suspect.[50] The government in fact concentrated its efforts on the third alternative: to permit the demonstration while insuring the security of the National Assembly. The practical failure of this effort was to shape the *journée* of May 15.

On the eve of the demonstration, the government made its final plans for the morrow. During the afternoon of May 14, the Executive Commission met with high

---

ister of the Interior and the police prefect to arrest those clubists best known for their extremism who have figured in recent agitation." *Procès-verbaux du gouvernement provisoire et de la commission exécutive* (Paris, 1950), p. 259. It is not surprising that neither the Minister of the Interior (who was a moderate republican) nor the police prefect (who was or had been close to such club leaders as Barbès and Sobrier) was willing to execute so vague an order. For details, see testimony Monnier (secretary at the police prefecture) and Recurt, Haute-Cour de Bourges, *Le Moniteur universel*, March 25, 1849, p. 1032; Caussidière, *Mémoires*, II, 122-123.

The government's objectives in issuing such an order remain obscure. Garnier-Pagès, who attended the meeting and who has otherwise narrated the events of May 15 in detail, omits the order, though he includes the minutes of May 15 in an appendix. Garnier-Pagès, *Histoire de la révolution*, IX, 145-147.

[50] "Opinion intime du comité Blanqui sur la situation actuelle," May 14, A.N., C. 933, CdE 1447. For an assessment of Carlier by an unnamed superior (Carteret, undersecretary of the Ministry of the Interior?), dated July 4, 1848, see A.N., C. 934, CdE 2754.

civilian officials and military commanders to resolve three problems. First, General Courtais, who headed the Paris National Guard, was made temporary supreme commander to create a unified military command. Second, to avoid both panic and provocation, one thousand men

5. Route of the demonstration of May 15, 1848

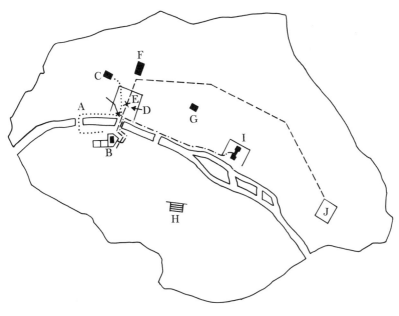

————— Demonstrators' March on the National Assembly
·········· Route of the First Legion "Relief Column"
—·—·—·— Insurgents' March on the Hôtel-de-Ville

A. Bridge of the Invalides; B. Palais Bourbon, seat of the National Assembly; C. Municipal building of the first *arrondissement*: D. Obelisk; E. Place de la Révolution (formerly: de la Concorde); F. Church of the Madeleine; G. Sobrier's headquarters, rue de Rivoli; H. Palais du Luxembourg, seat of the Executive Commission; I. Paris City Hall (Hôtel-de-Ville); J. Place de la Bastille; K. Bridge of the Revolution (formerly: de la Concorde).

from each of the twelve National Guard legions were quietly mobilized for service on the fifteenth. Finally, the Constituent Assembly was to be safeguarded by the blocking of bridges from the Right Bank, where the Centralizing Committee had scheduled the march from the Bastille to the Place de la Révolution by way of the boulevards, to the Left Bank, where the Palais Bourbon housing the Assembly was located. The key to the government's military plan was the blocking of a key bridge, the Pont de la Révolution (which faced the Assembly) by a force of five thousand men (later raised to six thousand).[51] During the evening of May 14, General Courtais called the colonels of the National Guard to a meeting at which these high-level decisions were translated into specific orders to each legion.[52]

The events of May 15 were to reveal a shocking gap between plan and execution. The marchers had started out from the Place de la Bastille about 11:00 A.M.[53] Not

[51] For the details of the preparations on the part of the government, see "Rapport de la commission exécutive à l'assemblée nationale," *Le Moniteur universel*, May 31, 1848, pp. 1211-1212. In fact, the planning had not been so clear-cut, since the minutes of the Commission du Pouvoir exécutif on May 14 indicate only the disposition of the National Guard units. *Procès-verbaux*, p. 257, only ordered the commander of the Garde mobile to send four battalions "dans le voisinage de l'assemblée."

[52] "Rapport de la commission exécutive à l'assemblée nationale," *Le Moniteur universel*, May 31, 1848, p. 1212. Most of the legion commanders testified at the Haute-Cour de Bourges (testimony Yautier, Courtais, Hingray, Ramond de la Croisette, de Tracy, Bourdon, Guinard, in *Les accusés*, pp. 115, 343, 245-249, 228-229, 230-231, 259-262).

[53] The progress of the demonstration may be traced in the following police reports: unsigned, May 15, 10:30 A.M. (*Enquête*, ii, 225-226); unsigned, 11:00 A.M. (A.N., C. 933, CdE 1464, 1465); signed Carlier, May 15, 11:45 A.M. (A.N., C. 933, CdE 1467); signed Aulin (A.N., C. 932A, CdE 1470); signed Carlier, May 15, noon (A.N., C. 933, CdE 1468); unsigned, May 15, noon (A.N., C. 933, CdE 1469).

until shortly before noon did General Courtais find out that, despite his supposed supreme command, the Garde mobile units assigned to the protection of the National Assembly paid no attention to his orders. Courtais also discovered that the mobilization of the National Guard was vitiated by absenteeism: some guards had failed to show up altogether; others had drifted off to lunch.[54] But most shattering was Courtais' discovery that the strategic bridge was occupied by a mere five hundred men instead of the called-for six thousand.[55] Three of the four battalions of the Garde mobile had been withdrawn to the Left Bank.[56] One battalion of the Fourth Legion, though stationed on the bridge, comprised a mere one hundred men instead of one thousand as planned.[57] A contingent

[54] The Commission du Pouvoir exécutif was later to claim that the requisite number of National Guards had indeed reported for service. *Le Moniteur universel*, May 31, 1848, p. 1211. While this may be true for some of the legions, we have the word of the commander of the battalion of the Fourth Legion that only 300 men had shown up for service. Testimony Clouvez, *Les accusés*, p. 236.

[55] Testimony Clouvez, Courtais, Fraix, Chevalier, Haute-Cour de Bourges, *Le Moniteur universel*, March 22, 1849 p. 969. The testimony of the lieutenant commander, Reverdy, of the Fourth Legion battalion indicates that several hundred Gardes mobiles were stationed at the bridge when the demonstrators approached. Testimony Reverdy, ibid., p. 966.

[56] General Tempoure, who attended the war council of May 14 and commanded the Garde mobile, did not reach the scene before the demonstration got out of hand. Testimony Tempoure, Haute-Cour de Bourges, *Le Moniteur universel*, March 14, 1849, p. 846; testimony Courtais, ibid., March 22, 1849, p. 869.

[57] The move of the battalion of the Fourth Legion to a station on the bridge represented a last-minute change of plans. Of about 300 men who had reported for service, two-thirds had been permitted to leave for lunch. Since the order to change stations arrived during their absence, they presumably did not know where to rejoin their unit. Testimony Clouvez, Haute-Cour de Bourges, ibid., p. 969; *Les accusés*, p. 236. Testimony

from the First Legion, also assigned to the blocking force, was nowhere to be seen. The government's security measures had collapsed at the moment when the roar of the demonstrators approaching the Madeleine could be heard in the distance.

Courtais' last-moment attempts to redress the situation had exactly the opposite effect. An adjutant found the missing unit waiting for written orders at the municipality of the first *arrondissement*, just off the rue du Faubourg Saint-Honoré, half a mile from the National Assembly palace.[58] Belatedly, the battalion set off in that direction. In the meantime General Courtais had disoriented the few troops on the bridge by ordering them to stand aside to permit the passage of some carts. It was at this moment, just as the immense column of demonstrators was drawing to a halt at the obelisk in the center of the Place de la Révolution, that the battalion of the First Legion irrupted into the square from a parallel street. Finding themselves on the flank of the demonstration, the National Guards, on the double, headed diagonally for the

Reverdy, *Le Moniteur universel*, March 22, 1849, p. 966. Clouvez and Reverdy were the commander and lieutenant commander of the battalion in question.

[58] The explanation of the absence of the battalion of the First Legion from its assigned station on the bridge hinges on a misunderstanding. The colonel of the First Legion claimed that he had waited for written orders to confirm the oral orders of the day before. For the tedious controversy over whether the oral orders were binding or not, see testimony Courtais, Saisset, Hingray, Ramond de la Croisette, de Tracy, Bourdon, Guinard (all commanding officers in the National Guard). *Les accusés*, pp. 343, 245-249, 228-229, 230-231, 259-262. My conclusion is that the oral orders were probably binding. Yet there is little doubt that the officers of the First Legion were genuinely convinced that they were to await written orders. Testimony Fitz-James, *Le Moniteur universel*, March 23, 1849, p. 988.

bridge to cut them off.[59] At the sight of the running troops, the marchers surged forward in a race for the undermanned Pont de la Révolution. The momentum of forty thousand men carried them across, where this human flood eddied and swirled around the Palais Bourbon until the gates yielded. The crowd lapped into the inner courtyards and into the Assembly Chamber itself. Though happenstance had served as catalyst, the inadequacy of the government's security arrangements had allowed the National Assembly to be invaded.[60]

iv

There is no need to retell the story of the violation of the National Assembly on May 15, 1848. Observers agree

[59] Given the chaotic situation, there is considerable agreement among witnesses that the column had halted and that it surged forward at the sight of the running National Guards. Testimony Huber, Danduran, Delbrouck, Hahn, Haute-Cour de Versailles, *Le Moniteur universel*, October 11, 12, 1849, pp. 3046, 3957, 3064; also Danduran, letter to the editor, *Le Représentant du peuple*, May 30, 1848. Indirectly this is confirmed by the lieutenant commander of the National Guard unit involved. Testimony Bourcard, Haute-Cour de Bourges, *Le Moniteur universel*, March 22, 1849, p. 966. On the other hand, it is easy to overestimate the discipline and cohesion of a large demonstration. I have come across a letter from a demonstrator, a member of the Club démocratique des Quinze-Vingt, who obviously had never heard of the planned halt on the Place de la Révolution. A.M.G., A. 1887, Dossier Camille Chellier; for Raspail's paranoid interpretation, see *Les accusés*, p. 326.

[60] It may be argued that even after the crossing of the bridge timely and intelligent action by the authorities might have prevented the violation of the National Assembly. At best it is a moot point. For some lost "opportunities," see testimony Huber, Haute-Cour de Versailles, *Le Moniteur universel*, October 11, 1849, p. 3046; testimony Delbrouck, Hahn, ibid., October 12, 1849, p. 3064; testimony Lemansois-Duprez, ibid., p. 3058.

on the essentials: that after having (illegally) read their petition in support of Poland from the floor of the Chamber, the leaders of the demonstration proved unable to persuade the tumultuous crowd to withdraw. Speeches were drowned out by the general hubbub. Leaders no longer led. The popular tide that had overwhelmed the National Assembly would not ebb.

Yet when Huber pushed his way to the rostrum hours later to bellow that the National Assembly was dissolved "in the name of the people betrayed by its representatives," an unruly demonstration abruptly turned into a journée.[61] Was this the move of an *agent provocateur*, the act of someone mentally deranged, or should one look elsewhere for some other, more tenable, explanation of this twist?

There is no evidence to support the charge that Huber was a government undercover agent or that he was anything other than he seemed.[62] The problem of his mental balance is less clear-cut: while he had never been afflicted with any obvious mental illness, Huber was a highly excitable type, a hothead with a record of impulsive behavior and ungovernable rages.[63] Certainly the overheated atmosphere—literally and figuratively—in the invaded Chamber was hardly conducive to reflection. Temperamentally, Huber was the wrong leader in the wrong place.

Yet the dissolution of the National Assembly cannot

[61] *Le Moniteur universel*, May 17, 1848, supplement, p. iv.

[62] I have examined the problem of Huber's background and good faith, probably at greater length than it deserves, in "The Huber Enigma," 190-203.

[63] To be specific, there are eyewitness accounts of what can only be called "tantrums" for May 12 (at the Dourlans meeting), May 13 (at the meeting of the Comité centralisateur), and May 15 (when Huber discovered that the demonstrators had forgotten their petition after the march had begun). A similar pattern of behavior is revealed at Huber's political trials in 1836 and 1838.

be written off merely as the erratic gesture of an impulsive individual. Huber's act sprang from the logic of the events themselves and of the Centralizing Committee's confused contingency planning. Around four o'clock on May 15, Huber, having joined one of the many unsuccessful attempts to clear the hall, was overcome by fatigue and hunger.[64] For about half an hour he remained unconscious in the antechamber. As soon as he recovered, his first concern was to learn whether P.-J. Buchez, the president of the National Assembly, had countermanded an earlier order calling the National Guard to arms. Huber was assured that the order had been rescinded.[65] Yet about this time the drumming of the *rappel* could be heard above the general din. Apparently even before Huber's dissolution of the Assembly the British ambassador had overheard orders for the occupation of the Chamber given to a band of demonstrators "with the intimation that too much time had already been lost, that they must finish at once."[66] This account corroborates Huber's claim that he had encountered a group of thirty or forty men who surrounded him in the antechamber, shouting that they had been betrayed, that the *rappel* was being beaten all over Paris. According to Huber, this group had already drawn up a list of prospective members for an insurrectionary government and was ready

[64] In Huber's case this is not particularly surprising, as he had never fully recovered from the chronic tuberculosis contracted when he was a political prisoner from 1838 to 1848. However, the turbulence in the invaded Assembly was such that at one time or another most of the demonstration's leaders became ill or faint, including Raspail, Barbès, Blanqui, Quentin, Albert, and Sobrier. Garnier-Pagès, *Histoire de la révolution*, IX, 243.

[65] Testimony Huber, Haute-Cour de Versailles, *Le Moniteur universel*, October 11, 1849, p. 3047, and October 13, 1849, p. 3078.

[66] Normanby, *Year of Revolution*, entry for May 15, II, 398.

to seize a supposed store of rifles belonging to members of the National Assembly in their private capacity as members of the National Guard. Huber wavered until he too heard the renewed drumbeat of the call to arms above the noise.[67]

Originally the leaders of the demonstration had agreed —witness Huber's letter to Marrast on May 14—that the *rappel* was tantamount to an attack on the demonstrators, who, should the case arise, would run home to take up arms. The impracticality of such a plan has already been noted. Huber was later to maintain that several alternatives had flashed through his head on hearing the *rappel*. The demonstrators could beat a retreat through streets bristling with National Guard bayonets, reenacting the workers' humiliation on April 16. Or they could remain in the Assembly Chamber, where the principal leaders of the popular party, by now irremediably compromised, would be caught as in a mousetrap. Or they could seize the revolutionary initiative, dissolve parliament, and proclaim an insurgent government, as the group Huber had encountered in the Assembly antechamber had just demanded.[68]

Yet in opting for this third alternative, Huber and the crowd responding to his proclamation were really reverting to earlier plans discussed at the Dourlans meeting of May 12, except—and this was a momentous exception— that the revolution was proceeding without arms. The logic of the situation that existed at 4:30 P.M. on May 15 called for the immediate arming of the impromptu insurgents. Though some of them seem to have been aware of the need for weapons, the practical obstacles in their way were insurmountable.[69] In any case, the issue was

[67] Testimony Huber, Haute-Cour de Versailles, *Le Moniteur universel*, October 11, 1849, p. 3047.

[68] Ibid.   [69] Normanby, *Year of Revolution*, ii, 399.

immediately obscured: the earlier seesaw battle between proponents and opponents of insurrection had created such a confused psychological climate that an unarmed crowd acted as though it were armed—and almost got away with it.

V

For about an hour, revolutionary illusions and reminiscences were to count for as much as the realities of power. Only in this atmosphere could the heavily guarded Hôtel-de-Ville have been briefly "conquered" by unarmed insurgents. The ritual of dissolving parliament and marching on the Paris City Hall was so evocative of the February Days that the forces of order were temporarily as bemused as the weaponless revolutionaries. How indeed could a regular army officer like General Tempoure (who commanded the Garde mobile stationed by the Palais Bourbon) distinguish between a genuine (i.e., successful) revolution like that of February and a fleeting convulsion before all the returns were in?[70] Though he refused Huber's summons to join the insurgents, Tempoure permitted the club leader to order his troops to open ranks to let the insurgents proceed to the Right Bank on their way to the municipal building.[71] Even some National Guards were swept along by the current, joining the insurgents on their march after the three hundred guards

[70] For a discussion of this "moral crisis of the French army" in 1848, see P. Chalmin, "La crise morale de l'armée française," *Etudes*, Bibliothèque de la Révolution de 1848, XVIII, 28-76. Traditionally, the army took its cue from the behavior of the Paris National Guard. If the Guard fired on the insurgents, they were rebels; if the Guard refused to fire, they were revolutionaries.

[71] Testimony Huber, Haute-Cour de Versailles, *Le Moniteur universel*, October 11, 1849, p. 3047; testimony Tempoure, *Les accusés*, p. 105.

stationed on the Palais Bourbon's steps had joined in the cry, "Long live the Provisional Government."[72]

The same mix of incompetence and revolutionary nostalgia explains how an unarmed crowd of less than ten thousand could penetrate the heavily guarded perimeter of the Hôtel-de-Ville, defended by several thousand guardsmen of the Ninth Legion and by a battalion of the elite Garde républicaine recruited among February insurgents. The latter's artillery commander, it may be recalled, had volunteered to march on the Assembly in concert with the Polish demonstrators. Other officers, many of whom would have qualified as the *chefs de barricade* invited to the Dourlans meeting of May 12, may also have been sympathetic to the insurgents, as one of them was to charge.[73] Even where there seems to have been no prior arrangement, personal friendship played its part: Colonel Rey, who commanded the Garde républicaine, was unlikely to shoot down his old comrade and fellow republican veteran, Armand Barbès, who led the insurgent column.[74]

The response of the National Guard units was more complex. At first one battalion blocking the *quai* repelled the approaching column. When the column returned with National Guards in the van, the demonstrators-turned-insurgents explained that the National Assembly had dissolved itself and that they merely wanted to carry the news to City Hall.[75] Left without orders or reliable infor-

[72] Testimony Huber, Haute-Cour de Versailles, *Le Moniteur universel*, October 11, 1849, p. 3047; testimony Guyon and Yautier, *Les accusés*, pp. 115-116, 119.

[73] The most detailed and credible eyewitness account of the behavior of the Garde républicaine is found in "Simple note sur le bataillon de l'Hôtel de Ville par Lermet, ex-capitaine de la garde républicaine de l'Hôtel de Ville," probably written in July 1848. A. S., V^bis 84, dossier 1.

[74] Testimony Guyon, *Les accusés*, pp. 119-120. Rey was indicted, but died before he could come to trial.

[75] Testimony Yautier, *Les accusés*, p. 115.

mation, officers like Colonel Yautier of the Ninth Legion were appalled at the prospect of shooting unarmed men; he ordered his units back to their home district. As he was later to point out in his defense, had not Jean Bailly, mayor of Paris in 1791, mounted the guillotine two years later for having ordered fire on the unarmed demonstrators of the Champ-de-Mars?[76] The retreat or defection of the defending forces permitted the insurgents to install themselves in the Hôtel-de-Ville in the least bloody and most ephemeral French revolution on record.

This temporary effacement of the forces of order accounts only in part for the events of the late afternoon. Even more significant was the fact that the demonstration of May 15 turned into an uprising only after the Paris National Guard had been called into the streets, and indeed this revolutionary metamorphosis took place in response to that call. The forces of repression were therefore afoot before those of rebellion had even been marshaled. This peculiarity explains the swiftness with which the insurrection was smothered once the National Guard had recovered its nerve. This dispatch in turn accounts for the inaction of such revolutionary sympathizers as the twenty-three thousand men of the Twelfth Legion, who had been widely expected to follow their elected colonel, Barbès; it accounts for the mutinous frustration at the police prefecture, where the police, recruited from among the revolutionaries of February, had been eager but unable to join the insurrectional movement.[77] The organizers' contingency plan for a defensive rising proved fatally flawed; the insurrection was defeated before it had begun.

[76] Ibid., p. 116.

[77] For the disappointed expectations in the Twelfth Legion, see Le Populaire, May 18, 1848; for the activities at the police prefecture, ibid., May 18, 1848; Caussidière, Mémoirs, ii, 132-161.

vi

The government took measures against the clubs as soon as City Hall was retaken. At 6:45 P.M., Recurt ordered a search of the palace of the rue de Rivoli that housed both the newspaper, *La Commune de Paris* published by Sobrier, and in a separate wing the offices of the Centralizing Committee, formerly the Club of Clubs. While the Minister of the Interior's order merely called for seizure of all papers, arms, and ammunition, the National Guards not only arrested some seventy-five men whom they found on the premises but proceeded to sack both the newspaper offices and the files of the Centralizing Committee.[78] Recurt had also given orders for the arrest of the executive committee of the Society of the Rights of Man, but the organization had just moved. When after nightfall a mob of excited National Guards finally found and searched the new headquarters, which turned out to be empty, they began to shoot at each other in the darkness and confusion. Three guards were shot accidentally by their comrades; these were the only fatalities on May 15.[79]

The official policy of the government toward the clubs was expounded by Garnier-Pagès in his address to the Constituent Assembly during the evening session of May 15. "The clubs that have conspired are closed. . . . We shall respect the right of assembly, for we owe the glorious revolution of February 24 to the right of assembly; but the clubs that are meeting in arms, that are meeting

[78] A.N., C. 933, CdE 1495. Saint-Amand, governor of the Tuileries, to the Commission du Pouvoir exécutif, evening of May 15, A.N., C. 933, CdE 1511. Longepied and Laugier, *Comité révolutionnaire*, p. 130; testimony Leboucher, Haute-Cour de Bourges, session of March 16, 1849, *Les accusés*, p. 189.

[79] Testimony Villain, Haute-Cour de Bourges, session of March 22, 1849, *Le Moniteur universel*, March 24, 1849, p. 1008. Garnier-Pagès, *Histoire de la révolution*, IX, 296-297.

threateningly, that are constantly menacing to invade the National Assembly, those clubs we are going to disperse, we are going to prosecute."[80] This relative moderation was also reflected in the Assembly itself, which on May 18 shouted down a motion to ban all political clubs even before it could be seconded.[81] The government's legislative initiative in the Constituent Assembly was confined to a decree against armed gatherings introduced by the Minister of the Interior on May 17. Though prompted by the events of May 15, the proposed law was better designed to propagate a myth than to deal with a problem; few, if any, of the clubs had ever met in arms.

Actually Recurt's explanation for not introducing further repressive legislation was more indicative of the direction of official policy. The Minister of the Interior publicly recognized the abrogation of the harsh September Laws of 1835. But all other laws dealing with "public order"—and much legislation against unlawful street gatherings, seditious cries, posting placards, incitement to rebellion or sedition dated back to the Empire and the Restoration—were once again to be enforced unless and until they were repealed by the Constituent Assembly.[82] Compared to this jolt, the decrees of May 22, dissolving the clubs formerly presided over by Raspail and Blanqui for their responsibility in the May 15 affair, were anticlimactic.[83]

From the evening of May 15 on, troops and National Guard units converged on Paris, which began to look like an armed camp.[84] The wildest rumors gained credence

[80] *Le Moniteur universel*, March 24, 1849, supplement to Nos. 137 and 138, 1848, p. vii.

[81] Ibid., May 19, 1848, p. 1090.

[82] Ibid., May 18, 1848, p. 1078.

[83] Ibid., May 23, 1848, p. 1123.

[84] *La Réforme*, May 17, 1848. Order from undersecretary of the Interior to General Fouché, May 15 evening. A.N., C. 933, CdE 1496; *La Réforme*, May 18, 1848.

in this atmosphere of uncertainty. Earnest citizens of Montmartre were willing to believe, for example, that the Montagnards, the police guard that was being disbanded because of its equivocal attitude on May 15, were about to burn the suburbs.[85] The same vague fears that had unnerved the capital after the April 16 demonstration again gripped the city and the roving squads of National Guards who patrolled it. But this time their cry was, "Long live the National Assembly! Down with the clubs! We want no more clubs!"[86] In these circumstances, Garnier-Pagès' nice distinction between good—or at least permissible—clubs and clubs to be shut down was bound to become somewhat shadowy.

For several days the mobilized National Guard dominated Paris. Within the Guard it was clearly the men of property, frightened by these latest revolutionary disorders, who set the tone. They considered clubs as hotbeds of anarchy, to be closed with no questions asked. When a crowd gathered in front of the rue Albouy branch of the Society of the Rights of Man on the evening of May 16, a company of National Guards not only dispersed the crowd but broke into the club premises to seize its files.[87] Similarly, several days before Raspail's Society of the Friends of the People was officially outlawed, club members found themselves locked out of their rented hall. When they persisted, they were assaulted by massed National Guards who came at them with rifle butts and the flats of their sabers.[88] It is difficult

[85] Mayor of Belleville to mayor of sixth district, May 16, A.N., C. 932A, dossier Mairies de Paris, CdE 1301; report from mayor of sixth district to Executive Commission, May 16, CdE 1277.

[86] Police report signed Carlier, May 16, 1848, A.N., C. 933, CdE 1481.

[87] Mayor of fifth district to Executive Commission, May 16, 10 P.M., A.N., C. 932A, dossier Mairies de Paris, CdE 1280.

[88] *Le Représentant du peuple*, May 21, 1848. *Le Courrier français*, May 22, 1848.

to assess how widespread this repression was, but scattered club announcements in the press suggest more than isolated incidents. The clubs' statements either disclaimed any part in the May 15 demonstration or, more frequently, asserted the inalienable right to continue meeting.[89] In one case, the executive board of the Club of the Salvation of the People demanded and obtained protection from their district mayor against threatened violence.[90]

More characteristically, the action of the municipal administration complemented and supported the initiative of the National Guard. On May 16, for example, the mayor of the working-class suburb of Belleville requested a company of National Guards from the mayor of Paris' sixth district to disperse the members of the Club of the Montagnards of Belleville. Since the members were accused of having met in arms on the evening of the fifteenth, this particular intervention followed Garnier-Pagès' guidelines.[91] The municipal authorities also had recourse to less dramatic but equally effective ways of dealing with the clubs. The recent decision to expel clubs from public buildings began to be enforced,[92] while it became increasingly difficult to hold meetings in rented quarters. On May 16 the Club of the Revolution found

[89] Club du progrès, *Le Représentant du peuple*, May 17, 1848; Club démocratique de l'Arsenal, letter of May 18, *La vraie République*, May 20, 1848; Club républicain démocratique central, ibid., May 18, 1848; Club de l'égalité et de la fraternité, May 20, ibid., May 24, 1848.

[90] Mayor of first district to police *commissaire* of first district, May 19, 1848, A.S., V3D⁶-23, No. 14.

[91] Mayor of Belleville to mayor of sixth district, May 16, A.N., C. 932A, dossier Mairies de Paris, CdE 1301. Report, May 16, mayor of sixth district to Executive Commission, A.N., C. 932A, dossier Mairies de Paris, CdE 1277.

[92] F. Pinel-Grandchamp, "Exposé de la conduite de M. Pinel-Grandchamp, ex-maire du 12ᵉ arr. du 16 mai au 25 juin," *Procès des insurgés des 23, 24, 25 et 26 juin 1848 devant les conseils de guerre* (Paris, 1848), p. 50.

the Salle des Spectacles Concerts, which it had been renting on a regular basis, suddenly unavailable. The district mayor had had a heart-to-heart talk with the hall's owner.[93] In other instances the authorities intervened to suspend the meetings of a club provisionally, as did the director of the Hospice of Quinze-Vingt, who temporarily withdrew the "resident" club's privileges so that the Club of Quinze-Vingt could not reconvene until May 23. By that date, the much more moderate Club of the Peoples' Emancipation was still under injunction by the second district's mayor to postpone its meetings "in the interest of order and public peace."[94] Altogether, the jeremiad of *La vraie République* in depicting the plight of the clubs was not too far from the point:

> Where will they meet? In public places, in national edifices? That is what should be, yet this is not what is. Gradually *public* buildings are being closed and will be closed to *public* meetings.
> On private premises? That takes a lot of money and, what is more, the good will of the owners, who are usually little inclined to attract the attention of the authorities by opening their halls to popular gatherings.
> There remains the street and the public square. . . . No, under the Republic of 1848, under the *Pentarchy* . . . things will be as they were under the monarchy. . . . The laws against unlawful assembly will be strictly enforced.[95]

The club movement had already undergone a major amputation after the April elections, which ended one of the *raisons d'être* of the popular societies, as many clubs failed to survive the postelectoral letdown. The campaign

[93] Landolphe, vice-president of the Club de la révolution, to editor, *La vraie République*, May 17, 1848, Thoré Papers, B.A.

[94] For Club des Quinze-Vingt, see testimony Soubert, Haute-Cour de Bourges, *Les accusés*, p. 256; and *La vraie République*, May 26, 1848. For Club de l'émancipation des peuples, *Le Représentant du peuple*, May 25, 1848.

[95] *La vraie République*, May 21, 1848.

of harassment that followed the May 15 affair resulted in a further drastic decline in the number of clubs, and presumably in the number of club members. By the end of May, when the impending supplementary elections to the Constituent Assembly evoked a Central Commission for Democratic Elections, only thirty-five clubs participated, as compared to the one hundred forty-nine that had taken part in the Club of Clubs.[96] Altogether for the period of May 16 to June 23 only forty-six clubs, four of them newly founded, have left some record of their activity.[97]

The May 15 affair was even more brutal in eliminating the best-known club leaders and disrupting, at least temporarily, the middle echelons. Barbès, Sobrier, and Raspail were arrested and imprisoned before the day was out, while Blanqui was cornered in a friend's apartment some ten days later. Huber and Villain went underground, not to emerge until March 1849, when they surrendered to stand trial before the High Court of Bourges. Many lesser lights of the club movement were rounded up at the Hôtel-de-Ville on May 15; for example, the former president of the Club of Clubs' commission, Longepied, who was held without charges for several weeks.[98] As late as May 28, Gadon, ex-president of the

[96] Eugène Longepied to Amable Longepied, about May 29, 1848, A.N., C. 942, CdE 9102; Club de la révolution, session of June 2, Le Travail, June 4-6, 1848.

[97] By itself, I would distrust this second set of figures, since evidence for club activity is largely drawn from newspaper announcements and stories. It is likely that clubs were less newsworthy—hence less reported—after the April elections. Yet both sets of figures—and the Club of Clubs affiliation is comparable to that of the Commission centrale des élections démocratiques—are in remarkable agreement in pointing to a four-fifths decline in the number of clubs.

[98] Longepied to E. Arago, May 18, 1848, A.N., C. 942, CdE 9083; Longepied to Lamartine (copy), May 25, 1848, A.N., C. 942, CdE 9037; Pelletier to Longepied, May 28,

Club of Free Men, had just been seized, though most arrests took place within forty-eight hours of the collapse of the putsch.[99] Figures for the number of arrests—there were several hundred—are almost meaningless, since this whole police operation was something of a revolving door.[100] Of fifty-two prisoners transferred to the Château de Vincennes in the night of May 15-16, seventeen had not yet been questioned, twenty-eight had been released after interrogation, while only nine were being held for pretrial investigation, according to a report of the evening of May 16.[101] Longepied, arrested at the Hôtel-de-Ville when it was retaken by the National Guard on May 15, was imprisoned with some twenty other prisoners, half of whom would be released by May 18.[102] Ultimately, of the hundreds of suspects arrested, only twenty-one were charged, of whom no more than half were prominently identified with the club movement. Nonetheless, police

---

1848, A.N., C. 942, CdE 9099; Longepied and Laugier, *Comité révolutionnaire*, p. 130.

[99] Pelletier to Longepied, May 28, 1848, A.N., C. 942, CdE 9099; Pelletier to Longepied, May 30, 1848, A.N., C. 942, CdE 9100.

[100] The 153 people reported as being held at the Château de Vincennes by 8:00 P.M. on May 16, 1848 (H. Fournery, special commissioner to members of the Provisional Government [sic], A.N., C. 933, CdE 1486), is obviously an incomplete figure, since we knew that some prisoners were held at the La Force prison (Longepied to E. Arago, A.N., C. 942, CdE 9083). On May 19 *Le Courrier français* reported "about 250 arrests," and on May 27 *La vraie République* cited a figure of 390. The most official (though not necessarily the most accurate) statement puts the number of arrests at 280. Procurator-general Baroche, Haute-Cour de Bourges, session of March 8, 1849, *Les accusés*, p. 42.

[101] H. Fournery to members of the Provisional Government [sic], May 16, [1848], A.N., C. 933, CdE 1486.

[102] Longepied to E. Arago, May 18, 1848, A.N., C. 942, CdE 9083.

roundups had created an atmosphere of insecurity that certainly contributed to the decline of the clubs during the second half of May.

On May 21 the Festival of Concord, after three post-ponements, was finally held, a "really barbarous republican extravagance, senselsss in its design and joyless in its progress," in the jaundiced view of the British ambassador.[103] Almost a million francs had been budgeted for the event and an elaborate pageantry planned, ironically enough, under the supervision of Louis Blanc's brother.[104] Although originally an invitation had been extended to the clubs, if any actually participated their role was too inconspicuous to be mentioned in newspaper accounts.[105] Tocqueville, sitting in the bleachers reserved for the National Assembly, watched the glinting of bayonets as two hundred thousand armed men marched and counter-marched across the undulating terrain of the Champ-de-Mars. The contrast between the uniformed veteran National Guards and the new recruits in their workers' smocks looked ominous to him; they resembled two armies in a civil war maneuvering during a truce.[106] Or was this the wisdom of hindsight? The troops filed past a colossal papier-mâché statue of Liberty "leaning on a sword," as one observer noted, "as though about to trans-fix herself upon it."[107]

[103] Normanby, *Year of Revolution*, entry for May 22, p. 407.
[104] For the official program, see *Le Moniteur universel*, May 11, 1848, p. 1003.
[105] For the convocation of club presidents to the commission of the Fraternal Banquet of the Constituent Assembly, see *Le Courrier français*, May 17, 1848. For at least one categorical club refusal to participate "on the grounds that the democratic party has more reason to wear mourning than to celebrate in the present circumstances," see the letter to the editor (May 19) from the Club des hommes lettrés, *La vraie République*, May 21, 1848.
[106] Tocqueville, *Recollections*, p. 142.
[107] Bonde, *Paris in 1848*, p. 156.

8 | Toward a Showdown

A new social crisis is approaching. Responsibility for it will fall on those who shall have provoked it, be it through lack of intelligence or through ill will. We say it with deep sorrow: this victory of February, that from the humanitarian stand-point was to have been the glorious complement to the work of our fathers, may go down in history but as a gust of wind between two storms.

Open letter to its imprisoned president,
A. Barbès, from the Club of the
Revolution, June 9, 1848

i

The weeks preceding the June insurrection generated a profound malaise felt by most Parisians who were at all politically sensitive. In this atmosphere of impending crisis, the club movement played only a marginal role. An increasingly irreconcilable social antagonism focused on concrete issues—disorder in the streets, Bonapartist agitation, the future of the National Workshops—that did not yield to petitions, proclamations, or verbal in-junctions. Nor were the clubs in any position to influence the decision makers. Never having seized any of the levers of power, the popular societies were restricted from their very beginnings either to the conventional pol-itics of electioneering or to the unconventional politics of mass confrontation. The latter having failed so miser-ably on May 15, in the following weeks this alternative looked unattractive to the club leadership. This left the

clubs with their other option, electoral politics, at the
exact moment when this kind of politics, with its dependence on reasonable give and take, had become meaningless. Just as the clubs had espoused an irrelevant legality,
"the people" for whom they professed to speak were
coming round to the idea that the February Revolution
had aborted and would therefore have to be fought all
over again. And on the barricades clubs were useless.

In tracing the final four weeks of the Paris club movement, I shall deal successively with the clubs' role in the
special elections of June, the Banquet of the People, the
response of the clubs to some major issues of the day,
and the government's policy toward the popular societies.

ii

While some of the clubs weathered the crisis of May 15
without interruption, many others did not reopen until
the last week of the month. Though the atmosphere of
an armed camp that Paris had assumed following the invasion of the National Assembly had no doubt impaired
club activity, the very threat to freedom of speech also
served to rally the clubs to exercise once again their inalienable rights.[1] Of the two clubs which the government
had dissolved by decree for their alleged complicity in the
May 15 affair, Raspail's Friends of the People remained
shut while protesting the Executive Commission's abuse
of power;[2] Blanqui's Central Republican Society, though
diminished in numbers, ignored the decree of outlawry
by meeting regularly from May 23 on without encounter-
ing police repression.[3] Nor did major popular societies

[1] Edouard Hervé to Thoré, undated (prior to May 25; after
May 15), Thoré Papers, B.A., 7916 (IX).
[2] Letter of May 27, *La Commune de Paris*, May 29, 1848.
[3] Police prefect's report, May 24, 1848, A.N., C. 932A,
CdE 1636. For evidence that a number of clubs regained the
premises they had occupied in public buildings, see announce-

like the Club of the Revolution have trouble renting suitable halls.[4]

Upon reopening, the clubs tried to come to terms with the experience of May 15. None of them was willing to defend the dissolution of the National Assembly publicly, yet neither could they disavow a popular demonstration in behalf of a sacred cause. Nor were they allowed to forget what had happened, for as the judicial investigation proceeded more club leaders were being imprisoned. The clubs responded by indirection, ranging from down-to-earth subscriptions for the benefit of "the arrested patriots" to elaborate petitions demanding compensation for anyone unjustly detained.[5] Equally pointed was their defense of leaders implicated in the May 15 affair: the incarcerated Barbès became the object of a minor cult, and not only in the club he had headed.[6] General Courtais, an unlikely object for revolutionary devotion, was offered a ceremonial sword to replace one broken by National Guardsmen angered by the general's "treachery" on May 15.[7] The most persistent and passionate adulation was

ment, Club fraternel de Quinze-Vingt, *Le Représentant du peuple*, May 27, 1848; Club de l'organisation sociale (formerly Club du progrès), *La vraie République*, May 29, 1848.

[4] Police prefect's report, May 26, 1848, A.N., C. 932A, CdE 1700, concerning the Société républicaine centrale, session of May 25; for Club de la révolution, session of May 25, *La Commune de Paris*, May 30, 1848; for announcement of the reopening, *La Réforme*, May 25, 1848.

[5] Announcement, Société des Droits de l'Homme, *La Commune de Paris*, May 28, 1848; Société pacifique des Droits de l'Homme, *La Commune de Paris*, May 28, 1848; the latter's petition was submitted to the Constituent Assembly on June 17 by Caussidière, *Le Moniteur universel*, June 18, 1848, p. 1410.

[6] For example, open letter to Barbès from Club de l'égalité et de la fraternité, *La vraie République*, May 29, 1848.

[7] Club populaire de la Sorbonne, *La Commune de Paris*, May 28, 1848; Société des Droits de l'Homme, session of June

reserved for Louis Blanc, the workers' champion, as he was under continual attack in and out of the National Assembly for having fraternized with the May 15 intruders. Various clubs drafted statements of support and sympathy both before and after Louis Blanc's (temporary) triumph over his accusers. "We shall never forget that you devoted a part of your life to studying the improvement and happiness of that calm, great, and generous class of workers. In return we consecrate to you our unbounded loyalty and devotion."[8] A medallion in his honor, to be designed by "one of the most distinguished artists of Paris," was also in the offing.[9]

iii

Yet a political movement does not thrive on reminiscences alone. The renewed club activity was spurred by the announcement of special elections to the National Assembly, ordered for June 4 and 5 by the Executive Commission.[10] Called to fill vacancies left by invalidations, by resignations, and by the success of some April candidates in more than one constituency, the new elections were slated to fill eleven of the capital's thirty-four seats. The vote was the first reading of the barometer of public

---

8, *L'Organisation du travail, journal des ouvriers*, June 11, 1848.

[8] Club Popincourt, session of May 26, *La vraie République*, May 29, 1848.

[9] In all likelihood, the prospective artist was the republican sculptor, David d'Angers. See Club démocratique de l'Arsenal, session of June 3, *La Commune de Paris*, June 7, 1848; also Club Popincourt, session of May 26, *La vraie République*, May 29, 1848; Club fraternel de Quinze-Vingt, session of May 31, ibid., June 2, 1848; Club de la révolution, ibid., June 10, 1848.

[10] *Le Moniteur universel*, May 23, 1848; for details of electoral and registration procedure, see the instructions of the mayor of Paris, ibid., May 25, 1848.

opinion since the National Assembly had begun to sit; the vanquished of April, on both the left and right, were tempted to blow up the elections into a national referendum.

By adapting themselves to the new election campaign, the clubs hoped to regain their vitality and reverse the attrition of their membership. Some clubs took the opportunity to publish their slate of (advanced) candidates immediately in the hope that all like-minded would rally around this banner. Others, like the sinking Central Democratic Society, tried to refloat themselves by public hearings for prospective candidates.[11] The Peaceful Society for the Rights of Man distinguished itself by promising to listen to all opinions with "reverend attention," though its tolerance, it turned out, had limits; when Victor Hugo —at that time a staunch conservative—forwarded his statement of principles, it was publicly incinerated before the cheering assembly.[12]

In view of earlier experiments, the idea of coordinating the campaign efforts of all Parisian clubs, workers' organizations, and the left-wing press came naturally. As early as May 25, two neighborhood clubs, the Democratic Club of the Arsenal and that of Saint-Maur, independently suggested common action.[13] Yet it took the more prestigious initiative of the Club of the Revolution (which had sponsored the Club of Clubs in March) to start a common organization; this time, however, the

[11] *La vraie République*, May 25, 1848; also Amann, *Minutes*, May 22, 1848, pp. 512-514.

[12] Announcement, Société pacifique des Droits de l'Homme, *La Commune de Paris*, May 27, 1848; session of May 26, ibid., June 1, 1848.

[13] *La vraie République*, May 26, 1848, for Club démocratique de l'Arsenal. See the testimony of the Lycée's *proviseur*, A.M.G., dossier Siméon-Chaumier, A. 5084; for Club de Saint-Maur, *La Réforme*, May 28, 1848; *La Commune de Paris*, May 28, 1848.

Club of the Revolution had to relinquish control over the club-coordinating committee even before it was properly formed.

Most of the clubs had, despite the charade of hearing candidates, already decided upon a slate of nominees made up entirely of socialists or communists. The Club of the Revolution did not merely advocate the unity of the Left (clubs, organized crafts, Garde mobile, National Workshops, revolutionary newspapers), but also an alliance with the moderate republicans on the basis of mutual concessions. As vice-president Landolphe maintained, "What good is this mania for exclusiveness which works only against ourselves? Why build a chapel all our own to raise altar against altar? This is inexpedient and clumsy. Let us band together to save the Republic. . . . Let us vote for non-socialist republicans rather than to endanger the existence of our beloved Republic."[14]

Landolphe and his fellows tacitly assumed that: (1) the other clubs would agree to cooperate with the moderate republicans; (2) the moderates themselves would respond to these overtures for republican solidarity; (3) the moderate republicans had retained their commanding lead in Paris. Not only did all three assumptions turn out to be wrong, but the Club of the Revolution proved unable even to open negotiations with the men of *Le National* prior to the first meeting of all the clubs.[15]

A preliminary meeting on May 28 in the offices of the

[14] Session of May 25, *Le Travail*, May 27, 1848; for a slightly different version of the same meeting, the first held since May 15, see *La Commune de Paris*, May 30, 1848.

[15] As it turned out, the moderate republicans themselves could not agree on a common list of candidates. There were two rival lists with about half the names overlapping, one posted by *Le National*, the other sponsored by the Comité central démocratique de la Seine, the direct successor of the pre-April Comité central des élections générales de la Seine. *Le National*, June 1 and 3, 1848.

Club of the Revolution was shifted to the rue Albouy
headquarters of the Society of the Rights of Man the following day, heralding a shift of the leadership from the
former to the latter.[16] The task of drawing up a Socialist
unity slate had been made easier, first of all, by the
choices already made by individual clubs. Most clubs had
consciously selected candidates who were known and
who dramatized the socialist cause.[17] Since the pool of
such potential candidates was small, there were at least
half a dozen nominees so obvious as to preclude discussion. Secondly, the Central Committee of the Workers
of the Seine, which had insisted on burdening the Club
of Clubs with twenty obscure worker candidates in the
April elections, by June had been cured of their *ouvrier-
ism*, their simple faith that only workers could achieve
proletarian emancipation. At their meeting of May 27,
the majority within the former stronghold of working-
class exclusiveness decided to endorse eight Socialist notables as against only three workers.[18] Before drawing up
the Socialist slate at the session of May 29, the assembled
delegates agreed to reserve three places for worker candidates chosen by the ex-Luxembourg workers, despite objections from the representatives of the Club of the Revolution. Determined to avoid the mistakes and delays of
the Club of Clubs, the delegates also decided to draw up
a definitive slate simply by throwing into a hat the names
of the nominees chosen in the individual clubs and pick-
ing the eleven who had proven the most popular—save
for the understanding about the Luxembourg candidates.
The proposal of the Club of the Revolution to await the

[16] *La vraie République*, May 28, 1848. Luxembourg workers, June 2, 1848, A.N., C. 942, CdE 9421; Club de la révolution, session of May 30, *Le Travail*, June 1, 1848.

[17] Discussion of the qualifications needed for candidates is
particularly revealing at the Société pacifique des Droits de
l'Homme, session of May 26, *La Commune de Paris*, June
1, 1848.

[18] A.N., C. 942, CdE 9410.

result of negotiations with the republicans of *Le National* was specifically voted down.[19]

About thirty clubs, as well as delegates from the ex-Luxembourg workers, the Garde républicaine, and the National Workshops participated in the balloting. There was unanimous agreement on Marc Caussidière, who, ousted as police prefect after the May 15 affair, had also resigned his Assembly seat and was bidding for a vote of confidence. The vote was nearly unanimous on Pierre Leroux, reigning sage of socialism, on Pierre-Joseph Proudhon, editor of *Le Représentant du peuple*, whose ideas on socializing credit were echoing in club discussions, on the pugnacious scientist-humanitarian-revolutionary François Raspail (since May 15 once more behind bars), and on Théophile Thoré, the socialist editor of *La vraie République*. Etienne Cabet, the prophet of Icarian communism, Théophile Guillard de Kersausie, as well as that chronic republican insurgent Charles Lagrange, also carried by substantial majorities. The three worker candidates endorsed by the Luxembourg delegates obtained only pluralities, and one of them, the bronze-worker Mallarmet, had to be advanced over the republican journalist Dupoty, who had outpointed him. Every one of the nominees chosen was an acknowledged socialist or communist.[20]

[19] There are four independent primary sources for this meeting, differing in emphasis as well as disagreeing on the number of clubs present. The latter discrepancy may be a matter of semantics—i.e., can the National Workshop delegates or the ex-Luxembourg workers' delegates be counted as a club? Société des Droits de l'Homme, (hereafter DH Minutes), A.M.G., dossier Guille, A. 6911; ex-Luxembourg delegates, session of June 2, A.N., C. 942, CdE 9421; Eugène Longepied to Amable Longepied (May 30, 1848), A.N., C. 942, CdE 9102; DH Minutes, May 30, 1848, pp. 532-536.

[20] At least two of the workers chosen, Mallarmet and Savary, were known as self-educated intellectuals who had founded the communist monthly, *La Fraternité de 1845*. For their biographical sketches, see *DBMOF*, III, 387-388, 21.

The May 29 gathering formalized its agreement by founding a Central Commission for Democratic Elections in the department of Seine, a latter-day Club of Clubs, to coordinate campaign efforts. From the start, the Central Commission was dominated by the Society of the Rights of Man, whose quarters it shared and whose stamp appeared on its official communications. Of the nine-man commission, four were members of the society, while the remaining five represented five different clubs, one of them the Club of the Revolution that had taken the initiative leading to unity.[21] During the two weeks of its activity, the Central Commission's primary task was to print proclamations and voting lists, assessing the member clubs for their share of the expense, which amounted to about 50 francs each or 1,500 in all.[22] At the same time, the commission became a front for the Society of the Rights of Man which used it to get general club support for its positions on various current problems.

As it was the Society of the Rights of Man that ani-

---

[21] A.N., C. 942, CdE 9285. The other clubs represented were the student-dominated Club du deux mars in the Latin Quarter and (probably) the working-class Club Popincourt du Faubourg Saint-Antoine. The nine members of the commission were A. Delettre, a building inspector; Jeantet (unidentified); Louis Guille, in 1848 a self-employed cap maker; Charles Blu, porcelain decorator employed as pay clerk at the National Workshops; Jerôme Langlois, a former naval officer turned republican journalist; François Pardigon, a twenty-one-year-old law student; Guillard, probably Théophile Guillard de Kersausie, a former army officer who had already been prominent in the original Société des Droits de l'Homme and who was an unsuccessful socialist candidate to the Assembly in June; André, probably Antoine André, naturalized Belgian and iron-molder by trade. *DBMOF*, II, 50, 320; I, 249; II, 432-433; III, 176-177; II, 319; I, 97.

[22] There appear to have been three assessments of 25, 12, and 10 francs. A.N., C. 942, CdE 9421, 9285; A.M.G., dossier Guille, A. 6911.

mated the club coalition of June 1848, the nature of the
organization and of its policy are worth noting.[23] Unlike
any of the other popular societies, the Society of the
Rights of Man was a hybrid—part club, part secret society—though it is almost impossible to judge which
aspect loomed larger at any given moment. As a club it
had originally sponsored public sessions at the Conserva-
tory of Arts and Crafts that were fully reported in the
left-wing press. The society also produced a number of
neighborhood affiliates, one of which, that of the rue
Albouy, became dominant after the central society had
been closed, its papers confiscated, and its leadership
driven underground in the aftermath of May 15. In reading the club's fragmentary minutes for late May and early
June, I have the impression of dealing no longer with a
popular society open to all comers, but with sessions of
the organization's cadres.

As a paramilitary, semisecret society, the Society of
the Rights of Man had not only deliberately revived the
ethos of its namesake of the early July Monarchy, but
had also inherited both the original leadership and the
organizational structure left over from that heroic age of
the republican movement. For the purposes of the society, Paris was broken down into districts served by a
military hierarchy somewhat confusingly divided into
neighborhood and section commanders on one hand,

[23] The ensuing analysis is based on the examination of the
society's minutes, seized when its secretary Guille was arrested
after the June insurrection. While the minutes proved revealing on a few key points, some of their limitations should be
stated: (1) they are obviously the raw minutes used in com-
piling the official (and missing) minutes; (2) they are the
work of an unusually clumsy as well as illegible notetaker and
are fragmentary more often than not; (3) they are undated,
though some of them can be dated fairly accurately on the
basis of internal evidence; (4) they only cover from about
May 26 to June 10.

centurions and decurions on the other. In the best secret society tradition, all members were pledged to unconditional obedience, which meant that they were to be ready to fight at their commanders' signal.[24] Some elements of such a structure really did exist, if only on paper—or at least they had existed in April when, for example, the society's secretary Guille (who in June also sat on the Central Commission for Democratic Elections) had, as section chief, carried twenty names on his roster.[25] How extensive a network was still in place in June is uncertain, but there seems to have been an attempt to tighten the society's military organization at about the time of the special elections. On June 5, for instance, military commanders were asked to report, and there is at least tenuous evidence to suggest that after June 10—when the Central Commission for Democratic Elections was also allowed to fade away—the Society of the Rights of Man shifted its emphasis from discussion to secret organization.[26]

Despite its militancy, the Society of the Rights of Man was never given to millennarian exaltation. While affirming the social nature of the February Revolution, it did not demand any instantaneous transformation of society. It professed "to stand between the pariahs and privileged of the old social order," recommending "unity and calm"

[24] For the "Practical Instruction on Joining the Society of the Rights of Man," see *Enquête*, II, 84.

[25] A.M.G., dossier Guille, A. 6911.

[26] I surmise this on the basis of the society's minutes, which do not go beyond June 10—suggesting a switch to complete secrecy—except for the minutes of June 18(?), which seem to deal entirely with military organization. I have not ventured a guess on the membership of the society. Alphonse Lucas' claim of no more than 3,000 sounds reasonable but cannot be checked. Lucas, probably a police spy who had infiltrated one of the society's affiliate clubs, is sensationalist but well informed. See Lucas, p. 118.

to the former, "repentance and reparation" to the latter.[27] Like most clubs sympathetic to socialism, the society preferred to take its stand on Robespierre's proposed Declaration of the Rights of Man of 1793, rather than to endorse more contemporary—and controversial—reform programs. The society had taken no part in the May 15 demonstrations, but this did not prevent its new headquarters from being sacked.[28] As its minutes in late May and early June testify, the *sociétaires* were no more monolithic in their views than the members of any other club. Though they were disenchanted not only with the moderates of *Le National* (and the government) but also with Ledru-Rollin's faction, they were wary of a premature armed confrontation.

On June 1, after consulting journalists from various socialist newspapers, the Central Commission for Democratic Elections released a "Proclamation to All the Workers of the Seine Department." Couched in simple unadorned language, the commission's manifesto nailed down a few home truths for the benefit of the Paris workers: (1) that only through complete unity could the people profit from the bitter lesson of April; (2) that only socialists were worthy of election, for "there are enough politicians, enough windbags in the National Assembly already"; (3) that only by winning this election could the Paris masses foil the machinations of those who, by dissolving the National Workshops, were planning to "send half of you into the army in order to use you against your brothers"; (4) and finally, that the proclamation carried the names of the candidates "freely and unanimously adopted by the united delegates of the crafts, the National Workshops, the Garde républicaine, the Garde mobile, and all the democratic clubs."[29]

[27] See pp. 192-193.
[28] See p. 240.
[29] *La vraie République*, June 3, 1848.

iv

Working-class Paris may have been agitated and bourgeois Paris frightened, yet the campaign and the elections
themselves were reasonably free. Radical complaints of
police interference, intimidation, and downright fraud
either referred to minor incidents or else were not sub-
stantiated. Down in the Gobelins section of the twelfth
district, three distributors of the club voting lists were
reported illegally arrested; and in one of his daily reports
the commander of the Paris National Guard, Thomas
Clément, made no bones about having detained a man
for handing out "lists of names of persons noted for the
eccentricity of their opinions."[30] In suburban Bercy, the
municipal authorities were accused of peddling their own
"authorized" list. No complaints were voiced about Paris,
where, as one of the district mayors later insisted, the
municipality had remained above the battle.[31] Unofficial
intimidation also seemed to be confined to the outskirts,
where life was less anonymous and notables could throw
their weight around. In La Villette, a correspondent of
La Réforme observed the director of the mail boats tear-
ing up one voter's printed ballot after telling him, "Do
you want to cut your own throat by voting for this
canaille?" and handing him a new list that included the
name of Adolphe Thiers, the *bête noire* of all good republicans.[32] Whether the poll-watching organized by the
Central Commission with the assistance of individual
clubs may have prevented what otherwise might have
been large-scale fraud is hard to say. *Le Représentant du
peuple* contended that in one section of the fourth district
votes for the revolutionary Lagrange—a club nominee—
were counted separately according to three different

[30] *La Réforme*, June 4, 1848; A.N., C. 932A, CdE 1842.

[31] Letter from Bercy, *La Réforme*, June 6, 1848. Testimony
of Pinel-Grandchamp, *Les insurgés*, p. 53.

[32] Letter to the editor, *La Réforme*, June 6, 1848.

labels: one pile for plain Lagrange, another for Lagrange of Lyon, and a third for Charles Lagrange.[33] Despite this claim, no such tallies showed up in the final results for the department of Seine, and Lagrange was elected. Other objections missed the point altogether. There was bitterness that by closing the polling places at 8:00 P.M. on the second and last day of voting the municipal authorities had disenfranchised as many as ten thousand workers who were on the way home from work at this hour.[34] True or not, the hours had been posted well in advance of the elections and in any case the polls had been open all day Sunday. All told, considering that the left-wing press was eager to publish any report of irregularities as a reserve alibi in the event of political defeat, the special elections in Paris were surprisingly clean.

At first sight, the result of the elections, officially announced on June 8, appeared bewildering. "How is anyone to make sense of the real opinion of Paris in this incredible mélange of opposing names, doctrines and sentiments," complained Le National, practically all of whose candidates had been wiped out. "How can one imagine that the Parisian workers are at the same time socialists with MM. Proudhon and Leroux, monarchist conservatives like M. Thiers, revolutionaries like MM. Caussidière and Lagrange, imperialists with M. Louis Bonaparte, and French peers with M. Victor Hugo?"[35] Le National's old

[33] Announcement, Club de la révolution, La Réforme, June 4, 1848; Club de la révolution, session of June 3, Le Travail, June 6-8, 1848, for information on poll surveillance; Le Représentant du peuple, June 7, 1848.

[34] La Réforme, June 6, 1848, cites a specific example from the eleventh section at the Louvre (fourth district) where sixty workers were waiting when the polls closed. L'Organisation du travail, journal des ouvriers, June 7, 1848, cites the 10,000 figure and talks of protests from the nightly crowd at the Porte Saint-Denis.

[35] Le National, June 10, 1848.

rival, *La Réforme*, took a more analytical tack. Its editors argued that the 91,000 votes received by Thiers represented the high-water mark of reaction. The vote for three other conservatives, Moreau, Boissel, and General Changarnier, was not politically significant. Parisians had voted for Moreau and Boissel not because they were former deputies of the dynastic opposition but because both men had long been associated with Paris municipal politics. The election of General Changarnier could be discounted, since it was no more than a popular tribute to the popularity of the army—though the newspaper failed to explain why the general's total vote should have shot up by 47,000 since the April elections in which he had been defeated. Still according to *La Réforme*, Louis Bonaparte, elected eighth of eleven running, owed his unspectacular success to the benighted suburbs where dynastic loyalties were rife. This left the four socialists, who had won. Caussidière, who had received the highest vote of any candidate, did not count because he had attracted support from all quarters; but the three others, Lagrange, Leroux, and Proudhon, accurately reflected the concentrated efforts of the socialists.[36] This modest success could be enlarged by pointing to the three nearest runners-up, all of whom also were "official" socialist nominees. As one sympathetic journalist crowed, "This is the social republic at the gates of the Assembly. It is knocking, so to speak, and makes the reactionaries turn pale on their benches."[37]

A close scrutiny of the election statistics permits several less impressionistic conclusions.[38] First of all, the

[36] *La Réforme*, June 11, 1848.

[37] *L'aimable Faubourien*, June 11-13, 1848.

[38] An extremely useful breakdown of the vote by both candidate and voting district can be found in *La vraie République*, June 10, 1848. The figures for the April elections are much less complete, hence any comparisons must remain approximate.

Central Commission for Democratic Elections had failed in its drive to increase registration and to get out the registered vote. While the number of registered voters remained practically unchanged, the total of those casting ballots in the twelve districts of the capital dropped by at least 30,000 compared to April. Were the new stay-at-homes conservatives or socialists, bourgeois or proletarians? The most that one can say is that registration was slightly down in the bourgeois western parts of the city and slightly up in the more working-class eastern section. The number of actual voters, while it declined in both areas, was down by 17 percent in the west as against only 11 percent in the east. Seemingly fewer working-class than middle-class voters had turned their backs on electoral politics. Secondly, and much more demonstrably, moderate republicanism had collapsed, its share of the votes dropping from 45 percent in April to 9 percent in June. Thirdly, the conservatives, eclipsed in April, now captured 41 percent of the vote while electing four candidates to the Assembly. Finally, the socialist minority, while also electing four representatives, had progressed from 26 percent in April to 38 percent of the vote in June. Its support had, moreover, been surprisingly well disciplined; not a single socialist received less than 59,000 votes, and the more proletarian the *arrondissement*, the more solid the socialist vote. In the eighth district, the Faubourg Saint-Antoine (which was also to be the last redoubt of the June insurgents three weeks later), all eleven candidates of the Central Commission for Democratic Elections won handily: in the sixth, seventh, ninth, and twelfth districts, eight of the eleven club nominees were ahead; in the fourth and fifth, the borderland between bourgeois and proletarian Paris, seven socialists were the winners.[39] Compared to what the Club of Clubs had accomplished in April in alliance with the Central Committee of the Workers of the Seine, the so-

[39] *La vraie République*, June 9, 1848.

cialists had converted 35,000 voters, though without making real inroads among abstainers. From a range of 20,000 to 65,000 votes in April, socialist strength in the Seine department had risen to between 60,000 and 90,000 in June. If the results of the balloting fell short of the most sanguine expectations, the clubs could take credit for considerable progress.

V

Just at the time when the new election campaign signaled the return of the club movement to conventional politics, the campaign for a monster Banquet of the People pulled it in the contrary direction. If the Central Commission for Democratic Elections had been the work of the revolutionary establishment, the banquet was being organized by mavericks closer in mood to the rank and file. On May 27 the government-ordered kidnapping of Emile Thomas, the director of the National Workshops, sharpened the fear of the workshops' impending dissolution among the unemployed. The nightly crowds on the boulevards reflected this popular restiveness and alienation. For people who saw their high hopes of social renewal fading, another election must have seemed beside the point, whereas the idea of a popular banquet promised at least emotional satisfaction. At once a concrete gesture and a nebulous project, the proposal for a vast proletarian gathering was attractive to people looking for some affirmation without yet being prepared to raise barricades again. The government opposed the banquet as a challenge to its authority from below; the club leadership sought to thwart the banquet as a trap.[40]

[40] There are two major source collections on the banquet, both of them in the cartons of the June 1848 insurgents at the A.M.G. at Vincennes. The complete archives of the Founding Commission created by the Club de la Montagne and located at 12, rue Ménars, are under dossier Thuillier et autres, A. 3669bis, filling a whole carton. Where my information is de-

The history of the banquet campaign opened with a coincidence. Almost at the same time, two separate and originally unrelated appeals for a gigantic banquet catering to the Paris working class were launched. The May 28 issue of *Le Père Duchêne, gazette de la révolution,* then the most widely read left-wing sheet, published the following notice:

BANQUET OF THE NATIONAL WORKSHOPS

The citizen-workers of the National Workshops have decided to hold a banquet at fifty centimes per person. They invite those among them who have not yet been notified to get together so that everybody may be there. Contact your brigade leader. The banquet will take place in the course of next week. There will be fraternizing and discussions concerning the interests of the proletarians. *Le Père Duchêne* will be there. . . .

Far more dramatic was the proposal placarded on Paris walls the next day:

BANQUET OF THE PEOPLE—
FRATERNIZATION OF THE WORKERS

Workers!
Children of the Republic!
Our Mother, France, is impoverished, . . . but our wealth consists of fraternity. They haven't been able to tear it out of our hearts. . . . May we come together in fraternal communion! The earth is rich in greenery; the grass of the meadows offers us its seats for the Banquet of the People. No unnecessary expenses, brothers. . . . That

rived from this collection and where the nature of the document is evident, I have omitted footnotes. Much less informative is *Le Père Duchêne*'s correspondence received in connection with the banquet, under dossier Colfavru, A. 982. For a somewhat more detailed treatment, see my "Prelude to Insurrection: The 'Banquet of the People,' " and "*Du neuf* on the Banquet of the People, June 1848," *French Historical Studies,* I (1960), 436-444; v (1968), 344-350.

is why we shall hold a banquet at five sous per person. . . .
The Almighty must hear but one acclaim, one wish from
our hearts, the sole cry of humanity: Long live the
democratic and social Republic.[41]

The names of the six founding commissioners followed
this announcement. A special invitation was extended to
National Workshops, brigadiers, club presidents, army
and craft delegates to pick up subscriptions at the offices
of the rue Ménars or at *Le Père Duchêne*. The newspaper story, after spelling out the proposed menu—a
bottle of burgundy to wash down bread and first-quality
cheese—also promised that following the artillery salvos
that would open the festivities there would be "patriotic
symphonies." With disarming candor, the founders went
on to invite volunteer musicians and artillery men to report to banquet headquarters.

On May 30 *Le Père Duchêne* again featured the announcement of the Banquet of the People, adding that
the Banquet of the National Workshops was also reduc-
ing its admission to twenty-five centimes. From that point
on, no one—neither the public nor the organizers nor the
police—ever managed to disentangle the Banquet of the
People from that of the National Workshops until, about
a week later, the two finally became one.[42]

If the Banquet of the National Workshops had really

[41] See *Enquête*, II, 286-288; *Le Père Duchêne, gazette de
la révolution*, May 29-June 1, 1848; *La Réforme*, evening ed.,
May 29, 1848; *La vraie République*, June 1, 1848.

[42] The fact that *Le Père Duchêne* proved to be a more popular ticket office than the rue Ménars increased the friction
between the two, as the newspaper refused to turn over the
funds collected. The wrangle is richly and tediously documented in the Founding Commission's archives. The commissioners seem to have taken the first step in a civil suit to
bring Thuillier to heel. For some of the public posturing, see
Le Père Duchêne, June 6-8, 1848; poster, "Banquet du Peuple,
le 8 juin," B.H.V.P., 1848, affiches.

originated within the workshops, its organizers succeeded in preserving their anonymity. Their (self-appointed?) spokesman from the start was *Le Père Duchêne*. For practical purposes, *Le Père Duchêne* consisted of two people: Emile Thuillier, its publisher, and Jean-Claude Colfavru, its editor-in-chief. Both were young, of respectable family, but slightly *déclassé*. A few years before the February Revolution, Thuillier had been set up by his father with an iron foundry, an enterprise the son succeeded in running into the ground, or rather into fraudulent bankruptcy, within a year.[43] His 1848 venture into revolutionary journalism was more successful. Dusting off Hébert's old formula of 1793, *Le Père Duchêne* impersonated the crusty and profane old patriot, whose gruff exterior could not hide his shrewdness and good sense. If violence of language cut loose from any definable program is the mark of demagoguery, *Le Père Duchêne* was indisputably demagogic. Yet whatever the abstract merits of the formula, in 1848 as in 1793 it sold newspapers. By June the paper's claimed circulation of 75,000 outstripped that of any other newspaper.[44]

Colfavru is a less shadowy figure than Thuillier. Twenty-seven years old, clerking in the back office of an established legal firm, "sole support of a pensioned soldier-father, a mother and sister living in poverty in Lyon," he must have been no different from dozens of other young provincial lawyers who had found Paris less hospitable than they had hoped.[45] The February Revolution catapulted Colfavru from dingy obscurity into the glamor world of

[43] A.M.G., A. 3669 and 3669bis.

[44] For the problems involved in verifying such figures for 1848, see R. Gossez, "La presse parisienne à destination des ouvriers (1848-1851)," 189-190. According to Gossez, *Le Père Duchêne*'s official press-run figures for June were 70,000; ibid., p. 143, n. 70.

[45] A.M.G., dossier Colfavru, A. 982, particularly a letter from his former employer.

political journalism and the club movement. By April he was presiding over the militant Club of Free Men, while copiloting the meteoric flight of *Le Père Duchêne.*

The sponsorship of the Banquet of the People, on the other hand, was clearly vested in a club—the Club of the Mountain of suburban Montmartre—rather than in particular individuals.[46] Founded by one Dulaurier, a member of the postrevolutionary town council of Montmartre, the club had gone through three or four presidents in three months. It retained the same nucleus of activists, who show up in a variety of offices in the club minutes. Except for its preoccupation with municipal affairs— something characteristic of the small-town atmosphere of the suburbs—the Club of the Mountain was typical of dozens of other popular societies with their rounds of demonstrating, electioneering, and playing Greek chorus in the revolutionary drama. The club had, like many others, participated in the Club of Clubs, though the one motion that it had submitted for approval seems to have been passed over. On May 15 the club's banner may have been seen in the hall of the National Assembly, but participation in the Polish demonstration was hardly a mark of originality. Nor was club membership impressive: in April attendance fluctuated between one and three hundred.[47] Certainly nothing in the club's antecedents could account for the notoriety of the banquet movement.

With one possible exception, the six founding commissioners (others were to be added later) were as obscure

---

[46] Aside from the club archives which peter out just prior to the April elections (A.M.G., dossier Thuillier et autres, A. 3669bis), fragments of information on the club may be found in *La Commune de Paris*, March 17, 1848; *La Voix des clubs*, March 24; for relations with the Club of Clubs, A.N., C. 941, CdE 9551, 8555, and *La Réforme*, March 29; Lucas, *Les clubs et les clubistes*, p. 182; for participation in May 15 demonstration, Louis-Benjamin Thomassin, *DBMOF*, iii, 450.

[47] Club de la Montagne, A.N., C. 941, CdE 8549, 8555.

as the Club of the Mountain from which they had emerged. The originator of the whole idea was the club president, Charles Edouard Deshayes, aged twenty-nine, a clerical worker, possibly employed by the municipality of Montmartre, who succeeded to his club office in early April.[48] Despite Deshayes' acknowledged precedence, the chief banquet spokesman was Louis-Benjamin Thomassin, who at forty-eight was the senior member of the commission. A former typographical worker and master printer, in 1848 he was Paris manager of a substantial insurance company, though the business slump had eroded his position. Thomassin was not only active in the Club of the Mountain but was also second lieutenant of his National Guard company in Montmartre. Quite apart from this, he stood near the top of the Society of the Rights of Man's military hierarchy as a neighborhood or possibly even a district commander. What is puzzling is that, despite the society's vaunted iron discipline, Thomassin should have continued to promote the banquet after the Society of the Rights of Man had formally disavowed it. Ideologically Thomassin may have been an Icarian disciple, if a request from prison for "the book of Cabet" is any indication. Another facet of Thomassin's career did not become known until after his arrest in mid-June: he had been active as a Bonapartist propagandist during the 1830's.[49] Mathias Leinen, another commissioner, aged twenty-nine, was a Prussian subject from the border town of Sarrelouis, who had settled in Paris to run a workingmen's rooming house and wineshop. Leinen, less active in the Club of the Mountain than some of the

[48] Registre des insurgés de juin 1848, B.H.V.P., Liesville Collection; Lucas, *Les clubs et les clubistes*, p. 182.

[49] A.M.G., dossier Thuillier et autres, A. 3669bis. Gossez' *notice*, Louis-Benjamin Thomassin, *DBMOF*, III, 450-451, may be in part based on documents that have eluded me. For Thomassin's role in the Société des Droits de l'Homme, DH Minutes, A.M.G., dossier Guille.

others, headed a committee of his compatriots living in Paris, whose main preoccupation was the rehabilitation of Sarrelouis' most famous native son, Marshal Ney, a victim of Bourbon vengeance in 1815.[50] A fourth member of the commission, Etienne Grossier-Barangé, also twenty-nine, listed himself as an *employé*, though he was a traveling salesman with Montmartre as his home base. By 1848 he already had a varied career behind him; successively soldier, hairdresser, ribbon dealer, wholesale ribbon merchant, and, most recently, bankrupt, Grossier-Barangé had been exposed to Blanqui's brand of communism in Tours before he came to the capital in 1847.[51] A fifth commissioner was noted as a student, while the last of the six remains a name only.[52] Aside from common membership in the Club of the Mountain, all of these founding fathers were residents of Montmartre, all of them had at least one foot in the door to middle-class standing, all but Thomassin were under thirty, and, with the same exception, all were unknown outside of their suburb.

What were the intentions of the promoters? Of the two groups, the organizers of the Banquet of the National Workshops (including the journalists of *Le Père Duchêne*) saw the banquet as an organized and disciplined protest against Emile Thomas' removal and a warning against any attempt to dissolve the workshops. Some of these anonymous organizers may well have been among the men who touched off the June insurrection four weeks later. The Club of the Mountain group was less militant, less class conscious, and less politically minded. Its

[50] Mathias Leinen, *DBMOF*, ii, 483. A.M.G., dossier Thuillier et autres, A. 3669[bis].

[51] Etienne Grossier, *DBMOF*, ii, 306. I have been unable to find this dossier at Vincennes.

[52] Archives of the Banquet Founding Commission, A.M.G., dossier Thuillier et autres, A. 3669[bis].

emphasis was on the fraternization of all those who, living by their brawn or brain, identified themselves as workers—and wives and children were included in the proceedings. According to notes found in the Banquet Commission's archives, the organizers hoped for 300,000 participants, 100,000 of whom would be drawn from the capital's fifty clubs, 150,000 from the organized crafts, and 50,000 from unattached patriots and from the National Workshops. In their appeals to the clubs and the craft groups, in their attempts to appease the government, in their correspondence with a multitude of wholesalers, the founding commissioners testified to an uncomplicated faith in a simple idea meant for humble people—though some of them must have known better.

In June of 1848 a monster banquet for the disinherited was anything but a simple proposition to be accepted at face value. Like a medieval reading of a Bible story, layers of meaning and of allusion could be unraveled, depending on the sophistication of the interpreter. From the authorities' viewpoint, the most uncomplicated level is represented by an investigating judge's stuffy reprimand to Colfavru of *Le Père Duchêne*: "You must have known very well that a banquet that was to bring together several thousand subscribers drawn from the least enlightened classes of the people would inevitably bring about the most serious excesses."[53] From the standpoint of "the least enlightened classes of the people," the banquet at five sous was the workingman's answer to those who had priced fraternity beyond his reach. The February Revolution had set in motion an orgy of public dinners in the name of republican brotherhood, some of them sponsored by clubs.[54] Yet most of these banquets had been

[53] Interrogation Colfavru, A.M.G., dossier Colfavru, A. 982.
[54] For example, Comité central du IIIe arrondissement, A.N., C. 941, CdE 8877; Banquet des Ecoles, *La Réforme*, June 2, 1848. The invitation to one such banquet (in April?) issued

held by units of the Paris National Guard, with its bourgeois core and proletarian accretions, often at prices that
the new Guard members could ill afford. As one member
of the Club of the Revolution was to complain, "These
meals at six francs are nothing but a lie! The banquet of
the proletarians at twenty-five centimes will be real fraternity."[55] Or, to quote the doggerel in one of the
ephemeral newssheets of the day:

> Five sous they've voted, five sous a head
> To celebrate fraternity.
> For nowadays we've neither bread
> Nor butter. Five sous! What a pity
> That we are like the Wand'ring Jew
> Forever on the march. 'Tis true
> The people have been on the go
> Ere Eden and the Ark of No',
> Dragging their way o'er dale and hill:
> No end in sight; they're looking still
> Just like the Jew, having withal
> But five sous jingling, and that's all.[56]

Yet it did not take great perspicacity to view the
planned banquet in terms of recent precedents, which
shifted the connotation drastically from fraternity to revolution. No one had to be reminded that in February
1848 the famous Banquet of the Twelfth District had

---

by the moderate Club de l'émancipation des peuples was in
the files of the Club de la Montagne (of Montmartre). Could
this be the source for the idea of the Banquet of the People?
However, the most likely precedent was a mass banquet for
popular societies organized by the little-known Club des incorruptibles on April 2, Place du Châtelet. This banquet, April
showers notwithstanding, attracted a number of clubs but was
generally ignored even by the revolutionary press. *Le Démocrate égalitaire*, April 18, 1848.

[55] See Club de la révolution, June 2, *Le Travail*, June 4-6,
1848.

[56] *Le Petit Homme rouge*, No. 9, June 1848.

sparked the insurrection that had swept away the July Monarchy. What the bourgeois banquet had done for the monarchy might not the proletarian banquet do for the bourgeois Republic?[57] Historical analogy could be pushed even further: the February banquet had miraculously saved the declining cause of the middle-class reformers.[58] Equally miraculously, could not the June banquet save the declining cause of the Paris workers and their socialist allies?

The organizational details of the banquet, the delays and postponements, the tug of war between *Le Père Duchêne* and the other commissioners settled only by virtual peace treaty on June 7, need not detain us. What is important is that within a matter of days the banquet at five sous had become the talk of the town. By June 1, the figure of 75,000 subscribers was bruited, even as police informers reported that practically the whole of the National Workshops—which stood at about 100,000 men— had signed up.[59] By June, questionable estimates had risen to 150,000 and the editors of *Le Père Duchêne* were hoping for the banquet commissioners' own target of 300,000 men, women, and children.[60] Rumor, fanned by the promoters, left reality far behind. After selling less than four hundred tickets in the first three days, the commissioners of the rue Ménars had the nerve to announce a doubling of their staff to handle the "influx" and to suggest that henceforth only blocks of tickets be sold, to

[57] Bonde, *Paris in 1848*, p. 176, letter of June 5, 1848; Normanby, *Year of Revolution*, i, 447, June 8 entry.

[58] See John Baughman, "The Banquet Campaign of 1847-48," *Journal of Modern History*, xxxi (1959), 1-15.

[59] *La Réforme*, June 2, 1848; police report, June 2, 1848, *Enquête*, ii, 197.

[60] Club de la révolution, June 2, *Le Travail*, June 6-8, 1848; *Le Père Duchêne*, June 4-6, 1848. The last "official" figures, supposedly released by the Banquet Commission, were 195,532 subscriptions sold. *La République rouge*, June 11-14, 1848.

avoid bottlenecks.[61] After this, business picked up
rapidly; by the evening of June 10, between the offices
of the rue Ménars and those of *Le Père Duchêne* 26,607
tickets had been sold and paid for.

vi

The clubs' initial response to the banquet had been enthusiastic. On June 1 the Blanquist Central Club of
United Workers summoned all its members to participate, while the Popular Club of the Second of March at
the Sorbonne advertised its pledge of complete attendance at "the communion of the disinherited" in the
press.[62] Suburban clubs seemed particularly eager to participate. The Democratic Club of La Chapelle bought a
block of four hundred tickets, while the notoriously militant Montagnards of Belleville took no less than twenty-
nine hundred.

The euphoria on the Left was short-lived. First, the
Club of the Revolution, then after some hesitation the
Society of the Rights of Man, moved to head off the banquet by concerted action. By June 2 few defenders of the
banquet could be found at the Club of the Revolution.
Speaker after speaker arose to voice his misgivings: "I
am constantly on guard against anything that may offer
a toehold to reaction. For several days now, bourgeois
bayonets have been on the lookout for a riot. I am afraid
that this banquet may offer them just the opportunity
they want. The past should serve as object lesson: let us
remember May 15," ran a typical tirade. Voting its dis-

[61] *La vraie République*, June 1, 1848. The manuscript announcement can also be found in the archives of the Banquet
Founding Commission.

[62] Police report, June 1, *Enquête*, II, 197; *Le Père Duchêne*,
June 4-6, 1848. Correspondence with the Club populaire du
deux mars may also be found in the Founding Commission's
archives and in A.M.G., dossier Colfavru, A. 982.

approval of the whole affair, the club appointed a commission to see what might be done to stop the banquet.[63] As its chairman reported the following evening, this first step was useless. A long interview with one of the *Père Duchêne* editors yielded little in the way of information. Instead, the newspaperman responded with an offer— declined by the club representatives—of a seat on the banquet organizing committee.[64] The Club of the Revolution therefore took a second step by convoking all club delegates to a meeting with the banquet promoters, a meeting which took place on June 6 or 7 at the rue Martel. Now facing delegates from a number of clubs rather than those of the Club of the Revolution alone, the banquet organizers proved no more cooperative than they had a few days earlier. The commissioners simply dug in behind their position that the Banquet of the People was theirs and theirs alone. They categorically refused to let outsiders pass on their preparations or peer into their books. Yet as an act of good faith they were willing to consult the subscribers to the banquet by calling a meeting of these "shareholders" (or rather of their delegates) for the evening of June 10 in the hall used by the Society of the Rights of Man.

It was this first encounter in the rue Martel which decided the Society of the Rights of Man to intervene decisively against the banquet, for its representatives had been thoroughly disquieted by the promoters' unaccountability. Before this the banquet had been a divisive issue among the *sociétaires*,[65] but now the society publicly announced its unanimous resolve to see the banquet at twenty-five centimes adjourned indefinitely: "The present

[63] Club de la révolution, session of June 2, *Le Travail*, June 4-6, 1848.

[64] Club de la révolution, session of June 3, *Le Travail*, June 6-8, 1848.

[65] DH Minutes.

agitated public opinion is the reason for this decision. It is to be feared that the agents of the antidemocratic cause might find opportunities for starting trouble in such a large gathering and by so doing undermine the rights of the real people."[66]

In a pattern reminiscent of the special election campaign, the Society of the Rights of Man now took over the leadership from the Club of the Revolution. Using the Central Commission for Democratic Elections as its front, the society called what amounted to a council of war against the banquet for June 8. Delegates representing thirteen clubs and seven left-wing newspapers attended.[67] It was at this meeting that the club strategy to stop the Banquet of the People must have beem hammered out. Since the club leadership had proved unable either to control the banquet promoters or to cancel the banquet because the organizers were impervious to outsiders, someone evidently got the idea that by becoming insiders—subscribers to the banquet—the clubists might be able to seize control. By packing the "stockholders" meeting called by the Founding Commission for June 10 with club delegates hostile to the project, the whole affair might be smothered. For this reason, the Society of the Rights of Man convened another—and, they hoped, more inclusive—meeting of club delegates to concert strategy only two hours before the scheduled Founding Commission's "stockholders" session.[68]

[66] The announcement appeared in several papers: *Le Représentant du peuple*, June 9, 1848; *La Réforme*, June 9, 1848; *L'Organisation du travail*, June 10, 1848.

[67] DH Minutes, June 8. Even though delegates from the Club de la révolution participated, the latter continued its unilateral efforts against the banquet by grilling Colfavru of *Le Père Duchêne* at its June 9 club session. *Le Travail*, June 11-13, 1848; letter from one Mesle to *Le Père Duchêne* (B.H.V.P., Liesville Collection) may refer to the same episode.

[68] *La Réforme*, June 9, 1848.

The club strategy proved only partly successful because the clubs had apparently counted on a smallish crowd of banquet representatives whom their delegates would easily dominate. Instead they found a mob of some thousand people, many of whom were apparently delegated only by themselves. Could it be that the founding commissioners, having gotten wind of the club stratagem, had tried their own hand at packing the meeting? The banquet organizers defended their project on the grounds that it was not only peaceable but deliberately designed to guard against possible violence. They denied as slander the rumors of Bonapartist influence and subsidy. They condemned every attempt to postpone the great working-class outing or to shackle the hands of the organizers.[69] To a delegate from the moderate-leftish Central Democratic Society, the journalists of *Le Père Duchêne* seemed persuasive, the founding commissioners of the Club of the Mountain remained suspect.[70] After the meeting, the Society of the Rights of Man released an "authorized" scenario, claiming that the delegates had voted overwhelmingly to overrule the banquet promoters by adjourning the great fraternization to July 14 and by setting up a commission to control the commissioners.[71]

A more dramatic—and likely—version made the rounds of the Club of the Revolution. Its delegates claimed that the unruly crowd had noisily applauded the banquet commissioners and their stand. Only a brilliant harangue by Hervé, one of their own club delegates, had swayed the audience to defeat the motion to hold the banquet on June 18.[72] At best, the concerted club drive had won a half victory, one month of grace rather than the banquet's

[69] Club de la révolution, session of June 13, *Le Travail*, June 14-16, 1848.

[70] DH Minutes, June 14, pp. 580-582.

[71] *La vraie République*, June 13, 1848.

[72] Session of June 13, *Le Travail*, June 14-16, 1848.

liquidation. The very choice of July 14 was the organizers' snort of defiance. To pick the anniversary of the storming of the Bastille among the 366 days of the calendar year 1848 was as unlikely to allay the misgivings of the club leaders opposing the banquet as it was to reassure public opinion in general.

Assailed by the clubs, the banquet promoters were not able to snatch a night's sleep before the government swooped down upon them. Just a day earlier, on June 9, the Founding Commission had sought to cover its flank by direct negotiations with the authorities. They had seen Panisse, director of the Ministry of the Interior's security police. According to a memorandum drawn up right after the meeting, the banquet commissioners had stressed five points: (1) That they, the commissioners, had always intended to submit their plans for prior approval to the authorities. They pointed to earlier letters to Trouvé-Chauvel, the police prefect, and to Lalanne, the new director of the National Workshops, as proof of their good faith. (2) That from the start they had rejected the idea of inviting integral units of the National Workshops—this was a sideswipe at *Le Père Duchêne*—except insofar as individual "workers of all classes" were welcome. (3) That only once had they proposed that the banquet be held along the outer fortifications of Paris and then only with the understanding that this proposal be ratified by delegates of the banquet subscribers themselves. (4) That none of their posters or announcements had ever set a specific date because they realized that this required official authorization. (5) That rumors that the banquet would be held in the vicinity of Vincennes were completely unfounded. Having deluded themselves into believing they had won Panisse's confidence, the banquet organizers must have been badly jolted by the arrest of their spokesman, Thomassin, at 3:00 A.M. on June 11. Evidently the government had awaited the outcome of the banquet "stockholders" meeting of June 10 before pouncing. While Thomassin's alleged complicity in the events of May 15 was cited as the official justification, this cover story was accompanied by a long account of his Bonapartist past.[73] The attempt to halt the banquet by discrediting its most prominent leader was both transparent and successful.

Whether the postponement to July 14 or the exposé of Thomassin's background contributed more to braking the momentum of the banquet campaign is debatable. The sudden and spectacular collapse of the movement is not. While on June 10 no less than 2,779 subscriptions were bought, on June 11 they were down to 310, on June 12 to 75. From May 30 through June 10, 26,607 tickets were purchased; from June 11 through June 20, no more than 2,800. Toward the end, the average daily "take" hovered around eight francs. As the campaign collapsed, the Founding Commission's manifestos became shriller.[74] Imperceptibly, but with ultimate finality, Le Père Duchêne dissociated itself from the banquet.[75] The Founding Commission itself was splintering: the incarcerated Thomassin declined responsibility for his colleagues' acts, while Charles Deshayes, the originator of the whole project, resigned, precipitating an unseemly squabble over finances. Yet until a new revolutionary tidal wave finally submerged the banquet, its remaining commissioners stayed at their post. On June 22, the very eve of the June insurrection, they sent a letter to the Min-

[73] The story was carried by most newspapers from June 13 on. La vraie République, June 13, 1848; Le Père Duchêne, June 15-18, 1848; L'Organisation du travail, June 18, 1848; Le Travail, June 18, 1848.

[74] Enquête, II, 291; L'Organisation du travail, June 20, 1848. The manuscript drafts, often in many versions, of such announcements and proclamations have been preserved in the files of the Banquet Founding Commission.

[75] Le Père Duchêne, June 18-20, 1848.

ister of the Interior confirming that the Banquet of the People, Fraternization of the Workers, would indeed be held on July 14; and that was the end of it.

vii

Along with the banquet campaign and the crisis over the National Workshops—never mirrored in the clubs— which the nightly street demonstrations reflected and sharpened, the sudden popularity of Louis Napoleon was one of the characteristic phenomena of June 1848. The Bonapartist agitation, both spontaneous and subsidized, had grown as a byproduct of the June elections once Louis Napoleon had announced his candidacy to the National Assembly. His election led to passionate debates on street corners and in ministerial councils over letting an acknowledged pretender to the French throne take a seat in a republican legislature. Bonaparte's resignation on June 16—a master stroke in furthering his career— avoided the immediate dilemma, though the agitation in his behalf continued.[76]

Like the Banquet of the People, Bonapartism was a divisive issue for the clubs, and in much the same way.

[76] For reports and comments on Bonapartist agitation in the left-wing press, see *La vraie République*, June 13, 14, 19; *La Réforme*, June 14, 1848, evening ed.; *L'Organisation du travail*, June 13, 1848; *La République rouge*, June 13, 1848; *L'Accusateur public*, June 14-18, 1848; *Le Représentant du peuple*, June 16, 18, 1848; *La Réforme*, June 19, 1848; the reports are also borne out by police reports: see unsigned report, June 17, *Enquête*, II, 208; report from police prefect's *chef du cabinet*, June 20, A.N., C. 933, CdE 2383. For a monographic account, see R. Pimienta, *La propagande bonapartiste en 1848* (Paris, 1911). His interpretation of Louis Napoleon's simultaneous appeal to the forces of both order and disorder is more convincing than a more recent analysis by Tudesq, "La légende napoléonienne en France en 1848," *Revue historique*, LXXXI (1957), 64-85, which stresses the nationalist appeal of Louis Napoleon.

It was generally recognized by contemporaries that Louis Napoleon drew more support from the suburbs than from the city proper, a generalization that also held true in the clubs. As in the case of the banquet, club leaders were more adamantly opposed than the casual member, who often identified with Louis Napoleon's tilting against the conservative republican establishment. It was the passivity of this very establishment that the Club of the Mountain of the rue Frépillon (which had no connection with the sponsors of the banquet) blamed for the sudden prominence of ridiculous pretenders such as "the Don Quixote of Strasbourg."[77] The Club of the Union circulated two successive petitions, the first requesting the National Assembly to unseat Louis Bonaparte on the grounds that he was not a French citizen and had twice led an armed invasion of French territory, the second one indignantly protesting against "the reactionary demonstrations which these last few days have been dishonoring the capital in behalf of an imperial pretender."[78] As late as June 17, after Louis Bonaparte's resignation from the Assembly, the Club of the Revolution adhered by a strong majority to a resolution sponsored by the Club of the Butte des Moulins demanding the prince's banishment and requesting an inquiry into the Bonapartist agitation.[79] Yet if the club leaders were united in resisting Bonapartist pretensions, their followers, particularly in the suburbs, wavered. The identical petition to which the Club of the Revolution had assented was shouted down at a club in Saint-Denis.[80] At the Democratic Club of

[77] Undated petition (ca. June 10), A.M.G., dossier Colfavru, A. 982.

[78] Petition of June 11, *Le Père Duchêne*, June 13-15, 1848; letter to the editor, *La vraie République*, June 13, 1848, Thoré Papers.

[79] *Le Travail*, June 21-24, 1848.

[80] Unsigned police report, June 22, referring to events of June 17, A.N., C. 933, CdE 2520.

Batignolles in the northwestern suburbs a speaker advo-
cating Louis Bonaparte's banishment had to compete
with shouts of "We want Napoleon! We'll get him yet!"
In this instance the orator, a left-wing lawyer named
Madier de Montjau, was finally allowed to resume his
plea. The club meeting broke up amidst recriminations
between pro- and anti-Bonapartist members.[81]

viii

In the aftermath of the Polish demonstration the clubs
paid less attention to day-by-day legislative debate than
in early May, when they had played echo chamber to the
Constituent Assembly.[82] Most radicals had probably
given up hope that anything constructive would emerge
from a parliament that kept underscoring its conserva-
tism. Only when some of the major achievements of the
February Revolution were threatened did the clubs react
sharply. During June there were at least three such occasions: in first place were the official attempts to deal with
nightly street crowds that upset both the government and
the National Assembly; in second and third place was the
drive against the left-wing press and against the clubs
themselves.

The domestic policy of the five-man Executive Com-

[81] Same report, but referring to events of June 20.

[82] There were exceptions. The Club central de l'organisation des travailleurs, for one, still considered it worth appealing to the Assembly to reverse its own committee's decision
against nationalizing the railroads. *La Réforme*, May 27, 1848.
More characteristic was the Club populaire de la Sorbonne's
mock petition in which the club invited the parliament which
"pays too much attention to the fate of the workers and very
little to that of the rich . . . also to do something for these latter by ordering an investigation among property owners to
determine if they are not too rich just like the one ordered to
find out if the poor are not too poor." *Journal des sans-culottes*,
May 28-June 1, 1848.

mission that governed France was to liquidate the revolution. I do not mean to suggest some diabolical bourgeois conspiracy against the Paris working class, nor that the officials responsible for this policy were consciously antirepublican. Yet three of the five members of the Executive Commission, as well as most of the ministers that had been appointed, had long been associated with *Le National*, a newspaper which, a generation before Thiers' famous dictum, had maintained that the Republic would be conservative or would not be at all.[83] No doubt this reasoned conviction was reinforced by the attitude of the National Assembly, which had elected the executive with a clear mandate to "normalize" an abnormal situation. To normalize did not, of course, mean simply to turn the clock back to January 1848. For the time being, for example, political democracy based on manhood suffrage was beyond tampering with; but the continuous agitation in the Paris streets, the noisy challenge to the established social order, the frenetic mass involvement that the February Revolution had sanctioned and even sanctified—all these were considered intolerable by executive and legislature alike. Even perfectly sincere republicans looked back to the monarchy—the only "normal" government they had experienced—for the proper norms of public tranquillity, just as they turned to prerevolutionary legislation for the means of restoring law and order. If, as Trotsky has it, revolution is defined as the irruption of the masses upon the stage of history, government and Assembly concurred in wanting that stage cleared.

It is in this context that controversy over legislation to control unlawful gatherings took shape. The government's bill had been introduced in parliament by the Minister of the Interior on June 5. To what extent the threat of the Banquet of the People contributed to its in-

[83] Georges Weill, *Histoire du parti républicain, 1814-1870* (Paris, 1928), p. 48.

10.–Antecedent of the June Insurrection

Bonapartist rumors:

   "I tell you that I saw Bonaparte at the race-course."

   "But that's impossible since I just heard him at the National Assembly."

   "You are both wrong, for I just passed Place Vendôme a moment ago and he was on top of the column."

troduction and passage is uncertain, for the debaters referred chiefly to the nightly crowds that clogged the eastern boulevards. There was nothing organized about these
thousands of milling workers who re-formed every time
they were dispersed by National Guard patrols. While the
crowds blocked traffic on several key arteries of pre-
Haussmann Paris, they were not insurrectionary; yet neither were they ordinary evening strollers. The idle and
embittered by the thousands turned the Porte Saint-Denis
and Saint-Martin into forums for venting their grievances. The balmy summer weather, the monstrous scope
of unemployment, the popular disenchantment with the
clubs' ineffectiveness, as well as the magnetic attraction
of any large mass of people, helped to swell the crowd
night after night. It was a free show that street orators
and National Guard patrols helped keep alive.

The government's rationale for a new law was not the
lack of old ones—major legislation dating back to 1791,
1819, and 1822 could have been invoked—but squeam-
ishness about using "monarchical" laws without special
endorsement by the Republic's representatives. At the
same time, the proposed new law turned out to be more
severe than anything on the statute books. Anyone in an
unarmed street gathering who did not disperse at the first
official summons could be charged with a misdemeanor;
anyone in an armed crowd was guilty of a misdemeanor
even if the crowd did disperse immediately, and with a
felony if it did not. The joker was to define an *armed*
gathering. According to the new law, if the crowd included a single individual openly bearing arms (a saber,
for instance), and if that individual was not expelled or
if the crowd included several persons bearing hidden
arms, it was to be considered armed. To top it off, the
legislation provided for criminal action against anyone
inciting an unlawful gathering by speech, picture, or
print, thus opening the door to the same "moral com-

plicity" which republicans had deplored during the July Monarchy. On June 7, after a day of debate, the bill passed with only minor changes, 478 to 82.[84]

Club condemnation was unanimous. Even before the bill had come up for discussion, the Club of the Emancipation of the Peoples, anything but radical on social issues, petitioned the Assembly against following "the Executive Commission along the deplorable road where it is dragging you. When we read this Draconian code, we don't know whether to be more astonished or more indignant. Citizens, were the men who have drawn up such laws chosen by the revolutionaries of 1848 or are they the ministers of Louis-Philippe?"[85] The Society of the Rights of Man waited for the bill to become law before drawing up its protest, in which it invited all other democratic clubs to join. The society's petition went beyond the usual "astonishment and indignation" by pointing out the lesson of history that repression always stimulates revolt. When, as was the case now, repressive legislation paralleled a concentration of troops in the capital, the situation was even more serious: "We must not hide from you, citizen representatives, that the people's feelings are very much aroused. It implores you to put an end to such unfortunate proposals. While it seeks to defend and safeguard its rights by reason and persuasion, it cannot believe that the goals of complete freedom promised by the Republic can come by means of a Draconian code carried on the points of bayonets." The petition concluded by demanding that the Assembly repeal the law and order a troop withdrawal from Paris.[86] These

[84] For the original proposal, see *Le Moniteur universel*, June 6, 1848, p. 1273; for the debate, ibid., June 8, 1848, pp. 1290-1298. For the amended text of the law as passed, ibid., June 9, 1848, p. 1301.

[85] *Le Représentant du peuple*, June 7, 1848.

[86] Session of June 9, *La vraie République*, June 14, 1848.

sentiments were shared even in the Club of the Revolution, which, forgetting its habitual caution, rang with fiery speeches about a people's duty to rise against a violation of its inalienable rights.[87] More judiciously, but with no more effect, the Club of the Mountain of the rue Frépillon called for modifications in the law to permit peaceful assembly wherever this did not impede traffic and to restrict penalties only to armed or tumultuous gatherings. The club also singled out the clause about moral complicity as one that had to go.[88]

With regard to the government's infringement of free speech, the clubs lodged some complaints, but the actual violations were less serious than the rumors of impending restrictive legislation. When the officers of the Club of the Sorbonne were protesting the police harassment of Constant Hilbey, ex-political prisoner and publisher of the crimson *Journal des sans-culottes*, they were reacting to sporadic incidents, not to official policy promulgated by the Executive Commission or legislated by the National Assembly.[89] Confidentially, the Executive Commission did call for the prosecution of all subversive publications, as well as for the enforcement of a law of 1830, never repealed but completely ignored since the Febru-

[87] Session of June 10, *Le Travail*, June 13-15, 1848; session of June 13, ibid., June 14-16, 1848.

[88] Petition to National Assembly, n.d., ca. June 10, A.M.G., dossier Colfavru, A. 982.

[89] For the protest, see *La Commune de Paris*, June 4, 1848. After an article listing the richest bankers in Paris published in both *L'Organisation du travail* and *La Réforme* had drawn sharp attacks from the floor of the National Assembly, the government mobilized the Minister of Justice, who in turn activated the procurator of the Republic. (Note of June 13, A.N., BB[18], 1464, dossier 5896a.) A week later a new scurrilous left-wing sheet, *L'aimable Faubourien*, was facing police interference, or rather its street vendors were. *Le Représentant du peuple*, June 22, 1848. Gossez, "Presse," passim, mentions several similar instances for June.

ary Revolution, prohibiting the placarding of unauthorized posters. The police prefect, upon whom enforcement would have fallen, protested against the poor timing of this return to legality.[90] Shortly before the outbreak of the June insurrection, rumors reached the clubs that all newspapers would again have to post bond, as under the July Monarchy, a requirement that would paralyze the entire left-wing press.[91] The Club of the Revolution and that of the Second of March immediately protested against such a violation of "the principles which, at the cost of its blood, the people had conquered on February 24."[92]

ix

The government's preoccupation with problems of public order in general, and specifically with Bonapartism, street mobs, and the National Workshops, led to an uncoordinated and somewhat absent-minded policy toward the clubs. The Executive Commission itself virtually ignored the clubs.[93] Recurt, the Minister of the Interior, was also too concerned with dispersing crowds to devote sustained attention to the popular societies. He left this to the discretion of his chief policeman, inherited from the monarchy. Carlier, "irresponsible, rash, with few scruples either as to legal procedures or as to principles that are beyond his grasp," did plan the arrest of twenty-six top

[90] See *Minutes de la Commission du Pouvoir exécutif*, June 18, p. 394; the police prefect's daily report of June 19 contains his advice. A.N., C. 933, CdE 2359.

[91] Cf. *Procès-verbaux*, session of June 21, p. 405.

[92] Club de la révolution, petition to National Assembly, n.d., *La vraie République*, June 22, 1848; for the similar petition of Club populaire du deux mars, *Le Représentant du peuple*, June 23, 1848.

[93] *Procès-verbaux*, sessions of June 2 and June 4, 1848, pp. 324, 338, for the only two mentions.

club leaders during the second week of June.[94] Even though he had obtained Recurt's consent, Carlier's coup never materialized because of a jurisdictional squabble with the police prefect, who refused to take his orders from an underling.[95] The police prefect's own scheme, proposed on May 28, to dissolve the Society of the Rights of Man and to arrest its military hierarchy, was vetoed by Recurt.[96] The police official's later suggestion, forwarded on June 19, that closing the clubs might now be feasible, drew no response either.[97]

In contrast to the inaction or vacillation of other officials, Marrast, as mayor of Paris, pursued an increasingly aggressive policy toward the political clubs in the capital. Originally this policy had been formulated, or at least sanctioned, by the Executive Commission on May 14, but the turmoil caused by the Polish demonstration had delayed implementation. Marrast's policy was to undermine the clubs by depriving them of the city-owned meeting places which they had enjoyed since the February Days. On May 30 Marrast presided over a meeting of municipal district officials at which he conveyed his order, baldly noted in the minutes: "Closing of all clubs located on premises belonging to the *arrondissements.*"[98]

[94] Unsigned semiofficial report on Carlier (by Carteret or Trouvé-Chauvel?), July 4, A.N., C. 934, dossier 7, CdE 2754.

[95] Anonymous undated report (by Carteret? July 1848?), A.N., C. 933, dossier 3, CdE 2627.

[96] Trouvé-Chauvel to Minister of the Interior, May 28, 7:00 P.M., A.N., C. 934, dossier 7, CdE 2745; testimony Trouvé-Chauvel, *Enquête*, I, 361.

[97] Police report, signed Trouvé-Chauvel, June 19, 1848, A.N., C. 933, CdE 2359.

[98] For the fact that clubs were still able to use (and to reopen) in public school buildings during the last week of May, see announcement of Club fraternel de Quinze-Vingt, ca. May 23, *Le Représentant du peuple*, May 27, 1848; announcement of Club de l'Organisation sociale (formerly Club du progrès), May 29, *La vraie République*, May 29, 1848. The minutes of

The official letter sent to the district mayors was more diplomatic. It justified the clubs' ouster as restoring the public schools to their proper function, denying any infringement upon "the sacred freedom of assembly."[99] Evidently the district mayors—unpaid officials sensitive to the mood of their constituents—were less than eager to comply, preferring that classic mechanism of bureaucratic delay, an investigation, to brutal action.[100] When a second, sharper letter from the deputy mayor of Paris followed, the district officials gave in. Between June 12 and 16, clubs still meeting in schools, hospitals, asylums, and palaces had their municipal authorization canceled. In some instances they simply found the school building where they met locked and barred.[101]

The clubs' response was predictably bitter. "Inexpedient, imprudent, antifraternal," was the verdict of the Democratic Club of Saint-Maur: inexpedient, for if the clubs were forced to meet in private they evaded public supervision; imprudent, because disillusioned republicans

---

the May 30 meeting at the mayor's office are in A.S., V 3 D⁶, 23, No. 14.

[99] Same carton and file.

[100] Félicie Hérouart, nursery school principal, to mayor of the first district, June 17; Teulière, nursery school principal to mayor of the first district, June 16; M. Delahaye, public school teacher, to mayor of the first district, June 16, 1848, same carton and file.

[101] Undated circular letter, signed Edmond Adam, deputy mayor, same carton and file. Form letter from mayor of the first district, presumably sent to presidents of clubs within his jurisdiction, June 16, 1848, same carton and file. For a notified club, see Société pacifique des Droits de l'Homme, session of June 14, *La vraie République*, June 16, 1848; for a locked-out club, open letter from J. Gosset, president of Club démocratique de Saint-Maur, to Marrast, mayor of Paris, *Le Représentant du peuple*, June 19, 1848.

would be driven into the arms of the Bonapartists.[102] The Club of Socialist Republicans of the sixth district struck a pathetic note: "Give us back our public schools, so that the fathers may learn about the Republic in the evening, where their children learn their ABCs in the morning."[103] The Club of the Antonins, born of a merger of four working-class clubs of the eighth district, moved from lofty rhetoric to veiled threat in its petition to the Executive Commission. "Thus on the day when the club opens, the tavern closes its doors. For us the club constitutes the evening service; it is a course in patriotism; it is the place where we still believe in liberty, equality, and fraternity."[104] The official explanation of their eviction left them incredulous. Was it likely, they argued, that they would deface the classrooms where their own children were taught in the daytime? The real reason had nothing to do with vandalism:

> . . . it is the poor who are again being struck down and gagged. . . . The doors of the . . . school rooms are being locked against us. There we were permitted to meet without having to defray rental costs. Yet it is very well known today that only our patriotism silences our empty stomachs and that, once we have given our children their inadequate share of bread, nothing is left for us in the evening save the fear of the morrow. But the rich will be able to meet. . . . The closing of the clubs of the poor is but the complement of the law against unlawful assembly.[105]

The fact that organized craft workers were being denied public meeting places while employer groups were not,

[102] *Le Représentant du peuple*, June 19, 1848.

[103] Ibid., June 22, 1848.

[104] Petition to Commission du Pouvoir exécutif from Club des Antonins, June 20, 1848, Pagnerre Papers, A.N., 67 AP, dossier 4.

[105] Ibid.

or that a displaced conservative club like the Democratic Club of the National Guard could turn to Marrast for help in finding a new home, lends weight to the charge of class discrimination raised by the Antonins.[106]

Detailed information about where individual clubs met and what alternatives were open to them are too scanty to assess the impact of Marrast's offensive. Their angry protests notwithstanding, the Antonins, for example, managed to find new premises within one city block of their former public school meeting place; on the other hand, the Peaceful Society of the Rights of Man canceled further meetings and relied on an explosive newssheet to keep the club going.[107] There is no way of gauging which was more typical, though it seems likely that the more prosperous western part of the capital had more halls for hire than the dank slums of the Cité or the Place Maubert. Marrast's eviction order surely imperiled some of the clubs that had survived the postelection slump and the crackdown that followed the Polish demonstration. Yet which ones and how many I cannot say.

The psychological—and hence political—effect of Marrast's order is clearer. During the weeks before the June insurrection, the club leaders had exercised a moderating influence on their followers; the club rank and file, accustomed to debate and discussion, was probably less militant than the workers who frequented the Porte Saint-Martin and Saint-Denis at night, or those who took their orders from the cadres of the National Workshops. Except for the brief sidetrack of the Banquet campaign, since May 15 the clubs had pursued the path of conven-

[106] *Les Boulets rouges, feuille du club pacifique des Droits de l'Homme*, June 22-25, 1848.

[107] Club [démocratique] de la Garde nationale, session of June 20, anonymous police report, A.N., C. 933, CdE 2377; *Journal des travailleurs*, June 18-22, 1848; *Les Boulets rouges*, June 22-25, 1848.

tional politics. In this sense, closing the clubs was to rule out the reformist option. "Today the people merely wants to discuss freely and peacefully its interests and those of its brothers. If you smother its words, by the energy of its efforts it may turn again to clamor. Let us therefore try to still the raucous voice raised on the barricades."[108] Disillusionment with the whole political process was expressed in even stronger terms by the president of the dispossessed Peaceful Society of the Rights of Man:

Since we no longer have our halls for political instruction, . . . our executive committee publishes this sheet to protest and to expose the turpitude of a bastard authority which, betraying its origins, has fallen back on the errors of a despotism against which we raised our barricades. From now on, we shall expect anything from these men. Nothing would surprise us. We shall merely watch them, noting their acts, until the Sovereign, weary of seeing its power abused, shall arise from its torpor to dismiss and chasten its servants.[109]

If these were typical reactions, Marrast's move against the clubs may have had paradoxical consequences. By disrupting club organization on the eve of the June insurrection, the mayor's policy may have led wavering individual club members to side with the insurgents when the chips were down.

[108] Announcement, Club démocratique des Antonins, June 16, B.N., Lb[54], 502; petition to Commission du Pouvoir exécutif from Club des Antonins, June 20, 1848, Pagnerre Papers, A.N., 67 AP, dossier 4.

[109] *Les Boulets rouges*, June 22-25, 1848.

9 | The June Days and After

Versez sur eux et l'injure et l'outrage
Vous que jamais n'atteindra le remords,
Le destin seul a trahi leur courage
Nous les aimions et nous pleurons nos morts.

You whose hearts are immune to contrition
Insult and outrage upon them heap.
Fate mast'ring courage led them to perdition,
Those whom we loved: our dead we weep.
                    Charles Gille,
                    Parisian chansonnier (July 1848)

i

Buoyant in March, sagging in April, compromised in
May, the club movement did not survive the agony of
June 1848. Already before the insurrection, the clubs
were in rapid decline as activists, wearied by fruitless discussion, deserted. Harassed by an increasingly repressive
government, the popular societies were forced to scram-
ble for the limited number of private halls. At best this
was a temporary expedient. In the long run, most owners of auditoriums and vacant dance palaces would have
caved in to informal police pressure—what else are fire
regulations and building codes good for?—by evicting
their "dangerous" tenants.

The insurrection of June 23-26 permitted the government to strike down the popular societies without further
resort to administrative subterfuge or hypocritical con-

cern for the welfare of Parisian school children. Already
on June 23, the day before General Eugène Cavaignac
was installed as republican dictator, the Paris police prefect, Trouvé-Chauvel, ordered all clubs provisionally
shut.[1] Characteristically, units of loyal National Guards
had already anticipated these official instructions by seal-
ing club doors in the areas of Paris that they controlled.[2]
The National Assembly reopened the issue in July 1848
by passing legislation permitting the ghostly revival of
isolated and severely controlled popular societies.[3] This
was no renascence, but rather an extended wake before
the final burial in 1849.

ii

My aim is not to tell the story of the June Days nor even
to provide a social analysis of the movement, but to indicate the role of the clubs in this "the most extensive and
most singular insurrection that has occurred in our history. . . . The most extensive because, during four days,
more than a hundred thousand men were engaged in it;
the most singular, because the insurgents fought without
a war cry, without leaders, without flags, and yet with a
marvelous harmony and an amount of military experience that astonished the oldest officers."[4] So spoke
Tocqueville, and so spoke another great observer, Karl

[1] To put it more precisely, at 5:00 P.M. on June 23 Trouvé-
Chauvel recommended to the Commission du Pouvoir exécutif
that all clubs be closed temporarily. The government then ordered its own police force to close what it considered the three
major clubs and arrest those in attendance. For Trouvé-Chauvel's letter, see A.N., C. 933, CdE 2506 (misdated June 22
in *Enquête*, II, 231). Also testimony Vassal, *Enquête*, I, 365.

[2] Testimony Vassal, *Enquête*, I, 365.

[3] The history of club legislation 1848-1850 is conveniently
documented in A.N., BB[18], 1474A.

[4] *Recollections of Alexis de Tocqueville*, p. 160.

Marx.[5] Unknowingly, between them they were laying the foundations of the conventional wisdom on the June 1848 insurrection. Yet their verdict took issue with the contemporary consensus, more accurately expressed in a speech by an obscure representative, Anathase Coquerel, to the National Assembly on July 22, 1848: "Public opinion understands already what our judicial system shall shortly make plain: while evil newspapers recruited the army fighting behind these bloody barricades, evil clubs furnished the general staff, the sappers, the battle plan, and the munitions."[6]

The truth lies somewhere between the insights of genius and the prejudice of frightened parliamentarians. There *was* a war cry: "The social and democratic Republic!" There *were* leaders, like the *lycée* professor Léon Lacollonge, who directed the Faubourg Saint-Antoine, or the commander of the Fourth National Guard battalion in the twelfth district. There *were* flags, some tricolor, some red. More important, the "marvelous harmony" and "military experience" are readily accounted for. Compared to the revolutionaries of July 1830 and February 1848, the June insurgents started with infinitely superior organization. Their problem was one of embarrassment of riches, of having to choose among several parallel organizations for the instrument best suited to insurrection.

The insurgents' alternatives may be illustrated by hypothetical exemplar. Let us take an average insurgent-to-be from the uprising's last redoubt, the Faubourg Saint-Antoine. As a militant republican, our future insurgent would have taken part in the fighting in February 1848, manning the local barricades with his friends and neighbors. As an able-bodied adult male, he would also

[5] Karl Marx, *Class Struggles in France (1848-1850)* (London, 1936), p. 58.

[6] *Le Moniteur universel*, July 25, 1848, p. 1752.

have belonged to one of the thirty-two companies and, less directly, to one of the four battalions of the Eighth Legion of the Paris National Guard. Since he was assigned to his company by residence, all of his four or five hundred company comrades would live within a block or two of each other. As a journeyman cabinetmaker by trade, our man was likely to adhere to his trade union that had come out in the open since February. Considering that 66 percent of all workers in the Faubourg Saint-Antoine and 73 percent of the furniture tradesmen in particular were out of work by June 1848, our man was likely to have enrolled in the National Workshops.[7] As an ardent republican he was surely a member of his neighborhood popular society, perhaps of the Club des Antonins, which in turn was loosely linked to the federated clubs of Paris since the last days of May. Did our man act as a veteran of February, a National Guard, a member of his craft union, an enrollee in the National Workshops, or a clubist? This question is as pointless as it is unanswerable: as the June insurrection developed, some institutions—hence some "identifications"—proved more useful than others.

No more than revolution is insurrection all of a piece *un bloc*. If we are to discern the role played by the clubs, at least five phases should be distinguished: first, strategic planning for the uprising, that is, the agreement on a general plan of action reached prior to the rising; second, tactical preparation for the fighting ahead, with all that this implies in terms of leadership, armed men, supplies; third, the actual triggering of the conflict; fourth, spreading the rebellion to transform scattered rioting into a genuine revolutionary rising; and, finally, the military contest itself.

[7] The percentage is computed from tables compiled by the Paris Chamber of Commerce, *Statistique de l'industrie*, p. 977.

iii

Whether the June Days were preceded by a systematic consideration of military and political strategy by which the revolutionaries hoped to seize power is a question as obscure today as it was in 1848. It is difficult to believe that no one talked about the prospects of a revolution that everyone felt to be coming. The Union of Brigadiers of the National Workshops, who emerged as genuine spokesmen for the workers on relief, or the paramilitary Society of the Rights of Man must at least have weighed alternatives. Strangely enough, the apparently timely convocation of the member clubs of the Central Commission for Democratic Elections for June 23 aimed at nothing more exciting than winding up business left over from the supplementary elections earlier in the month.[8] There is no solid evidence pointing to overall planning or to its prerequisite, the existence of a disciplined, hierarchical revolutionary organization with a devoted mass following. In 1848 we know of no Bolshevik party plotting an October Revolution.

Nineteenth-century French revolutionary tradition may also have had a deterrent effect. Concerted strategy and disciplined conspiracies were associated with impotent sectarians, with phenomena like the futile rising of the "Seasons" which Barbès and Blanqui led in 1839. Successful revolutions, on the contrary, were assumed to be spontaneous (and therefore unplannable) upheavals of the masses—witness July 1789, July 1830, and February 1848. By June 1848 everyone foresaw violence, widespread popular violence provoked by a hostile

[8] For the announcement, see *L'Organisation du travail*, June 23, 1848, and other left-wing papers. For its actual business, François Pardigon, *Épisodes des journées de juin 1848* (London, 1852), p. 73. Pardigon, a club president, attended the meeting.

government. But no revolutionary organization dreamed that it could control the direction, intensity, and timing of that violence. Noting the storm clouds was one thing, harnessing the hurricane another.

iv

The apparent absence of any master plan did not preclude tactical preparation for the expected showdown. When, where, and how the insurrection would break out might remain unpredictable, but anyone could foresee some down-to-earth, practical problems. The democratized Paris National Guard had handed a rifle to every able-bodied man, but the rifle was unloaded. Bullets and cartridges were stored in district municipal armories. On this level, preparations did take place, though we know less about them than we would like. As François Pardigon, law student, president of the Club of the Second of March, and June insurgent, noted from the vantage point of exile in 1852: "The June insurrection came about, it is true, without any overall plan, without conspiracy in the full meaning of the word, without general staff; but it did not come about without preparation, without prior cooperation."[9]

For such immediate tasks, the clubs were more serviceable than other available institutions. Despite its tauter organization, the National Guard was useless. It was impossible to gauge in advance which officers would throw in their lot with the revolutionaries, which would remain neutral, and which would actively side with the government. Preparations such as the manufacture of gunpowder and the casting of bullets would therefore have to take place in some other setting. The trade unions were inconvenient because their members were scattered all over Paris and because they seem to have been far

[9] Pardigon, *Episodes*, p. 69. For biographical information, see *DBMOF*, III, 176-177.

more preoccupied with collective bargaining than with collective violence. The cohesion of the National Workshops was too brittle, its upper cadres too clearly the authorities' minions, its outdoor work sites too unsuitable for the sort of preparatory effort for which the situation called. This left the clubs. Despite police infiltration, the popular societies offered the best opportunity for secret preparation. An informer attending the session of the Society of the Rights of Man on June 21 reported something more than the usual "threats against the government" and "anarchist exaltation"—the staple fare of the run-of-the-mill police report: "When one of the speakers remarked that they had to get organized, the president reproached him with not keeping quiet, adding: we are organizing, but you must not talk about it."[10]

Similarly, just before the June Days the Club of the Second of March had begun reviving the pattern of *décuries*, self-contained platoons of ten men modeled on the republican secret societies, while the Club of the Mountain, rue Frépillon, was considering imitating the military "sections" of the Society of the Rights of Man.[11] These instances suggest that many clubs may have come to grips with preparations for a new, increasingly inevitable revolution.

v

In assessing the clubs' role in triggering the June conflict we can be more definite than in weighing their part in preparing for battle. It is now generally agreed that the government's policy toward the National Workshops (and

[10] Unsigned police report, résumé des clubs, June 21, 1848, A.N., C. 933, CdE 2520.

[11] Pardigon, *Episodes*, p. 73, for Club du deux mars, A.M.G., A. 4745; dossier Charles Courbon for Club de la Montagne.

the response it evoked from lower-class Paris) was the catalyst for popular violence. Despite his partisan involvement, Pardigon's assessment still stands:

> ... a crisis had become imminent ever since the beginning of the month [of June]. The return of the troops and the law against unlawful assembly had been the first spur. The measures taken against the National Workshops: the enrollment of all members seventeen to twenty-five years old in the army; the order given on June 21 to close registration [for the Workshops] in the municipal offices; the departure of several of these brigades to the provinces; the setbacks encountered by these workers at Courbevoie, Puteaux, Orléans, and elsewhere; the fruitless interview of the delegates with the director; the threats on both sides at the end of the last of these interviews had finally put forward and defined the *casus belli*.[12]

Historians have rightly stressed this catalytic role of the National Workshop delegates, headed by Louis Pujol, on the evening of June 22. That evening excited crowds gathered both on the Right Bank near the Hôtel-de-Ville and at least on two different occasions on the Place du Panthéon in the Latin Quarter.[13] A minor historical myth to the contrary, the crowd that agreed to meet in an early morning demonstration on June 23, the day that was to mark the actual start of the uprising, was made up of National Guards from the Twelfth Legion rather than of men from the National Workshops.[14] Be this as it may, the fateful decision of a morning rendezvous was reached outside the club movement.

[12] Pardigon, *Episodes*, pp. 69-70.
[13] Price, *The French Second Republic*, pp. 158-159.
[14] According to Clément Thomas, commander of the Paris National Guard, A.N., C. 933, CdE 2428. It should be noted that the police prefect did not make this distinction in informing the chairman of the National Assembly of the evening's events. *Enquête*, II, 231.

vi

Where the clubs were actively involved was in spreading the news of the demonstration planned for 6:00 A.M. By so doing, they helped to transform what might otherwise have been a local tumult into a revolution. Apparently even the clubs in the Latin Quarter had had no advance notice of the open-air meeting on the Place du Panthéon on the evening of June 22. Receiving word that the square was lit up by torches—uncommon for such goings-on—the local clubs sent delegates to join the crowd and listen to the speakers. Although these club delegates do not seem to have participated, once a decision had been acclaimed by the crowd, they immediately took action:

We dispersed among the clubs, spreading news of the decision of that meeting and exhorting all members to be there for the morning's rendezvous. . . . The women and many of the people who attended clubs out of curiosity or to kill time left, a little frightened . . . by the silence that greeted the news. Young people of various professions and workers of all ages joined in groups, continuing to talk about it, promising to cooperate in the insurrection. . . . No doubt what we did in the eleventh and twelfth district was done in other sections of Paris to prepare the *journées* of the twenty-third through the twenty-sixth.[15]

Pardigon's surmise is confirmed by a police report drawn up on the morning of June 23 announcing that the Society of the Rights of Man, whose headquarters were on the Right Bank, rue Albouy, was meeting in unlimited emergency session, having just dispatched "delegates . . . to organize the movement in the suburbs, in the north, in Montmartre, Belleville, and Charonne."[16] Another higher-level policeman noted that "I meet individuals from the

[15] Pardigon, *Episodes*, pp. 71-72.
[16] Unsigned police report, June 23, 1848, A.N., C. 933, CdE 2528.

Club of the People . . . rallying men in working-class garb and others."[17] No doubt dramatic news has a way of spreading just by word of mouth. Nonetheless, the clubs' action may have changed what would otherwise have been wild rumor to a call to combat.

vii

Once the fighting began in earnest, the clubs played a very modest part. On the whole, the June insurgents pursued the tactics that had worked in February: they put up hundreds of barricades, which, until the rebel-held area shrank, were defended mostly by local people. Many of these barricades, erected on the same spots where they had been raised four months earlier, must have been manned by the same teams of neighbors as in February.[18] In addition, some brigades from the National Workshops, cooperating employees of a few large enterprises such as railroad repair shops, and a handful of clubs played subsidiary roles in the fighting.[19] Yet, given the essentially

[17] Police report signed Carlier, undated. A.N., C. 933, CdE 2608.

[18] I do not suggest that the *area* of the two revolutionary outbreaks coincided. In June the three westernmost *arrondissements*—the first and second on the Right Bank, the tenth on the Left Bank—proved immune to insurrection. As to personnel, the only statistically detectable difference between the average February revolutionary and the average June insurgent was one of age: recruitment into the Garde mobile drained off the very young, who, in June, ended up on the other side of the barricades. Remi Gossez, verbal communication, 1964. Official interrogators carefully avoided asking about revolutionary participation in February, but did ask June suspects about club membership and attendance.

[19] The fairly successful attempt by the government to divert the National Workshop members by arranging payday is well known. The collective intervention by employees of large enterprises was made difficult because many had laid off the bulk of their work force. Moreover, most of such firms were located in the northern and northwestern suburbs, far removed

static character of combat in the streets in June 1848, insurgents naturally turned to the existing neighborhood military organization: units of the National Guard constituted the organizational skeleton of the June uprising because no other instrument was as serviceable.[20]

---

from the action. For the inconclusive evidence on the textile printing firm Depouilly at Puteaux, see *DBMOF*, entries on Depouilly *père* and his sons, ii, 62-63.

[20] See also the brief discussion in Louis Girard, *La garde nationale*, pp. 312-317. The raw material available for analysis of the June insurrection is a corpus of 11,400 dossiers of arrested suspects, each of which comprises from half a dozen to several hundred documents. Since my own interest in the June insurrection is peripheral rather than central, I sampled this mass in the following manner:

(1) A random sample of one carton of dossiers (2 rolls of microfilm).

(2) A perusal of the biographical *notices* (provided by Gossez) of all June insurgents listed in *DBMOF*, 1789-1864, i-iii, which must run to perhaps 1,000. Unfortunately, I am at a loss to understand what criteria have governed their selection, as the number deported was nearer 4,000.

(3) I followed up all listed club officers by studying their file in A.M.G., série A, "Insurgents de juin 1848."

(4) From my own file of club activists, I selected those club officers about whom I had sufficient data to permit conclusive identification (unusual name and/or profession and/or home address). I had this list checked against the dossiers of the June insurgents, microfilming all relevant files from A.M.G., série A.

(5) The total number of individual dossiers studied amounted to about 400, or about 3 percent of all individual files.

(6) I also spent a few days perusing the dispatches of various army commanders during the June insurrection, A.M.G., F¹, 9, but these are less concerned with social and structural analysis than with military tactics and problems.

Control of the local National Guard structure seems to have determined the allegiance of whole districts of the capital. For example, the presence of large contingents of men from the National Workshops was not in itself decisive, or else the tenth *arrondissement*, where thousands of relief workers were leveling the Champ de Mars, should have been one of the insurrection's focal points. Similarly, if club militancy alone had mattered, the first district might well have joined the uprising. Neither of these westernmost districts budged, though in both cases their number of workers was small, both proportionately and absolutely. Yet the second *arrondissement* (with 34,000 workers constituting 29 percent of the population) was equally quiescent. Evidently the concentration of workers in a given area did not by itself determine allegiance; despite their highest proportion of workers in Paris (43 percent and 47 percent), insurgents never established unchallenged control of the third and fifth districts.[21] What made the difference, apparently, was the loyalty to the

[21] All statistics cited are derived from figures gathered by the investigation of the Paris Chamber of Commerce in 1848-1849. They must be treated cautiously for the following reasons:

(1) The numbers and proportion of workers to residents is misleading in that the figures refer to workers whose work place but not necessarily residence is in a given district (though most Parisians lived close to their place of work). The discrepancy is probably most striking in the very poor twelfth and ninth districts, which show up as low in workers because little industry was located there.

(2) The inquiry's definition of worker tends to understate their numbers. Excluded by definition is the large *Lumpenproletariat* of occasional day laborers and the poorest strata of self-employed artisans or street vendors, who are indistinguishable from workers in social outlook. Also missing is the large group of servants concentrated in western Paris.

government of a nucleus of National Guard cadres; this denied the use of the militia organization to the rebels.[22]

The clubs' inability to compete in military efficiency with a locally rooted militia explains the modesty of their contributions to the June fighting. In truth, the clubs never pretended to be taken seriously as a military force. The "sacred right of insurrection" to which popular societies had so frequently appealed was a ritual invocation, not a program of action.

viii

This incompatibility between popular societies that centered around talk and an insurrection concerned with war might have been overcome had it not been for other more tangible problems. In the first place, a number of militant clubs were cut off in hostile territory, in sections of Paris dominated from the outset by government forces. For example, the Club of Free Men, housed at the Palais de l'Institut in the aristocratic tenth district, would have had to break through a veritable military cordon to take part in the fighting. Although its president, Jean-Claude Colfavru, was later arrested and deported, no evidence linked him to the insurrection. On the contrary, he was able to prove that he had fought with the "forces of order." He was evidently deported for editing the rabble-rousing newspaper *Le Père Duchêne* and for his connection with the Banquet of the People.[23]

Second, the action of the National Guard in neighborhoods that did not fall to the insurgents until June 24 pre-

[22] My hunch is that the results of the officer elections (April 1848) on the company level decided control of National Guard units in June. I am convinced that, if data were available, there would be a strong positive correlation between the number of "new" officers elected in April and the local intensity of the June insurrection.

[23] A.M.G., dossier Colfavru, A. 982. For reasons unknown, the *notice* in *DBMOF*, i, 438, overlooks this source.

vented organized club action. As already mentioned, "loyalist" National Guard patrols prevented club doors from opening on the evening of June 23 (just before the barricades were built) when, according to a police spy, "agitators have agreed to meet . . . in the clubs."[24] For a brief time, progovernment militia occupied the rue Albouy that housed both the Club of the Revolution (formerly presided over by Barbès) and the central office of the Society of the Rights of Man, which was to have served as one of the three general headquarters of the insurrection, according to another agent.[25] Meanwhile the Club of the People (successor to Blanqui's Central Republican Society), locked out of its hall on the boulevard Bonne Nouvelle, met furtively in a courtyard, where its members were identified by a plainclothes policeman.[26] Paradoxically, this lockout may have saved hundreds of clubists from detention by "ruining" a raid on the major popular societies carried out by the special police of the Executive Commission.[27] Nonetheless, the lockout also

[24] Police prefect Trouvé-Chauvel (to Commission du Pouvoir exécutif), June 23, 1848, 5:00 P.M. A.N., C. 933, CdE 2506.

[25] For the fact that the National Guard controlled the rue Albouy, preventing the clubs from meeting, and for the fact that the Club de la révolution (not one of the three against which Vassal's police raid was aimed) had moved there, see unsigned police report, June 23, 1848, 6:00-11:00 P.M., A.N., C. 933, CdE 2507. Also testimony Vassal, *Enquête*, I, 365. For Société des Droits de l'Homme as would-be headquarters, see unidentified police report, June 23, 1848, A.N., C. 933, CdE 2528. Similar reports apparently reached Inspector Yon, special police chief to the National Assembly; *Enquête*, II, 231.

[26] Police report signed Carlier, no date [evening of June 23?], A.N., C. 933, CdE 2608. For the fact that the Club du peuple was closed, see also unsigned police report, June 23, 1848, 6:00-11:00 P.M. A.N., C. 933, CdE 2507.

[27] Testimony Vassal, *Enquête*, I, 365; Vassal apparently was given only the addresses but not the official names of the clubs

foiled the attempt by key clubs to take a lead in the struggle.

Finally, fragmentary evidence suggests that the one club that did take pride in its military tradition, the Society of the Rights of Man, was organized for the wrong revolution. The surviving records of one section leader arrested after the June Days show that his twenty section members lived inconveniently far from each other.[28] They would never have made it to a rendezvous; certainly by June 24 armed men would have been drafted en route by the defenders of the first barricade short of manpower. The society's structure, meant to be infiltration-proof, was not geared to participation in a massive popular uprising. This is why the society's official claim that it never participated in the insurrection *as an organization* is probably correct: it was not equipped to participate.[29] Like other insurgents, individual section members seem to have fought in the ranks of their National Guard units or joined street crowds.[30]

Under special circumstances, particularly in the suburbs, popular societies overcame some of these handicaps

---

he was ordered to raid (which he described inaccurately as "branches of the Club Blanqui").

[28] A.M.G., A. 6911, Louis Guille. For biographical résumé, see *DBMOF*, II, 320.

[29] Announcement in *Le Représentant du peuple*, July 1, 1848. Restated by L.-J. Villain (or Vilain), president of the Société des Droits de l'Homme, at his trial for complicity in the affair of May 15, 1848, before the Haute-Cour de Bourges in 1849.

[30] See, e.g., *DBMOF*, *notices* in II, 211, on Louis Francart; and in II, 395, on Jacques Klein, treasurer and vice-president of the club, respectively. *DBMOF* has entries for 26 members of the Société des Droits de l'Homme arrested after the June Days (23 of whom were deported), a larger number than any other Parisian club, with the single exception of the Montagnards de Belleville.

to take a more active role. As indicated, in the west of the capital, those sympathizing with the insurrection were fenced off by an impenetrable barrier of National Guards, Gardes mobiles, and regular troops strung out along a north–south axis. The working-class suburbs, stretching clockwise from La Chapelle-Saint Denis in the north to Montrouge in the south, were in a different position. Though not cordoned off from the fighting, they were out of the battle's reach geographically. Militant suburbanites had to march into Paris to join the revolution. Usually they did so as a group, banded together in their National Guard companies, but occasionally they marched under club leadership. The clearest instance of such club initiative appears in the action of the Montagnards of Belleville. The Montagnards, mobilizing the local National Guard over the protest of their commander (who would later denounce them to the authorities), led a trek to the Faubourg du Temple, which the Bellevilleans defended throughout the insurrection. Hundreds of men, perhaps as many as three thousand, were involved.[31]

Elsewhere club roles are ill-defined because popular society affiliation cannot be disentangled from other sources of authority. Take the Republican Society of La

[31] Of some 30 *notices* of insurgent Montagnards de Belleville in *DBMOF*, the most interesting are those of P. Carpentier (i, 355), H. Dubois (ii, 107-108), and P.-J. Regnier (iii, 293). See Price, *The French Second Republic*, p. 178, for the 3,000 figure. I have been unable to use the Soviet historian A. E. Molok's account of the June Days in the Paris suburbs save for a brief synopsis in French, *Annuaire d'études françaises*, 1963 (Moscow, 1964), pp. 90-119.

It should be added that some suburban workers seem to have participated as "workshops," particularly some of the railway workers. Remi Gossez, "Diversité des antagonismes sociaux vers le milieu du XIX⁰ siècle," *Revue économique*, i (1956), 451. Also the perceptive account by George Rudé, *The Crowd in History, 1730-1848* (New York, 1964), pp. 176-177.

Chapelle-Saint Denis, three-quarters of whose twenty-five hundred members are said to have joined the rising. Technically they did so as National Guards, yet several of their companies, made up largely of club members, were led by club officers, including the society's secretary, vice-president and, possibly, president.[32] In another instance, how can one tell whether J.-J. Chautard, president of the Club of United Republicans of Montmartre, owed his command of one thousand insurgents defending the barricades of the Barrière Poissonnière to his club post, to his local reputation, or to personal charisma?[33] Then there is the case of F. Voissard, who organized a blockade of the Ivry freight station to deny the government the use of the Orléans railway line. Voissard was both assistant stationmaster and president of the Ivry Club of Fraternal Union. In what capacity was he acting?[34]

Even in Paris itself club militants with energy and presence of mind could make themselves useful. After all, the framework of the National Guard had certain limitations, particularly since few guard officers above the rank of captain fought on the insurgent side. These junior officers joining the rising were unprepared to make far-reaching military and political decisions. In the Faubourg

[32] For the estimate of participation, see testimony Winter (*commissaire de police* at La Chapelle-Saint-Denis), *Enquête*, I, 369. *DBMOF* lists 14 insurgents as members of the club.

[33] Under interrogation Chautard admitted having stopped at the club first, but supposedly only to find out whether it was meeting. There is no question about his leading role. Testimony Collard; A.M.G., dossier J.-J. Chautard, A. 9326. The *notice* in *DBMOF*, I, 403-404, is less revealing.

[34] A.M.G., dossier F. Voissard, A. 8111. For brief mention of the incident based on other sources, see Jean-Pierre Amalric, "La révolution de 1848 chez les cheminots de la compagnie du Paris Orléans," *Revue d'histoire économique et sociale*, XLI (1963), 368-369.

Saint-Antoine such a power vacuum was filled by the *lycée* professor, Léon Lacollonge, editor of the newspaper *L'Organisation du travail* and president of a club of the same name, who turned out to be the ablest leader uncovered by the insurrection. Though his efforts were confined to the eighth district, Lacollonge, relying on the activists of the Club des Antonins, organized an effective, if short-lived, local administration (after evicting the legal district mayor, Victor Hugo, from his office), capitalizing on its control of the National Printing Works.[35]

More prosaic tasks also fell to some clubs. From its inception, the June uprising was plagued by ammunition shortages which the seizure of the municipal armories in the eighth and ninth *arrondissements* did not fully remedy. For the most part, individual initiative took over, with sympathetic pharmacists manufacturing gunpowder instead of filling prescriptions. However, the most ambitious ammunition manufacturer seems to have been the Republican Democratic Club of Quinze-Vingt. For three days running some of its members were holed up in a requisitioned foundry of the Faubourg Saint-Antoine, casting and distributing some ten thousand cartridges. Meanwhile the club president, the mathematics professor O. Brutinel-Nadal, sallied forth to the barricades every so often to keep his club members apprised of the battle's progress.[36]

ix

Aside from this collection of impressionistic bits, is there any reliable way of measuring whether and to what extent

[35] *DBMOF*, ii, 405-406. Gossez, "Presse," pp. 155-156. Lacollonge (alternate spellings: La Collonge, Lacolonge) also has a dossier at A.M.G., A. 5112, and at A.N., BB[24], 489-493, 2252. For his trial, see *Le Droit journal des tribunaux*, March 9 and April 28, 1849.

[36] *DBMOF*, i, 317. I have also examined his dossier, A.M.G., A. 5112.

individual activists of the popular societies played a greater role in June than comparable Parisians without such club affiliations? Conservatives had not the slightest doubt that they could answer in the affirmative. The parliamentary investigative commission assumed that clubs and clubists played a central role in the rebellion, though its report provided little solid backing for this thesis.[37] The military judges, trying captured suspects, were of similar convictions. A typical summary report (quoted in full) on Théodore Coutard, grocer by trade and president of the Club of L'Homme-Armé, illustrates their attitude: "This accused was found with illegally manufactured powder in his possession. He confesses to having been on the barricades. The Club of L'Homme-Armé was one of the most dangerous centers of the insurrection. Coutard admits belonging to it. He is known and feared in his neighborhood for his anarchist views. He is a dangerous individual."[38] Club "subversion" damned Coutard more than his part in the fighting, as the military panels proclaimed open season on anyone prominently identified with the popular societies between February and June. Informers were only too eager to furnish them with names of club officers.[39] The reverse side of such discrimination showed up in the interrogation of suspects, who habitually and understandably denied or minimized their club ties.

[37] *Enquête*, I, 36-37, 40.

[38] A.M.G., dossier A. 2180.

[39] There were a number of club officers deported even in the absence of any report attesting to their participation in the insurrection, though they usually made no claim to have fought on the side of order. Among many others, see the following *notices* in *DBMOF*: Claude Feuillâtre, II, 185-186; Louis Guille, II, 320. On the other hand, Charles Blu, (paid) secretary of the Société des Droits de l'Homme, was freed, and so was General Sebastien Jorry, president of the "incendiary" Club des Intérêts du peuple, A.M.G., A. 8889.

The official bias against club leaders only underscores the general unreliability of what might otherwise be the marvelously quantifiable data on the June rebels. Consider some figures. Historians have estimated the number of June insurgents as ranging from a low of 10,000 to a high of 100,000, of whom probably less than 5,000 were killed in combat or by summary execution.[40] As a matter of convenience, let us postulate 35,000 surviving participants. Against this, set the figures for the repression following the victory of the "forces of order": 12,000 suspects arrested and booked, of whom about 4,000 were "deported" or sentenced to prison terms, the remaining 8,000 set free as "innocent."[41]

The 4,000 convicted provide a tempting and apparently substantial sample. In fact, it is far from the random sample of which statisticians' dreams are made, because different sections of insurgent Paris were subject to differing intensities of repression. Early in the fighting the defenders of an overrun barricade had a fair chance of retreating and eluding capture. Insurgents from "border" districts like the third and eleventh are therefore underrepresented among both arrested and convicted. The last-ditch defenders of the Faubourg Saint-Antoine, on the other hand, had nowhere to flee and were therefore more likely to be apprehended. Actually, in the last phase of combat, military repression took its most extreme forms: for instance, a mass sweep rounded up all the male resi-

[40] One recent assessment puts the total of combatants on the insurgent side at between 40,000 and 50,000. Price, *The French Second Republic*, pp. 168, 171.

[41] These figures are approximations, since the register of those arrested (A.N., F7, 2585) lists 11,727; but there are individual dossiers numbered to about 12,600 at the A.M.G. at Vincennes. There is also a discrepancy of several hundred between the A.N. register and an apparently equally official-looking "Liste alphabétique des transportation maintenues," Liesville Collection, B.H.V.P.

dents of the Cité Popincourt, a back alley in the eighth *arrondissement*, and many of these were ultimately deported. In short, there is considerable doubt that the suspects punished were representative of the June insurgents in general both because known radicals were singled out and because repression fell most heavily on certain geographical areas of Paris.[42] No statistical analysis that I could devise can answer the question whether club activists were more or less involved in the June uprising than the general run of Parisians.[43]

In this instance, speculation based on common sense may edge closer to the truth than misleading statistics can. Insofar as club membership signified lower-class political involvement, the membership card might easily be traded for the insurgent's badge. At the same time, commitment to a popular society, with its emphasis on rational discussion, testified to some flickering faith in political—as against military—solutions. To this extent

[42] Price (*The French Second Republic*, pp. 163-176) has unfortunately compounded confusion by analyzing all suspects arrested, an analysis which is meaningless, since the two-thirds released were for the most part innocent of participation. He also failed to go behind the statistics to examine the selection process of those arrested, the relationship of the insurrectional geography of Paris to the occupational geography of the capital as detailed in *Statistique de l'industrie*, etc.

[43] Originally I attempted to deal with this question by comparing a sample of identifiable club activists but not club presidents who might be singled out for repression with the general adult male population. This sample yielded 3 percent of club activists versus 1 percent general male adults deported after the June insurrection. But a closer examination of my sample—some 300 "missionaries" sent by the Club des clubs to the provinces in March and April—forced me to reject my findings: (1) a disproportionate number of the 300 lived in eastern (read "insurgent") Paris; (2) several of the deported *were* club presidents by June and may have owed their condemnation to their club role. Club delegates are listed in A.N., C. 930, dossier 3, CdE 209.

club activity tended to neutralize violence. Here, then, lay the paradox: those whom the clubs had awakened were more likely to fight than the apathetic and the apolitical, yet by stressing persuasion rather than coercion the clubs had also muffled their members' rage. But by June there were many whom the popular societies had originally initiated but whom the clubs' ineffectiveness had ultimately repelled. In a real sense, therefore, the June Days may have been the revolution of the club dropouts.

x

The epilogue to the club movement's story is quickly told. Invested with unlimited powers by the National Assembly on June 24, 1848, General Cavaignac, the legislators assumed, would close all "dangerous" clubs by executive fiat.[44] If such an order was actually issued, it never found its way into the Republic's official journal. An annotated list of Parisian popular societies, drawn up by the chief of general security in the Ministry of the Interior on June 26, seems to have had no practical effect —though it may serve as testimonial to official ignorance and misinformation.[45] That same day, the Faubourg Saint-Antoine surrendered; it is unlikely that any clubs, "dangerous" or not, survived the defeat of the insurrection in a Paris flooded by National Guards from all over France. The state of siege was not conducive to niceties regarding the right of free assembly.

It was in this oppressive atmosphere that two weeks later, on July 11, Interior Minister Sénard introduced the

[44] Session of June 26, *Le Moniteur universel*, June 27, 1848, p. 1502; session of June 27, ibid., June 28, 1848, p. 1505. In both cases the mention appears in an introductory speech by the chairman of the National Assembly.

[45] *Enquête*, II, 95-98. This report by Panisse does speak of "a book of clubs prohibited by the citizen head of the executive power." No such book has been found as far as I know.

government's bill regulating clubs. Sénard, a conservative
republican from Normandy, owed his ministry to having
put down the postelection riots in Rouen and Elbeuf two
and a half months earlier. After paying lip service to the
right of assembly and to the social utility of free discussion, the minister stressed the need to reconcile these with
"the surveillance and control imperiously demanded by
the interests of society and of public tranquility."[46] The
law proposed by the Minister of the Interior, tightened
by a legislative committee and ultimately adopted by the
overwhelming margin of 629 to 100, preserved clubs but
killed the club movement. In essence, the decree permitted popular societies to reopen, provided they welcomed official surveillance, weighed every word spoken
at their meetings, avoided all contact with each other,
and eschewed meaningful political activities.[47]

Consider the key provisions. Forty-eight hours before
a club could open its doors, its founders had to provide
the authorities with information about themselves and
about the time and place of their meeting. Popular societies, now officially barred from public buildings, could
name themselves only for the street or hall in which they
gathered. Club sessions were to be open to the general
public at all times, though women and minors were not
permitted to attend. An official, either in uniform or
wearing the insignia of his office, might sit in on any session to determine whether the discussion infringed on

[46] *Le Moniteur universel*, July 12, 1848, p. 1621.

[47] The debates are in *Le Moniteur universel*, sessions of July
22 (pp. 1751-1753), July 25 (pp. 1759-1761), July 26 (pp.
1774-1776), July 27 (pp. 1785-1789), July 28 (pp. 1796-
1801). In *Le Moniteur* the sessions of July 25 and 27 are
both erroneously dated July 26. The official text is in *Le
Moniteur universel*, August 2, 1848, p. 1837. The various
versions of this and later club legislation, including article by
article comparisons, may be found in A.N., BB[18], 1474A, *Clubs
et associations*.

—On m'a dit qu'il y avait un club dans cette rue, n'est-il pas dangereux d'y passer? — C'est au moins une haute imprudence. — C'est aussi mon avis.

11.–The twilight of the club movement

Left:
"They've told me that there is a club on this street; isn't it dangerous to go by?"

"It's at least highly imprudent."

"That's my opinion also."

Below: Closing the clubs in 1849

7.7 CHAM

"good order and morality," whether it "tended to provoke acts considered crimes or misdemeanors," whether
it witnessed "attacks on individuals or persons," or
whether any threats were voiced. For any or all of these
infractions the club's officers were held criminally responsible. Clubs, moreover, could not affiliate, cooperate,
or even communicate—by writing or by delegates—with
any other club. They were forbidden to issue any poster,
proclamation, or collective petition, or to pass any resolution "in imitation of public authorities." In the event
that a participant or officer was indicted, the courts could
order the provisional but immediate closing of the popular society concerned, an order that was without appeal.
If the accused were convicted, "his" club remained permanently closed. The rest of the decree detailed a gamut
of penalties.[48]

How could a republican government propose and a
democratically elected legislature enact such a law only
five months after a revolution precipitated by restrictions
on free assembly had supposedly conquered? There is no
reason to question the sincerity of the moderate republicans, who saw in their proposal a reasonable compromise
between license and suppression. The dominant strand
within the French revolutionary tradition had never con-
doned continuous popular interference in the serious
business of politics: the libertarians of 1789 had outlawed the clubs in 1791; the Jacobins ended by disarming and disowning the sans-culottes that had brought
them to power. As conservative republicans saw it in
1848, the French people had delegated its sovereignty
to a National Assembly whose duty it was to regulate the
exercise of abstract "rights"; and in this case surely this
did not mean abetting a rival authority. In the words of
the Minister of the Interior: "We mean to consecrate the
right of the citizen, but we do not mean to set up within

[48] *Le Moniteur universel*, August 2, 1848, p. 1837.

the state an entity, a power with its own right to act. . . . Thus we will never agree to consider the clubs as moral beings with their own identity, separate even from those taking part in them; as capable of deciding, acting, and moving as a club."[49]

Yet the majority of the National Assembly was not made up of republicans, conservative or otherwise, but of monarchists of various hues for whom the moderate Republic was a temporary and unloved shield against social upheaval.[50] Despite the trauma of June, this majority of Orleanists, Legitimists, and Bonapartists still remembered February 1848; they were still fearful of setting back the clock altogether, aside from being unable to agree by which dynasty to set it. Though none said so openly, the new club legislation was a welcome first step on the road back to sanity; and sanity, for them, meant a world without clubs. In the meantime, the antirepublicans had merely to sit back quietly, voting article after article by crushing majorities.

The passivity of the left-wing republicans was a more astonishing phenomenon. No doubt the June Days had been an unnerving experience for these men, torn as they were between sentiment and legality, socialist rhetoric and political realism. Yet the lack of vocal opposition must have reflected more than the aftershock of the insurrection: there may have been genuine relief that, despite administrative fetters, the principle of free assembly was at least safe. Many may have agreed with the Fourierist Victor Considérant, who admitted half way through

[49] Session of July 25 (misdated July 26), *Le Moniteur universel*, July 26, 1848, p. 1762.

[50] For independent analyses of the political complexion of the National Assembly, see George W. Fasel, "The French Election of April 23, 1848: Suggestions for a Revision," *French Historical Studies*, v (1968), 287-290; and Frederic A. de Luna, *The French Republic under Cavaignac, 1848* (Princeton, 1969), pp. 188-193.

the debate, that he had voted for all but the exclusion of women: "I voted that way because I do not wish the precious liberty that we are regulating today to be abridged tomorrow, in consequence of excesses to which liberty's abuse may have given rise."[51] Be this as it may, the Left accepted the central (and most damaging) provisions of the bill virtually without debate. They reserved their protests and their eloquence for tangential issues like the fate of private, nonpolitical societies, the applicability of jury trials to the various infractions, the definition of the "secret societies" which the bill outlawed. In the final vote, even the neo-Jacobin ex-members of the Provisional Government, Flocon and Ledru-Rollin, approved the law.[52]

Club activists were to discover one minor loophole. Though affiliation between clubs had been outlawed, it remained legal for one individual to belong to several clubs. For example, the mathematics professor Edouard Merlieux, who before June had been president of the Club of the Union, reappeared as president of the Club of Vieux-Chêne and as member of the Club of the Antonins' executive board, and was condemned separately in both capacities.[53] Another escape hatch, exempting "preparatory electoral meetings" from the restrictions, was written into the law. It permitted a group of Montagnard republican representatives to launch what amounted to a left-wing national party, calling itself Re-

[51] Session of July 25 (misdated July 26), *Le Moniteur universel*, July 26, 1848, p. 1760.

[52] Session of July 28, *Le Moniteur universel*, July 29, 1848, p. 1801.

[53] *Le Moniteur universel*, March 26, 1849, p. 1049. For Merlieux' career, see *DBMOF*, iii, 83. His encounters with the law are also documented in A.N., BB[18], 1474B. For his pre-June club career, see an open letter of June 13, 1848, from the Club de l'Union, Thoré Papers, Bibliothèque de l'Arsenal.

publican Solidarity, prior to the presidential elections. Immediately after the inauguration of President Louis Napoleon Bonaparte that hatch was battened down: the headquarters of Republican Solidarity were raided on December 12, a move which the new Minister of the Interior, Léon Faucher, followed up by an order to his prefects declaring the organization illegal and dissolved.[54]

On the whole, however, the legislation regulating the clubs accomplished all that its champions expected. A bulky file accumulated by the Ministry of Justice testifies to the zeal with which the new law was enforced against Parisian popular societies.[55] Omitting all pending cases from the count, forty-two individuals had been tried for violations before police courts by February 1849 and thirty of them were convicted, accounting for the closing of two clubs. Trial juries heard fourteen more serious cases involving forty-five individuals belonging to eleven different clubs. Though only tweny-one persons were convicted of club-related misdemeanors, eight clubs with which they had been connected were dissolved. As of January 1849, an additional five popular societies were under suspension pending a series of unresolved court cases. Evidently the law, perhaps aided by growing political apathy, was a smashing success: where thirty-seven clubs had been active in the Paris area in August 1848, only six survived into the new year.[56]

---

[54] For the text of Faucher's circular, see *Le Moniteur universel*, January 27, 1849, p. 273; for the debate on this issue following an *interpellation*, session of January 31, ibid., February 1, 1849, pp. 331-332.

[55] A.N., BB[18], 1474B. These were utilized by J. Tchernoff, *Associations et sociétés secrètes sous la Deuxième République* (Paris, 1905), who reproduces many documents, pp. 210-246.

[56] From the committee's report to the National Assembly, delivered by Adolphe Crémieux (Minister of Justice under the Provisional Government), session of February 20, *Le Moniteur universel*, February 24, 1849, p. 626.

The final outlawing of the clubs in 1849 therefore had no practical import. It was meant as a symbolic blow against the hated Republic for which the clubs served as convenient surrogate, a blow meant to gratify all right-minded conservatives. In defending his proposal, Léon Faucher, the new Minister of the Interior, almost admitted as much. Granted that clubs had been dissolved and militants prosecuted, "the spectacle of these maneuvers [the efforts of the clubs to avoid extinction] offends our sense of the fitness of things. It disturbs people and slows the expansion of our industry. . . . It is a last echo of street uproars that one is astonished to hear under what is henceforth a regular and constituted government."[57] However, the minister was unable to convince either the committee to which it had been referred or the National Assembly itself that the government's bill should be treated as an emergency measure.[58] Furthermore, the committee, headed by a republican, showed unexpected spirit in reporting out a legislative proposal that merely amended slightly the law still on the statute books. Faucher nonetheless got his way. On March 20 the majority accepted a laconically worded substitute motion: by 378 to 359 the National Assembly voted that "clubs are forbidden."[59] Thereafter the debate was anticlimac-

[57] Session of January 26, *Le Moniteur universel*, January 28, 1849, p. 276.

[58] Session of January 27, *Le Moniteur universel*, January 28, 1849, p. 294; session of February 20, ibid., February 24, 1849, p. 626. One curious incident in the government's campaign to drum up support while the bill was in committee involved the American minister to Paris, Richard Rush. Rush was induced by an official of the Ministry of Justice to comment on clubs in the early days of the American republic; he stated that, although there was no positive legislation forbidding them, they were "under disapprobation" and discredited with the fall of Robespierre. A.N., BB[18], 1474A.

[59] The debate began on March 19 (*Le Moniteur universel*, March 20, 1849, pp. 933-939) and continued on March 20

tic.⁶⁰ Before the end of March the club bill, never quite completed, was put aside for more pressing business as the various ministries began to submit their annual budgets. In the rush to adjournment, made mandatory by new general elections called for May 1849, the bill banning clubs was apparently forgotten. Technically, popular societies were tolerated until June 19, 1849, when a new legislature pushed through a law authorizing the government to close all clubs.⁶¹

(ibid., March 21, 1849, pp. 949-956), at which time the decisive vote was cast.

⁶⁰ Session of March 21, *Le Moniteur universel*, March 22, 1849, pp. 971-979; session of March 22, ibid., March 23, 1849, p. 992.

⁶¹ The bill was introduced by the Minister of the Interior, J. Dufaure, on June 14, reported out of committee on June 18, and voted almost without debate on June 19. The text of the law was officially published on June 23, 1849. See *Le Moniteur universel*, pp. 2077, 2100-2101, 2106, 2110, 2135. I believe that Price, *The French Second Republic*, p. 253, is mistaken in seeing in the June 1849 *échauffourée* the catalyst for the club law. It was simply unfinished business.

10 | Reflections and Retrospect

i

After analyzing its career, its *histoire événementielle* as some French historians would scornfully call it, I would like to draw back from the incidental to recapitulate and reflect on the general nature of the club movement. At the very least we can now identify it as a significant response to a revolutionary situation, a response intermediate between the ritual of collective violence and effective political organization along "modern" lines.

First, let me scan once more the problem of origin: old-line republicans, among whom veterans of the revolutionary underground predominated, played God the Father in the creation of the popular societies. Yet the initiative of these activists would have been fruitless had the February revolution of 1848 not succeeded in politically mobilizing vast numbers of the previously inert; the clubs met an obvious need. This awakening of the masses assumed what might be called different "densities." The minimum consisted of the act of registering and voting, a step some three-quarters of the Parisian electorate was willing to take. Enrollment in the Paris National Guard, which involved very occasional inconvenience, meant a slightly more intense commitment: the Parisian militia swelled from 56,000 to 237,000. Attendance at sessions of popular societies, however passive, was more demanding in that it marked a change of everyday habits. Active membership in political clubs or in craft unions (there may have been considerable overlapping) was the most meaningful expression of mass participation and of what political scientists would call "mobilization." The fact that some hundred thousand men were active as club members and that some forty thousand adhered to the *corporations ouvrières*, the revitalized craft unions, underlines the depth of the revolutionary upheaval in 1848.

The political clubs, it need hardly be emphasized, were never unified, though historians would do well to look beyond the picturesque feud between Barbès and Blanqui to account for the fissures. Attachment to the neighborhood, devotion to local control and local prejudices, an anarchical reluctance to accept dictation—anyone's dictation—counted for more in blocking unity than the much publicized rivalry between the Club of the Revolution and the Central Republican Society. Yet it is equally true that leaders and well-wishers of the popular societies consistently contended that "the clubs" constituted a collective reality that amounted to more than that hazy alliance of kindred spirits that contemporaries labeled the "republican party." Though the term had yet to enter the French political vocabulary, the clubs did constitute a movement. Not only were the majority of them dedicated to a new deal for the working class, but popular societies managed to collaborate on important occasions, on March 17 and May 15, in the National Guard elections, in the campaign in two installments for representatives to the National Assembly, and finally in coping with the ground swell of activism that centered on the Banquet of the People in June.

Much as one may speak of a club "movement," one should not assume that it remained unaltered throughout the critical four months of the French revolution of 1848. Club participation reached its peak shortly before the national elections in April, a time when the existence of more than two hundred popular political societies within intramural Paris can be documented. A 50 percent decline in their number in early May reflects the panic of April 16 and after, the letdown once the ballots were counted, perhaps disgust with the campaign failure of the clubs and with evidence of their general powerlessness. In mid-May the fiasco of the Polish demonstration once again halved the number of clubs: somewhere around fifty survived into June. Though the evidence is too fragmentary for hard-and-fast conclusions, my impression is that between March and June 1848 the same core of club leaders remained active (save for those arrested or forced into hiding after May 15), but that a good portion of the original rank and file drifted away. This erosion, I suspect, was caused less by specific political events than by the increasingly desperate economic plight of the lower classes, which no amount of club oratory could touch. The tempting hypothesis that this drift merely reflected the gradual (and "normal") depolitization of the masses as revolutionary fervor subsided is probably wrong; though the clubs shrank in numbers and membership, more voters voted for club-sponsored candidates in June than in April, when popular societies were riding the crest of the wave. Furthermore, neither the excitement over the Banquet of the People nor the breadth of the June insurrection itself points to growing apathy as the root cause of the club movement's decline.

ii

As long as they remained a vital force, the popular societies pursued three main goals: first, to educate and indoctrinate the lower-class electorate of Paris, whom the clubs considered their natural constituency; second, to force lower-class aspirations on the attention of the authorities—first the Provisional Government, later the National Assembly—by means of pressure ranging from petitions and delegations to mass demonstrations; third, to organize the revolutionaries' political campaign in successive Parisian elections. These objectives, it is important to stress, were relatively modest. The clubs' brand of participatory democracy fell far short of what Trotsky would tag "dual power." In 1848 the clubs never developed that taste for direct democracy, for self-administration in all its aspects, that had made the Paris sections of 1792 and 1793 such formidable rivals to constituted government, whatever its political complexion.

Among the three main tasks the clubs performed—indoctrination, confrontation, and campaigning—that of propaganda was always the neglected stepchild. Usually ideology was introduced from the outside, by candidates soliciting endorsement or, in the case of Robespierre's Declaration of the Rights of Man, by the authority, such as it was, of the Club of Clubs. Scattered admonitions by club officers suggest that the rank and file had a short attention span when it came to finely honed theories or elaborate schemes of social renovation. Exceptions to this anti-ideological bias could be found in societies headed by professed ideologues, what contemporaries called *chefs d'école*, whose doctrines served as drawing cards.

Though real revolutions may offer an inherently unpropitious climate for detached ideological speculation, the priority given to practical problems does not fully explain the clubs' neglect of ideology. Save for the handful of the converted, club activists, however sympathetic to "socialism," however responsive to its accepted slogans, were perplexed by the welter of competing doctrines. Occasionally they voiced the hope that open discussion among reformers and theorists would ultimately lead to a consensus on a common socialist program. But these same leaders of the popular societies were reluctant to "waste" their own club sessions and confuse their own membership by offering hospitality to such debate. This posed a dilemma: as long as ideological Babel prevailed, with what doctrine could the clubs indoctrinate their members?

However lightly the popular societies touched on ideology, they played a major role in what might be called "mythical" indoctrination. Sorel's concept of a political myth as a cluster of emotion-laden ideas that inspire men to act applies readily to the Parisian revolutionaries of 1848. The clubs' contribution to the clarification of such catchwords as "organization of labor" or "social and democratic republic" may have been minimal, but the popular societies' continual harping on such slogans helped enshrine them as political myths in the Sorelian sense. My impression—and in the absence of public opinion polling in 1848 it can be no more than that—is that in February these revolutionary slogans stirred only a few thousand republican militants; by June these same slogans, serving as focus for a diversity of genuine grievances, moved tens of thousands to raise the barricades once again, or at least to support those who did, practically or morally. This is not to say that the popular societies deliberately manipulated a set of symbols or that they necessarily welcomed the use to which these symbols were put. I am also far from suggesting that the clubs had an exclusive patent on myth-making. Street crowds, the popular press, the labor movement, even the National Workshops in their last phase, must have contributed to the dominance of the myths of social revolution prevailing in June 1848.

Another educational achievement that may be attributed to the club movement was the weaning of the masses —or at least those susceptible to club advice—from the simple-minded, undifferentiated republicanism so popular in the first weeks of the Second Republic. The clubs, their instruction reinforced by events themselves, taught people to distinguish between revolutionary and conservative republicans, between what a few months later would be called "red" as against "blue" republicans. The veterans forming the club cadres had known all along that the republican party bristled with mutually hostile factions. They were immediately aware that the members of the Provisional Government were at odds over serious ideological and political questions. Militants knew an Armand Marrast or a Garnier-Pagès for what they were: sincere political democrats, but equally sincere upholders of the social *status quo*. They knew that as neo-Jacobins, Flocon and Ledru-Rollin would favor paternalistic intervention on behalf of the weak but would have no truck with Louis Blanc's state-aided cooperative socialism. To impart these insights to a politically unsophisticated rank and file, who looked to the divided Provisional Government as the anointed of the revolutionary masses, was no easy chore. The election in Paris of every last member of that government in the teeth of club opposition testifies to the power of this popular mystique. But club failure in April was not the end of the story. By early June, when special supplementary elections were held in the capital, a substantial minority of the Parisian electorate had learned to shun moderate republicanism with ambiguous results: the winning candidates were either revolutionary republicans or frankly antirepublican conservatives. It would be foolhardy to claim that club indoctrination alone had led to this polarization—the mood for a showdown was rising in various sections of the population—but the popular societies were able to capitalize on the new disillusionment through their organ, the Central Commission for Democratic Elections.

iii

The club movement's propaganda function was never more than incidental. The popular societies' involvement in direct action and electioneering was central. These two functions cannot be depicted as mutually exclusive, for most twentieth-century revolutionary parties have marched off in both directions. Yet such dualism does pose problems. Organizing successful street demonstrations requires an ambiance of revolutionary enthusiasm fueled by apocalyptic rhetoric and fanned by charismatic leaders. A well-oiled political machine, by contrast, cries out for careful organization, for patient attention to tedious detail, for an orderly chain of command to insure that an army of precinct and block captains conscientiously fulfills its prosaic task of keeping the voters in line.

The club movement dealt with this contradiction by tacking back and forth between confrontation in the streets and conventional campaigning, though this zigzag course was never thought out in advance. The popular societies went through four, possibly five, distinct oscillations: First, from the overthrow of the monarchy to the great but indecisive demonstration of March 17, the clubs played the card of popular pressure, hoping to force the Provisional Government into a genuinely revolutionary path. Second, with the creation of the Revolutionary Committee, Club of Clubs, just after March 17, the popular societies veered toward electioneering, taking on successively the selection of National Guard officers and the general elections. Third, by the end of April, in the wake of the clubs' electoral defeat in Paris and with the Rouen "massacre" serving as catalyst, the club movement again swung back to direct agitation, culminating in the disastrous Polish demonstration of May 15. Fourth, sobered by the shock of that aborted putsch, the popular societies changed course again to re-enter conventional politics by organizing the campaign for the special elections called for June 4 to fill the Seine department's eleven vacant seats in the National Assembly. Their respectable showing seems to have converted most club leaders to electoral politics. Fifth, this conversion explains the skirmishing between "politicals" and "direct actionists" that characterized the final phase of the club movement. An increasingly cautious club leadership resisted the growing mood that favored dramatic and reckless reassertion of the popular will. Having barely managed to postpone the Banquet of the People, a scheme symptomatic of the new mood, the club leaders were bypassed by events. The June insurrection originated outside club circles, though by this time official harassment may have persuaded some club leaders that they had nothing to lose through violence.

iv

Why did the Parisian club movement fail? On the most down-to-earth level, popular societies in 1848 benefited from a gush of revolutionary enthusiasm that never succeeded in funneling it. The very psychological success of the clubs in providing a sense of civic participation and importance to tens of thousands of ordinary people helped defeat the attainment of more tangible objectives. Anarchical mass movements may be exhilarating for the participants, but they are rarely effective instruments for achieving limited, practical goals. Alternatives that come to mind—subordination of revolutionary enthusiasm to a hero-leader (the "On with Fidel" syndrome) or integration into a revolutionary party supposedly legitimized by history itself—were not available. The revolutionary party as a focus of popular energies is an invention of the later nineteenth century; and the urge to democratic self-expression was too strong for charismatic leadership to act as a controlling device. Auguste Blanqui, for instance, had great personal presence and commanded intense loyalties, yet his Central Republican Society was just as loose as other clubs. Blanqui himself favored chairmanship as the proper role of a leader: he was no Führer.

332 | Reflections and Retrospect

In attempting to counter official reluctance and inertia with the massed strength of lower-class Paris, the club movement consistently misread the lessons of the February Revolution. On that occasion, lower-class insurgents had triumphed only because the regime had lost its nerve (or, according to a more charitable interpretation, preferred defeat to the horrors of civil war) and because the sizable and armed Parisian middle class turned out to be unwilling to defend the constitutional monarchy.[1] The street-fighters of February never made explicit social demands that would have stiffened the resistance of all those with something to lose. The clubs did make such demands. They were never able to wear down the determination of the Provisional Government, its revolutionary credentials notwithstanding, to preserve the social order. Had the popular societies overcome this initial obstacle, they would have encountered far more formidable defenses manned by the possessing classes. As it was, the popular societies dispatched ultimatums but never laid serious plans to counter their possible—in fact, probable—rejection. The club movement claimed to embody the popular will, yet never envisaged seizing power if that will were thwarted.

Though the clubs' electoral role needs to be assessed, it should not be measured against lofty standards of political professionalism. Even in our own day most democratic election campaigns are the work of more-or-less gifted or lame-brained amateurs. Admittedly, nowadays these amateurs can tap a vast pool of collective political experience and have access to a variety of specialists who, for a price, will poll prospective voters, film campaign advertisements, and purchase television time. The electoral campaign of 1848, a trial run for mass democ-

[1] William L. Langer, "The Pattern of Urban Revolution in 1848," in Evelyn M. Acomb and Marvin L. Brown, Jr., eds., *French Society and Culture since the Old Regime* (New York, 1966), pp. 97-100, 110-112.

racy in France, was unusually amateurish and inept. Historians of French elections write off April 1848 as both atypical and unrevealing, for it marked the encounter of a bewildered electorate with only the crudest forms of political organization at a moment when the traditional elite had been panicked into temporary retirement.[2] Yet, measured against this inadequate norm, club performance in the spring 1848 elections in Paris was nontheless abysmal: the record of the Revolutionary Committee, Club of Clubs, as a campaign organization is indefensible by any standard. By contrast, the Central Commission for Democratic Elections, though it had very little time for campaigning in June, was surprisingly successful in increasing the size and discipline of the revolutionary vote. A comparison of April and June shows that the clubs did profit from experience.

This improvement, however, would not have continued indefinitely even if there had been no June insurrection. The political effectiveness of the club movement was up against built-in limitations. Most obviously, Paris was not the nation and, save for a few provincial cities like Lyon and Limoges, the club movement was essentially a political phenomenon of the French capital. To send a few representatives from the department of the Seine to the National Assembly may have been hailed as a moral triumph, but it did not hand power to the revolutionary republicans. What is less well known is that even within the constituency of the capital the revolutionaries, despite two years of trying, were never able to overcome stubborn political facts. Even a cursory examination of election results reveals that, despite growing political sophistication, despite more experienced political organization (even after the club movement's disappearance), despite the half-a-dozen general and special elections

[2] On this last point, see Tudesq, *Les grands notables*, pp. 989-1072, for what he depicts as the "great fear" of the traditional ruling class.

held between 1848 and 1850, the electorate consistently supporting revolutionary candidates fluctuated between two-fifths and one-half. In the general elections of May 1849, for example, which political scientists often single out as a sort of *Ur*-election revealing the political complexion of France, if not for all time, at least into the 1960's, the results in Paris illustrate what seemed to be the natural limits of the revolutionary electorate: a few of the "demo-soc" candidates, most notably Ledru-Rollin, won handsomely, yet the majority of the revolutionary nominees lost—by paper-thin margins of 1 to 5 percent of the vote. Conservatives and "demo-socs" were almost evenly matched, though the former retained a slight edge.[3] There is no strong reason to suppose that had the club movement survived it would have been able to improve on that performance in the short run. What campaigning could achieve was limited not only because Paris was not France, but also because revolutionary republicanism never gained a clear preponderance even on its home ground.

v

If we extend our focus from the French revolution of 1848 to take in all of France's history since the late eighteenth century, the club movement appears in a still different light. As a French historical phenomenon, revolutionary clubs catering to the masses—popular societies

[3] The official figures for Paris may be found in *Le Moniteur universel*, May 22, 1849. An older account of the 1849 elections, Gaston Génique, *L'élection de l'assemblée législative en 1849; essai d'une répartition géographique des partis politiques en France* (Paris, 1921), has been largely superseded by Jacques Bouillon, "Les démocrates-socialistes aux élections de 1849," *Revue française de science politique*, VI (1956), 70-95. As for 1849 (not 1848) as the fountainhead of French *géo-sociologie électorale*, see, among others, René Rémond, *La vie politique en France* (Paris, 1969), II, 81. I cite a textbook to emphasize the extent to which this view has become part of conventional wisdom since the 1950's.

comparable to those which this book has traced—occurred on three occasions: in the 1790's, in 1848, and in 1870-1871 during the Prussian siege and the Paris Commune.[4] In short, the club movement accompanied the three most profound revolutionary upheavals of these years. This observation in no way implies that other revolutionary institutions did not play major roles. During the 1790's the Paris sections and during the Terror the "revolutionary armies," so lovingly detailed by Professor Cobb, also expressed popular ferment.[5] Even in 1848 the same revolutionary consciousness that filled club halls also accounted for the astounding, though short-lived, blossoming of the labor movement and the press. In the Paris of 1870-1871 organized labor and the organized cadres of the National Guard both played important revolutionary roles. Even while admitting these qualifications, I would continue to insist that during these three major crises popular societies provided the most significant outlet for the revolutionary energies of the lower classes.

As a historical phenomenon in France, the club move-

[4] Isabelle Bourdin, *Les sociétés populaires à Paris pendant la révolution* (Paris, 1937), takes the story to 1792 only, but it can be pursued in less detail in Albert Soboul, *Les sans-culottes parisiens en l'an II* (Paris, 1958), pp. 614-648. For the clubs of 1870, we have only the tendentious Gustave de Molinari, *Les clubs rouges pendant le siège de Paris* (Paris, 1871); and for the Commune of 1871, Eugene Schulkind, "The Activity of Popular Organizations during the Paris Commune of 1871," *French Historical Studies*, I (1960), 394-415. The structure and role of political clubs during the Fifth Republic owes nothing to those of the period 1789-1871. See Jean-André Faucher, *Les clubs politiques en France* (Paris, 1965), which is devoted to contemporary clubs stemming from dissatisfaction with the ideological barrenness of the left-wing parties.

[5] R. C. Cobb, *Les armées révolutionnaires: instrument de la Terreur dans les départements, avril 1793-floréal an II*, 2 vols. (Paris, 1961-1963).

ment has a sharply defined time span. Popular societies
do not seem to have played a role in that great revolutionary upheaval of seventeenth-century France, the
Fronde.[6] They had no importance in any of the three or
four twentieth-century crises that mobilized great masses
of people in ways that may be described as revolutionary
or at least pseudorevolutionary: 1934, 1936, 1944, and
1968. In his masterful analysis of the power elite that
dominated France during much of the nineteenth century
André-Jean Tudesq speculated that this elite, whom he
labels the "Great Notables," was characteristic of a transitional society. Enjoying landed wealth, prestige, and
visibility, the notables served as intermediaries and bro-
kers at a time when corporate solidarity had eroded and
traditional hierarchies had lost legitimacy but before
modern mass organizations had taken root.[7] In France
this period of transition extended, Tudesq suggested,
from the late eighteenth century to the 1870's, precisely
the time span during which, in moments of major revolution, popular societies flourished. The function that the
Great Notables performed of binding men together during periods of relative social stability through an elaborate network of patron–client relationships, the clubs
performed during the social crises. The new era of parliamentary democracy, mass parties, and, somewhat
later, a mass labor movement founded on large-scale industry, relegated Great Notables and revolutionary clubs
alike to the dustbin of history.

As a phenomenon characteristic of a society on the
road to modernity, was the revolutionary club movement
uniquely French? Or was it rather a common reflection

[6] I have examined the two leading (and most analytical)
works on the Fronde: E. H. Kossmann, *La Fronde* (Leiden,
1954); and A. Lloyd Moote, *The Revolt of the Judges: The
Parlement of Paris and the Fronde* (Princeton, 1971).

[7] Tudesq, *Les grands notables*, pp. 1230-1241, esp. pp.
1230-1231.

of a particular stage in the political emergence of the masses in the West? Might not the earnest British "Jacobins" of the 1790's whom the Home Office hounded with King-and-Country mobs, *agents provocateurs*, and Treason Acts, or the mass meetings of the Chartists more than a generation later, be valid analogues to the French experience and explicable in similar terms? And what about popular "bonding" during the American Revolution, or the clubs of the 1790's against which the Alien and Sedition Acts were invoked? Within the last fifteen years, thanks to scholars like Rudé, Hobsbawm, E. P. Thompson, Soboul, Tønnesson, Tilly, Gurr, and many others, we have gained some sense of "the crowd"; we have learned to understand popular violence as an authentic and eloquent expression of the inarticulate and the oppressed.[8] Perhaps it is time to examine with equal care that next rung on the rickety ladder to human dignity: the revolutionary club movement.

[8] For representative works not previously cited, see Eric J. Hobsbawm, *Primitive Rebels: Studies in the Archaic Forms of Social Movement in the 19th and 20th Centuries* (Manchester, 1959); E. P. Thompson, *The Making of the English Working Class* (London, 1963); R. C. Cobb, *The Police and the People: French Popular Protest, 1789-1820* (Oxford, 1970); George Rudé, *The Crowd in the French Revolution* (Oxford, 1959), and *Paris and London in the Eighteenth Century: Studies in Popular Protest* (New York, 1971); K. D. Tønnesson, *La défaite des sans-culottes; mouvement populaire et réaction bourgeoise en l'an III* (Oslo, 1959); Isser Woloch, *Jacobin Legacy: The Democratic Movement under the Directory* (Princeton, 1970); Charles Tilly, "The Changing Place of Collective Violence," in Melvin Richter, ed., *Essays in Social and Political History* (Cambridge, Mass., 1970), and "How Protest Modernized in France, 1845 to 1855," in William O. Aydelotte, ed., *The Dimensions of Quantitative Research in History* (Princeton, 1972); Louise A. Tilly, "The Grain Riot as a Form of Political Conflict in France," *Journal of Interdisciplinary History*, II (1971), 23-57; Ted R. Gurr, *Why Men Rebel* (Princeton, 1970).

Bibliography

Manuscript Sources [cartons examined]

ARCHIVES NATIONALES

BB[18], 1460-1465B, 1468-1469, 1472-1474B, 1474.
BB[21], 520, 524-525, 527, 561-562, 622.
BB[23], 63-64.
BB[30], 281, 285, 299-321, 328, 336-337, 363, 365-366.
C. 908, 915, 922, 924-942.
F[1a], 353-361[3].
F[1b], ii, Seine, 26.
F[1c], ii, 97.
F[1c], iii, Seine, 12, 30.
F[1d], iii, 83-98.
F[7], 3894-3899, 4163-4165, 12178[a-c], 12357, 12710.
F[9], 422[bis]-423, 655, 684-689, 1076, 1093, 1117-1122, 1124, 1170, 1177-1178, 1181, 1246, 1248, 1250-1255.
F[15], 3884.
F[90], 770-776.

ARCHIVES DE LA SEINE

1-AZ, 165, 170, 171.
2-AZ, 269.
3-AZ, 168-169, 293-294 i.
4-AZ, 32, 95, 171, 174, 179-180, 214, 243, 288, 299, 390, 394, 459, 463.
D[3], 1-7.
D[1]M2, 1-4.
DM[2], 57, 59, 61-64.
DM[4], 10.
DM[13], 3, 6-7.
DR[4], 1-31.

D³R⁴, 20-38ᵇⁱˢ, 57, 114, 256-265.
DR⁵, 1-2.
H³, 1-9.
M², 57-67.
M¹³, 1-3.
Vᵇⁱˢ, 15, 19, 31-33, 51, 84, 224, 229, 257, 267-268, 335-337, 428, 429, 431.
VD³, 5-7.
VH³, 1, 4.
VK³, 12-15.
VK⁵, 4 cartons on 1848 elections.

BIBLIOTHÈQUE HISTORIQUE DE LA VILLE DE PARIS

Série 25, Collection Liesville. (The dozen cartons I saw in this series were in process of being rearranged and reclassified at the time. I am therefore unable to provide more specific references.)

ARCHIVES HISTORIQUES DU MINISTÈRE DE LA GUERRE

F¹, cartons 1-8.
A, dossiers des insurgés de juin. (I examined slightly more than 3 percent of the approximately 11,500 individual dossiers.)

ARCHIVES DE LA PRÉFECTURE DE LA POLICE

F⁷, A/A, 427-431.
Aᴬ, 370-417.

PERSONAL PAPERS

Thoré-Bürger Papers, Bibliothèque de l'Arsenal, Nos. 7908-7922.
François Arago, Bibliothèque de l'Institut de France.
Raspail Papers, Archives de la Seine.
Buchez Papers, Bibliothèque historique de la Ville de Paris, Liesville Collection.
Cabet Papers, Bibliothèque historique de la Ville de Paris, Liesville Collection.
Ledru-Rollin Papers, Bibliothèque historique de la Ville de Paris, Liesville Collection.
Pagnerre Papers, Archives Nationales, 67 AP.
Considérant Papers, Archives Nationales, 10 AS, cartons 36-42 (with Archives sociétaires).

Printed Sources

The bibliography that follows is deliberately restricted to newspapers, articles, and books actually cited in this work. Posters, handbills, announcements, and other ephemera cited in the footnotes are omitted from the bibliography.

Any scholar is indebted to hundreds of historians who have dealt not only with his own topic but with its broader setting— in this case the French Second Republic. Yet to acknowledge this indebtedness by bloating one's bibliography strikes me as both pretentious and superfluous. For good critical bibliographies of nineteenth-century writings on the revolution of 1848 in France, I would refer the reader to Calman, *Ledru-Rollin and the Second French Republic*, McKay, *The National Workshops*, and Wassermann, *Les Clubs de Barbès et de Blanqui*. For more recent work, my bibliographical article "Writings on the Second French Republic," *Journal of Modern History*, XXXIV (1962), 409-429, while concentrating on publications of the period 1949 to 1961, lists relevant bibliographies for earlier periods. For work on the French revolution of 1848 published between 1961 and 1971, see de Luna, *The French Republic under Cavaignac*, and the even more recent study by Price, *The French Second Republic: A Social History*.

NEWSPAPERS

L'Accusateur public
L'aimable Faubourien
L'Ami du peuple en 1848
L'Assemblée nationale
Les Boulets rouges, feuille du Club pacifique des Droits de l'Homme
La Commune de Paris
Le Courrier français
Le Démocrate égalitaire
La Démocratie pacifique
Le Droit—journal des tribunaux
Les Droits de l'Homme
Le Garde national
Gazette des tribunaux
Journal des sans-culottes
Journal des travailleurs
Le Messager
Le Monde républicain

Le Moniteur universel
Le National
L'Organisation du travail, journal des ouvriers
Le Père Duchêne—gazette de la révolution [title varies]
Le petit Homme rouge
Le Peuple constituant
Le Peuple souverain
Pilier des tribunaux, compte rendu des cours d'assises
Le Populaire
La Presse
La Réforme
Le Représentant du peuple
La République
La République rouge
La Sentinelle des clubs
Le Tam-Tam républicain
Le Travail
Le Tribun du peuple, organe de la Montagne
La Voix des clubs, journal quotidien des assemblées populaires
La Voix du peuple (1849)
La vraie République

BOOKS AND ARTICLES

Alméras, Henri d'. *La vie parisienne sous le règne de Louis-Philippe*. Paris: A. Michel [1911].

Amalric, Jean-Pierre. "La révolution de 1848 chez les cheminots de la compagnie du Paris Orléans." *Revue d'histoire économique et sociale*, XLI (1963), 332-373.

Amann, Peter. "*Du neuf* on the 'Banquet of the People,' June 1848." *French Historical Studies*, V (1968), 344-350.

―――, ed. "A French Revolutionary Club: The *Société démocratique centrale*." Ph.D. diss., University of Chicago, 1958.

―――. "The Huber Enigma—Revolutionary or Police Spy?" *International Review of Social History*, XII (1967), Part 2, 190-203.

―――. "Prelude to Insurrection: The 'Banquet of the People.'" *French Historical Studies*, I (1960), 436-444.

―――. "Revolution: A Redefinition." *Political Science Quarterly*, LXXVII (1962), 36-53.

Andrews, Richard M. "Laboring Classes and Dangerous Classes." *New York Times Book Review*, November 4, 1973, pp. 7-8.

Angrand, Pierre. *Etienne Cabet et la République de 1848.* Paris: P.U.F., 1948.

Annuaire général du commerce et de l'industrie. Paris: Firmin Didot, 1847, 1848, 1849.

Assemblée Nationale. *Rapport fait au nom de la commission chargée de l'enquête sur l'insurrection qui a éclaté dans la journée du 23 juin et sur les évènements du 15 mai.* 3 vols. Paris: Imprimerie nationale, 1848.

Audebrand, Philibert. *Souvenirs de la tribune des journalistes, 1848-1852.* Paris: Dentu, 1867.

Aydelotte, William O., ed. *The Dimensions of Quantitative Research in History.* Princeton: Princeton University Press, 1972.

Balzac, Honoré de. *The Works of Honoré de Balzac.* New York: Harper, n.d.

Bastié, Jean. *La croissance de la banlieue parisienne.* Paris: Presses Universitaires, 1964.

Baughman, John. "The Banquet Campaign of 1847-48." *Journal of Modern History,* XXXI (1959), 1-15.

Bernstein, Samuel. "Le néo-babouvisme d'après la presse (1837-1848)." In Maurice Dommanget et al., *Babeuf et les problèmes du babouvisme: Colloque international de Stockholm, 21 août 1960.* Paris: Editions sociales [1963].

Blanc, Louis. *Révélations historiques.* Brussels, 1859. Trans. into English as *1848: Historical Revelations.* London: Chapman & Hall, 1858.

————. *Pages d'histoire de la révolution de février 1848.* Paris: Bureau du Nouveau Monde, 1850.

Bonde, Baroness Florence. *Paris in 1848: Letters from a Resident Describing the Events of the Revolution.* Ed. C. E. Warr. New York: J. Pott & Co.; London: J. Murray, 1903.

Bouillon, Jacques. "Les démocrates-socialistes aux élections de 1849." *Revue française de science politique,* VI (1956), 70-95.

Bourdin, Isabelle. *Les sociétés populaires à Paris pendant la Révolution.* Paris: Sirey, 1937.

Bouton, Victor. *Attentat de la police républicaine contre la souveraineté du peuple.* Paris: V. Bouton, 1848.

Brelingard, Désiré. "La vie parisienne à travers les âges." In *De 1600 à 1945.* Vol. III. [Paris]: Connaissance du Passé, n.d.

Brochon, Pierre, ed. *La chanson française: Le pamphlet du pauvre (1834-1851).* Paris: Editions sociales, 1957.

Bulletin des lois du la République française, X^e série, 1er semestre de 1848. Vol. I. Paris: Imprimerie Nationale, July 1848.

Calman, Alvin R. *Ledru-Rollin and the Second French Republic.* New York: Columbia University Press, 1922.

Caussidière, Marc. *Mémoires de Caussidière, ex-préfect de police et représentant du peuple.* 2 vols. Paris: Lévy, 1849.

Chalmin, Pierre. "La crise morale de l'armée française." *Etudes*: "Bibliothèque de la révolution de 1848," XVIII (1955), 28-76.

Chauvet, Paul. *Les ouvriers du livre en France de 1789 à la Fédération du Livre.* Paris: Rivière, 1956.

Chazelas, V. "Un épisode de la lutte de classe à Limoges." *La révolution de 1848*, VII, 161-180, 240-256, 326-349, 389-412; VIII, 41-66.

Cherest, Aimé. *La vie et les œuvres de A.-T. Marie.* Paris: Durand, 1873.

Chevalier, Louis. *Classes laborieuses et classes dangéreuses à Paris pendant la première moitié du XIXe siècle.* Paris: Plon, 1958.

————. *La formation de la population parisienne au XIXe siècle.* Paris: Presses Universitaires, 1950.

Cobb, Richard Charles. *Les armées révolutionnaires: instrument de la Terreur dans les départements, avril 1793-floréal an II.* 2 vols. Paris: Mouton, 1961-1963.

————. *The Police and the People: French Popular Protest, 1789-1820.* Oxford: Clarendon Press, 1970.

Collins, Irene. "The Government and the Press during the Reign of Louis-Philippe." *English Historical Review*, LXIX (1954), 262-282.

Crémieux, Adolphe. *En 1848—discours et lettres.* Paris: Calmann-Lévy, 1883.

Cuvillier, Armand. *Un journal d'ouvriers: l'Atelier (1840-1850).* Paris: Editions Ouvrières [1954].

Daumard, Adeline. *La bourgeoisie parisienne, 1815-1848.* Paris: S.E.V.P.E.N., 1963.

————. *Maisons de Paris et propriétaires parisiens au XIXe siècle, 1809-1880.* Paris: Editions Cujas, 1965.

————. "Les relations sociales à l'époque de la monarchie constitutionnelle d'après les registres paroissiaux des mariages." *Population*, XII (1957), 457-461.

Delahodde, Lucien. *Histoire des sociétés secrètes et du parti républicain de 1830 à 1848.* Paris: Julien, Lanier & Co, 1850.

[Delmas, Gaëtan]. *Curiosités révolutionnaires: Les affiches rouges, reproduction exacte et histoire critique de toutes les affiches ultra-républicaines placardés sur les murs de Paris depuis le 24 février 1848, avec une préface par un Girondin.* Paris: Giraud & Dagneau, 1851.

————. *Curiosités révolutionnaires: Les journaux rouges, histoire critique de tous les journaux ultra-républicains publiés à Paris depuis le 24 février jusqu'au 1ᵉʳ octobre 1848.* Paris: Giraud, 1848.

de Luna, Frederic A. *The French Republic under Cavaignac, 1848.* Princeton: Princeton University Press, 1969.

Delvau, Alfred. *Histoire de la révolution de février.* Paris: Garnier, 1850.

————, ed. *Les murailles révolutionnaires.* Paris: Gayot, 1852.

————, ed. *Les murailles révolutionnaires.* 2 vols. 2nd ed. Paris: Picard, 1868.

Dommanget, Maurice. "Blanqui et le document Taschereau—Attitude et règle de conduite de Blanqui en matière de défense personnelle." *Revue d'histoire économique et sociale,* 1953, pp. 50-70.

————. *Un drame politique en 1848.* Paris: Les Deux Sirènes, 1948.

————. "Les 'faveurs' de Blanqui: Blanqui et le document Taschereau." *1848,* XLIII (1950), 137-166.

Dubuc, André. "Les émeutes de Rouen et d'Elbeuf (27, 28 et 29 avril 1848)." *Etudes d'histoire moderne et contemporaine,* II (1948), 243-275.

Duquai, Ernest, ed. *Les grands procès politiques: Les accusés du 15 mai devant la Haute-Cour de Bourges.* Paris: Le Chevalier, 1869.

Duveau, Georges. *La vie ouvrière sous le Second Empire.* Paris: Gallimard, 1946.

Fasel, George W. "The French Election of April 23, 1848: Suggestions for a Revision." *French Historical Studies,* V (1968), 285-298.

————. "The French Moderate Republicans, 1837-1848." Ph.D. diss., Stanford University, 1965.

Faucher, Jean-André. *Les clubs politiques en France.* Paris: Editions J. Didier, 1965.

Fourastié, F. and J., eds. *Les écrivains témoins du peuple.* Paris: Editions J'ai Lu, 1964.

Fournier, A. "George Sand en 1848." *Europe*, February 1948, pp. 140-150.

France. *Statistique générale de la France, Dénombrement des années 1841, 1846 et 1851*. Paris: Imprimerie Nationale, 1855.

Garnier-Pagès, Louis-Antoine. *Histoire de la révolution de 1848*. 11 vols. 2nd ed. Paris: Pagnerre, 1861-1872.

Génique, Gaston. *L'élection de l'assemblée législative en 1849: essai d'une répartition des partis politiques en France*. Paris: Riedes, 1921.

Geoffroy, C. *L'enfermé*. Paris: Charpentier, 1897.

Girard, Louis. *La garde nationale*. Paris: Plon, 1964.

Glotz, Gustave, ed. "Les papiers de Marie." *La Révolution de 1848*, I (1904-1905), 151-158, 181-193.

Goriély, B. "La Pologne en 1848." In *Le printemps des peuples dans le monde*, ed. F. Fejtö. 2 vols. Paris: Editions de Minuit, 1948.

Gossez, Rémi. "Diversité des antagonismes sociaux vers le milieu du XIXe siècle." *Revue économique*, I (1956), 439-457.

———. *Les ouvriers de Paris*. Vol. I: *L'organisation (1848-51)*. Paris: Société de l'histoire de la révolution de 1848, 1967.

———. "La presse parisienne à destination des ouvriers (1848-1851)." In "Bibliothèque de la Révolution de 1848." Vol. XXIII: *La presse ouvrière, 1819-1850*. Paris, 1966.

Guichonnet, Paul, ed. "William de la Rive: un témoins genevois de la révolution de 1848." *Etudes*, "Société de l'histoire de la révolution de 1848," XV (1953), 143-163.

Guillemin, Henri. *La tragédie de quarante-huit*. Geneva: Milieu du Monde, 1948.

Gurr, Ted R. *Why Men Rebel*. Princeton: Princeton University Press, 1970.

Handelsman, M. "1848 et la question polonaise." *La révolution de 1848*, XXIX, No. 179, 24-38.

Hobsbawm, Eric J. *Primitive Rebels: Studies in Archaic Forms of Social Movement in the 19th and 20th Centuries*. [Manchester]: Manchester University Press, 1959.

Hollingsworth, T. H. *Historical Demography*. Ithaca, N.Y.: Cornell University Press, 1969.

Husson, Armand. *Les consommations de Paris*. Paris: Guillaumin, 1856.

Les insurgés de 23, 24, 25 et 26 juin 1848 devant les conseils de guerre. Paris: Giraud, 1848.

[Izambard, H.]. *Le croque-mort de la Presse, ou la presse parisienne, journal non-politique, littéraire et bibliographique.* [Paris]: Bonaventure & Ducessois, 1848-1849.

Izambard, H. *La presse parisienne, statistique bibliographique et alphabétique de tous les journaux, revues et canards périodiques, nés, morts, ressucités ou métamorphosés à Paris depuis le 22 février 1848 jusqu'à l'empire.* Paris: Krabbe, 1853.

Jeanjean, F.-F. *Armand Barbès (1809-1870).* 2 vols. Vol. I: Paris: Cornély, 1909; Vol. II: Carcassonne: privately printed, 1947.

Johnson, Christopher H. "Communism and the Working Class before Marx: The Icarian Experience." *American Historical Review,* LXXVI (1971), 642-689.

————. "Etienne Cabet and the Problems of Class Antagonism." *International Review of Social History,* XI (1966), 403-443.

————. *Utopian Communism in France: Cabet and the Icarians.* Ithaca, N.Y.: Cornell University Press, 1974.

Kaes, René. "Mémoire historique et usage de l'histoire chez les ouvriers français." *Le mouvement social,* No. 61 [1967], pp. 13-32.

Kossmann, E. H. *La Fronde.* Leiden: University of Leiden Press, 1954.

Labrousse, Ernest. *Le mouvement ouvrier et les théories sociales en France de 1815 à 1848.* Paris: Cours de Sorbonne [1952].

Lamartine, Alphonse de. *History of the French Revolution of 1848.* London: Bohn, 1852.

Langer, William L. "The Pattern of Urban Revolution in 1848." In Evelyn M. Acomb and Marvin L. Brown, Jr., eds., *French Society and Culture since the Old Regime.* New York: Holt, Rinehart & Winston, 1966.

Larnac, J. *George Sand, révolutionnaire.* Paris: Editions Hier et Aujourd'hui, 1948.

Lasserre, André. *La situation des ouvriers de l'industrie textile dans la région lilloise.* Lausanne: Nouvelle Bibliothèque de droit et de jurisprudence, 1952.

Lees, Lynn, and Charles Tilly. "The People of June 1848." Working Paper No. 70. Ann Arbor: Center for Research on Social Organization, February 1972.

Léon, Paul. "Les transformations de Paris du Premier au Second Empire." *Revue des deux mondes*, No. 14 (1954), pp. 204-225.

Lévy-Schneider, L. "Les préliminaires du 15 mai 1848." *La révolution de 1848*, VII, 219-232.

Longepied [Amable], and Laugier. *Comité révolutionnaire, Club des clubs et la commission.* Paris: Garnier, 1850.

Loubère, Leo. *Louis Blanc.* Evanston, Ill.: Northwestern University Press, 1961.

Lucas, Alphonse. *Les clubs et les clubistes.* Paris: Dentu, 1851.

McKay, Donald C. *The National Workshops.* Cambridge, Mass.: Harvard University Press, 1933.

Maîtron, Jean, ed. *Dictionnaire biographique du mouvement ouvrier français.* 3 vols. Part 1: *1789-1864.* Paris: Editions sociales, 1964-1966.

Markovitch, J. "La crise de 1847-1848 dans les industries parisiennes." *Revue d'histoire économique et sociale*, XLIII (1965), 256-260.

Mazoyer, Louis. *La banlieue parisienne des origines à 1945.* "La vie parisienne à travers les âges," VI. [*Paris*]: Connaissance du Passé, n.d.

Ménard, Louis. *Prologue d'un révolution, février-juin 1848.* Paris: Bureau du Peuple, 1849.

Merriman, John. "Radicalization and Repression: The Experience of the Limousin, 1848-1851." Ph.D. diss., University of Michigan, 1972.

Molinari, Gustave de. *Les clubs rouges pendant le siège de Paris.* Paris: Garnier, 1871.

Molok, A.-I. "Les mouvements révolutionnaires dans la banlieue de Paris pendant l'insurrection de juin 1848" [in Russian]. In *Annuaire d'études françaises*, 1963. Moscow: Editions Nauka, 1964.

Moote, A. Lloyd. *The Revolt of the Judges: The Parlement of Paris and the Fronde.* Princeton: Princeton University Press, 1971.

Nadaud, Martin. *Mémoires de Léonard, ancien garçon maçon.* Bourganeuf: Duboueix, 1895.

Normanby, Constantine Henry, Marquis of. *A Year of Revolution from a Journal Kept in Paris in 1848.* 2 vols. London: Brown, Green, Longmans & Roberts, 1857.

Pardigon, François. *Episodes des journées de juin 1848.* London: Jeffs, 1852.

Paris Chambre de Commerce. *Statistique de l'industrie à Paris pour les années 1847-1848.* Paris: Imprimerie Nationale, 1851.

[E. Pelletan]. *Physionomie de la presse ou catalogue complet des nouveaux journaux qui ont paru depuis le 24 février jusqu'au 20 août avec le nom des principaux rédacteurs.* Paris, 1848.

Perreux, Georges. *Aux temps des sociétés secrètes: La propagande républicaine au début de la Monarchie de juillet (1830-1835).* Paris: Hachette, 1931.

Pierrard, Pierre. *Lille et les lillois.* Paris: Bloud & Gay, 1967.

Pimienta, Robert. *La propagande bonapartiste en 1848.* Paris: Bibliothèque de la Révolution de 1848, 1911.

Pinkney, David H. *Napoleon III and the Rebuilding of Paris.* Princeton: Princeton University Press, 1958.

Pornin [Bernard]. *La vérité sur la préfecture de police pendant l'administration de Caussidière. Réfutation des calomnies Chenu.* Paris: Palais-National, 1850.

Pouthas, Charles H. *La population français pendant la première moitié du XIXᵉ siècle.* Paris: P.U.F., 1956.

Price, Roger. *The French Second Republic: A Social History.* Ithaca, N.Y.: Cornell University Press, 1972.

Procès-verbaux du gouvernement provisoire et de la commission du pouvoir exécutif (24 février-22 juin). Paris: Imprimerie Nationale, 1950.

[Proudhon, P.-J.]. *Carnets de P.-J. Proudhon.* Vol. III: *1848-1850.* Paris: Rivière, 1968.

———. *Les confessions d'un révolutionnaire pour servir à l'histoire de la révolution de 1848.* Paris: La Voix du Peuple, 1849.

Rasch, Gustav. "Ein Immortellenkranz auf das Grab eines Martyrers [Max Dortu]." In *Der Deutsche Eidgenosse* (London), March 1865, pp. 21ff.

Regnault, Elias. *Histoire du gouvernement provisoire.* Paris: Lecou, 1850.

Rémond, René. *La vie politique en France.* 2 vols. Paris: A. Colin, 1969.

Robert, Adolphe, Gaston Cougny, and Edgar Bourloton. *Dictionnaire des parlementaires français.* 5 vols. Paris: Bourloton, 1889-1890.

Rougerie, Jacques. "Remarques sur l'histoire des salaires à Paris au XIXᵉ siècle." *Annales,* XXIII (1968), 71-108.

Rudé, George. *The Crowd in History, 1730-1848.* New York: Wiley, 1964.

――――. *The Crowd in the French Revolution.* Oxford: The Clarendon Press, 1959.

――――. *Paris and London in the Eighteenth Century: Studies in Popular Protest.* New York: Viking Press [1971].

Sand, George. *Correspondance.* Vol. vii. Paris: Garnier, 1964-.

――――. *Œuvres autobiographiques.* Vol. ii. Paris: Editions Gallimard, 1971.

Schulkind, Eugene. "The Activity of Popular Organizations during the Paris Commune of 1871." *French Historical Studies,* i (1960), 394-415.

Sencier, Georges. *Le babouvisme après Babeuf.* Paris: Rivière, 1912.

Simpson, J. Palgrave. *Pictures from Revolutionary Paris.* 2 vols. Edinburgh and London: Blackwood, 1849.

Soboul, Albert, *Les sans-culottes parisiens en l'an II.* 2 vols. Paris: Clavreuil, 1958.

Spitzer, Alan B. "Bureaucrat as Proconsul: The Restoration Prefect and the police générale." *Comparative Studies in Society and History,* vii (1965), 371-392.

Tchernoff, Iouda. *Associations et sociétés secrètes sous la Deuxième République.* Paris: Alcan, 1905.

Thompson, Edward Palmer. *The Making of the English Working Class.* London: Gollancz, 1963.

Tilly, Charles. "The Changing Place of Collective Violence." In Melvin Richter, ed., *Essays in Social and Political History.* Cambridge, Mass.: Harvard University Press, 1970.

――――. "How Protest Modernized in France, 1845 to 1855." In Robert Fogel, ed., *The Dimensions of Quantitative Research in History.* Princeton: Princeton University Press, 1972.

Tilly, Louise A. "The Grain Riot as a Form of Political Conflict in France." *Journal of Interdisciplinary History,* ii (1971), 23-57.

Tocqueville, Alexis de. *Recollections of Alexis de Tocqueville.* London: Harvill Press, 1948.

Toesca, M. "George Sand et la révolution de 1848." In *L'Esprit de 1848.* Paris: Bader-Dufour, 1948.

Tønnesson, K. D. *La défaite des sans-culottes: mouvement populaire et réaction bourgeoise en l'an III.* Oslo, 1959.

Trotsky, Leon. *The Russian Revolution.* Ed. F. W. Dupee. New York: Doubleday-Anchor, 1959.

Tudesq, André-Jean. "La crise de 1847 vue par les milieux d'affaires parisiens." *Etudes*, "Société de l'histoire de la révolution de 1848," xix (1956), 4-36.

————. *Les grands notables en France (1840-1849)*. 2 vols. Paris: Presses Universitaires, 1964.

————. "La légende napoléonienne en France en 1848." *Revue historique*, lxxxi (1957), 65-85.

Vapereau, Louis-Gustave, ed. *Dictionnaire universel des contemporains*. 1st ed. Paris: Hachette, 1858.

Vedrenne-Villeneuve, Edmonde. "L'inégalité sociale devant la mort dans la première moitié du XIXe siècle." *Population*, xvi (1961), 665-698.

Villermé, Dr. [Louis-René]. *Tableau de l'état physique et moral des ouvriers*. Paris: Renouard, 1840.

Wallon, H.-A. *La presse de 1848 ou revue critique des journaux publiés à Paris depuis la révolution de février jusqu'à la fin de décembre*. Paris: Pillet fils, 1849.

Wassermann, Suzanne. "Le club de Raspail." *La révolution de 1848*, v (1908-1909), 589-605, 655-674, 748-762.

————. *Les clubs de Barbès et de Blanqui en 1848*. Paris: Cornély, 1913.

Weill, Georges. *Histoire du parti républicain, 1814-1870*. Paris: Alcan, 1928.

Weiner, Dora B. *Raspail: Scientist and Reformer*. New York: Columbia University Press, 1968.

Woloch, Isser. *Jacobin Legacy: The Democratic Movement under the Directory*. Princeton: Princeton University Press, 1970.

Zévaès, Alexandre. "La fermentation sociale sous la Restauration et sous la monarchie de juillet." *Revue internationale d'histoire politique et constitutionnelle*, No. 11 (1953), pp. 206-234.

Index

L'Accusateur public, 51
Adam, 142
Adam, Edmond, 176, 221, 290
adult education, 30
Agricultural Committee, 213
Alberny, 121
Albert, 32, 72, 76, 187, 225, 235
Alien and Sedition Acts, 337
Alsatian Club, *see* Republican Club of Alsatian Workers
D'Alton-Shée, Colonel, 148, 159, 202
L'Ami du peuple en 1848, 38, 49, 79, 188
André, Antoine, 256
Arago, Etienne, 79, 142, 220, 245, 246
Arago, François, 72, 110, 145, 212
L'Atelier, 29, 80
Aude, 196
Aulin, 230
Austria, 205, 206, 208
Auvergne, 21

Bailly, Jean, 239
Balard, 68
Balzac, Honoré de, 13
Banquet of the National Workshops, 265, 266, 270
Banquet of the People, 50, 249, 264-280, 283, 331: club

response, 50, 274-278; origins of, 264-266; founding commission of, 264-265, 268, 270, 276-279; promoters of, 267-271; significance of, 271-273; failure of, 278-280
Banquet of the Schools, 271
Banquet of the Twelfth District, 272
Barbès, Armand, 61, 115, 116, 142, 191, 194, 195, 199, 221, 225, 235, 248, 250, 298, 325: as club president, 64; role in founding Club of the Revolution, 120-121; connection with Society of the Rights of Man, 130-131; elected colonel of the Twelfth Legion of the Paris National Guard, 148; role on April 16, 183-186; failure of candidacy in Paris, 189; response to Rouen "massacre," 196; opposition to May 15 demonstration, 220; relation to Caussidière, 228; and demonstration of May 15, 238-239; arrest of, 245
Barnabo, 171
Baroche, Procurator-general, 246
Baudin, Dr. Alphonse, 93, 158
Belgians, 169
Berlin, 210

Bertrand, 220
Bianchi, 120
Blanc, Louis, 72, 96, 142, 212, 329: political position within the Provisional Government, 75-76; as club ally, 88; favoring postponement of elections, 95; role in March 17 demonstration, 108; role in Central Committee of the Workers of the Seine, 118, 174; as last in social reform, 164-165; role on April 16, 175, 177-178; elected in Paris to National Assembly, 187; demands Ministry of Progress, 210-211, 213; club adulation of, 250-251
Blanqui, Auguste, 31, 49, 97, 116, 235, 298, 325: Blanqui upon release, 33, 40; as president of the Central Republican Society, 1-62, 68, 73, 156, 331; Taschereau charges against, 70, 123; relations with Lamartine, 75; relations with Louis Blanc, 76; connection with March 17 demonstration, 89-91, 94, 97, 103, 105; bypassed by Club of Clubs, 119; sponsoring Revolutionary Committee for the Elections to the National Assembly, 120-123; as advocate of proselytizing provinces, 125-126; connection with April 16 demonstration, 173, 178-182, 183, 184, 186; as unsuccessful candidate to National Assembly, 189-190; and Rouen "massacre," 194-195; opposition to May 15 demonstration, 220; official dissolution of his club, 241; arrest of, 245
Blue, Charles-Jules, 60, 312
Boissel, 262

Bonaparte, Louis Napoleon, 5, 261, 262, 280-282, 321
Bonapartist agitation, 248, 280, 282
Boulard, 136
Les Boulets rouges, 51
Bourcard, 233
Bourdon, 230, 232
Bouton, Victor, 50, 97
British "Jacobins," 337
Brutinel-Nadal, O., 311
Bulletin de la République, 95
Bunchez, Philippe, 179, 184, 223-224, 235

Cabet, Etienne, 31, 36, 269: under the July Monarchy, 29; as president of Central Fraternal Society, 61, 62-63, 67; response to February Revolution, 78; connection with March 17 demonstration, 93, 94-96, 119; as candidate to National Assembly, 116, 189; influence of April 16 on, 184-185; as candidate in supplementary elections of June 1848, 255
Cabrel de Nurelé, 160
Cahaigne, Louis, 120, 129-133
Carlier, 75, 100, 151, 168, 183, 207, 214, 216, 228, 230, 242, 288, 289, 303, 307
La Carmagnole, 38
Carpentier, P., 309
Carteret, 75, 108, 183, 186, 219, 228, 289
Castro, Fidel, 331
Catholic-Socialists, 29
Caussidière, Marc, 129, 250: authorizing clubs to use public buildings, 57; political position of, 72, 76; connection with March 17 demonstration, 97, 103-104, 108; as club-sponsored candidate,

142, role during April 16 crisis, 183, 185, 188; role during May 15 demonstration, 212, 223-224, 228; as candidate in the supplementary elections of June 1848, 255, 261-262
Caussidière senior (father of Marc C.), 30
Cavaignac, General Eugène, 227, 295, 315
Central Club for the Organization of Labor, 161
Central Club of the Organization for Workers, 282
Central Club of United Workers, 274
Central Commission for Democratic Elections, 245, 256, 258, 259, 260, 263, 264, 276, 298, 329, 333
Central Committee for general Elections to the National Assembly, 111, 113-116, 128, 133
Central Committee of Elections, 112, 122-124
Central Committee of the Electors of the Seine, 112, 253
Central Committee of the Schools, 116
Central Committee of the Third District, 102, 271
Central Committee of the United Clubs, 94-95
Central Committee of the Workers of the Seine Department, 76, 111-112, 154, 187, 254, 263: cooperation with Central Democratic Society, 113; origin of, 117-118; organization of, 118-119; alliance with Club of Clubs, 141-142; political failure of, 196
Central Democratic Club of the National Guard, 195

Central Democratic Committee of the Seine, 253
Central Democratic Republican Club, 243
Central Democratic Society, 79, 80, 111, 117, 175, 201, 203-204, 211, 252, 277: origins of, 35-36; as elite organization, 43; structure and policy of, 112-114; cooperation with Central Committee of the Workers of the Seine, 118; role in April 16 crisis, 181
Central Fraternal Society, 36, 56, 60, 67, 80, 87, 93-94, 161: character of, 61-63; role in preparations of March 17 demonstration, 93-94
Central Republican Committee of the Third District, 55, 83, 93
Central Republican Society, 35, 42, 156, 249, 250, 325, 331: foundation of, 33; as elite club, 43; relation to *Le Courrier français*, 49; meeting places of, 58; character of, 61-62, 70, 331; Ledru-Rollin's attitude toward, 73; connection with March 17 demonstration, 79-96; and 45% surtax, 162; attitude toward foreign revolutionaries, 171-172; and Rouen "massacre," 194; succeeded by Club of the People, 307
Centralizing Committee, 234: as successor to Club of Clubs, 191-199; initial attitude toward Polish demonstration, 208-210; role in May 15 demonstration, 215-222, 235; seizure of files of, 240
Cercle de la liberté, *see* Circle of Liberty
Changarnier, General, 262

Chartists, 171
Chautard, J.-J., 310
Chellier, Camille, 233
Chevalier, 231
Chevalier, E., 145
Children of Lutèce, Choral Society of, 30
Chilmann, 225
Circle of Liberty, 146
Clouvez, 231, 232
Club central de l'organisation des travailleurs, see Central Club of the Organization for Workers
Club central de l'organisation du travail, see Central Club for the Organization of Labor
Club central démocratique de la Garde nationale, see Central Democratic Club of the National Guard
Club central des travailleurs réunis, see Central Club of United Workers
Club de la Commune de Paris, see Club of the Commune of Paris
Club de la Convention nationale, 38
Club de la fraternité des ouvriers, see Club of the Workers' Faternity
Club de la fraternité universelle, see Club of Universal Fraternity
Club de la garde nationale mobile, see Club of the Garde Nationale Mobile
Club de la Liberté, see Club of Liberty
Club de la Montagne, see Club of the Mountain
Club de l'avenir, see Club of the Future
Club de l'Homme armé, see Club of the Homme Armé
Club de l'organisation du tra-
vail, see Club of the Organization of Labor
Club de l'union des travailleurs, see Club of the Workers' Union
Club de l'union, see Club of the Union
Club de l'union fraternelle, see Club of Fraternal Union
Club démocratique central de la garde nationale, see Democratic Central Club of the National Guard
Club démocratique de la rue St.-Bernard, see Democratic Club of the Rue Saint Bernard
Club démocratique fraternel du Faubourg Saint-Antoine, see Democratic Fraternal Club of the Faubourg Saint-Antoine
Club démocratique de l'Arsenal, see Democratic Club of the Arsenal
Club démocratique de la rue Popincourt, see Club Popincourt
Club démocratique de la rue Traversiere, see Democratic Club of the Rue Traversiere
Club démocratique de Saint-Maur, see Democratic Club of Saint-Maur
Club démocratique des Quinze-Vingt, see Democratic Club of Quinze-Vingt
Club démocratique du Vᵉ arrondissement, see Democratic Club of the Fifth District
Club démocratique du travail, see Democratic Club of Labor
Club de la propagande républicaine, see Club of Republican Propaganda
Club de la Réforme, see Club of Reform
Club de la sentinelle constitu-

ante, *see* Club of the Constituent Sentinel

Club de la société unitaire de la propagande démocratique, *see* Club of the United Society for Democratic Propaganda (Passy)

Club de l'égalité, *see* Club of Equality

Club de l'égalité et de la fraternité, *see* Club of Equality and Fraternity

Club de l'emancipation des peuples, *see* Club of the Emancipation of the Peoples

Club de l'organisation sociale, *see* Club of Social Organization

Club de l'unité démocratique, *see* Club of Democratic Unity

Club de l'unité républicaine du VIᵉ arrondissement, *see* Club of Republican Unity of the Sixth District

Club démocratique de la rue Charonne, *see* Democratic Club of the Rue Charonne

Club démocratique du Quartier Montorgueil, *see* Democratic Club of the Montorgueil Quarter

Club démocratique du Rhone, *see* Democratic Club of the Rhone Department

Club des amis fraternels, *see* Club of Fraternal Friends

Club des clubs, comité révolutionnaire, *see* Club of Clubs, Revolutionary Committee

Club des devoirs et des Droits de l'Homme, *see* Club of the Duties and Rights of Man

Club des Droits de l'Homme, *see* Society of the Rights of Man

Club des francs républicains, *see* Club of Frank Republicans

Club des Halles, *see* Club of the Halles

Club des hommes lettrés, *see* Democratic Society of Educated Men without Employment

Club des hommes libres, *see* Club of Free Men

Club des incorruptibles, *see* Club of the Incorruptibles

Club des intérêts du peuple et de la Garde Nationale Mobile, *see* Club of the People's Interests and of the Garde Nationale Mobile

Club des intérêts populaires, *see* Club of Popular Interests

Club des locataires-commerçants, *see* Club of Commercial Renters

Club des Montagnards de Belleville, *see* Club of the Mountaineers of Belleville

Club des ouvriers de la fraternité (XIᵉ arrondissement), *see* Club of the Workers of Fraternity (Eleventh District)

Club des patriotes indépendants, *see* Club of Independent Patriots

Club des prévoyants, *see* Club of the Foresighted

Club des prévoyants tenaces, *see* Club of the Tenacious Foresighted

Club des républicains socialistes, *see* Club of Socialist Republicans

Club des républicains unis (de Montmartre), *see* Club of United Republicans (of Montmartre)

Club des socialistes réunis, *see* Club of United Socialists

Club des Templiers, see Club of the Templars
Club des travailleurs, see Club of the Workers
Club des travailleurs du 1er arrondissement, see Club of the Workers of the First District
Club des travailleurs unis, see Club of United Workers
Club du mars see Club of the Second of March
Club du Xe arrondissement, see Club of the Tenth District
Club du Marais, see Club of the Marais
Club du peuple, see Club of the People
Club du progrès, see Club of Progress
Club du progrès démocratique, see Club of Democratic Progress
Club du salut du peuple, see Club of the Salvation of the People
Club du triomphe, see Club of Triumph
Club du Vieux-Chêne, see Club of Vieux-Chêne
Club fraternel des Quinze-Vingt, see Fraternal Club of Quinze-Vingt
Club of Bercy, 143
Club of Chaillot, 60, 67, 85, 86, 87, 214
Club of Clichy, 116
Club of Clubs, Revolutionary Committee, 34, 41, 46, 50, 58, 111, 112, 118, 167, 182, 190, 240, 245, 252, 254, 256, 263, 327, 330, 333: origins of, 119; foundation of, 120-123; rivalry with Blanqui-sponsored organization, 121-124; dual role of, 124-143; provincial role of, 125-128; leadership of, 129-134; electoral role in Paris, 134-143; clubs' response to campaign instructions of, 150, 152, 157, 158, 161, 169; fate of candidates endorsed by, 187-188; disintegration of, 197-198
Club of Commercial Renters, 34
Club of Democratic Progress, 144
Club of Democratic Unity, 195, 202, 207
Club of Equality, 87, 94, 122, 202
Club of Equality and Fraternity, 51, 160, 171, 172, 195, 211, 212, 243, 250
Club of Frank Republicans (Montmartre), 158
Club of Fraternal Friends, 197
Club of Fraternal Union (Ivry), 143, 146, 310
Club of Fraternity, 40, 183
Club of Fraternity (of the Latin Quarter), 56
Club of Free Men, 85, 87, 93, 94, 95, 140, 143, 151, 162, 163, 167, 224, 246, 268, 306
Club of Independent Patriots, 52
Club of L'Homme Armé, see Club of the Homme Armé
Club of Liberty, 70
Club populaire de la Sorbonne, see Republican Society of the Sorbonne
Club of Popular Interests, 52, 55, 171
Club of Progress, 82, 84, 120, 163, 170, 172, 243, 250, 289
Club of Progress, see also Club of Social Organization
Club of Puteaux, 116
Club of Quinze-Vingt, see Fraternal Club of Quinze-Vingt,

Democratic Club of Quinze-Vingt
Club of Reform, 134
Club of Republican Propaganda, 199
Club of Republican Unity of the Sixth District, 139, 197
Club of Saint-Maur, *see* Democratic Club of Saint-Maur
Club of Social Organization, 250, 289
Club of Socialist Republicans, 164, 165
Club of Socialist Republicans of the Sixth District, 53, 197, 291
Club of Socialist Republicans of the Twelfth District, 54
Club of the Abbaye, 116
Club of the Amandiers, 152
Club of the Antonins, 51, 195, 197, 291, 292, 293, 297, 311, 320
Club of the Butte des Moulins, 57, 69, 70, 139, 281
Club of the Commune of Paris, 38
Club of the Constituent Sentinel, 158
Club of the Duties and Rights of Man, 52, 55
Club of the Emancipation of the Peoples, 70, 155-156, 170, 244, 272, 286
Club of the Etoile, 52
Club of the Foresighted, 52, 87, 94, 164, 184
Club of the Friends of the People, *see* Society of the Friends of the People
Club of the Future, *see* Democratic Club of the Future
Club of the Garde Nationale Mobile, 170
Club of the Halles, 146
Club of the Homme Armé, 163, 312

Club of the Ile St.-Louis, 52
Club of the Incorruptibles, 86, 167, 272
Club of the Independents (of Charonne), 52
Club of the Jacobins (of the Faubourg du Roule), 39, 55
Club of the Marais, 92
Club of the Mountain (of the Carré St.-Martin), 39, 53, 155, 171, 172
Club of the Mountain (of Montmartre), 54, 56, 86, 87, 160, 264-265, 268-270, 272, 277
Club of the Mountain (of Passy), 52
Club of the Mountain (of the rue Frépillon), 281, 287, 300
Club of the Mountaineers of Belleville, 56, 195, 243, 274, 308, 309
Club of the National Convention, *see* Club de la Convention nationale
Club of the Organization of Labor, 311
Club of the People, 51, 303, 307-308
Club of the Peoples' Emancipation, *see* Club of the Emancipation of the Peoples
Club of the People's Interests and of the Garde Nationale Mobile, 208
Club of the Provençaux, 116
Club of the Revolution, 43, 50, 58, 61, 64, 73, 116, 119, 120, 121, 123, 130, 142, 145, 164, 165, 182, 183, 194, 197, 220, 243, 244, 245, 250, 251, 252, 253, 254, 256, 261, 272, 273, 274-276, 277, 281, 287, 288, 307, 325
Club of the Salvation of the People, 143, 168, 202, 243

Club of the Second of March, 56, 159, 256, 274, 288, 299, 300

Club of the Sorbonne, see Republican Society of the Sorbonne

Club of the Templars, 56, 60

Club of the Tenacious Foresighted, 138

Club of the Tenth District, 203

Club of the Union, 281, 320

Club of the United Society for Democratic Propaganda (Passy), 116

Club of the Workers, 88, 96

Club of the Workers' Fraternity, 163

Club of the Workers of Fraternity (Eleventh District), 55

Club of the Workers (of the First District), 40, 52, 56

Club of the Workers' Union, 165

Club of Triumph, 197

Club of United Republicans of Montmartre), 195, 203, 310

Club of United Socialists, 210

Club of United Workers, 34, 117, 118, 159, 212

Club of Universal Fraternity, 82, 93, 152, 158

Club of Vieux-Chêne, 320

Club of Workers, see Club of United Workers

Club pacifique des Droits de l'Homme, see Peaceful Club of the Rights of Man

Club patriotique des Blancs-Manteaux, see Patriotic Club of the Blancs-Manteaux

Club Popincourt, 86, 197, 251, 256

Club populaire de la Sorbonne, see Republican Society of the Sorbonne

Club populaire du Xe arron-dissement, see Popular Club of the Tenth District

Club républicain de Batignolles-Monceaux, see Republican Club of Batignolles-Monceaux

Club républicain de l'Atelier, see Republican Club of L'Atelier

Club républicain de l'avenir, see Democratic Club of the Future

Club républicain de la fraternité, see Republican Club of Fraternity

Club républicain de l'Etoile, see Republican Club of the Etoile

Club républicain démocratique central, see Central Democratic Republican Club

Club républicain de Montmartre, see Republican Club of Montmartre

Club républicain de Passy, see Republican Club of Passy

Club républicain des ouvriers alsaciens, see Republican Club of Alsatian Workers

Club républicain des travailleurs, see Republican Club of Workers

Club républicain des travailleurs libres, see Republican Club of Free Workers

Club républicain du Faubourg du Roule, see Republican Club of the Faubourg du Roule

Club républicain du Faubourg Saint-Marceau, see Republican Club of the Faubourg Saint-Marceau

Club républicain du progrès, see Republican Club of Progress

Club républicain du Temple, see Republican Club of the Temple

Club républicain national, *see* Republican National Club

Club Saint-Georges, 95, 163

Club Saint-Maur, 146

Club Servandoni, 195, 203

Club Soufflot, 158

Clubs: beginnings of, 33-35; origins of, 35-39; influence of French revolution on, 37-39; influence of July Monarchy's secret societies on, 39; leadership among pioneer clubs, 40-42; social composition of, 43-47; relationship to organized labor movement, 44-47; relationship to revolutionary press, 47-51; professed aims of, 51-55; formal structure of, 55-56; meeting places of, 55-60; financial problems of, 60; frequency of sessions, 61; day-to-day functioning, 65-71; attitude of Provisional Government towards, 71-76; and stamp tax crisis, 78-80; concern with problems of National Guard, 81-88; protest against "premature" national elections, 89-91; policy toward the return of a garrison to Paris, 91-93; preparation of the March 17 demonstration, 93-98, 101-108; confrontation with Provisional Government, March 17, 108-109; attempts at unity, 111-143; reluctant acceptance of Paris garrison, 145-147; and National Guard elections (April 5-7), 147-152; and national elections, 141-143, 152-161; ideological content of, 161-172; attitude toward tenant-landlord conflict, 166-167; attitude toward freedom of the press, 167-168; attitude toward antiforeign agitation, 168-169; attitude toward foreign revolutionaries, 170-173; stance toward April 16 demonstration, 181-184; impact of April 16 on clubs, 186-187; club influence on election results, 187-191; and Rouen "massacre," 191-196; postelection decline of, 196-197; postelection readaptation of, 199-202; stance toward National Assembly, 202-204; attitude toward Polish cause, 206-210; preparations of demonstration in behalf of Poland, 209-222; involvement in demonstration of May 15, 230-239; measures against following May 15, 240-247; attitude toward Banquet of the People, 264-280; preparation of supplementary elections of June 4 and 5, 251-261; influence on supplementary election results, 261-264; attitude toward Bonapartist agitation, 280-282; attitude toward crowd control legislation, 286-288; eviction from public buildings, 288-293; role in June insurrection, 297-315; legislation restricting, 315-323; political function of, 326-331; reasons for failure of, 331-334; historical significance of, 334-337

"name," 61-65: Central Republican Society, 61-62; Central Fraternal Society, 62-63; Society of the Rights of Man, 63-64; Club of the Revolution, 64; Society of the Friends of the People, 64-65

Cobb, R. C., 335

Colfavru, Jean-Claude, 143, 265, 267-268, 271, 276, 306

Collard, 310

Collet, P., 184
Comité central démocratique de
la Seine, *see* Central Demo-
cratic Committee of the Seine
Comité central démocratique du
XIᵉ arrondissement, *see*
Democratic Central Commit-
tee of the Eleventh District
Comité central des clubs
réunis, *see* Central Committee
of the United Clubs
Comité central des écoles, *see*
Central Committee of the
Schools
Comité central des électeurs de
la Seine, *see* Central Commit-
tee of the Electors of the
Seine
Comité central des élections, *see*
Central Committee of Elec-
tions
Comité central des élections
générales, *see* Central Com-
mittee for General Elections
to the National Assembly
Comité central des ouvriers de
la Seine, *see* Central Com-
mittee of the Workers of
Seine
Comité central du IIIᵉ arron-
dissement, *see* Central Com-
mittee of the Third District
Comité centralisateur, *see* Cen-
tralizing Committee
Comité central polonais, *see*
Polish Central Committee
Comité de l'émigration polon-
aise, *see* Committee of Polish
Emigration
Comité démocratique de la
Porte Montmartre, *see* Demo-
cratic Committee of the Porte
Montmartre
Comité démocratique du Vᵉ ar-
rondissement, *see* Democratic
Committee of the Fifth Dis-
trict

Comité démocratique du Xᵉ arrondissement, *see* Democratic
Committee of the Tenth District
Comité électoral du XIᵉ arrondissement, *see* Electoral Committee of the Eleventh District
Comité républicain du IIIᵉ arrondissement, *see* Republican
Committee of the Third District
Comité révolutionnaire, *see*
Club of Clubs, Revolutionary
Committee
Comité révolutionnaire des élections a l'Assemblée Nationale,
see Revolutionary Committee
for the Elections to the National Assembly
Commissaire, Sebastien, 27
Commission centrale des élec-
tions démocratiques, *see* Cen-
tral Commission for Demo-
cratic Elections
Commission des récompenses
nationales, *see* Commission of
National Rewards
Commission des 30, *see* Com-
mission of Thirty
Commission for the propagation
of Social Science, 161
Commission Founded to Call All
Tested Patriots to the Defense
of the Republic, 104, 119
Commission instituée pour ap-
peler tous les patriotes
éprouvés à la défense de la
République, *see* Commission
Founded to Call All Tested
Patriots to the Defense of the
Republic
Commission of National Re-
wards, 76, 224-225
Commission of the Fraternal
Banquet of the Constituent
Assembly, 247

Commission of Thirty, 94, 101-108, 119, 120, 122
Commission pour la propagation de la science sociale, *see* Commission for the Propagation of Social Science
Committee of Public Safety, 183, 214
Committee of the Polish Emigration, 206
La Commune de Paris-Moniteur des clubs, 38, 50, 58, 104, 142, 147, 185, 198, 212, 213, 240
"Communists," 184
"Communist-Socialist," 72-76
compagnonnage, 30
Conseil typographique, *see* Typographical Council
Considérant, Victor, 116, 158, 319-320
Constitution of 1791, 121
Le Constitutionnel, 168
Coquerel, Anathase, 160, 296
Corbon, Anthine, 27
Courbon, Charles, 300
Cournot, 198
Le Courrier, français, 49
Courtais, General, 179, 185, 229, 230, 231, 232, 250
Coutard, Théodore, 312
Cracow, 205, 206
Crémieux, Adolphe, 72, 178, 321
Creuse, 125

Dagneaux, 215, 216
Danduran, J.-J., 49, 199, 208, 209, 217, 218, 219, 233
Danse de Boullonges, 138
Daumier, 100
David (d'Angers), 251
Decree against armed gatherings, 241
Delahaye, 290

Delahodde, Lucien, 30
Delaire, Adrien, 116, 127, 128, 129-133, 141, 154
Delbrouck, *see* Delbrueck
Delbrueck, 138, 209, 233
Deleau, 197
Delettre, A., 256
Delpech, 183
"demo-soc," 334
Democratic Central Club of the National Guard, 116, 292
Democratic Central Committee of the Eleventh District, 211, 223
Democratic Club of Batignolles, *see* Republican Club of Batignolles-Monceaux
Democratic Club of Blancs-Maneaux, *see* Patriotic Club of Blancs-Manteaux
Democratic Club of Labor, 52, 55
Democratic Club of La Chapelle, *see* Republican Society of La Chapelle
Democratic Club of Quinze-Vingt, 54, 172, 197, 203, 233, 244, 311
Democratic Club of Saint-Maur, 195, 252, 290
Democratic Club of the Arsenal, 51, 58, 201, 202, 243, 251, 252
Democratic Club of the Fifth District, 56
Democratic Club of the Future, 67, 82, 85, 92, 93, 102, 158, 204
Democratic Club of the Montorgueil Quarter, 207
Democratic Club of the National Guard, *see* Democratic Central Club of the National Guard
Democratic Club of the Rhone Department, 34

Democratic Club of the Rue Charonne, 197
Democratic Club of the Rue Saint Bernard, 197
Democratic Club of the Rue Traversière, 197
Democratic Committee of the Fifth District, 95
Democratic Committee of the Porte Montmartre, 80
Democratic Committee of the Tenth District, 150
Democratic Fraternal Club of the Faubourg Saint-Antoine, 202, 204
Democratic Meeting of the Fraternity of the Faubourg St.-Antoine, 83
Démocratic pacifique, 158
Democratic Society of Educated Men Without Employment, 34, 247
Democratic Society of La Villette, 146, 159
Democratic Society of the Fifth District, 55
Democratic Society of the First District, 53
Democratic Society of the Sorbonne, see Republican Society of the Sorbonne
Deplanque, Louis, 129-133, 225
Depouilly, 304
Deshayes, Charles Edouard, 269, 279
Despeux, 160
Detours, 220
Dourlans meeting, 214, 216, 218, 219, 234, 236, 238
Doussat, 217
Dubois, H., 309
Dufaure, J., 323
Dulaurier, 268
Dupont (de l'Eure), 72
Dupoty, 255
Durrieu, Xavier, 49

Ecole Polytechnique (delegates from), 216
Egalitarian Workers, 39
Elbeuf, 191
Electoral Committee of the Eleventh District, 87
England, 31, 41, 208
Esquiros, Alphonse, 51, 155
Executive Commission: preparations prior to the May 15 demonstration, 227-230; measures against the clubs, 240-241; holds Festival of Concord, 247; domestic policy of, 282-283; introduces legislation vs. unlawful gatherings, 283-286; policy toward the clubs, 288-289

Faucher, Léon, 321, 322
Festival of Concord, 247
Feuillâtre, Claude, 312
Fitz-James, 232
Flaubert, Gustave, 65
Flocon, Ferdinand, 41, 72, 187, 320, 329
Flotte, 42
Fomberteaux, 220
Fontaine, 144
Forestier, Colonel Henri-Joseph, 148, 149
Fouché, General, 241
Foulquier, 184, 198
Fourierists, 28-29, 161
Fournery, H., 246
Fraix, 231
Francart, Louis, 308
Frank-Carré, 191, 195
Frankfurt, 210
Fraternal Club of Quinze-Vingt, 159, 250, 251, 289
La Fraternité de 1845, 28, 255
French Central Committee for the Liberation and Defense of Poland, 170

French Democratic Society
(London), 39
Frichot, 220
"friendly societies," 30

Gadon, Hippolyte, 129-133,
225, 245-246
Gallois, Léonard, 184, 220
Garde mobile, 70, 259, 303
Garde républicaine, 219, 255,
259
Garnier-Pagès, L.-A., 72, 177,
178, 221, 228, 240-241, 242,
243, 329
Gayot de Montfleury, 57, 226
German Democratic Legion,
172
Germans (in Paris), 172
Germany, 170
Gille, Charles, 294
Girard, 219
Girardin, Emile de, 167
Gosset, 179
Gosset, J., 290
Gouache, J., 114
Goudchaux, 79
Grandmesnil, 40
"great notables," 189, 336
Grégoire, Ernest, 138, 183, 184
Griardon, General, 143
Grossier, Barangé, Etienne, 270
Guillard de Kersausie, Thé-
ophile, see Kersausie, Theo-
phile Guillard de
Guille, 255, 256, 257, 258,
308, 312
Guillemette, Charles, 154-155
Guinard, Joseph, 41, 82, 113,
149, 175, 225, 230, 232
Gurr, T. R., 337
Guyon, 238

Hahn, 233
Haussmann, Baron, 5
Hébert, 267

Hérouart, Félicie, 290
Hervé, Edouard, 249, 277
Herwegh, 172
High Court of Bourges, 245
Hilbey, Constant, 287
Hingray, 230, 232
Hobsbawm, E. J., 337
Huber, Aloysius, 116, 208, 209:
elected president of Club of
Clubs, 129; background of,
130-133; role as president,
137; as club and worker en-
dorsed candidate to National
Assembly from Seine, 142;
failure to be elected, 189;
calls final meeting of Club of
Clubs, 198; role in May 15
demonstration, 208-209,
214-228, 233-238, 245
Hugo, Victor, 11, 14, 252, 261,
311

Icarians, 29, 36, 56, 62-63,
184-185, 269
Indre-et-Loire, 133
Italians (in Paris), 172
Italy, 170, 208

Jeantet, 256
Jorry, Général Sebastien, 312
Journal des sans-culottes, 38,
287
Juin d'Allas, see Michelot

Kersausie, 142, 255, 256
King-and-Country mobs, 337
Klein, Jacques, 180, 308

Lachambeaudie, 220
La Collonge (or Lacollonge),
Léon, 51, 296, 311
Lacordaire, Father, 157

Lagrange, Charles, 149, 260-261, 262
Lalanne, 278
Lamartine, Alphonse de, 90, 245: political stance of, 72; relations to club leaders, 75; receives delegation from Central Republican Society, 91; response to March 17 demonstration, 109-110; role in April 16 crisis, 173, 179, 182; contact with Club of Clubs leaders, 198; receives club delegation demanding support for Poland, 208-209
Lambert, Emile, 199
Lamennais, 79, 80, 142
Lamieussens, 163
Landolphe, 244, 253
Langlois, Jerôme, 256
Larochejaquelein, Henri de, 156
Laugier, 129-133, 198, 225
Lavaux, 159
Lavoie, 179
Laws of September, 71, 80, 90
Lebas, Philippe, 114-115
Lebon, Napoléon, 41, 61, 64, 116, 129-133, 156, 198, 199
Leboucher, 240
Lechevalier, Jules, 161
Ledru-Rollin, 41, 72, 82, 148, 149, 207, 259, 329, 334: neo-Jacobin stance of, 73-75, 329; dissolves National Guard elite companies, 88; apparent attitude toward postponing elections, 95; National Guard attitude toward, 98-100; and demonstration of March 16, 100-101, 102; political alliance with Caussidière, 103; confrontation with Commission of Thirty March 17, 109; relations with Club of Clubs, 126-127, 129; endorsed as candidate by Club of Clubs,

142; and Belgian "invasion," 169; grants relief to families of departing Poles, 172; role in April 16 crisis, 179, 183-185, 187, 190; receives club demand for special seating, 201; vote on law restricting clubs, 320; electoral success in 1849, 334
Lefèvre, 140
Leger, Captain, 83
Legré, 220
Lehsner, 220
Leinen, Mathias, 269
Lemansois-Duprez, 233
Lermet, 238
Leroux, Pierre, 255, 261, 262
Leroyer, G. A., 125
Lille, 7
Limoges, 125, 191-192, 333
Limousin, 21
Lombards, 171
Longepied, Amable, 136, 184, 255: role in founding Club of the Revolution, 122-123; elected chairman of Commission of Club of Clubs, 129; background of, 130-133; resigns from Club of Clubs, 197; contacts with Lamartine, 198; contacts with Marrast, 225; founds Society of the Friends of the Republic, 225; arrested in wake of May 15 demonstration, 245-246
Longepied, Eugène, 245, 255
Louis-Philippe, 40, 203, 286
Lucas, Alphonse, 258
Luxembourg Labor Commission, 72, 142, 154, 165, 210
Luxembourg Labor Commission worker delegates to, 211: scanty role in club leadership, 42, 44-45; political evolution of, 46-47; creation of Central Committee of the Workers of

the Seine by, 117-119; role in April 16 crisis, 174, 176-177, 181, 183, 188; cooperate in the Central Commission for Democratic Elections, 254-255
Lyon, 333

Madier de Montjau, 282
Mairet, 177
Malarmé, 142, 255
Mallarmet, see Malarmet
Manifeste des sociétés secrètes, see Manifesto of the Secret Societies
Manifesto of the Secret Societies, 104, 119
Marchal (de Calvi), 157
Marie, A. T., 57, 72-73, 179, 226
Marrast, Armand, 82, 148, 329: member of Provisional Government's moderate majority, 72; role in April 16 crisis, 179, 183; rumors of his intervention in the pro-Polish May demonstration, 208; receives letter from Huber, 220-221, 228; Marrast's policy toward clubs prior to May 15, 224-227; Marrast's policy toward clubs, May-June 1848, 289-290; club response to same, 290-293
Martin-Bernard, 120, 142
Marx, Karl, 295-296
Marx-Engels, 200
materialist communists, 28
Maurice, 215
Maury, 42
Mazzini, 172
Merlieux, Edouard, 320
Mesle, 276
Michelot, 124
"Ministry of Progress," 177, 213

Monnier, 228
Montagnards, 242
Moreau, 262
Mornet, 150
Moscowa, Prince de la, 157
Moulin, 169, 215

Nadaud, Martin, 27
Napoleon III, see Bonaparte, Louis-Napoléon
Le National, 114, 115, 190, 253, 259, 261, 283
National Guard: democratization of, 81-83; impending elections within, 83-84; dissolution of elite companies of, 88; demonstration of old-line March 16, 98-101; demand for postponement of elections within, 87-88; results of elections of April 5-7, 147-152; decisive intervention of, April 16, 175, 185, 187; reaction to Rouen "massacre," 195; role on May 15, 229-232, 238-240; role in June insurrection, 299, 304-306
National Republican Club, 145, 146
Neo-Babouvists, 28
neo-Jacobins, 28, 72-73, 75, 76
Newspaper stamp tax, 78-79
Ney, Marshal, 157, 270
Nogué, 152
Normanby, Marquis of, 235
Normandy, 191

L'Organisation du travail, 51, 311
"organization of labor," 164

Pagnerre, 97
Panisse, 278, 315

Pardigon, François, 256, 298, 299, 301, 302

Paris: physical appearance in 1848, 3-6; nineteenth-century growth of, 6-7; administrative geography of, 10-11; human geography of, 11-17; poverty in, 17-18; employment situation in, 18-20 *working class of*, 20-23: unemployment among, 23-24; "moral profile" of, 24-27; political attitudes of, 27-31

Paris Commune (of 1871), 335

Patriotic Club of the Blancs-Manteaux, 151, 156, 158, 159, 200

Peaceful Club of the Rights of Man, 51, 250, 252, 254, 290, 292, 293

Peaceful Society for the Rights of Man, *see* Peaceful Club of the Rights of Man

Pecquer, 116

Pelletier, 245, 246

Perdiguier, Agricol, 27, 188

Le Père Duchêne, 38, 65, 265-268, 270, 271, 273, 274, 275, 276, 277, 278, 279, 306

Peupin, 211-212

Le Peuple constituant, 79

Piat, General, 156

Piedmont, 171, 208

Pinel-Grandchamp, 260

Pireault, 220

Poitiers, 133

Poland, 170, 172, 205-210, 217, 234

Poles (in Paris), 171, 172

Polish Central Committee, 172

Le Populaire, 29, 62, 145

Popular Club of the Second of March, *see* Club of the Second of March

Popular Club of the Sorbonne, *see* Republican Society of the Sorbonne

Popular Club of the Tenth District, 88, 93

Popular Society of the Eleventh District, 40, 51

Posen, 205, 206, 210

La Presse, 167-168

La Propagande républicaine, 49

Prot, 176, 177, 180

Proudhon, Pierre-Joseph, 111, 116, 182, 200, 255, 261, 262

Provisional Government: ambiguous position of, 32; divisions within, 71-76; policy toward repeal of newspaper stamp tax, 79-80; response to demonstration of March 17, 95-96, 100, 108-110; relations of Club of Clubs with, 126-127; response to the crisis of April 16, 173-176, 178-179; reintroduction of troops into Paris by, 186

Prussia, 171, 205, 208, 210

Pujol, Louis, 301

Quentin, 220, 235

Railroad, Stagecoach & Teamster Employees Association, 42

Ramond de la Croisette, 230, 232

Raspail, François, 49, 61, 64-65, 67, 79, 80, 116, 189, 205, 207, 224, 233, 235, 241, 242, 245, 255

Raymond, Abbé, 143

Recurt, Dr., 114, 213, 221, 226, 228, 240, 241, 288, 289

Reform Banquet of the XIIth district, 31

La Réforme, 76, 79, 114, 186, 190, 192, 207, 222, 260, 262

Regnier, P.-J., 309

Le Représentant du peuple, 200, 255, 260
Republican Club of Alsatian Workers, 34, 218
Republican Club of *L'Atelier*, *see* Republican Society of *L'Atelier*
Republican Club of Batignolles-Monceaux, 82, 157, 159, 172, 281-282
Republican Club of Fraternity, 201
Republican Club of Free Workers, 33, 155
Republican Club of Montmartre, 85
Republican Club of Passy, 52, 154, 162
Republican Club of Progress, 204
Republican Club of the Etoile, 52
Republican Club of the Faubourg du Roule, 116, 125
Republican Club of the Faubourg St.-Marceau, 102
Republican Club of the Future, *see* Democratic Club of the Future
Republican Club of the Temple, 39, 55
Republican Club of Workers, 43-44, 82, 154-155, 164, 166, 167
Republican Committee of the Third District, 203
Republican Democratic Club of Quinze-Vingt, *see* Democratic Club of Quinze-Vingt
Republican National Club (of Belleville), 54
Republican Society of La Chapelle, 42, 274, 309-310
Republican Society of *L'Atelier*, 36, 80, 88, 95
Republican Society of Passy, *see* Republican Club of Passy
Republican Society of the Faubourg St.-Denis, 56, 95, 96, 102, 104, 136, 137, 152, 163, 167
Republican Society of the Panthéon, 140
Republican Society of the Sorbonne (or Popular Club of the Sorbonne), 80, 82, 92, 124, 162, 250, 282, 287
Republican Solidarity, 320, 321
Réunion démocratique de la fraternité du Faubourg St.-Antoine, *See* Democratic Meeting of the Fraternity of the Faubourg St.-Antoine
Reverdy, 231, 232
Revolutionary Committee, Club of Clubs, *see* Club of Clubs, Revolutionary Committee
Revolutionary Committee for the Elections to the National Assembly, 120
Revue retrospective, 123
Rey, Colonel, 238
Robert, 212
Robert (du Var), 155
Robespierre's Proposed Declaration of the Rights of Man (1793), 39, 87, 140, 156, 157, 161, 259, 327
Roubaix, 7
Rouen "massacre," 191-196, 205, 218, 330
Royer, Dr., 213, 220
Rudé, G., 337
Rush, Richard, 322

Saint, Amand, 240
Saisset, Colonel, 94, 232
Sand, George, 35, 182, 188
Sarrelouis, 269
Savary, 255
Savoyards, 169

Schmit, J.-B., 203-204, 205
Schoelcher, Lieutenant-colonel, 148
"the Seasons," 29-30, 298
Seigneuret, 213, 214
Sénard, 191, 315
Sentimental Education, 65
La Sentinelle des clubs, 50
Siméon-Chaumier, 252
Soboul, A., 337
Sobrier, Joseph, 116, 126, 136, 199, 228, 235, 245: as publisher of *La Commune de Paris*, 50; granted a palace, rue de Rivoli, 58; relations with Lamartine, 75; relations with Caussidière, 76; role in March 17 demonstration, 104, 108; as founder of Commission to Call All Tested Patriots to the Defense of the Republic, 119; role in organizing Club of Clubs, 120; houses Club of Club's Commission, 127; elected officer of Club of Clubs, 129; background of, 130-133; role in April 16 crisis, 182, 184-185; resigns from Club of Clubs, 198; club delegates meet at his palace daily, 201; role in May 15 demonstration, 212-214, 219-220; his newspaper sacked, 240; arrested, 245
socialism, 164
Socialist Club of the Future, *see* Democratic Club of the Future
socialist, 72
Société démocratique centrale, *see* Central Democratic Society
Société démocratique de La Villette, *see* Democratic Society of La Villette
Société démocratique des

hommes Lettrés sans emploi, *see* Democratic Society of Educated Men Without Employment
Société démocratique du 1er arrondissement, *see* Democratic Society of the First District
Société démocratique française (Londres), *see* French Democratic Society (London)
Société des amis de la République, *see* Society of the Friends of the Republic
Société des amis du peuple, *see* Society of the Friends of the People
Société des droits de l'homme, *see* Society of the Rights of Man
Société des droits de l'homme du IIIe arrondissement, *see* Society of the Rights of Man of the Third District
Société des gens de lettres, *see* Writers' Society
Société fraternelle centrale, *see* Central Fraternal Society
Société populaire de la Sorbonne, *see* Republican Society of the Sorbonne
Société populaire du XIe arrondissement, *see* Popular Society of the Eleventh District
Société républicaine centrale, *see* Central Republican Society
Société républicaine de Chaillot, *see* Club of Chaillot
Société républicaine de La Chapelle, *see* Republican Society of La Chapelle
Société républicaine de la Sorbonne, *see* Republican Society of the Sorbonne
Société républicaine de l'Atelier, *see* Republican Society of *L'Atelier*

Société républicaine de Passy, *see* Republican Society of Passy

Société républicaine du Faubourg St.-Denis, *see* Republican Society of the Faubourg St.-Denis

Société républicaine du Panthéon, *see* Republican Society of the Panthéon

Society of the Club of Ardèche, 57

Society of the Friends of the People, 49, 61, 64-65, 67, 156, 157, 207, 208-209, 242, 249

Society of the Friends of the Republic, 225

Society of the Rights of Man, 55, 60, 61, 82, 115, 116, 133, 137, 145, 151, 156, 157, 158-159, 163, 186, 198, 250, 269, 298: relation to July Monarchy's secret societies, 39; and short-lived newspaper, 49; permitted use of public buildings, 57; meeting place of, 58; character of, 63, 64; demands expulsion of army garrison, 92; role in March 17 demonstration, 96, 99; position on National Guard election, 150; speech by Delaire before, 154; anti-ideological bias of, 161, 162; faith in Louis Blanc, 165; defends *Constitutionnel*, 168; opposes demonstration in April, 181; role in April 16 crisis, 182-184, 185; response to Rouen "massacre," 192-193, 195-196; in support of Poland, 206-207; alleged military preparation prior to May 15, 219; executive committee of ordered arrested on May 15, 240; shoot-ing in local of, May 15, 240; role in Central Commission for Democratic Elections, 256, 259; character of, in June 1848, 256-259; response to Banquet of the People, 274-276; protests vs. law against unlawful gatherings, 286; police prefects proposal, May 28 to dissolve the, 289; military organization of imitated by other clubs, 300; response to June insurrection, 302, 307-308

Society of the Rights of Man (Albouy branch), 242, 254, 256, 274-276, 300, 302, 307

Society of the Rights of Man of the Third District, 143, 147, 159, 163, 164

Society of the Rights of Man (of the Twelfth District), 42, 212

Solidarité républicaine, *see* Republican Solidarity

Soubert, 244

Spain, 41

Stévenot, 215

Tard, 127

Taschereau, 49, 70, 123, 180

Tempoure, General, 231, 237

Teulière, 290

Thiers, Adolphe, 260, 261, 262, 283

Thomas, Clement, 217, 260, 301

Thomas, Emile, 264

Thomassin, Louis Benjamin, 268, 269, 278-279

Thompson, E. P., 337

Thoré, Théophile, 49-50, 120, 249, 255

Thuillier, Emile, 265, 266, 267, 268, 269, 270

Tilly, C., 337

Tocqueville, Alexis de, 247, 295
Tonnesson, K. D., 337
Tourcoing, 7
Tours, 40
de Tracy, 230, 232
Le Travail, 50
Le Travailleur, 51
Treulé, 138
Trinité, 220
Trotsky, 201, 283, 327
Trouvé-Chauvel, 278, 289, 295, 307
Turkey, 209
Typographers' Council, 211

Union des brigadiers des ateliers nationaux, see Union of Brigadiers of the National Workshop
Union of Brigadiers of the National Workshops, 298

Vassal, 295, 307-308
Vavin, 217
Vendôme, 139
Vidal, 68
Villain, Léopold J., 61, 64, 150, 168, 181, 184, 186, 192, 240, 245, 308
Viollet-le-Duc, 5
Voissard, F., 310
La Voix des clubs, 50
La vraie République, 50, 188, 190, 244, 255

Wenge, Bige, 127
Winter, 310
Wolowski, 210, 213
Workers' Club of Fraternity, 43
Writers' Society, 80

Yautier, Colonel, 148, 238, 239

Library of Congress Cataloging in Publication Data

Amann, Peter, 1927-
   Revolution and mass democracy.

   Bibliography: p.
   1. France—History—February Revolution, 1848.
2. Political clubs. I. Title.
DC270.A55   944.06'3   74-2959
ISBN 0-691-05223-9   9-2-75